A Glossary of English Food Terms

When you're in London, you speak English. American English is perfectly fine, of course. Like a major credit card, it's accepted everywhere. But you may come across a few unfamiliar terms, particularly when the subject is food. The following can help (see the reverse side for general terms):

English English	American English	English English	American English
Afters	Dessert	Haricots vert	Green beans
Aubergine	Eggplant	Liquor	Green, salty, parsley-based gravy
Bangers	Sausages	Mange tout	Snow peas
Bap	Soft sandwich bun	Marrow	Squash
Biscuit	Cracker or cookie	Mash	Mashed potatoes
Black or white	Refers to coffee; white is coffee with cream	Mince	Ground meat, usually beef
Broad bean	Lima bean	Ploughman's lunch	Pub grub consisting of crusty bread with cheese or pâté
Bubble and Squeak	Mashed potatoes mixed with cabbage or meat and then fried	Pudding	Dessert
Chicory	Endive	Rasher	Slice of bacon
Chips	French fries	Rocket	Arugula
Cornish pasties	Pastry filled with meat, onion, and vegetables	Salt beef	Corned beef
Cottage pie	Ground meat and mashed potatoes baked in a pie	Scotch egg	Hard-boiled egg fried in jacket of ground sausage and bread crumbs
Courgettes	Zucchini	Shepherd's pie	Baked pie of meat and vegetables covered with gravy and mashed potatoes
Crisps	Potato chips	Spotted dick	Sponge cake with fruit and raisins steamed and served with custard sauce
Crumpet	Holier version of an "English muffin"	Steak and kidney pie	Pastry-topped pie of steak, kidneys, and mushrooms in gravy
French beans	Green beans	Sticky toffee pudding	Spotted dick (see preceding entry) without the fruit and served with warm butterscotch sauce
Fry-up	Big English breakfast of eggs, sausage/bacon, baked beans, tomatoes, and more	Sultana	Raisin
Gateau	Cake	Sweet	Dessert
Jacket potato	Baked potato served with various toppings		
Jelly	Jello		rry, erves, , and
Joint	Meat roasted on the bone		cheese and mustard or Worcestershire sauce served on toast
Kipper	Smoked fish	Whitebait	Small, whole, deep-fried fish

London For Dummies, 2nd Edition

Minding Your Teas and Queues

British English differs a bit from the English spoken in the New World. You may encounter the following "foreign" words and phrases, which are listed below with their American English translations (see the reverse side for food terms):

English English	American English	English English	American English
Bonnet	Hood of a car	Mate	Male friend
Boot	Trunk of a car	Nappy	Diaper
Brilliant	All-purpose, enthusiastic superlative	Peckish	Hungry
Brolly	Umbrella	Petrol	Gasoline
Cheers	Goodbye (or said when raising a glass in a toast)	Queue	To line up (The Brits are excellent queuers.)
Cinema	Movie ("Theatre" is only live theater)	Quid	One pound sterling (£1)
Coach	A long-distance bus	Mac (macintosh)	Raincoat
Concessions	Special discounts for , students, seniors, and the disabled	Return ticket	Round-trip ticket
Cooker	Stove (sometimes called an Aga, a brand name)	Ring	Call on the phone ("Ring me in the morning.")
First floor	Second floor (and so on)	Rubber	Eraser
Flat	Apartment	Serviette	Napkin
Fortnight	Two weeks	Single ticket	One-way ticket
Ground floor	First floor	Subway	Underpass
Jumper	Sweater	Ta	Thanks
Knackered	Tired	Teatime	Period between 3:30 and 6:00 p.m.
Knickers	Underwear ("Don't get your knickers in a twist.")	Tights	Pantyhose
Lift	Elevator	Torch	Flashlight
Loo	Toilet/restroom ("I need to use the loo.")	Underground/Tube	Subway
Lorry	Truck		

Hungry Minds™

For Dummies: Bestselling Book Series for Beginners

London
FOR
DUMMIES®
2ND EDITION

by Donald Olson

Hungry Minds™

Best-Selling Books • Digital Downloads • e-Books • Answer Networks
e-Newsletters • Branded Web Sites • e-Learning

New York, NY ◆ Cleveland, OH ◆ Indianapolis, IN

London For Dummies® 2nd Edition

Published by:
Hungry Minds, Inc.
909 Third Avenue
New York, NY 10022
www.hungryminds.com
www.dummies.com

Library of Congress Control Number: 2001099320

ISBN: 0-7645-5416-6

ISSN: 1531-1457

Printed in the United States of America

10 9 8 7 6 5 4 3 2 1

2B/QW/QS/QS/IN

Distributed in the United States by Hungry Minds, Inc.

Distributed by CDG Books Canada Inc. for Canada; by Transworld Publishers Limited in the United Kingdom; by IDG Norge Books for Norway; by IDG Sweden Books for Sweden; by IDG Books Australia Publishing Corporation Pty. Ltd. for Australia and New Zealand; by TransQuest Publishers Pte Ltd. for Singapore, Malaysia, Thailand, Indonesia, and Hong Kong; by Gotop Information Inc. for Taiwan; by ICG Muse, Inc. for Japan; by Intersoft for South Africa; by Eyrolles for France; by International Thomson Publishing for Germany, Austria and Switzerland; by Distribuidora Cuspide for Argentina; by LR International for Brazil; by Galileo Libros for Chile; by Ediciones ZETA S.C.R. Ltda. for Peru; by WS Computer Publishing Corporation, Inc., for the Philippines; by Contemporanea de Ediciones for Venezuela; by Express Computer Distributors for the Caribbean and West Indies; by Micronesia Media Distributor, Inc. for Micronesia; by Chips Computadoras S.A. de C.V. for Mexico; by Editorial Norma de Panama S.A. for Panama; by American Bookshops for Finland.

For general information on Hungry Minds' products and services please contact our Customer Care department; within the U.S. at 800-762-2974, outside the U.S. at 317-572-3993 or fax 317-572-4002.

For sales inquiries and resellers information, including discounts, premium and bulk quantity sales and foreign language translations please contact our Customer Care department at 800-434-3422, fax 317-572-4002 or write to Hungry Minds, Inc., Attn: Customer Care department, 10475 Crosspoint Boulevard, Indianapolis, IN 46256.

For information on licensing foreign or domestic rights, please contact our Sub-Rights Customer Care department at 212-884-5000.

For information on using Hungry Minds' products and services in the classroom or for ordering examination copies, please contact our Educational Sales department at 800-434-2086 or fax 317-572-4005.

Please contact our Public Relations department at 212-884-5174 for press review copies or 212-884-5000 for author interviews and other publicity information or fax 212-884-5400.

For authorization to photocopy items for corporate, personal, or educational use, please contact Copyright Clearance Center, 222 Rosewood Drive, Danvers, MA 01923, or fax 978-750-4470.

Hungry Minds™ is a trademark of Hungry Minds, Inc.

About the Author

Donald Olson is a novelist, playwright, and travel writer. His novel *The Confessions of Aubrey Beardsley* was published in the United Kingdom by Bantam Press, and his play, *Beardsley*, was produced in London. His travel stories have appeared in the *New York Times*, *Travel & Leisure*, *Sunset*, *National Geographic* guides, and many other national publications. He is also the author of *England for Dummies* and has written guidebooks to Italy, Berlin, and Oregon. London is one of his favorite cities.

Dedication

To G and his guiding eyes.

And to the memory of Ron Boudreau, dedicated editor.

Author's Acknowledgments

I'd like to thank British Airways, Rail Europe, and Paul Duboudin of the British Tourist Authority for their generous help while I was researching and writing this guide. Special thanks also go to Deirdra Morris in London.

Publisher's Acknowledgments

We're proud of this book; please send us your comments through our Hungry Minds Online Registration Form located at www.dummies.com.

Some of the people who helped bring this book to market include the following:

Editorial

Editors: Allyson Grove, Lisa Torrance

Copy Editor: Christina Guthrie

Cartographer: Nicholas Trotter

Editorial Manager: Jennifer Ehrlich

Editorial Assistant: Brian Herrmann

Senior Photo Editor: Richard Fox

Assistant Photo Editor: Michael Ross

Front Cover Photo: © Yellow Dog Productions/Image Bank

Back Cover Photo: © Lisl Dennis/ Image Bank

Production

Project Coordinator: Maridee Ennis

Layout and Graphics: Joyce Haughey, LeAndra Johnson, Betty Schulte, Julie Trippetti, Erin Zeltner

Proofreaders: Andy Hollandbeck, Charles Spencer, TECHBOOKS Production Services

Indexer: TECHBOOKS Production Services

General and Administrative

Hungry Minds Consumer Reference Group

> **Business:** Kathleen Nebenhaus, Vice President and Publisher; Kevin Thornton, Acquisitions Manager

> **Cooking/Gardening:** Jennifer Feldman, Associate Vice President and Publisher; Anne Ficklen, Executive Editor; Kristi Hart, Managing Editor

> **Education/Reference:** Diane Graves Steele, Vice President and Publisher

> **Lifestyles:** Kathleen Nebenhaus, Vice President and Publisher; Tracy Boggier, Managing Editor

> **Pets:** Kathleen Nebenhaus, Vice President and Publisher; Tracy Boggier, Managing Editor

> **Travel:** Michael Spring, Vice President and Publisher; Brice Gosnell, Publishing Director; Suzanne Jannetta, Editorial Director

> **Hungry Minds Consumer Editorial Services:** Kathleen Nebenhaus, Vice President and Publisher; Kristin A. Cocks, Editorial Director; Cindy Kitchel, Editorial Director

> **Hungry Minds Consumer Production:** Debbie Stailey, Production Director

Contents at a Glance

Cartoons at a Glance

By Rich Tennant

page 45

page 205

page 155

page 123

page 313

page 7

page 339

Cartoon Information:
Fax: 978-546-7747
E-Mail: richtennant@the5thwave.com
World Wide Web: www.the5thwave.com

Maps at a Glance

Table of Contents

$\cdots\cdots\cdots\cdots\cdots\cdots\cdots\cdots\cdots\cdots\cdots\cdots\cdots\cdots$

Introduction

For all its historic panache, time-honored traditions, quaint corners, and associations with royal pomp and ceremony, London is very much a modern European city (maybe I should say half-European, because the Brits continue to resist full incorporation with the European Union). London is a rich blend of the very old and the very new — from the 900-year-old Tower of London to the 2-year-old Tate Modern gallery. And the city is big, in both size and population; more than 9 million people reside in the 622-square-mile megalopolis known as Greater London.

For first-time visitors, London can be a bit of a challenge. The streets aren't laid out in a grid, and the crowds and traffic in Central London can be intimidating, especially if you're not used to big cities. When you cross the street, you have to look right instead of left; remember that Brits drive on the "wrong" side of the road. And the currency is different. These differences don't present major obstacles, however. If anything, they add to the pleasure of a trip to London because they're reminders that you are, after all, in a different country — albeit one where you (sort of) speak the same language as the natives (see the Cheat Sheet for a list of British terms that may be unfamiliar).

If you have a bit of advance planning and some useful information under your belt, making the trip will be easier than you thought. London may be far from where you live, but for many people a trip to England is like going home.

About This Book

London For Dummies, 2nd Edition is meant to be used as a reference. You can, of course, start at the first page and read all the way through. If you do, you'll end up with an unusually complete knowledge of London essentials. On the other hand, you may not need parts of this guide because you've already been to London and/or know the basics of international travel. You're after quick, easy-to-find specifics. In that case, you can easily flip to the part that you need or hone in on a specific chapter — hotels, for example (see Chapter 8). The philosophy behind this book is quite simple. I wanted to create the kind of guide that I wished I'd had on my first trip to London: informative, practical, down-to-earth, and fun.

When you travel, the unexpected surprises create the most memorable moments and provide the stories you take back with you. But the other side of travel is details and planning: What are the most important sights, how can I reach them, what do they cost, and how much time do I need to see them? Where should I eat? Where should I sleep? These questions aren't small issues when you're away from home. They can make or break a trip — I know that. So what I offer here is based on my own experience in traveling, living, and working in London. I don't want you to have a good trip — I want you to have a great one!

You should know, however, that travel information is subject to change at any time — especially prices. Therefore, I suggest that you write or call ahead for confirmation when making your travel plans. The authors, editors, and publisher cannot be held responsible for the experiences of readers while traveling. Your safety is important to us, however, so we encourage you to stay alert and be aware of your surroundings. Keep a close eye on cameras, purses, and wallets — all favorite targets of thieves and pickpockets.

Conventions Used in This Book

I recently tried to extract some information from a guidebook and found so many symbols that I needed training in hieroglyphics to interpret them all. I'm happy to report that the user-friendly *London For Dummies, 2nd Edition* travel guide isn't like that. I keep the use of symbols and abbreviations to a minimum, as follows:

- The credit card abbreviations are AE (American Express), DC (Diners Club), MC (MasterCard), and V (Visa).

- I include the London postal area (SW7, for example) in all street addresses in case you want to look up the street in a *London A to Z* or other London street reference map.

- I give the nearest tube/Underground (subway) stop for all destinations (for example, Tube: Piccadilly Circus).

- I list all prices first in British pounds sterling (£), and then in U.S. dollars ($) rounded to the nearest dollar (when prices are under $5, I don't round them). Although the exchange rate fluctuates daily, in this guide I use the rate £1 = $1.50.

- All London telephone numbers in this guide are preceded by 020, the London city code (a different code applies in a few cases), followed by the local London number. If you are calling London from outside the United Kingdom, you must dial the U.K. country code (44) followed by 020 and the local number. If you're calling London from elsewhere within the United Kingdom, drop the zero and dial 20 before the number. If you're calling London from within London, just dial the local number.

I also apply a few conventions to the listings of hotels, restaurants, and attractions, as follows:

✔ I list the hotels, restaurants, and top attractions in A-to-Z order, so moving among the maps, worksheets, and descriptions is easy.

✔ I give exact prices for every hotel, restaurant, and attraction. Please note, however, that prices are subject to change and an additional 17.5% *VAT* (value added tax) is added to restaurant meals and may be added to hotel bills (I note in the individual hotel listings if the price does not include the VAT).

✔ I use a system of dollar signs ($) to show a range of costs for hotels or restaurants. The dollar signs for hotels correspond to *rack rates* (nondiscounted standard rates) and reflect a hotel's low to high rates for a double room. For restaurants, the dollar signs denote the *average* cost of dinner for one person, including appetizer, main course, dessert, a non-alcoholic drink, tax, and a tip. Check out the following table to decipher the dollar signs:

Cost	*Hotel*	*Restaurant*
$	$150 and under	$25 or under
$$	$151 to $225	$26 to $35
$$$	$226 to $300	$36 to $50
$$$$	$301 to $400	$51 and up
$$$$$	$401 and up	

✔ I divide the hotels into two categories — my personal favorites and those that don't quite make my preferred list but still get my hearty seal of approval. Don't be shy about considering these "runner-up" hotels if you can't get a room at one of my favorites or if your preferences differ from mine — the amenities that the runners-up offer and the services that each provides make all these accommodations good choices to consider as you determine where to rest your head at night.

Foolish Assumptions

As I wrote this book, I made some assumptions about you, dear reader, and what your needs may be as a traveler. Here's what I assumed about you:

✔ You may be an inexperienced traveler looking for guidance when determining whether to take a trip to London and how to plan for it.

✔ You may be an experienced traveler, but you don't have a lot of time to devote to trip planning, or you don't have a lot of time to spend in London after you get there. You want expert advice on how to maximize your time and enjoy a hassle-free trip.

✔ You're not looking for a book that provides all the information available about London or that lists every hotel, restaurant, or attraction available to you. Instead, you're looking for a book that focuses on the places that will give you the best or most unique experience in London.

If you fit any of these criteria, then *London For Dummies, 2nd Edition* gives you the information you're looking for!

How This Book Is Organized

London For Dummies, 2nd Edition has seven parts plus an appendix and worksheets. The parts can all be read independently — so if you want to zero in on restaurants or hotels, you can turn right to those parts. Or you can read the book sequentially to find out all you need to know about planning and visiting the City by the Thames. The parts include the following:

✔ **Part I: Getting Started** introduces London and gives you some excellent reasons for going there. I help you decide on the best time of year for your visit, give you sound advice on planning a realistic budget, and provide special tips for families, travelers with disabilities, seniors, and gays and lesbians.

✔ **Part II: Ironing Out the Details** helps take some of the wrinkles out of trip planning. You can find all the options for airlines and tips on how to get the best fare, plus the lowdown on package tours and whether they can save you money. (They certainly can!) The thumbnail sketches of London neighborhoods help you decide where you want to stay. I explain what kind of accommodation you can expect for your money, provide details on booking a room, and describe London's best hotels. This part helps you tie up any pre-trip loose ends (passports and so on) *before* you enter the aircraft and fasten your seatbelts for the flight to London.

✔ **Part III: Settling into London** tells you what you need to know after you arrive. A bit of airport orientation is in order, followed by detailed information on the ways, means, and costs of getting from the airport into the city. To help you get your bearings, I provide another quick rundown of London's diverse neighborhoods. I tell you everything you need to know about getting around town — whether you travel on foot, on the Underground or bus, or in a taxi. And because you must use pounds and pence, I talk money, such as where to find a currency exchange or an ATM.

✔ **Part IV: Dining in London** begins with an appetizing survey of London's dining scene before moving on to the delectable main course: London's best restaurants, complete with easy-to-use indexes for price, location, and type of cuisine. This part ends with some suggestions for meals on the run and special places to go for tea, fish-and-chips, or a picnic.

✔ **Part V: Exploring London** is dedicated to seeing the sights — from the absolute must-sees (Buckingham Palace, Westminster Abbey, and the British Museum) to lesser-known haunts and fascinating places nearby (Hampton Court Palace and Windsor Castle). I suggest all kinds of guided tours and provide shopping coverage that steers you to a whole range of big stores (yes, Harrods) and small specialty shops that I think you want to know about. I also provide sample daily itineraries that won't leave you gasping for breath. And if you want to explore beyond London, check out my five great day or overnight trips — to Bath, Stonehenge, and more.

✔ **Part VI: Living It Up after the Sun Goes Down: London Nightlife** introduces you to the theater scene, the performing arts, and all manner of after-dark entertainment possibilities. I clue you in to the best sources for finding out what's going on around town and tell you how to get tickets. Then I fill you in on some of the city's best pubs, clubs, bars, and discos.

✔ **Part VII: The Part of Tens** allows me to squeeze in some extra places and sights I think are special but don't really fit in elsewhere in the book. My lists include ten famous London statues, ten special London churches, and ten historic pubs.

✔ The **Quick Concierge** in the Appendix includes an A-to-Z directory of fast facts that you need to know, such as how the telephone system works, what numbers to call in an emergency, and what taxes you must pay. I also provide a list of toll-free telephone numbers and Web sites for airlines and hotel chains serving London, and tell you where to go for more information on London. I give names, addresses, and phone numbers and/or Web sites of relevant agencies and sources.

✔ I also include a bunch of **worksheets** to make your travel planning easier — among other things, you can determine your travel budget, create specific itineraries, and compare costs on airfares and hotels. You can find these worksheets easily because they're printed on yellow paper.

Icons Used in This Book

These five icons appear in the margins throughout this book:

Bargain Alert is my favorite icon — and I suspect it may be yours, too. I'm not cheap, but I love to save money. I love to know about special deals. Every time I tell you about something that can save you money, I include the Bargain Alert icon.

The Tip icon highlights useful bits of information that can save you time or enhance your London experience. A Tip alerts you to something (like a special guided tour or a way to avoid standing in long lines) that you may not otherwise consider or even know about.

I'm not an alarmist, so you won't find too many Heads Up icons. If you see one, it means that I want you to be aware of something, such as ticket agencies claiming to sell "reduced-price tickets" or the double-tipping scam you may encounter in a restaurant. London, you'll be pleased to know, isn't the kind of city that requires too many warning labels.

Traveling with children? Keep your eyes peeled for the Kid Friendly icon. If the icon is in front of a hotel name, the hotel welcomes families with children and may even provide extras for kids. If it's in front of a restaurant name, the kids will enjoy the food or the atmosphere, and the staff will be welcoming to youngsters. And if the icon is in front an attraction name, kids will (probably) enjoy something about the place.

When was the last time you read a travel book that filled you in on local gossip as well as all the mundane facts? For the London Tattler icon (named after the famous London newspaper, *The Tatler,* published from 1709–1711), I include only the most newsworthy scandals — I mean stories — to report on. I throw in these tidbits about well-known Londoners and curious bits of London lore just for the fun of it.

Where to Go from Here

To London, of course! This book, which gives you the tools you need to make the most of your trip, is a very good place to start your journey. You can also take the book with you to a travel agent or reference it as you look into various tours or package deals. Because the book covers all the basics, it's an excellent guide to help you plan, anticipate, and understand exactly what you want to see and do in London. Whatever your plan, I hope that you think of me as your guide or companion on the journey. I love London. My goal is to help you have a great time while you're there — however you read the book and plan out your trip.

Part I
Getting Started

"I think Philip was inspired by our trip last year touring the Great Gothic Decks of London."

In this part...

Are you a stranger to London? Well, now's the time to introduce yourself to the city, and this part helps you put a face to the place. In Chapter 1, I give a general overview of this great city, sketching in some details so you know what you can find there — including the newest attractions. If you haven't decided when to go, Chapter 2 fills you in on what London offers during each season and why some times may be better than others for a visit. Chapter 3 is about planning your budget — a workable budget based on real London prices — and it includes cost-cutting tips. And Chapter 4 is full of special advice for London-bound families, seniors, travelers with disabilities, and gays and lesbians.

Chapter 1

Discovering the Best of London

- -

In This Chapter

▶ Discovering historic, royal, and modern landmarks

▶ Taking a bit of Modern British cuisine

▶ Exploring London's parks, streets, and museums

▶ Shopping around town

▶ Raising the curtain on the city's performing arts

- -

So, you're going to London. Gives you a thrill just thinking about it, right? The capital of the United Kingdom is one of the world's top destinations, visited year-round by millions from all corners of the globe. In fact, an international survey done in 2001 ranked London as the third-most popular holiday destination in the world. After you arrive, you can make your way through one of the most historic, cultured, and exciting cities on earth. You have every reason to feel a tingle of anticipation.

But maybe you're not absolutely certain London is your cup of Earl Grey. "What's it *really* like?" you want to know. So, in this chapter, I talk a bit about London's flavor — or flavour, as the Brits spell it — and answer the question: What will you find in the City by the Thames?

From Londinium to London: Landmarks of History

Did you know you can see Roman ruins in London? Two millennia ago, London was Londinium, a colony of the Roman Empire. On one London street, you can actually see the excavated remains of a temple where Roman soldiers worshiped a Persian god named Mithras. Although the temple is one of London's oldest archaeological sites, the **Temple of Mithras** is relatively unknown to visitors.

On the other hand, some of London's sights may have percolated through your consciousness because you've seen them in countless movies or photos, heard about them from friends, or read about them somewhere. Places like the **Tower of London** and **Westminster Abbey** have a legendary quality, but these sights are quite real — and they're open to visitors throughout the year. The Tower and the Abbey represent almost *1,000 years* of history. And that's why the great landmarks in London stir the imagination: They've been witness to so much — from glorious triumphs to bloody tragedies.

When visiting the Tower, you walk on a piece of ground where the great dramas and terrors of a turbulent kingdom were played out, where Elizabeth I was held captive while still a princess, and where Sir Thomas More and Anne Boleyn (second wife of Henry VIII and mother of the future Elizabeth I) were beheaded. When stepping into Westminster Abbey, you enter the place where England's kings and queens have been crowned since William the Conqueror claimed the throne in 1066. In this guide, check out Chapters 16 and 17 for descriptions of all the great historic landmarks.

Pomp, Ceremony, and Scandal: The Royals

I never really gave much thought to royalty, except as a footnote to history, until one day several years ago. I was passing St. James's Palace just as Princess Diana and Princess Anne were being hustled into a waiting limousine. There they were, two famous princesses, going about the mysterious routines of royalty. I glimpsed them for maybe three seconds and stood there like a slack-jawed yokel as the limo pulled away.

In London, the royals are spied on the way movie stars are in America. The paparazzi furor lessened a bit after Princess Diana's death but still exists. In 2001, a major royal scandal erupted concerning Prince Edward's wife, Sophie Rhys-Jones, who was caught tackily exploiting her royal connections to promote her public-relations firm; the Queen told her, in no uncertain terms, that she must give up her business. Prince Phillip was overheard yelling at his son, Prince Andrew (former husband of Sarah Ferguson), to shape up and assume more royal responsibilities. Speculation also circulated in 2001 that the Queen had finally given the green light to a marriage between Prince Charles and his long-time companion, Camilla Parker-Bowles. Prince William, primary heir to the throne after his father, Prince Charles, is now a major item in the thriving royal gossip industry. From the Queen on down, the monarchy is a huge business (they actually call themselves "The Firm"), and you can't avoid it. Buy a London paper any day you're there and you find some juicy tidbit about the Queen Mother (who turned 101 in 2001), Prince Edward (whose documentary film business didn't show a profit in seven years), Princess Margaret (who had a stroke and was rumored to be seriously depressed), Prince William, or some other member of **The Firm.** (I provide a few juicy items of my own in this guide with my "London Tattler" asides.)

Queen's golden anniversary

I was in London during the Queen's Silver Jubilee celebrations and still remember the parties and festive brouhaha throughout the city. Another big royal event is coming up in 2002, the year the Queen celebrates her 50th anniversary on the throne. Although the popularity of the monarchy has never been lower, London will certainly celebrate the Queen's anniversary with pomp and pageantry. Unfortunately, dates and details were not yet available at press time. The only other monarch to hold the throne for this long was Queen Victoria.

Okay, so you're probably not going to get invited to the Queen's Garden Party or be asked to go on a hunt with Prince Charles and Camilla Parker-Bowles. But you can have fun seeing **Buckingham Palace,** the royal seat of power and intrigue (see Chapter 16), and traipsing through **Windsor Castle** (see Chapter 17), an hour away. Although you can't see the rooms where Diana actually lived, you can get into her former home, **Kensington Palace,** and see the **Princess Diana Memorial Playground** in Kensington Gardens (see Chapter 16).

Cool Britannia: 21st-Century London

Trend-setting London is to the United Kingdom what New York City is to the United States: the place where it happens first (or ultimately ends up). London is where you can put the eyeball on what's hot, British style. You see the latest hardcore street fashions side by side with the quintessentially traditional. And this ancient city is now as high-tech as a hyperlink, with mobile phones, cyber cafes, and e-communications part of everyday life.

London celebrated the arrival of 2000 in a big way, building several new, large-scale attractions. The Millennium Dome was a real turkey and is no longer open, but the **British Airways London Eye** observation wheel (see Chapter 16) is still revolving beside the Thames. Even more exciting is the **Tate Modern** art gallery (see Chapter 16). A new **Millennium Bridge** now spans the Thames between Tate Modern and St. Paul's Cathedral. Sleek new Underground (subway) stations have opened on the **Jubilee Line.** The courtyard of the hallowed British Museum has been transformed into a stunning glass-roofed **Great Court,** adding much needed space. And **Hertford House,** home of the Wallace Collection (see Chapter 17), has opened its new interior atrium.

Food, Glorious Food: Modern British Cuisine

Once upon a time, you could always count on getting lousy meals in London and the rest of the United Kingdom. The cooking — all too often dull, insular, and uninspired — was the joke of Europe. That reputation began to change in the 1980s, with the influx of new cooking trends that favored foods from France and Italy. Since then, London has become a food capital (allegedly with more Michelin-starred restaurants than Paris). London is certainly the best place to find restaurants serving inventive Modern British cuisine. But don't despair: All those wonderful "Old English" faves are still around — eggs, kippers, beans, and fried tomatoes for breakfast; bubble and squeak; roast beef and Yorkshire pudding; meat pies; fish-and-chips; toad in the hole; cottage pie; sticky toffee pudding; and trifle. (For a guide to English cuisine, see the Cheat Sheet at the beginning of this book.)

And don't forget that London boasts more ethnic restaurants than anywhere else in the United Kingdom, so almost any kind of cuisine can be literally on the tip of your tongue. For more about English food, see Chapter 13. My recommended restaurants are in Chapter 14, and I include tips on where to find teas and cakes and more informal meals in Chapter 15.

Perambulating and Lounging: London's Parks

I love big cities. I love being right in the thick of the action. But at times, the urban rumble and roar get to be a bit much, and I instinctively seek out a place with peace and quiet and lots of green. Fortunately, London is blessed with marvelous parks.

You may have heard of them: **Hyde Park, Kensington Gardens, St. James's Park, Green Park,** and **Regent's Park** (see Chapter 16). These carefully groomed havens, where you can stroll beneath stately trees, lounge on the grass, watch ducks in a pond, or admire the color of the spring-time daffodils, were former royals-only hunting grounds. Now they're part of every Londoner's life and life's blood, the green lungs of an otherwise congested city.

Altogether Charming: London's Streets

What could be more fun than just wandering around London's streets? Try it. Pick a neighborhood. The City? Soho? Chelsea? Then just stroll at will, taking note of the wealth of architectural styles, the curious reminders of days gone by, and the array of local sights such as the blue "famous-person-lived-here" plaques on house fronts. On some streets, you can almost hear the horses' hooves clopping on the cobblestones as they did up until about 1915.

Because the Great Fire of 1666 burned down most of medieval London, the building and house styles that you see tend to range from the sober neoclassical of the early 18th century to the more elegantly light-hearted Regency style of the early 19th century to the heavier and less graceful Victorian period of the mid- to late 19th century. The human scale of London streets, with their long terraces of attached brick, stone, and stucco homes built around leafy squares, gives the city a charm and character that intrigues and delights the eye. London grew from a series of villages, and you can still find that village-like character in many London neighborhoods (for a list of them, see Chapters 6 and 10).

Treasures All Around: Magnificent Museums

What can I say about London's museums? If you're a dedicated museum maven, London's selection will keep you going for days, weeks, months, even years. This city is loaded with every conceivable kind of treasure from all over the world.

If you tire of the great Western European masterworks hanging in the **National Gallery,** you can walk next door to see images of pop icons like Elton John and Princess Di in the **National Portrait Gallery** (see Chapter 16 for both). London's **South Bank** is really buzzing now that the stunning **Tate Modern** (see Chapter 16) has opened; the museum exhibits an international roster of contemporary greats. You can also enjoy masterpieces in museums that were built as private palaces, such as **Spencer House,** former home of Princess Diana's family; **Apsley House,** home of the first duke of Wellington; and **Hertford House,** home of the Wallace Collection (all described in Chapter 17).

Among the "museum museums," the venerable **British Museum** (see Chapter 16), with its unparalleled collection of antiquities, comes out on top — the magnificent Parthenon sculptures (formerly called the Elgin Marbles) understandably hold pride of place there. If you're keen on decorative and applied arts, you can head over to the **Victoria & Albert Museum** (see Chapter 16), a linchpin in the cluster of great South Kensington museums. And you can also tour the **Museum of London** (see Chapter 17), probably the world's most comprehensive city museum, and **Tate Britain** (see Chapter 16), formerly the Tate Gallery, holding the world's greatest collection of British art.

Many London museums are favorites with kids as well as adults. The dinosaurs (and the gemstones) at the **Natural History Museum** are dazzling. One of the exhibits in the **Science Museum** is the scorched and battered Apollo 10 Command Module. You find a whole slew of intriguing museum possibilities for kids in Chapters 16 and 17.

From Harrods to Markets: London's Shopping

It's not just my credit cards speaking: I'm here to tell you that London is one of the world's great shopping cities. Possibly the greatest. Why? The sheer variety of what's available. From mighty **Harrods** and **Fortnum & Mason** to the super-chic boutiques of **Bond Street,** from the 200-year-old shops on **Jermyn Street** to the wonderland of book-stores on **Charing Cross Road,** London offers a seemingly endless array of goods and goodies.

Custom-made shirts and suits, hand-tooled leather shoes, high-quality woolens from all over the United Kingdom — in London, you can still find such things. You can hunt for an old engraving, paw through bric-a-brac at an outdoor market stall, or wander through the London silver vaults in your quest for a soup ladle. In Chapter 19, I put you onto some of the best shopping in London.

All the City's on Stage: Theater, Performing Arts, and the Club Scene

I never tire of listening to those magnificently distinctive English voices, whether the accent is East End cockney or upper-crust Queen's English. (If you're puzzled about East End, West End, and other parts of town, see Chapter 6.)

That's why, when I'm in London, I go to the theater every chance I have. On a recent trip, in less than a week, I saw productions with such famous British actors as Vanessa Redgrave, John Hurt, Zoe Wanamaker, Alan Bates, and Dame Maggie Smith, all known for their stage work. When actors of this caliber are on the boards — as they always are in London — you don't need to think twice about going to the theater. You just go.

The London theater scene is phenomenal, and seeing a West End play adds to any trip's enjoyment. Take your pick (you have to because so much is available): long-running international-hit musicals, Gilbert and Sullivan operettas, light comedies, hard-hitting dramas, everything from Shakespeare to Wilde to Mamet and beyond. Theater is so much a part of London that I devote all of Chapter 22 to it. Culture vultures can also flip to Chapter 23 for a rundown on the other performing-arts possibilities — grand opera, symphony concerts, chamber music, and dance. And don't forget, ticket prices are lower in London than they are in New York.

But theater and music are only part of the story. Are you a club person? Do you want to slip into your slinkiest gown and go dance to a band or listen to a DJ spinning the latest sounds? Or maybe having a pint or two in a neighborhood pub is more to your taste? Or would you like to dress up in your swellest clothes and glide into one of London's legendary hotel bars for a cocktail? For your after-dark entertainment, you also find jazz joints, blues bars, cabarets, and more. Have a look at your many options in Chapter 24.

Chapter 2

Deciding When to Go

● ●

In This Chapter

▶ Going in season or out?

▶ How rainy is it, really?

▶ Can the calendar make a difference?

● ●

*L*ondon is one of those cities that's popular year-round. So popular, in fact, that according to the British Tourist Authority, more than 12.5 *million* tourists from around the globe visited London in 2000 (the last year for which figures are available), with nearly 2.9 million of them from the States (21% of the total).

Arriving in London at any time of year without advance hotel reservations is not a wise idea. If you plan to be here between April and mid-October, making hotel reservations is essential. Although you can find agencies in London that can help you find a hotel or a B&B in peak season (see Chapter 7), the lines for these services are usually long, and you never know quite what you're getting or where it will be. In Chapter 8 you find descriptions of my recommended London hotels.

Disclosing the Secret of the Seasons

London weather is what you might call "changeable." Predicting what the weather will be like in any given season is hard. Remember that England is an island, and the seas surrounding it, as well as its northerly location, determine its weather patterns. In general, however, the climate is fairly mild year-round, rarely dipping below freezing or rising above 80°F/27°C (at least for extended periods). Table 2-1 gives you an idea of London's temperature and rainfall variations.

Table 2-1	London's Average Temperatures and Rainfall	
Month	*Temp (°F/°C)*	*Rainfall (in.)*
January	40/4	2.1
February	40/4	1.6
March	44/7	1.5
April	49/9	1.5
May	55/13	1.8
June	61/16	1.8
July	64/18	2.2
August	64/18	2.3
September	59/15	1.9
October	52/11	2.2
November	46/8	2.5
December	42/6	1.9

London can be drizzly, muggy, dry and hot, and clammy. It can also be glorious. Some days you get a combination. But whatever the weather, whatever the season, London is well worth seeing. The following sections let you know what's happening in London season by season so that you can pick the best time to go for you.

A-bloom in the spring

London is at its green, blooming best in April and May. Highlights of the season include:

✔ The great London parks and gardens and the surrounding country-side are at their peak of lushness. The Chelsea Flower Show is the quintessential spring event.

✔ Airfares are lower than in summer.

✔ The sky stays light well into the evening.

But keep in mind these springtime pitfalls:

✔ During the half-term school holidays in late February and for three weeks around Easter, visitors pour into London. As a result, the major attractions have longer lines (queues in Britspeak) and hotel rooms may be harder to find.

✔ The weather is always unpredictable.

✔ Public transportation is reduced during holiday periods.

✔ Many museums, stores, and restaurants close on Good Friday, Easter, and Easter Monday.

Summer fun in the sun

Notoriously chilly London becomes irresistible under the sun. Unfortunately, many tourists flock to London throughout the summer to enjoy the fine weather, which can often turn into rain in July and August. The crowds descend for several reasons:

✔ Everyone moves outdoors to take advantage of the fine weather with alfresco theaters, concerts, and festivals (see Chapters 22 and 23).

✔ The evenings are deliciously long and often cool, even if the day has been hot.

✔ The evening stays light until 9 p.m. or even later.

But keep in mind:

✔ July and August are the months of highest rainfall in London, so skies can stay gray and cloudy.

✔ Occasional summer heat waves can drive the mercury into the 80s and even 90s, making July and August hot and muggy. Many businesses and budget-class hotels don't have air conditioning.

✔ Aggravated by London's soot and gas and diesel fumes, a hot spell can lead to excessive air pollution.

✔ Most overseas visitors (30% of travelers) converge on the city from July to September. Lines for major attractions can be interminably long.

✔ Centrally located hotels are more difficult to come by, and their high-season rates apply.

✔ Booking your hotel in advance is essential during this time of year (see Chapter 8).

Chock full of culture in the fall

The golden glow of autumn casts a lovely spell over London. The air is crisp, and the setting sun gives old stone buildings and church spires a mellow patina. Fall is my favorite time of year to be in London, and I can think of only one disadvantage to counteract the many advantages, which include:

✔ After mid-September, fewer tourists are around, so the city feels less crowded and you encounter more Londoners than visitors.

✔ With the drop in tourism, hotel rates and airfares may go down as well.

✔ London's cultural calendar springs to life.

✔ Although you may experience rain at this time of year, you're just as likely to encounter what Americans call "Indian summer."

But one thing to look out for: Like every season in England, autumn can bring rain.

Wonderful in winter

Londoners love to be cozy, and there's no better time for coziness than winter. Although most overseas visitors to London arrive in July and August, the number of visitors from *within* the United Kingdom is highest between January and March. What do they know that you should know? Consider the points that make winter wonderful:

✔ London in winter is a bargain. London's off-season is November 1 to December 12 and December 25 to March 14. Winter off-season rates for airfares and hotels can sometimes be astonishingly low — airline package deals don't get any cheaper (see Chapter 5). At these times, hotel prices can drop by as much as 20%. If you arrive after the Christmas holidays, you can also take advantage of London's famous post-Christmas sales (more on these sales in Chapter 19).

✔ Although the winter winds may blow, nothing in London stops — in fact, everything gets busier. The arts — theater, opera, concerts, and gallery shows — are in full swing.

✔ London develops a lovely buzz during the Christmas season: The stores are decorated, lights are lit, carols are sung, special holiday pantomimes are performed, and the giant Norwegian spruce goes up in Trafalgar Square.

Naturally, winter has its downside. Consider some bad points of London in winter:

✔ Although the Yuletide holidays are always jolly, they also add up to another peak tourist season from mid-December to Christmas. You know what that means: bigger crowds and higher prices. The city is virtually shut down on December 25 and 26 and January 1. Stores, museums, and other attractions are closed, and public transportation is severely curtailed. On December 26 (Boxing Day), finding any kind of open restaurant is difficult.

✔ Wintertime London may be gray and wet for weeks on end; by mid-winter, the skies get dark by about 3:30 p.m. The English usually keep their thermostats set about 10° lower than Americans do. Rather than turn up the heat, the English don their *woollies* (long underwear). You should do the same — or be prepared for a chronic case of goose pimples.

Getting the Lowdown on London's Main Events

London hums with festivals and special events of all kinds, some harking back to centuries past. Before you leave for London, write or call the **British Tourist Authority** (see the Appendix for addresses and phone numbers) and request a copy of its monthly *London Planner,* which lists major events, including theater and the performing arts.

For recorded information on weekly events, call the London Tourist Board's 24-hour **London Line** at ☎ **09068/663-344;** calls cost 60 pence (about 80¢) per minute. You can't call the London Line from outside the United Kingdom.

January

In January, the **London Parade** features marching bands, floats, and the Lord Mayor of Westminster traipsing in a procession from Parliament Square to Berkeley Square. Call ☎ **020/8566-8586** for more details. January 1 (noon–3pm).

February

February brings in the **Chinese New Year,** marked by colorful street celebrations on and around Gerrard Street in Soho's Chinatown. Date varies.

March

St. Patrick's Day is a big to-do in London, which has the third-largest Irish population after New York and Dublin. There are no parades, but you see lots of general merriment. March 17.

The **Chelsea Antiques Fair** draws antiques lovers to Chelsea Old Town Hall (King's Road) for ten days. For more information, call ☎ **01444/ 482-514.** Mid-March (also held in mid-September).

April

At the **Oxford and Cambridge Boat Race** between Putney Bridge and Mortlake Bridge, rowing eights from the two famous universities compete for the Beefeater Cup. The Hammersmith Mall makes a good viewing spot. Last Thursday in March or first Saturday in April (check local press for exact date).

The **London Marathon** was first held in 1981 and has become one of the most popular sporting events in the city. In 2001, an estimated 32,000 runners took part, men and women, champion athletes and first-timers. The 26.2-mile race begins in Greenwich, winds its way past the Tower of London and along the Thames, and finishes in The Mall in front of Buckingham Palace, one of the best viewing spots. For more information, call ☎ 020/7620-4117. Mid-April.

May

The **Football Association FA Cup Final** is held at Wembley Stadium. Remember that *football* in the United Kingdom is what people in the United States call *soccer,* and tickets are difficult to obtain given the sport's popularity. Contact the Box Office, Wembley Stadium Ltd., Wembley HA9 0DW, ☎ 020/8902-0902. Mid-May.

One of London's most famous spring events, the **Chelsea Flower Show,** held on the grounds of the Chelsea Royal Hospital, draws tens of thousands of visitors from around the world. Ordering tickets in advance is a good idea; in the States you can order them from Keith Prowse at ☎ 800/669-7469 or 914/328-2357. For more information, call the Royal Horticultural Society at ☎ 020/7834-4333. Late May.

June

The juried **Royal Academy Summer Exhibition** presents more than 1,000 works of art by living artists from all over the United Kingdom. For more information, call the Royal Academy at ☎ 020/7439-7438. Early June to mid-August.

June 4 is the **Queen's birthday,** but her birthday parade, Trooping the Colour, takes place about a week later. The Horse Guards celebrate "Ma'am's" birthday in Whitehall with an equestrian display full of pomp and ceremony. For free tickets, send a self-addressed stamped envelope from January 1 to February 28 to Ticket Office, Headquarters, Household Division, Chelsea Barracks, London SW1H 8RF, ☎ 020/7414-2279. Mid-June.

Kenwood, a lovely estate at the top of Hampstead Heath, is the pastoral setting for the **Kenwood Lakeside Concerts,** a summer season of Saturday-night open-air concerts. For more information, call ☎ 020/8233-7435. Mid-June to early September.

The world's top tennis players whack their rackets at the **Wimbledon Lawn Tennis Championships,** held at Wimbledon Stadium. Getting a ticket to this prestigious event is complicated. August 1 to December 31, you can apply to enter the public lottery for next year's tickets by send-ing a self-addressed stamped envelope to All England Lawn Tennis Club, P.O. Box 98, Church Rd., Wimbledon, London SW19 5AE. For more infor-mation, call ☎ **020/8944-1066** or 020/8946-2244 (recorded information) or visit www.Wimbledon.com on the Web. Late June to early July.

The **City of London Festival** presents a series of classical concerts, poetry readings, and theater in historic churches and buildings, includ-ing St. Paul's Cathedral and the Tower of London. For more information, call ☎ **020/7377-0540** or 020/7638-8891 (box office). Late June to mid-July.

July

In July, you can see the much-loved **BBC Henry Wood Promenade Concerts.** Known as The Proms, this series of classical and popular concerts is held at the Royal Albert Hall. To book by credit card, call the box office at ☎ **020/7589-8212.** Mid-July to mid-September.

August

Buckingham Palace opens to the public August through September (see Chapter 16 for details).

During the **Notting Hill Carnival,** steel bands, dancing, and Caribbean fun take over in the streets of Notting Hill (Portobello Road, Ladbroke Grove, All Saints Road). This enormous street fair is one of Europe's largest. For more information, call ☎ **020/8964-0544.** Bank Holiday weekend in August (last Monday in August).

September

The **Thames Festival** celebrates the mighty river, with giant illuminated floats. For more information, call ☎ **020/7401-2255.** Mid-September.

The **Chelsea Antiques Fair** draws antiques lovers to Chelsea Old Town Hall (King's Road) for ten days. For more information, call ☎ **01444/ 482-514.** Mid-September (also held in mid-March).

November

Although based at the National Film Theatre on the South Bank, the **London Film Festival** presents screenings all over town. Call ☎ **020/ 7928-3232** in November for recorded daily updates on what's showing where. Throughout November.

On **Guy Fawkes Night,** bonfires and fireworks commemorate Guy Fawkes's failure to blow up King James I and Parliament in 1605. Check the weekly entertainment magazine *Time Out* (Internet: www.timeout. com) for locations. November 5.

For the **State Opening of Parliament,** the Queen in all her finery sets out from Buckingham Palace in her royal coach and heads to Westminster, where she reads out the government's program for the coming year. (This event is televised.) For more information, call ☎ **020/7971-0026.** First week in November.

The new Lord Mayor of London goes on the grand **Lord Mayor's Procession** through the City from Guildhall to the Royal Courts of Justice in his gilded coach; festivities include a carnival in Paternoster Square and fireworks on the Thames. For more information, call ☎ **020/7971-0026.** Early November.

December

Christmas lights go on in Oxford Street, Regent Street, Covent Garden, and Bond Street. Mid-November to early December.

The **lighting ceremony** of the huge Norway spruce Christmas tree in Trafalgar Square officially announces the holiday season. First Thursday in December.

Trafalgar Square is the focus of **New Year's Eve** celebrations. December 31.

Chapter 3

Planning Your Budget

● ●

In This Chapter

▶ Planning a realistic budget for your trip

▶ Pricing things in London

▶ Uncovering hidden expenses

▶ Using credit cards, traveler's checks, and ATMs

▶ Considering money-saving tips

● ●

*O*kay, you want to go to London. You're excited and eager to pack, but can you really afford it? At this point, a financial reality check is in order. London is an expensive city, no two ways about it. Although you may think the trip is prohibitively expensive because of the transatlantic flight, you can often find bargain airfares to this popular spot that, in some cases, are cheaper than what you'd pay when flying within the United States. Adding everything up, your trip to London can actually be comparable in cost to a trip to New York, San Francisco, or Los Angeles (also expensive cities to visit).

Adding Up the Elements

You can easily budget for your London trip, but holding down costs while you're in London may be another matter. (The city's shopping and dining is so enticing — and did I say expensive?) You can use the worksheets at the back of this book to get an approximate idea of what you'll spend.

A good way to get a handle on all costs is to walk yourself mentally through your trip, as follows:

    ✔ Begin with the cost of transportation to the airport.

    ✔ Add the cost of your flight and the price of getting from the London airport to your hotel.

    ✔ Add the total cost of hotel rooms for the duration of your trip.

    ✔ Factor in a daily allowance for meals and snacks (exclude breakfast if it's included in the hotel rate).

✔ Figure in costs for public transportation (you really don't want to drive in London).

✔ Add admission prices to museums, the theater, and other entertainment expenses (don't forget the cost of film and processing).

✔ Determine what you'd like to spend on souvenirs, and add that to your total.

✔ Add the cost of getting back to the London airport and of traveling from your originating airport to your home.

✔ Finally, tack on another 15% to 20% for good measure.

Budgeting for your biggest expense: Lodging

The cost of accommodations takes the biggest bite from your budget. Fortunately, because you have to book your rooms well in advance, you'll know this expense before you leave on vacation.

Chapter 6 gives you an idea of London neighborhoods and their suitability as your home base. Chapter 7 discusses what you can expect for your money and how to get the best rate. After you get a firm handle on the benefits of price and location, peruse Chapter 8 for my recommendations of top-notch B&Bs (bed-and-breakfast inns) and hotels in all price ranges and locations.

Rates vary considerably from B&B to B&B and from hotel to hotel, so I can't really give you a reliable average. For the recommendations in this guide, however, the rates are *generally* £83 to £100 ($125–$150) for an inexpensive property, £100 to £150 ($150–$225) for a moderately priced one, and £150 to £200 ($225–$300) for an expensive one. After that, you hit the stratosphere of £200-plus ($300-plus) for a luxury B&B or hotel. Keep in mind that many mid-range London hotels and all B&Bs include at least a continental breakfast as part of the room rate, so you can save a few pounds there.

Saving with Travelcards: Transportation

I have some good news that will save you a bundle: You don't need to rent a car in London. (If you want to rent a car to explore the areas surrounding London, see Chapter 9). The London Underground (called **the Tube**) is fast, convenient, and easy to use. Special reduced-price transportation passes, called Visitor Travelcards, make getting around the city relatively inexpensive.

Visitor Travelcards are not sold in England. In the United States and Canada, you can buy a voucher for a Visitor Travelcard before you leave home. After you arrive in England, you exchange the voucher for the appropriate card at any London Underground ticket window. Two kinds of cards are available: the *All Zone* and the *Central Zone,* which is good for everything in Central London, the area that contains the city's main attractions (see Chapter 6). Both allow unlimited travel on the Tube and bus and are available in three-, four-, or seven-day increments. Prices for the Central Zone card are $20 for adults and $9 for children for three days; $25 for adults and $10 for children for four days; and $30 for adults and $13 for children for seven days. You can buy Visitor Travelcards by contacting a travel agent, by calling **Rail Europe** at ☎ **888/382-7245,** or by going online at www. raileurope.com/us/.

If you plan to travel around England by train, consider getting a **BritRail pass.** You must buy these passes before you arrive (they are not sold in England), but they offer considerable savings over individual fares. You can select from a slew of options: a choice of either first or standard class, senior passes for those over 60, travel-time periods from eight consecutive days to one month, and Flexipasses allowing you to travel a certain number of days within a set time period. The cost for first-class adult travel for any four days in a two-month period is $349; standard-class is $235. You can order BritRail passes from **BritRail Travel International,** 500 Broadway, New York, NY 10036 (☎ **866/BRITRAIL** or 877/677-1066 in the U.S.; Internet: www.britrail.net).

Eating cheaply or splurging: Restaurants

The food in England used to be the butt (or shank) of many a joke, but in recent years London has emerged as one of the great food capitals of the world. Of course, that means eating at the top restaurants is going to cost you. However, you can find countless pubs and restaurants where you can dine cheaply and well — and where you can enjoy your meal along with the locals. In addition, many of the best London restaurants offer two- and three-course fixed-price meals that can be real bargains.

If you eat lunch and dinner at the moderately priced restaurants recommended in Chapter 14, you can expect to pay £20 to £47 ($30–$70) per person per day for meals, not including alcoholic drinks (assuming that breakfast is included in your hotel rate). If you have breakfast at a cafe instead of your hotel and are content with coffee and a roll, expect to pay about £2.70 to £3.30 ($4–$5). Depending on the restaurant, an old-fashioned English breakfast with eggs, bacon or sausage, toast, and tea or coffee can run anywhere from £5 to £10 ($8–$15). Likewise, a simple afternoon tea at a cafe (see Chapter 15 for these lighter meals) sets you back about £5 to £6 ($8–$9), but a lavish high tea at one of the great London hotels may total £20 ($30) or more.

Paying as you go: Attractions

Your budget for admission fees depends on what you want to see, of course. But you may not want to cut costs for sightseeing. After all, the sights are what you came all this way to see. Sure, an adult ticket to the **Tower of London** is £11 ($16), but do you really want to miss out on seeing this historic landmark and the extraordinary Crown Jewels housed there? Keep in mind that if you're a senior or a student, you can often get a reduced-price admission. Plus, some attractions offer reduced family rates that are good for two adults and two children.

Check out the sights in Chapters 16 and 17 and determine which are on your list of "must sees." Then add them to the worksheet entitled, "Places to Go, People to See, Things to Do" at the back of this book. Some of the top sights — the **British Museum, National Gallery, National Portrait Gallery, Tate Britain,** and **Tate Modern** — are free. In late 2001, three of the great South Kensington museums — the **Natural History Museum, the Science Museum,** and the **Victoria & Albert Museum** — abolished their admission fees as well. Plus, strolling through London's great parks or viewing **Buckingham Palace** (okay, from the outside) and the **Changing of the Guard** is also free.

Controlling costs: Shopping and nightlife

Shopping and entertainment are the most flexible parts of your budget. You don't have to buy anything at all, and you can hit the sack right after dinner instead of seeing a play or dancing at a club. You know what you want. Flip through the shopping options in Chapter 19 and the entertainment and nightlife venues in Chapters 22, 23, and 24. If anything strikes you as something you can't do without, budget accordingly. (Keep in mind that a pint in a pub sets you back about £2 [around $3.50], whereas a theater ticket can go for anywhere between £17 and £63 [$25 and $95].)

Table 3-1 gives you an idea of what things typically cost in London, so you can avoid some price shock.

Table 3-1	What Things Cost in London
Item	*Cost in U.S. $*
Transportation from Heathrow to Central London by Underground	$5
Transportation from Gatwick to Central London by train	$15
One-way Underground fare within Central London	$2.25
Double room at The Savoy	$435–$637

Item	Cost in U.S. $
Double room at Hazlitt's 1718	$262
Double room with breakfast at Hotel La Place	$202–$262
Double room at Hotel 167	$135–$148
Double room at Aston's Apartments (self-catering)	$125–$180
Pub meal for one at The Museum Tavern	$10
Meal for one at Oxo Tower Brasserie, excluding wine	$60
Set-price dinner for one at Rules, excluding wine	$30
Dinner for one at The Oratory, excluding wine	$22
Pizza at Gourmet Pizza Company	$10
Afternoon tea for one at the Lanesborough	$31
Coffee and cake at Pâtisserie Valerie	$8
Pint of beer at a pub	$3.50
Admission to the Tower of London (adult/child)	$16/$11
Admission to Madame Tussaud's (adult/child)	$18/$11
Theater ticket	$25–$95

This statistic may be of some use when planning your budget. In 2000 (the latest year for which figures are available), U.S. visitors stayed an average of 5.4 days in London and spent an average of £604 ($906), which comes out to about £112 ($167) per day. The figures include expenditures only while in London. So, for example, if visitors paid in advance for their accommodations as part of a package tour, that payment wasn't included in the figure, but if they paid for the room in London, the payment was included.

Keeping the VAT and Hidden Costs in Check

Allow me to introduce you to Britain's version of a sales tax, called the **value-added tax (VAT)**. Brace yourself: The tax amounts to 17.5%. The VAT is part of the reason that prices in London are so high. The tax is added to the total price of consumer goods (the price on the tag already includes it) and to hotel and restaurant bills. The VAT is not a hidden expense, but not all quoted room rates, especially in the luxury tier, include the tax. Make sure to ask whether your quoted room rate is inclusive or exclusive of VAT. (In the hotel listings in Chapter 8, I tell you if the rate does not include the VAT.)

 If you're not a resident of the European Union, you can get a VAT refund on purchases made in the United Kingdom (this doesn't include hotels and restaurants). See Chapter 19 for details.

 On top of the VAT, a few restaurants add a service charge of 12.5% to 15% to your bill. If they do, the menu must state this policy. This charge amounts to mandatory tipping, so if your charge receipt comes back with a space for you to add a tip, put a line through it. This extra charge is one of those little things that's important for you to be aware of; I mention it again in Chapter 13.

As a general rule, except for tips in restaurants (12.5%–15%) and to cab drivers (15%), London isn't a city where you tip excessively. An exception is if you stay in an expensive hotel with porters who carry your bags (£1 per bag) and doormen who hail you cabs (£1 per hailed cab).

The telephone in your hotel room is convenient, but I recommend that you avoid using it if you're on a budget. A local call that costs 20 pence (30¢) at a phone booth may cost you £1 ($1.50) or more from your hotel room. If you plan to make a number of calls during your trip, get a phone card (see the details under "Telephone" in the Appendix) and use pay phones.

Choosing Traveler's Checks, Credit Cards, ATMs, or Cash

Money makes the world go around, but dealing with an unfamiliar currency can make your head spin. In London, you pay for things in pounds and pence, meaning you have to convert your own currency into British pounds sterling (see Chapter 12 for detailed information about pounds and pence). When it comes to carrying money in London, should you bring traveler's checks or use ATMs? What about paying with credit cards? In this section, I tell you what you need to know about each option.

Toting traveler's checks: Safer than cash

Today, traveler's checks (*cheques* in the U.K.) are something of an anachronism from the days when people used to write personal checks all the time instead of using credit cards or going to the not-yet-invented

ATMs. These days, you don't really need traveler's checks because London, like most European cities, has 24-hour ATMs linked to an international network that most likely includes your bank at home (see the next section, "Using ATMs: They're everywhere"). Still, if you want the security of traveler's checks and don't mind the hassle of showing your passport every time you want to cash one, you can get them at almost any bank before you leave home.

Traveler's checks are issued from your home bank in your local currency. You generally pay a 1% commission fee to buy the checks. After you arrive in London, you need to convert them to pounds and pence. (I explain the transaction process in Chapter 12.)

The good thing about carrying traveler's checks instead of cash is that you can get a refund if your checks are lost or stolen. Be certain that you keep the checks separate from the official receipt that you receive for buying them, and write down each check number as you cash it. You need this record for any refund.

Never pay for hotels, meals, or purchases with traveler's checks denominated in any currency other than British pounds. You get a bad exchange rate if you try to use them as cash.

Using ATMs: They're everywhere

In less than a decade, ATMs have revolutionized the money side of travel. You can travel to London with as little as $20 in your pocket, using your bank card to withdraw the cash you need, in pounds, on arrival. ATMs offer a fast and easy way to exchange money at the bank's bulk exchange rate, which is better than any rate you can get on the street. If you withdraw only as much cash as you need every couple of days, you won't feel the insecurity of carrying around a huge wad of bills.

If you plan to use ATMs, make certain you have a four-digit personal identification number (PIN) *before* you arrive. You need a four-digit PIN to use ATMs in London — if you have a six- or an eight-digit PIN, you need to have a new one assigned to you. (You can also use ATMs to get credit-card cash advances, but you need a PIN suitable for overseas use. Check with your bank or credit-card company for details.)

You find 24-hour ATMs all over London: outside banks, in large supermarkets, and in some Underground (Tube) stations. **Cirrus** (☎ 800/424-7787; Internet: www.mastercard.com) and **Plus** (☎ 800/843-7587; Internet: www.visa.com) are the most popular networks; check the back of your ATM card to see which network your bank uses. The toll-free numbers and Web sites give you locations of ATMs where you can withdraw money while in London.

Many U.K. banks impose a fee of 50¢ to $3 every time you use an ATM. Your own bank may also charge you a fee for using ATMs from other banks. Obviously, you need to think twice about the amount you're withdrawing to keep bank fees low by limiting your need to use an ATM.

If you try to withdraw cash from an ATM and get a message saying your card isn't valid for international transactions, most likely the bank just can't make the telephone connection to check your account. Don't panic. Try another ATM or wait until the next day.

Paying with plastic: Classy and convenient

Credit cards are invaluable when traveling — they're a safe way to carry money, and they provide a convenient record of all your travel expenses. American Express, Diners Club, MasterCard, and Visa are widely accepted in London. A Eurocard or Access sign displayed at an establishment means that it accepts MasterCard.

When traveling, I've come to rely more and more on credit cards to pay for hotel rooms, meals, theater and concert tickets, and many other purchases. I don't do this because I'm a chargeaholic. I just find it much easier than carrying around a wad of pound notes, stopping to cash traveler's checks, or using ATMs all the time.

Credit-card purchases are usually translated from pounds to dollars at a favorable rate and show up on your monthly statement, so keeping track of expenditures is easy.

You can also use credit cards to get cash advances at any bank or from ATMs (see the preceding section, "Using ATMs: They're everywhere"), but you start paying interest on the advance the moment you receive the cash. (You won't receive frequent-flyer miles on an airline credit card, either.)

British retailers now have the option to charge more for goods and services paid for by credit card, but they're required to display a clear indication that differentiated pricing applies.

Bringing cash: Always appropriate

Britain has no exchange controls, so you can bring as much cash and as many traveler's checks into the country as you want. Some folks like to change a small amount (say $100) of currency into pounds before leaving for London. This small emergency fund is always enough to cover transportation from the airport to the hotel. You can trade dollars for pounds at currency exchanges in airports offering international flights to the United Kingdom.

Nowadays, though, waiting until you arrive in London to change money may be simpler. The currency-exchange windows at Heathrow and Gatwick (see Chapter 10) will almost certainly be open when your flight arrives, or you can use one of the airport's ATMs. Getting and changing money in London has never been so convenient.

Cutting Costs

Throughout this book, Bargain Alert icons highlight money-saving tips and/or great deals. Check out some additional cost-cutting strategies:

- ✔ **Go in the off-season.** If you can travel at non-peak times (October to mid-December or January to March), you'll find hotel prices can be as much as 20% less than during peak months.

- ✔ **Travel on off days of the week.** Airfares vary depending on the day of the week. If you can travel on a Tuesday, Wednesday, or Thursday, you may find cheaper flights to London. When you inquire about airfares, ask if you can obtain a cheaper rate by flying on a specific day.

- ✔ **Try a package tour.** For popular destinations like London, you can make just one call to a travel agent or packager to book airfare, hotel, ground transportation, and even some sightseeing. You'll pay much less than if you tried to put the trip together yourself (see Chapter 5).

- ✔ **Reserve a hotel room with a kitchen** (in London these are called "self-catering units") and do at least some of your own cooking. You may not feel as if you're on vacation if you do your own cooking and wash your own dishes, but you'll save money by not eating in restaurants two or three times a day. Parents traveling with small children may often find this stratagy useful.

- ✔ **Always ask for discount rates.** Membership in AAA, frequent-flyer programs, trade unions, AARP, or other groups may qualify you for discounts on plane tickets, hotel rooms, or even meals.

- ✔ **Ask if your kids can stay in your room with you.** A room with two double beds usually doesn't cost any more than one with a queen-size bed. And many hotels won't charge you the additional person rate if that person is pint-sized and related to you. Even if you have to pay a few pounds extra for a rollaway bed, you save hundreds by not taking two rooms.

✔ **Try expensive restaurants at lunch instead of dinner.** At most top restaurants, prices at lunch are considerably lower than those at dinner, and the menu often includes many of the dinnertime specialties. Also, look for the fixed-price menus.

✔ **Walk a lot.** London is large but completely walkable. A good pair of walking shoes can save you money in taxis and other local transportation. As a bonus, you get to know the city and its inhabitants more intimately, and you can explore at a slower pace.

✔ **Skip the souvenirs.** Your photographs and your memories should be the best mementos of your trip. If you're worried about your budget, do without the T-shirts, key chains, tea mugs, and other "royal" trinkets.

Chapter 4

Planning Ahead for Special Travel Needs

● ●

In This Chapter

▶ Visiting London with children

▶ Getting discounts and special tours for seniors

▶ Locating wheelchair-accessible attractions

▶ Finding lesbigay communities and special events

● ●

*M*any of today's travelers have special interests or needs. Parents may want to take their children along on trips. Seniors may like to take advantage of discounts or tours designed especially for them. People with disabilities may need to ensure that sites on their itineraries offer wheelchair access. And gays, lesbians, and bisexuals may want to know about welcoming places and events. In response to these needs, this chapter offers advice and resources.

Taking Your Children Along

Traveling with children, from toddlers to teens, is a challenge — no doubt about it. Bringing the brood can put a strain on the budget and influence your choices of activities and hotels. But in the end, isn't sharing your experiences as a family great?

Look for the Kid Friendly icon as you flip through this book. I use it to highlight hotels, restaurants, and attractions that are particularly family friendly. Zeroing in on these places can help you plan your trip more quickly and easily.

In addition, the following resources can help you plan your trip:

✔ **About Family Travel** (424 Bridge St., Ashland, OR 97520; ☎ **800/ 826-7165** or 541/488-3074; Fax: 541/488-3067; Internet: www. about-family-travel.com) can tailor a tour specifically for families traveling to London. Its services include arranging airfares, hotel rooms, transportation, and theater tickets, as well as providing tips on sights and destinations.

✔ **Family Travel Forum** (☎ **212/665-6124;** Fax: 212/661-6136; Internet: www.familytravelforum.com) offers a call-in service for subscribers. To order a subscription ($48 per year), write FTF, 891 Amsterdam Ave., New York, NY 10025, or call to request its free information packet.

Admission prices for most London attractions are generally reduced for children 5 to 16 years old. Children under 5 almost always get in for free. If you're traveling with one or two children 5 to 15, always check to see whether the attraction offers a money-saving family ticket, which considerably reduces the admission price for a group of two adults and two children.

Locating family-friendly accommodations and restaurants

Most hotels can happily accommodate your family if you reserve your rooms in advance and make the staff aware that you're traveling with kids. The establishment may bring in an extra cot or let you share a larger room; these types of arrangements are common. Smaller bed-and-breakfasts (B&Bs) may present problems, such as cramped rooms and shared toilet facilities, and some places don't accept children at all. Ask questions before you reserve.

London has plenty of American-style fast-food places, including **Burger King, McDonald's, Pizza Hut,** and **KFC.** Teens probably want to check out the **Hard Rock Café** in Mayfair or the scene at the **Pepsi Trocadero** in **Piccadilly Circus,** which offers theme restaurants such as **Planet Hollywood** and the **Rainforest Café** (see Chapter 17).

Expensive restaurants are less welcoming toward young children. The menus aren't geared to the tastes of U.S. youngsters, the prices can be high, and the staff can be less than accommodating.

To keep costs down, you can rent a hotel room with a kitchen (in England these are called "self-catering units") and prepare your own meals, as long as you don't mind cooking while on vacation. Another option, when the weather cooperates, is to take the family on a picnic. **Kensington Gardens** or **Hyde Park** may be just the ticket for an enjoyable afternoon (see Chapter 15 for more suggestions). You can also take advantage of pre-theater, fixed-price menus (usually served 5:30 to 7:00 p.m.), which are usually a good deal.

Planning your trip together

Your children may be more excited about their London trip if they know some of the special sights and events in store for them. Before you leave, sit down with your kids and make a plan. Go over the sights and activities in Chapters 16 and 17, and let your children list a few of the things they'd like to see and do, in order of preference. Make a similar list of your own. Older children may want to do some London research on the Internet (see the Appendix for the best Web sites). Together, plot out a day-by-day schedule that meets everyone's needs. You can use the "Places to Go, People to See, Things to Do" and "Going 'My' Way" worksheets at that back of this book.

Letting your younger children read *Peter Pan* or *Peter Pan in Kensington Gardens,* and telling them about his statue there, can generate excitement about the trip. Slightly older children may want to read the *Harry Potter* series, which takes place in real and fictional settings in London and around the country. (If your kids have already read the *Harry Potter* series, they know that Harry lives in London — in fact, he leaves from Paddington Station to go off to sorcerer's school.) Older children may enjoy thinking about traveling around London in the Underground (called the Tube) or taking a boat trip down the Thames. With the information in this book, and some online investigating, you can also incite your kids' curiosity about historic sites such as the **Tower of London** and **H.M.S. Cutty Sark.** And most young people enjoy the prospect of a meal at the **Hard Rock Café** or a trip to **Madame Tussaud's** wax museum.

Some kids and adult activities can easily overlap. You may want to spend one afternoon in **Kensington Gardens.** After the entire family visits Kensington Palace, the kids can blow off steam in the new **Princess Diana Memorial Playground.** Many kid-oriented activities in London are just as interesting for parents. From the dinosaur exhibit in the **Natural History Museum** to the animatronic robots re-creating historic scenes in Madame Tussaud's, you *and* your kids have plenty that you can experience and enjoy together.

Don't over schedule your days with your children. You can't enjoy your trip if both you and your children are worn out.

Preparing for a long trip

The shortest international trip to London (from New York) is about six hours (unless you're traveling on the Concorde); airtime from Australia may be 25 hours, which is a lot of time for kids to sit still and be quiet. Although children can spend some of the journey time watching a movie (or two) on the plane, come prepared with extra diversions: games, puzzles, books — whatever you know will keep your kids entertained.

Request a special kids' menu at least a day in advance from the airline. If your child needs baby food, bring your own and ask a flight attendant to warm it. Dealing with jet lag can be hard on adults but even harder on small children. Don't schedule too much for your first day in London. Get everyone comfortably settled and then take it from there.

Hiring a babysitter while on your trip

What you really need is a relaxing evening at the opera and a romantic late dinner. But you can't take Junior along on this special evening. What are your options? Ask your hotel staff if they can recommend a local babysitting service. Most of the hotels marked with a Kid Friendly icon in Chapter 8 can arrange for babysitting. London also has several respected and trustworthy babysitting agencies that provide registered nurses and carefully screened mothers, as well as trained nannies, to be sitters. Check the London Yellow Pages.

A fully licensed children's care facility, **Pippa Pop-ins** (430 Fulham Rd., SW6 1DU; ☎ **020/7385-2458;** Fax: 020/7385-5706) provides a lovely toy-filled nursery (staffed by experienced caregivers) where you can safely park the little ones. Babysitting is available until 11:30 p.m. at £8.50 ($13) per hour; the staff cares for your child for the day for a fee of £50 ($75).

Going Over Sixty: Tips and Bargains for Seniors

London won't present any problems for you if you're a senior who gets around easily. If you do have trouble getting around, be aware when you plan your trip that not all hotels — particularly less expensive B&Bs — have elevators. The steep staircases in some places are a test for *anyone* with luggage. When you reserve a hotel, ask whether you'll have access to a *lift* (an elevator in Britspeak).

Although London is often crowded, people are generally polite and courteous. The British are orderly when *queuing up* (standing in lines), and they usually respect personal space. And you don't need to be overly concerned about crime. Yes, it does occur, but with far less frequency than in many other major cities.

In most cities, including London, being a senior often entitles you to some terrific travel bargains, such as reduced admission at theaters, museums, and other attractions. Carrying ID with proof of age can pay off in all these situations. **Note:** In London and the United Kingdom, you may find that some discounts are available only to members of a British association; public transportation reductions, for example, are available only to U.K. residents with British Pension books. But always ask, even if the reduction isn't posted.

The following sources can provide information on discounts and other benefits for seniors:

- ✔ **AARP (American Association of Retired Persons**, 601 E St. NW, Washington, DC 20049; ☎ **800/424-3410;** Internet: www.aarp.org) offers member discounts on car rentals and hotels. AARP offers $10 yearly memberships that include discounts of 12% to 25% on Virgin Atlantic flights to London from eight U.S. cities.

- ✔ **Elderhostel** (75 Federal St., Boston, MA 02110-1941; ☎ **877/426-8056;** Internet: www.elderhostel.org) offers people 55 and older a variety of university-based educational programs in London and throughout England. These courses are value-packed, hassle-free ways to learn while traveling. The price includes airfare, accommodations, meals, tuition, tips, and insurance. And you'll be glad to know that you don't receive any grades. Popular London offerings have included "Inside the Parliament," "Legal London," "Classical Music and Opera in London," and "Treasures of London Galleries."

- ✔ **Saga International Holidays** (222 Berkeley St., Boston, MA 02116; ☎ **877/265-6862;** Internet: www.sagaholidays.com) offers inclusive tours for those 50 and older. Although its tours cover places outside London (such as Cornwall), you can often arrange to spend a few days in London before or after the tour.

- ✔ **Grand Circle Travel** (347 Congress St., Boston, MA 02210; ☎ **800/597-3644;** Internet: www.gct.com) is another agency that escorts tours for mature travelers. Call or order online for a copy of its publication *101 Tips for the Mature Traveler.*

 Most of the major domestic airlines, including American, United, Continental, US Airways, and TWA, offer discount programs for senior travelers — be sure to ask whenever you book a flight.

Accessing London: Information for People with Disabilities

A disability needn't stop anybody from traveling, because more options and resources are available than ever before. Many hotels and restaurants are happy to accommodate people with disabilities.

If you use a travel agent, be sure to discuss with him or her the means of travel (train or plane, for example) that can accommodate your physical needs; special accommodations or services you may require (transportation within the airport, help with a wheelchair, and special seating or meals); and the type of special assistance you can expect from your transportation company, hotel, tour group, and so on.

Persons with disabilities are often entitled to special discounts at sight-seeing and entertainment venues in Britain. These discounts are called *concessions* (often shortened to "concs").

Before departing on your trip, contact the British Tourist Authority (see the Appendix for addresses and phone numbers) to be mailed a copy of its *Disabled Traveler Fact Sheet,* which contains some helpful general information.

The United Kingdom has several information resources for disabled travelers. The best of these include:

✔ **Artsline** at ☎ **020/7388-2227** provides advice on the accessibility of London arts and entertainment events. The Society of London Theatres (32 Rose St., London WC2E 9ET; Internet: `www.officiallondontheatre.co.uk`) offers a free guide called *Access Guide to London's West End Theatres.*

✔ RailEurope's **British Travel Shop** (551 Fifth Ave., 7th floor, New York, NY 10176; ☎ **212/490-6688**) sells *Access in London* ($19.95), the best and most comprehensive London guide for the disabled and anyone with a mobility problem. The book provides full access information for all the major sites, hotels, and modes of transportation. The publication costs £7.95 ($13) in the United Kingdom and is available at many London bookstores.

✔ **Holiday Care Service** (2nd Floor, Imperial Buildings, Victoria Road, Horley RH6 7PZ; ☎ **01293/774-535** or 01293/776-943 [TTY]; Fax: 01293/784-647) offers information and advice on suitable accommodations, transportation, and other facilities in England.

✔ **RADAR (Royal Association for Disability and Rehabilitation,** 12 City Forum, 250 City Rd., London EC14 8AF; ☎ **020/7250-3222;** Fax: 020/7250-0212) publishes information for disabled travelers in Britain.

✔ **Tripscope, The Courtyard** (Evelyn Road, London W4 5JI; ☎ **020/8994-9294**) provides travel and transport information and advice, including airport facilities.

Some other helpful resources in the United States include the following:

✔ **Travel Information Service** (☎ **215/456-9603** or 215/456-9602 [TTY]; Internet: `www.mossresourcenet.org`) provides general information and resources for the disabled traveler.

✔ The **Society for Accessible Travel & Hospitality** (347 Fifth Ave., Suite 610, New York, NY 10016; ☎ **212/447-7284;** Fax: 212/725-8253; Internet: `www.sath.com`) is a membership organization with names and addresses of tour operators specializing in travel for the disabled. You can call to subscribe to its magazine, *Open World.*

✔ **American Foundation for the Blind** (11 Penn Plaza, Suite 300, New York, NY 10001; ☎ **800/232-5463;** Internet: www.afb.org) offers information on traveling with Seeing-Eye dogs; the foundation also issues ID cards to the legally blind.

Joining escorted tours

You can find tours designed to meet the needs of travelers with disabilities. One of the best operators is **Flying Wheels Travel** (143 West Bridge, P.O. Box 382, Owatonna, MN 55060; ☎ **800/525-6790;** Internet: www. flyingwheelstravel.com), which offers various escorted tours and cruises, as well as private tours in minivans with lifts.

Here are some other tour operators for London-bound travelers with disabilities:

✔ **Accessible Journeys** (☎ **800/846-4537;** Fax: 610/521-6959; Internet: www.disabilitytravel.com) offers tours of Britain and London in minibuses or motorcoaches.

✔ **The Guided Tour** (☎ **800/783-5841;** Fax: 215/635-2637; E-mail: gtour400@aol.com) has one- and two-week guided tours for individuals, with one staff member for every three travelers.

✔ **Undiscovered Britain** (☎ **215/969-0542;** Fax: 215/969-9251; Internet: www.undiscoveredbritain.com) provides specialty travel and tours for individuals, small groups, or families traveling with a wheelchair user.

Dealing with access issues

The United Kingdom doesn't yet have a program like the Americans with Disabilities Act. By 2004, however, some form of legislation will be in place and more and more businesses will become accessible.

Not all hotels and restaurants in Britain provide wheelchair ramps. Most of the less expensive B&Bs and older hotels don't have elevators, or the elevators are too small for a wheelchair. Ask about this issue when you reserve your room or table.

All the top sights in Chapter 16 and many of the attractions in Chapter 17 are wheelchair accessible, but in some cases you must use a different entrance. Call the attraction to find out about special entrances, ramps, elevator locations, and general directions. Theaters and performing-arts venues are often wheelchair accessible as well (again, call first).

Trains throughout the United Kingdom now have wide doors, grab rails, and provisions for wheelchairs. To get more information or to obtain a copy of the leaflet *Rail Travel for Disabled Passengers,* contact

The Project Manager (Disability), British Rail, Euston House, Eversholt Street, London NW1 1DZ; ☎ **020/7922-6984.** You can also check out the **National Rail** Web site at www.nationalrail.co.uk, which has a section on disabled travel and contact details for the various train operating companies.

Disabled travelers will want to keep the following in mind when traveling around London:

✔ Although London's streets and sidewalks are generally kept in good repair, the city is old, so you won't find many modern curb cuts.

✔ Not all the city's Underground (subway) stations have elevators and ramps.

✔ Public buses aren't wheelchair accessible.

✔ The city's black cabs are roomy enough for wheelchairs.

✔ Victoria Coach Station in Central London has Braille maps.

The following organizations provide access information and services for disabled travelers in London:

✔ **London Transport's Unit for Disabled Passengers** (172 Buckingham Palace Rd., SW1 W9TN; ☎ **020/7918-3299;** Fax: 020/7918-3876) publishes a free brochure called *Access to the Underground.* The organization also provides information on the wheelchair-accessible minibus service (called Stationlink) between all the major BritRail stations.

✔ **Wheelchair Travel** (1 Johnston Green, Guildford, Surrey GU2 6XS; ☎ **1483/233-640;** Fax: 1483/237-772; Internet: www. wheelchair-travel.co.uk) is an independent transport service for the disabled traveler arriving in London. The organization offers self-drive cars and minibuses (although I strongly discourage anyone, disabled or not, from driving in London) and can provide wheelchairs. Drivers who also act as guides are also available on request. Bring your own disabled stickers and permits from home if you're going to rent a self-drive vehicle.

Taking health precautions

Before you leave on your trip, talk to your physician about your general physical condition and your prescriptions for the time you're traveling, medical equipment you should take, and how to get medical assistance when you're away. Carry all prescription medicines in their original bottles with the contents clearly marked, along with a letter from your doctor.

Make a list of the generic names of your prescription drugs in case you need to replace or refill them during your visit. Pack medications in your hand luggage. If you're in a wheelchair, have a maintenance check before your trip and take some basic tools and extra parts if necessary. If you don't use a wheelchair but have trouble walking or become easily tired, consider renting a wheelchair to take with you as checked baggage.

Finding Sites and Events Friendly to Gays and Lesbians

London has always been a popular destination for gays and lesbians, even in the days (prior to 1967) when homosexuality was a criminal offense in Britain. Today, with a more tolerant government at the helm, gay pride is prominent. The city government has actually *spent money* to promote gay tourism. You can find gay theaters, gay shops, more than 100 gay pubs, famous gay discos, and gay community groups of all sorts. Click the "Gay and Lesbian" bar on the British Tourist Authority's Web site at www.btausa.com for information on gay venues and events throughout England.

Old Compton Street in Soho is the heart of London's Gay Village, filled with dozens of gay pubs, restaurants, and upscale bars/cafes. The Earl's Court area, long a gay bastion, has several gay/lesbian hotels and restaurants, including the **Philbeach Hotel** and the **New York Hotel** (see Chapter 8).

Lesbigay events in London include the **London Lesbian and Gay Film Festival** in March, the **Pride Parade** and celebrations in June, and the big outdoor bash known as **Summer Rites** in August. You can obtain information and exact dates from the London Lesbian and Gay Switchboard at ☎ 020/7837-7324 or online at www.llgs.org.uk.

Brighton (which I describe in Chapter 21) is one of the gayest seaside resort towns in Europe. From London, you can get there on the train in under an hour.

You may want to check out the following Web sites as you plan your trip. All are specifically geared to gay and lesbian travelers to London and the United Kingdom:

- ✔ www.pinkpassport.com
- ✔ www.demon.co.uk/world/ukgay
- ✔ www.gaytravel.co.uk

✔ www.gayguide.co.uk

✔ www.gaybritain.co.uk

✔ www.timeout.com, the online edition of *Time Out* magazine, with a gay and lesbian section

The newest and most useful travel guide — covering London, Brighton, and many other hot European destinations — is *Frommer's Gay & Lesbian Europe* (published by Hungry Minds, Inc.), available at most bookstores.

In addition, several gay magazines, useful for their listings and news coverage, are available in gay pubs, clubs, bars, and cafes. The most popular are *Boyz* (www.21stcenturyboyz.com), *Pink Paper* (www.pinkpaper.com), and *QX* (*Queer Xtra*; www.qxmag.co.uk). *Gay Times* (www.gaytimes.co.uk) is a high-quality monthly news-oriented mag available at most news agents. *Gay to Z* (www.freedom.co.uk/gaytoz) is the United Kingdom's "pink telephone directory." Indispensable for its city-wide listings (including gay listings), *Time Out* appears at newsstands on Wednesdays.

Gay's the Word (66 Marchmont St., WC1; ☎ 020/7278-7654; Tube: Russell Sq.) is the city's only all-round gay and lesbian bookstore; the store stocks a fine selection of new and used books and current periodicals.

Part II
Ironing Out the Details

The 5th Wave   By Rich Tennant

"Welcome to our nonstop flight to London. Will you be sitting among the heather with us sir, or back in the moors?"

In this part...

This part is all about the nitty-gritty of trip planning. How will you get to London, and where will you stay after you arrive? Chapter 5 covers the pros and cons of using a travel agent and gives you some tips on escorted tours, package tours, and airlines. Chapter 6 describes what you can expect in terms of accommodations and their price ranges, and discusses London's neighborhoods. Chapter 7 focuses on finding a good hotel for the best possible rate. You may want to turn directly to Chapter 8, my list of London's best hotels, all described and cross-indexed by price and location. And Chapter 9 goes through some last-minute details and ties up a bunch of loose ends: getting a passport, making advance reservations, packing, and more.

Chapter 5

Getting to London

● ●

In This Chapter

▶ Evaluating the benefits of using a travel agent

▶ Deciding whether to travel on your own or take an escorted tour

▶ Discovering the advantages of package tours

▶ Planning the trip on your own

▶ Traveling by plane, train, or ferry

● ●

You just wanted to take a nice little trip to London. But now, trying to make all the necessary decisions, you're overwhelmed. Do you need a travel agent? Do you want to travel with a tour group and have all the decisions made for you, or do you want to strike out on your own? How do you find the best airfares to London? This chapter helps you find the answers.

Consulting a Travel Agent: A Good Idea?

A travel agent can help you find a bargain airfare, hotel room, or rental car. The best travel agents can tell you how much time to budget for a destination, find you a cheap flight that doesn't require you to change planes in off-the-beaten-path airports, get you a better hotel room for about the same price, and even give recommendations on restaurants.

Word of mouth is the best way to find a good travel agent. Check with family members, neighbors, or friends who've had experiences with travel agents. Make sure that you pick an agent who knows London.

To make sure that your travel agent meets your needs, find out all you can about London (you've already made a sound decision by buying this book) and pick out some hotels and attractions you think you'll like. If you have access to the Internet, check prices on the Web. Then bring your guidebook and Web information with you to the travel agency. If the agent offers you a better price than what you found on your own, ask him or her to make the arrangements for you.

Because a travel agent has access to more resources than even the most complete travel Web site, he or she should be able to get you a better price than you can get by yourself. And an agent can issue your tickets and vouchers on the spot. If the agent can't get you into the hotel of your choice, ask for an alternative recommendation; then look for an objective review in your guidebook while you are still at the travel agency. Remember, too, that a travel agent can take care of BritRail passes (see Chapter 3), airport-to-city transfers (see Chapter 10), Visitor Travelcards for the London bus and Underground system (see Chapter 3), and sightseeing tours (see Chapter 18).

Travel agents work on commission. The good news is that *you* don't pay the commission; the airlines, accommodations, and tour companies do. The bad news is that you may run into some unscrupulous travel agents who will try to persuade you to book the vacations that bring them the highest commissions.

Some airlines and resorts have begun limiting or eliminating travel agent commissions altogether. The immediate result has been that agents don't bother booking certain services unless the customer specifically requests them. If more airlines and companies throughout the industry lower commissions, travel agents may have to start charging customers for their services.

Considering Escorted Tours

Do you like letting a bus driver worry about traffic while you sit in comfort and listen to a tour guide explain everything? Or do you prefer renting a car and following your nose, even if you don't catch all the highlights? Do you like having events planned for each day, or would you rather improvise as you go along? The answers to these questions determine whether you should choose the guided tour or travel à la carte.

Some people love escorted tours. The tour company takes care of all the details and tells you what to expect at each attraction. You know your costs up front, and you don't encounter many surprises. **Escorted tours** can take you to the maximum number of sights in the minimum amount of time with the least amount of hassle.

Other people need more freedom and spontaneity. They prefer to discover a destination by themselves and don't mind getting caught in a thunderstorm without an umbrella (*brolly* in Britspeak) or finding that a recommended restaurant is no longer in business — those mishaps are just part of the adventure.

If you decide to go with an escorted tour, I strongly recommend purchasing travel insurance, especially if the tour operator asks you to pay up front. But don't buy insurance from the tour operator! If the tour operator doesn't fulfill its obligation to provide you with the vacation you paid for, you have no reason to think it'll fulfill its insurance obligations, either. Get travel insurance through an independent agency. (I provide more info about the ins and outs of travel insurance in Chapter 9.)

Talking with tour operators

If you decide to take an escorted tour, ask a few simple questions before you make a commitment. Along with finding out whether you need to put down a deposit and when final payment is due, ask the following questions:

- ✔ **What is the cancellation policy?** How late can you cancel if you can't go? Do you get a refund if you cancel? Do you get a refund if the operator cancels?

- ✔ **How jam-packed is the schedule?** Does the tour schedule try to fit 25 hours into a 24-hour day, or does it give you ample time to relax or shop? If getting up at 7 a.m. every day and not returning to your hotel until 6 or 7 p.m. sounds like a grind, certain escorted tours may not be for you.

- ✔ **How big is the group?** The smaller the group, the less time you spend waiting for people to get on and off the bus. Tour operators may be evasive about the number of travelers because they may not know the exact size of the group until everybody has made their reservations, but they should be able to give you a rough estimate.

- ✔ **Does the tour require a minimum group size?** Some tour operators require a minimum group size and may cancel the tour if they don't book enough people. If a quota exists, find out what it is and how close they are to reaching it. Again, tour operators may be evasive in their answers, but the information may help you select a tour that's sure to take place.

- ✔ **What exactly is included?** Don't assume anything. You may be required to get yourself to and from the airports at your own expense. A box lunch may be included in an excursion, but drinks may be extra. Beer may be included, but not wine. How much flexibility does the tour offer? Can you opt out of certain activities, or does the bus leave once a day, with no exceptions? Are all your meals planned in advance? Can you choose your entree at dinner, or does everybody get the same chicken cutlet?

Finding escorted tours

Dozens of companies offer escorted tours to London. Many of them cater to special interests, such as theater or history buffs, and others are more general. To find a tour that suits your interests, your best bet is to check with a travel agent. You can also scan the travel section in your local paper or check the Web sites of the major airlines (see the Appendix for their Web addresses), most of which offer escorted tours.

A few companies that offer escorted tours to London include the following:

- ✔ **Globus and Cosmos** (Internet: www.globusandcosmos.com) are well-known budget tour companies working in partnership. Current Cosmos offerings include an eight-day tour of London starting at $715, airfare included. Globus offers a week in London starting at $835, airfare included. These are not fully escorted tours because much of the time you're on your own; however, someone is available at all times to answer any questions, and sightseeing tours are part of the package. The prices can't be beat.

- ✔ **Maupintour** (Internet: www.maupintour.com) has a three-day/two-night London City Stay package that starts at $725, not including airfare.

- ✔ **Trafalgar Tours** (Internet: www.trafalgartours.com) offers a CostSaver London Week package starting at £315 ($457), which includes six nights in a London hotel, a half-day sightseeing tour, a three-day Visitor Travelcard for Tube and bus, and a seat at a West End show. This package doesn't include airfare.

Weighing the Benefits of Package Tours

Package tours are different from escorted tours. **Package tours** allow you to buy your airfare and accommodations at the same time. And for popular destinations, such as London, they can really be the smart way to go because with a package tour you can save a *ton* of money.

A London package tour that includes airfare, hotel, and transportation to and from the airport may cost less than the hotel alone if you book the room yourself. The reason is that package tours are sold in bulk to tour operators, who resell them to the public. Each destination usually has one or two packagers that offer better deals than the rest because they buy in even greater volume.

Packages — and their prices — vary considerably. Some offer a better class of hotel than others. Some offer the same hotels for lower prices. Some offer flights on scheduled airlines; others book charters. Your choices of accommodations and travel days may be limited; however, in some cases, adjusting your travel dates by a week (or even a day) can yield substantial savings. Some packages let you choose between escorted vacations and independent vacations; others allow you to add on just a few excursions or escorted day trips (also at prices lower than if you book them yourself) without booking an entirely escorted tour. Shop around and ask plenty of questions before you book your trip. The time you spend doing research will be worth the bucks you save.

Locating package tours

Information about package tours is available from a variety of sources. A few companies that offer packages to London include the following:

- ✔ **British Travel International** (☎ 800/327-6097; Internet: www. britishtravel.com), is a good source for discount packages.

- ✔ **Liberty Travel** (☎ 888/271-1584; Internet: www.libertytravel. com), one of the biggest packagers in the northeastern United States, offers reasonably priced packages.

- ✔ **Trailfinders** (Internet: www.trailfinders.com.uk), another good source for discount packages, has several offices in Australia: Sydney (☎ 02/9247-7666), Melbourne (☎ 03/9600-3022), Cairns (☎ 07/4041-1199), Brisbane (☎ 07/3229-0887), and Perth (☎ 08/9226-1222).

Good places to look for additional package tours include:

- ✔ **Local newspaper:** Look in the travel section of your local Sunday newspaper for advertisements. One reliable packager that you may see is **American Express Vacations** (☎ 800/346-3607; Internet: http://travel.americanexpress.com/travel).

- ✔ **National travel magazines:** Check the ads in the back of magazines, such as *Arthur Frommer's Budget Travel, Travel & Leisure, National Geographic Traveler,* and *Condé Nast Traveler.*

- ✔ **Online at www.vacationpackager.com:** At this Web site, you plug in your destination and interests, and the site makes many suggestions of companies that you can contact on your own or through a travel agent.

Checking out airline and hotel packages

Airlines are good sources for package tours, especially to London, because they package their flights together with accommodations. When you pick an airline, you can choose the one that has frequent service to your hometown and on which you accumulate frequent-flier miles.

Although disreputable packagers are uncommon, they do exist. By buying your package from an airline, you can be fairly sure that the company will still be in business when your departure date arrives.

The following airlines offer packages to London:

- ✔ **American Airlines Vacations** (☎ 800/321-2121; Internet: www.aavacations.com)

- ✔ **British Airways Holidays** (☎ 800/AIRWAYS; Internet: www. britishairways.com/holiday)

- ✔ **Continental Airlines Vacations** (☎ 800/634-5555; Internet: www.continental.com)

- ✔ **Delta Vacations** (☎ 800/872-7786; Internet: www. deltavacations.com)

- ✔ **Northwest Airlines World Vacations** (☎ 800/800-1504; Internet: www.nwaworldvacations.com)

- ✔ **Trans World Airlines Getaway Vacations** (☎ 800/438-2929; Internet: www.twa.com)

- ✔ **United Airlines Vacations** (☎ 800/328-6877; Internet: www. unitedvacations.com)

To give you an idea of cost, here's a quick look at some sample airline package prices — based on per person, double occupancy. (Single supplements are available for solo travelers, but they increase the price considerably — aggravating, isn't it?) These packages don't include airport taxes and surcharges, which typically amount to about $80. All hotels have private bathrooms (with tubs or shower stalls) and include breakfast. The packages in the following list were available at press time; they may or may not be available when you travel, but they can give you an idea of typical offerings.

- ✔ **British Airways:** "A Taste of London" packages are $479 to $1,099 for four days/three nights and $649 to $1,589 for seven days/six nights. Prices include airfare, transportation to your hotel from Heathrow or Gatwick, accommodations, and an open-top bus tour.

  "Treasures of London," a seven-day/six-night package for $729 to $1,809, adds a seven-day Travelcard for the bus and Underground (subway) and a more comprehensive sightseeing tour.

  Starting at $699 per adult and $389 per child for four days/three nights, "London Family Vacations" offers a meal at Planet Hollywood and a choice of a theater ticket or a sightseeing tour.

- ✔ **Continental Airlines:** The "London City Stay" package includes round-trip airfare and three nights in a hotel for $449 to $1,079, depending on the city of departure and class of hotel. Many add-ons are available, including tours and theater tickets.

✔ **Delta:** "City Stay" London theater packages range from $789 to $1,159, including airfare, hotel accommodations for three nights, and a top-price ticket to a West End show.

✔ **TWA:** The "Majestic London" package — at $1,829 to $2,249 depending on the season and point of departure — includes airfare, chauffeur-driven airport-to-hotel transfers, a chauffeured sightseeing tour of the West End (or private car and driver at your disposal for six hours), three nights in a deluxe hotel, and two dinners.

✔ **Virgin Atlantic:** For $909 to $1,789, the seven-day/six-night London packages include airfare, airport transfers, accommodations, two London tours, a theater pass, and an afternoon tea.

The biggest hotel chains also offer packages. The following are among large hotel groups with properties in London:

✔ **Forte & Meridien Hotels & Resorts** (☎ **800/225-5843;** Internet: www.forte-hotels.com and www.lemeridien-hotels.com)

✔ **Hilton Hotels** (☎ **800/HILTONS;** Internet: www.hilton.com)

✔ **Hyatt Hotels & Resorts** (☎ **800/228-3336;** Internet: www.hyatt.com)

✔ **Inter-Continental Hotels & Resorts** (☎ **800/327-0200;** Internet: www.interconti.com)

✔ **Sheraton Hotels & Resorts** (☎ **800/325-3535;** Internet: www.sheraton.com)

✔ **Thistle Hotels Worldwide** (☎ **800/847-4358;** Internet: www.thistlehotels.com)

If you already know where you want to stay, call that hotel and ask whether they offer land/air packages.

Making Your Own Arrangements

Are you a totally independent traveler? Maybe you're a control freak and can't stand even a single detail being out of your hands, or you're into spontaneity and hate having anything pre-arranged except for what's absolutely essential (like, say, your flight). Or perhaps you just like to be on your own. Whatever your reason, I'm happy to supply some basic transportation data for those who want to make their own travel arrangements.

Snagging the best airfare

If you need flexibility, be ready to pay for it. Full-price fare usually applies to last-minute bookings, sudden itinerary changes, and round trips that get you home before the weekend. On most flights, even the shortest routes, a full-price fare can approach $1,000.

 You pay far less than full fare if you book well in advance, can stay over Saturday night, or can travel on Tuesday, Wednesday, or Thursday. A ticket bought as little as 7 to 14 days in advance costs only 20% to 30% of the full fare. If you can travel with just a couple days' notice, you may also get a deal (usually on a weekend fare that you book through an airline's Web site — see the section "Getting away on the weekend" later in this chapter for more).

 Airlines periodically lower prices on their most popular routes (such as London). Restrictions abound, but the sales translate into great prices — usually no more than $400 for a transatlantic flight to London from the East Coast of the United States. Watch newspaper and television ads and airline Web sites, and when you see a good price, grab it. These sales usually run during slow seasons (in London, November 1 to December 12 and December 25 to March 14) and rarely coincide with peak travel times (in London, late April to mid-October) when people often fly regardless of price.

See the next three sections for information on how consolidators and airline Web sites can save you big money.

Cutting ticket costs with consolidators

 Consolidators, also known as *bucket shops,* are good places to find low fares. Consolidators buy seats in bulk and resell them at prices that undercut the airlines' discounted rates. Be aware that tickets bought this way are usually nonrefundable or carry stiff cancellation penalties (as much as 75% of the ticket price). **Important:** Before you pay, ask the consolidator for a confirmation number and then call the airline to confirm your seat. Be prepared to book your ticket through a different consolidator if the airline can't confirm your reservation.

Consolidators' small ads usually appear in major newspapers' Sunday travel sections at the bottom of the page. **Council Travel** (☎800/226-8624; Internet: www.counciltravel.com) caters to young travelers but offers bargain prices to people of all ages. Other reliable consolidators include **1-800/FLY-CHEAP** (☎ 800/359-2432; Internet: www.1800flycheap.com); **TFI Tours International** (☎ 800/745-8000 or 212/736-1140) serves as a clearinghouse for unused seats; and **rebaters,** such as **Travel Avenue** (☎ 800/333-3335 or 312/876-1116; Internet: www.travelavenue.com), rebate part of their commissions to you.

Shopping for bargains on the Web

Use the Internet to search for deals on airfare, hotels, and car rentals. Among the leading Web sites are **Arthur Frommer's Budget Travel Online** (www.frommers.com), **Travelocity** (www.travelocity.com), **Lowestfare** (www.lowestfare.com), **Microsoft Expedia** (www.expedia.com), **The Trip** (www.thetrip.com), **Smarter Living** (www.smarterliving.com), and **Yahoo!** (http://travel.yahoo.com).

Each site provides roughly the same service, with variations that you may find useful or useless. Enter your travel dates and route, and the computer searches for the lowest fares. Several other features are standard, and periodic bell-and-whistle updates make occasional visits worthwhile. You can check flights at different times or on different dates in hopes of finding a lower price, sign up for e-mail alerts that tell you when the fare on a route that you specified drops below a certain level, and gain access to databases that advertise cheap packages and fares for those who can get away at a moment's notice.

Remember that you don't have to book online; you can ask your flesh-and-blood travel agent to match or beat the best price you find.

Getting away on the weekend

Airlines make great, last-minute deals available through their Web sites once a week, usually on Wednesday. Flights generally leave on Friday or Saturday (that is, only two or three days later) and return the following Sunday, Monday, or Tuesday. Some carriers offer hotel and car bargains at the same time.

You can sign up for e-mail alerts through individual Web sites or all at once through **Smarter Living** (Internet: www.smarterliving.com). If you already know what airline you want to fly, consider staying up late on Tuesday and checking the Web site until the bargains for the coming weekend appear. Book right away and avoid losing out on the limited number of seats.

Traveling with a queen

Sail from New York to Southampton, 77 miles from London, on board the Cunard Line's *Queen Elizabeth II.* The ship crosses once in May, twice in June, and once per month from July to November. The trip takes six days. Fares begin around $2,500 for double occupancy in the smallest cabins and include airfare back to the States. For more information, contact **Cunard** (☎ 800/5CUNARD; Internet: www.cunardline.com).

Finding out who flies where

Your London adventure really begins when you land, and where you land can make a difference in how easy it is to get about. Four airports serve regularly scheduled flights to the London metropolitan area, with a fifth airport that's less frequently used. Public transportation service is available into Central London from all five airports (see Chapter 10).

Where you arrive depends on the city you're flying from and your airline. If you're on a regularly scheduled international flight from the States, you'll arrive at Heathrow or Gatwick. If you're on a flight from the Continent, you may land at Heathrow, Gatwick, Stansted, or London City. Luton is much smaller than the others and is used mostly for charter flights from the Continent. Here's a brief description of each of the five airports (see the Appendix for contact information of the airlines mentioned):

✔ **Heathrow,** the main international airport, is about 15 miles west of Central London. It's served by Air New Zealand, American, British Airways, Continental, Delta, Icelandair, United, and Virgin Atlantic. You can get into London on the Underground (the Tube) in about 40 minutes for £3.60 ($5). The Heathrow Express Train travels between Heathrow and Paddington rail station (in 15 minutes) for £12 ($18), and the Airbus gets you to Victoria and Euston rail stations (in about 75 minutes) for £7 ($11).

✔ **Gatwick** is smaller than Heathrow and about 25 miles south of London. It's served by American, British Airways, Delta, Continental, Northwest, Icelandair, TWA, and Virgin Atlantic. Gatwick Express trains travel from the airport to Victoria Station in Central London in about half an hour for £10.20 ($15).

✔ **Stansted,** about 50 miles northeast of London, is used for national and European flights. The Stansted Sky Train to Liverpool Street Station takes 45 minutes and costs £10 ($15).

✔ **London City,** only 6 miles east of Central London, services European destinations. A bus charges £5 ($8) to take passengers on the 25-minute trip from the airport to Liverpool Street Station.

✔ **Luton,** 28 miles northwest of London, services mostly charter flights. Travel by train from the airport to King's Cross Station for £10 ($15); the trip takes about an hour.

Arriving via the Channel or Chunnel

If you're traveling to London from another destination in Europe, flying isn't the only way to get there. Train and car ferries and high-speed hovercrafts cross the English Channel throughout the year from ports in France, Holland, and Belgium. And the Eurostar, a high-speed train, zips through the Chunnel, a tunnel beneath the English Channel.

Taking the train

London has several train stations, and the one you arrive at depends on your point of departure from the Continent. The fabulous three-hour Eurostar service connecting Paris and Brussels to London via the Chunnel arrives at Waterloo International Station (some Eurostar trains even offer a drive-on/drive-off service for people heading to London in a car). Trains from Amsterdam arrive at Liverpool Street Station. People traveling to London from elsewhere in the United Kingdom may arrive at Victoria, Paddington, King's Cross, or Euston Stations. Every London train station has an Underground link.

The trains in the United Kingdom are separate from those in the rest of Europe, so a Eurail pass isn't valid there. If you're going to travel within the United Kingdom, check out the various BritRail passes available by calling ☎ **866/BRITRAIL** in the United States or by checking out www.britrail.net (see Chapter 3 for more on BritRail passes).

Several types of Eurostar fares are available. Senior fares for those over 60 and youth fares for those under 26 can cut the price of a first-class fare ($279 at press time) by 20% or more. The same reductions apply for passengers traveling with validated Eurail and BritRail passes. Visit Rail Europe's Web site at www.raileurope.com to check out current and special promotional fares for Eurostar.

Riding a ferry or hovercraft

Crossing time for the car, train, and passenger ferries that regularly crisscross the English Channel can be anywhere from 90 minutes to 5 hours, depending on the point of departure. Various hovercrafts (high-speed ferries with propellers that lift them off the surface of the water) skim over the water in as little as half an hour. Any train ticket that has London as its final destination figures the price of these channel crossings into its cost. Frequent train service to London is available from all the channel ports. The following is a list of the major ferry and hovercraft companies:

✔ **Hoverspeed UK Limited** (☎ **08705/240-241** in the United Kingdom; Internet: www.hoversped.co.uk) operates hovercrafts that zip across the channel between Calais and Dover in 35 minutes; the SuperseaCats (jet-propelled catamarans) run between Newhaven and Dieppe in 55 minutes.

✔ **P&O European Ferries** (☎ **561/563-2856** in the U.S. or 870/242-4999 in the United Kingdom; Internet: www.poportsmith.com) offers daily ferry/car crossings between Cherbourg and Portsmouth (crossing time is five hours) and Le Havre and Portsmouth (crossing time is 5½ hours).

✔ **P&O Stena Line** (☎ **561/563-2856** in the U.S. or 0870/600-0600 in the U.K.; Internet: www.posl.com) operates ferries between Calais and Dover (crossing time is 75 minutes).

✔ **Sea France Limited** (☎ **01304/212-696** in the U.K.; Internet: www.seafrance.co.uk) runs ferries between Dover and Calais (crossing time is 90 minutes).

Chapter 6

Deciding Where to Stay

. . . .

In This Chapter

▶ Getting the lowdown on London's accommodation types

▶ Choosing a neighborhood that's right for you

▶ Knowing what to expect from a hotel in your price range

. . . .

*L*ondon hotel rooms run the gamut from a basic tiny bedroom with a shared bathroom down the hall to elegant, sumptuous splendor. Many travelers don't care where they stay, so long as it's cheap. The reasoning is, "I'm only going to be in a hotel room to sleep." That assumption may be true, but I also know that a cheap-at-all-costs hotel room can color your mood and turn a potentially memorable vacation into something unnecessarily dreary.

The choice is up to you. Do you want to wake up in a dark, drafty room that makes you want to bolt outdoors as quickly as possible? Or do you want to stay in a place with a reasonable amount of charm where you can comfortably relax and put your feet up between forays into London? Or do you want to treat yourself to marble bathrooms, luxurious surroundings, and 24-hour room service? Additionally, in what kind of neighborhood do you want to stay? Do you prefer a location in the center of the action or off the beaten path?

In Chapter 8, I give you details about specific hotels and B&Bs that I heartily recommend. In this chapter, I tell you what you need to know about London's neighborhoods and the kinds of accommodation you'll find, so you can make a choice.

Determining Your Kind of Place

Accommodations in London are available in varying price ranges and degrees of luxury. Places to stay generally fit into one of two categories: hotels and bed-and-breakfast inns (B&Bs). Nothing will be as inexpensive as that low-rate motel on the freeway back home, but London offers good budget hotels and plenty of B&Bs that won't render you unconscious when you see the bill. If price is less of an issue, you can choose among unique boutique hotels, large chain hotels, and several ultra-luxurious places known the world over. The following sections provide a rundown on the quirks and perks of each type of accommodation.

Understanding the pros and cons of B&Bs

B&Bs in Europe differ from what you may have experienced elsewhere. Most are former homes (some are current homes; you stay with the family) — usually old homes — and the comfort and service varies widely. The plumbing can be unpredictable, as can the water temperature. Space is often scarce. But they do offer a slice of domestic London life that you can't get anywhere else.

Because B&Bs are often private homes and not hotels, typical amenities also vary widely, especially in the bathroom facilities. Nearly all B&B rooms contain washbasins, but you may have to share a bathroom down the hall. The facilities are usually kept scrupulously clean, but many travelers prefer private bathrooms. Keep in mind, however, that *en-suite* (in the room) baths are generally so small that you feel as if you haven't left the airplane, and the super-small showers can be a trial.

The decor in many of the lowest-priced B&Bs is fairly unimpressive. Coming back to a small room with mismatched furniture, pink walls, and a tiny bathroom down the hall with no hot water may be an inconvenience that you're willing to suffer for the sake of saving money, but I don't recommend any such places in Chapter 8. The more popular and well-appointed B&Bs are, of course, more expensive, but their comforts and conveniences are worth the price.

What about the breakfast part of the B&B? Well, gone are the days when the staff of every B&B cooked you up a "full English breakfast" (also known as a *fry-up*) of eggs, sausages, bacon, fried tomatoes, and beans. Some still do, but others put out a *continental buffet*, which is a breakfast of cereals, fruits, and breads. The B&B descriptions in this book say "English breakfast included" or "Continental breakfast included," so you know what to expect.

Licensed B&Bs, like hotels, are inspected regularly, and the quality of B&Bs has improved considerably over the years. I recommend them for people who don't require many extras, although the most successful B&Bs continually upgrade their services or offer some enticing amenities. For example, many B&Bs now provide cable TVs and direct-dial phones in the rooms.

If you want to do some additional B&B research, the following two agencies have useful Web sites:

- ✔ **Worldwide Bed & Breakfast Association:** www.londonbandb.com (☎ **800/872-2632** in the United States).

- ✔ **London Bed and Breakfast Agency Ltd.:** www.londonbb.com (☎ **020/7586-2768** in London).

If you're physically disabled or infirmed in any way, B&Bs may not be the choice for you. B&Bs usually don't have elevators, so you may have to carry your luggage up steep narrow stairs. Be sure to check how accessible the B&B is before you make your reservations.

Exploring hotel choices

You find a wide choice of hotels in London. Most of the moderate-price hotels provide breakfast with a room rental. At a four- or five-star hotel, you pay a hefty price to eat breakfast on the premises. The rooms in a self-catering hotel are equipped with small kitchens so you can make your own breakfast in your room or go out to a nearby cafe or restaurant.

Boutique and deluxe hotels

London offers a few *boutique hotels*. These hotels are mid-range in size but not price; sumptuously furnished, they offer state-of-the-art amenities and full service. The **Covent Garden Hotel** and the **Dorset Square Hotel** in Marylebone are two of the best.

A more traditional choice is one of London's older deluxe hotels. The **Cadogan** in Knightsbridge, the **Gore** in South Kensington, and **Hazlitt's 1718** in Soho have all been around for a century or more. These hotels offer a distinctly English kind of style, full of charm and character.

The older deluxe hotels are offset by the hippest-of-the-hip: the **St. Martin's Hotel,** an Ian Schrager concoction in a converted office block.

Chain properties

But maybe you *always* stay at one of the chain hotels — a **Hyatt,** a **Crowne Plaza,** or a **Marriott,** places that are basically the same no matter where they are: They rely on their brand name and a no-surprise approach to win customers. London is chock-full of chain hotels, if that's what you fancy. Most of them cater to large groups, and you may feel rather anonymous in them. On the other hand, these hotels are usually well equipped for people with disabilities and families with children.

Landmark hotels

At the top of the hotel spectrum, in both price and prestige, are the landmark hotels: the **Dorchester, Claridge's,** the **Park Lane Sheraton,** and **The Savoy.** These famous hotels are among the best in the world. In each of them, you can expect glamorous public salons (and glamorous fellow guests), a generously proportioned and well-decorated room with a large private bath, an on-site health club or access to one nearby, and top-of-the-line service.

Self-catering options

You can also consider staying at a *self-catering hotel,* where *you* do the cooking in the kitchen in your own hotel room. For short stays and for one or two people, self-catering hotels don't always beat the competition's price. But for families and those who can't afford or don't want to eat every meal out, self-catering hotels can be a budget-saver. I note the best in Chapter 8.

Finding the Perfect Location

You can make your trip to London work more smoothly if you pay some attention to the neighborhood in which you choose to stay. Can you get a good night's sleep there? Is it close to attractions or public transportation? Can you take a brisk walk at night without fear? This section gives you the pluses and minuses of London's chief hotel neighborhoods, so you can match the amenities and drawbacks against your own needs.

Central London, considered the city center, is divided into three areas: **The City,** the **West End,** and **West London** (or Central London beyond the West End). The following sections provide brief descriptions of the Central London neighborhoods containing the hotels I recommend in Chapter 8 (see the map in this chapter for the hotels' locations). I don't cover all of Central London because it's unlikely that you'll stay in The City (which is the home of many tourist sites but few hotels) or Holborn (London's legal heart). Crime is less prevalent in London than in many other major cities, and all the neighborhoods in the following list are safe areas. See Chapter 10 for a more complete description of Central London's neighborhoods.

The West End

The West End (that is, west of The City) is what you might loosely call "downtown" London. Most people think of the West End as synonymous with the theater, entertainment, and shopping areas around Piccadilly Circus and Leicester Square. The following sections describe West End areas and attractions.

Covent Garden and The Strand

Covent Garden is the home of the **Royal Opera House** and **Covent Garden Market,** one of the city's most popular gathering spots. The entire area is chockablock with shops, restaurants, and pubs, but not many hotels. However, the **Fielding,** one of London's most centrally

located budget hotels, and the **Covent Garden Hotel,** a luxurious boutique hotel created from an old hospital, are both here. The Covent
Garden and Leicester Square Tube (subway) stops provide the closest
access, but you can easily walk to anywhere in the West End or neighboring Soho. South of Covent Garden is **The Strand,** a major street
flanked with theaters, shops, and restaurants. Architecturally, however,
The Strand is far less distinctive than the Covent Garden area. **The
Savoy** is the most famous hotel on The Strand. If you stay in this area,
you should know:

- ✔ Covent Garden and The Strand are the heart of the West End,
  close to theaters, shopping, and entertainment.

- ✔ The area is busy all day long and far into the night, so noise can
  be a problem.

Bloomsbury

North of Covent Garden is the Bloomsbury district, location of the **British
Museum,** the **University of London,** and many other colleges and bookstores. The formidably Victorian **Hotel Russell** peers down on **Russell
Square,** the largest park in Bloomsbury. Hotels and B&Bs long-favored by
budget travelers line the streets around the square, especially Cartwright
Gardens. **Tottenham Court Road** and **Goodge Street** are Bloomsbury's
major shopping streets and, with Russell Square, the main Tube stops.
This centrally located area tends to be quiet and rather staid, but it offers
many restaurants and pubs. If you stay in this area, you should know:

- ✔ Bloomsbury is close to the British Museum and is within walking
  distance of the West End.

- ✔ You need to go elsewhere for your nightlife.

Piccadilly Circus, Leicester Square, and Charing Cross

Central London's major theater, entertainment, and shopping streets are
to the west of Covent Garden. **Piccadilly Circus** is one of the world's
best-known tourist meccas, full of megastores, glitzy arcades, and restaurants catering to the hordes. Commercial West End theaters and
first-run movie palaces lie on or adjacent to **Leicester Square** and
Shaftesbury Avenue. Charing Cross Road is famed for its bookstores
and booksellers. The **Regent Palace Hotel** is one of the older tourist
hotels in this area, where the streets tend to be crowded, noisy, and
rather anonymous. The state-of-the-art **St. Martin's Lane,** designed by
Philippe Starck, is the area's newest and coolest hot spot. Transportation is easy, with Tube stations at Piccadilly Circus, Leicester Square,
and Charing Cross Road. If you stay in this area, you should know:

- ✔ This area is in the commercial heart of London, close to major
  shopping streets and entertainment.

- ✔ You need to be prepared for lots of street action, day and night.
  On weekends, this area can become boisterous and rowdy.

London Accommodations Overview

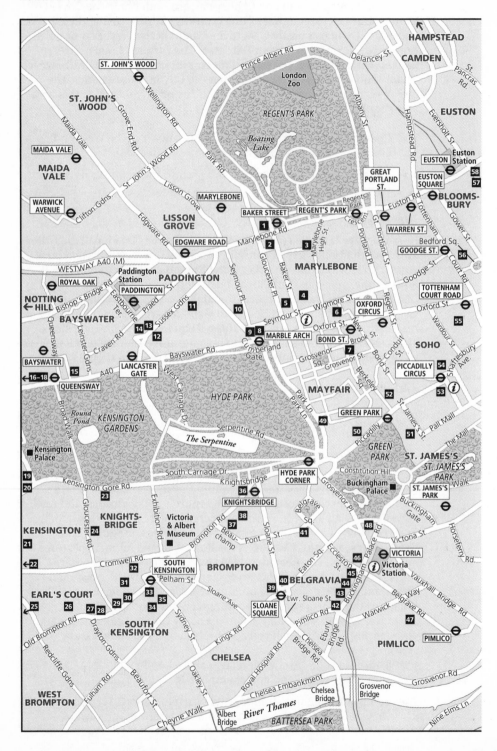

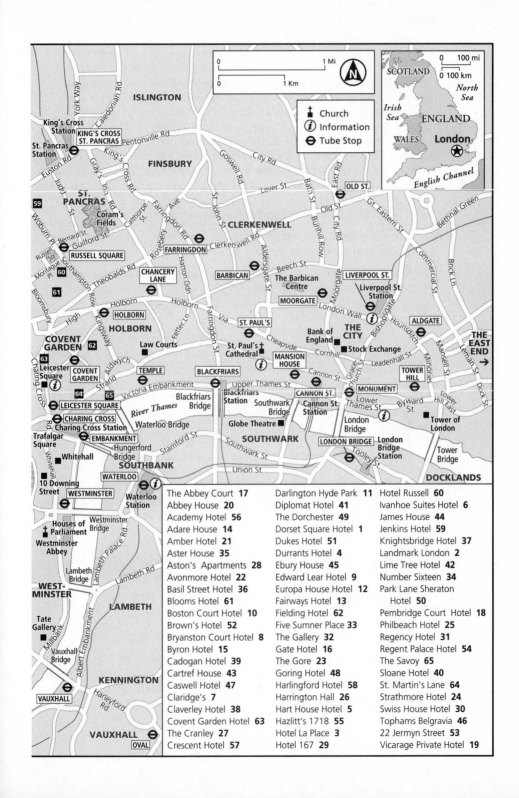

The Abbey Court **17**
Abbey House **20**
Academy Hotel **56**
Adare House **14**
Amber Hotel **21**
Aster House **35**
Aston's Apartments **28**
Avonmore Hotel **22**
Basil Street Hotel **36**
Blooms Hotel **61**
Boston Court Hotel **10**
Brown's Hotel **52**
Bryanston Court Hotel **8**
Byron Hotel **15**
Cadogan Hotel **39**
Cartref House **43**
Caswell Hotel **47**
Claridge's **7**
Claverley Hotel **38**
Covent Garden Hotel **63**
The Cranley **27**
Crescent Hotel **57**

Darlington Hyde Park **11**
Diplomat Hotel **41**
The Dorchester **49**
Dorset Square Hotel **1**
Dukes Hotel **51**
Durrants Hotel **4**
Ebury House **45**
Edward Lear Hotel **9**
Europa House Hotel **12**
Fairways Hotel **13**
Fielding Hotel **62**
Five Sumner Place **33**
The Gallery **32**
Gate Hotel **16**
The Gore **23**
Goring Hotel **48**
Harlingford Hotel **58**
Harrington Hall **26**
Hart House Hotel **5**
Hazlitt's 1718 **55**
Hotel La Place **3**
Hotel 167 **29**

Hotel Russell **60**
Ivanhoe Suites Hotel **6**
James House **44**
Jenkins Hotel **59**
Knightsbridge Hotel **37**
Landmark London **2**
Lime Tree Hotel **42**
Number Sixteen **34**
Park Lane Sheraton
 Hotel **50**
Pembridge Court Hotel **18**
Philbeach Hotel **25**
Regency Hotel **31**
Regent Palace Hotel **54**
The Savoy **65**
Sloane Hotel **40**
St. Martin's Lane **64**
Strathmore Hotel **24**
Swiss House Hotel **30**
Tophams Belgravia **46**
22 Jermyn Street **53**
Vicarage Private Hotel **19**

Soho

The warren of densely packed streets east of Leicester Square is **Soho.** The area has always been known for its restaurants and clubs but had a seedy air until about a decade ago, when gentrification took over big time. Soho remains a major tourist hub for shopping, eating, and nightclubbing. It has also become London's Gay Village, with dozens of gay pubs, restaurants, and upscale cafe/bars around Old Compton Street. London's **Chinatown** is centered around Gerrard Street. Soho isn't particularly known for its hotels, but you do find a few, including **Hazlitt's 1718,** one of London's oldest and most charming. The closest Tube stops are Leicester Square, Covent Garden, and Tottenham Court Road. If you stay in this area, you should know:

- ✔ The West End theaters and museums are minutes away.

- ✔ Soho is a nightclub, restaurant, and cafe mecca, with a few porn shops and strip clubs thrown into the mix.

- ✔ The narrow streets can be confusing, and they're often packed and noisy far into the night.

Westminster and Victoria

Westminster has been the seat of British government since 1050, when Edward the Confessor moved his court there. **Trafalgar Square,** a famous gathering point for tourists (and pigeons) across from the **National Gallery,** marks its northern periphery. From there, the Westminster area extends south, running beside the Thames and east of St. James's Park to **Westminster Abbey** and the **Houses of Parliament.**

The Victoria area around massive **Victoria Station** is a good spot to track down convenient and moderately priced B&Bs and hotels, especially on Ebury Street, the site of old favorites such as the **Lime Tree Hotel.** Victoria Station is one of London's major transportation hubs, a nucleus for the Tube, BritRail, and Victoria Coach Station. If you stay in this area, you should know:

- ✔ Inexpensive to moderately priced hotels and B&Bs are plentiful along Ebury Street.

- ✔ The neighborhood is much livelier during the day than at night. For some, that's a real plus.

St. James's

St. James's is the site of many stylish hotels, including **22 Jermyn Street,** an elegant boutique hotel. Named after the Court of St. James's, this posh neighborhood, which begins at Piccadilly Circus and moves southwest to include **Pall Mall, the Mall, St. James's Park,** and **Green**

Park, is often called Royal London. The Queen herself lives here, at **Buckingham Palace.** St. James's may be the most convenient area in the West End because it includes the American Express office on the Haymarket and upscale shopping emporiums such as **Fortnum & Mason** (one of the Queen's grocers) on Regent Street. If you stay in this area, you should know:

- St. James's is near the seats of royal power and privilege and some great shopping, as well as two lovely parks.

- You pay top dollar (or pound, I should say) for the choice location.

Mayfair

Luxury hotels cluster along the quiet streets of Mayfair, an area filled with elegant Georgian townhouses and exclusive shops. The **Park Lane Sheraton,** one of London's most famous (and expensive) hotels, overlooks Green Park. Marvelous little finds such as the inexpensive **Ivanhoe Suites** allow the rest of us to stay in this posh neighborhood. Mayfair is the most fashionable section of London, but offers no major tourist attractions. The **American Embassy** is at **Grosvenor** (pronounced *Grove*-nur) **Square** and, according to song legend, a nightingale once sang in **Berkeley** (pronounced *Bark*-lee) **Square.** You can access Mayfair to the north by the Bond Street or Marble Arch Tube stations and to the south by the Hyde Park Corner or Green Park stations. If you stay in this area, you should know:

- You are in a lovely place — if you can afford it. Most of the hotels are extremely expensive luxury establishments.

- You have to go elsewhere for your fun.

Marylebone

Marylebone (pronounced *Mar*-lee-bone), which includes **Regent's Park** (home of the **London Zoo**), is north of Bloomsbury and Mayfair. Here you can find that perennial tourist favorite, **Madame Tussaud's** wax museum. **Baker Street** continues to draw sleuthing Sherlock Holmes aficionados. Dating from Mr. Holmes's era is the gigantic **Landmark London,** a luxuriously restored railway hotel; **Durrants,** a traditional English small hotel, is even older. Marylebone has some lovely squares, such as **Portman Place,** laid out in the late 18th century, but later development robbed the area of much of its village character. If you stay here, you should know:

- Marylebone offers plenty of shopping and restaurants, as well as a huge park that's great for kids.

- You find this neighborhood less convenient if you're going to spend every night seeing a West End show. The area is business oriented, so the side streets are generally deserted after 8 p.m.

Central London beyond the West End

The following are considered West London (as opposed to the West End) neighborhoods. All in Central London, they contain some prime shopping, beautiful parks and gardens, and popular museums.

Knightsbridge

A fashionable and fashion-conscious area south of Hyde Park and west of Green Park, Knightsbridge is famed for its shopping. **Harrods,** one of the world's great department stores, is located there. Expensive chic boutiques and upscale restaurants are found along **Beauchamp** (pronounced *Beech*-um) **Place,** dating from the Regency era (1811–1820). The area has some superexpensive high-rise and boutique hotels and a few mid-range hotels, such as the **Claverley Hotel** and **Knightsbridge Hotel.** If you stay in this area, you should know:

- ✔ Knightsbridge is close to Hyde Park.

- ✔ Hotels are generally in the expensive-plus category.

- ✔ Although the area is an upscale-shopper's and gourmand's dream during the day, you won't find much action at night. Even finding a local pub can be difficult.

Belgravia

Extending south of Knightsbridge to the river, Belgravia has been a residential quarter for London aristocrats since Queen Victoria's time. The area rivals Mayfair for poshness and wealth and, like Mayfair, doesn't have any major museums or tourist attractions. **Belgrave Square,** its centerpiece, was completed in 1835. The hotels here tend to be on the upper-end of the price scale, with just a few moderately priced possibilities such as the **Diplomat Hotel,** sprinkled into the mix. If you stay in this area, these tips will be helpful:

- ✔ Be prepared for steep prices and empty streets at night.

- ✔ Here you find plenty of quiet, and you can pretend you're a *toff* (Britspeak for the upper class).

- ✔ This area is London's version of Embassy Row.

Chelsea

Full of expensive and charming town houses and quiet *mews* (former stables converted into residences), Chelsea flanks the river to the southwest of Belgravia. Upper crusts (including the late Princess Diana before her marriage) who lived and/or shopped around **Sloane Square,** Chelsea's northern boundary, were called the "Sloane Rangers" in the 1980s. In the 19th century, Chelsea was the preferred place of residence for artistic and literary luminaries and "bohemians." Flamboyant personalities such as Oscar Wilde and actress Lillie Langtry held court in the **Cadogan Hotel,** today one of London's most delightfully old-fashioned establishments. You can find the lovely 17th-century **Chelsea Physic Garden,** which also plays host to the annual Chelsea Flower Show, on the grounds of the Chelsea Royal Hospital. Trendy **King's Road,** Chelsea's major shopping (and traffic) artery, has been in the forefront of contemporary London street fashion since the 1960s. Here are some tips when considering a stay in this area:

- ✔ Although the area is charming, getting to and from the West End can be time consuming.

- ✔ King's Road is a hip shopping street, but it closes down after 6 p.m.

Kensington and Holland Park

The Royal Borough of Kensington lies west of **Kensington Gardens,** one of London's most beautiful parks. In the park itself is **Kensington Palace,** former home of the late Princess Diana and current home of Princess Margaret and other lesser royals. Two major shopping streets, Kensington High Street to the south and Kensington Church Street to the east, cross the area. Nearby **Holland Park,** another stylish neighborhood, boasts an open-air theater and makes a lovely place for a quiet stroll. The area's **Vicarage Private Hotel, Abbey House,** and the **Avonmore Hotel** are all fine inexpensive places in converted Victorian town houses. If you stay in this area, you should know:

- ✔ Its nearness to Kensington Gardens and Holland Park, along with the abundance of shopping, make this a great area during the daytime.

- ✔ You may feel a bit lonely at night when the shops close and the neighborhood's residential nature takes over. In addition, you need to allow extra time for getting to and from the West End.

South Kensington

A busy residential neighborhood south of Kensington Gardens, South Kensington is prime hotel and restaurant territory. Popular with European and American travelers, its streets and squares are lined with frequently identical Victorian terrace houses, many of them converted into B&Bs and small hotels. Four Victorian houses form **Aston's Apartments,** a good choice for those interested in self-catering rooms; the **Strathmore** is the former residence of 14th earl of Strathmore, the Queen Mother's late dad. The Gloucester Road Tube station provides easy access into the rest of London and is a stop on the Piccadilly Line from Heathrow airport. South Kensington is the other major Tube station in the area. South Ken is frequently referred to as Museumland because the **Natural History Museum,** the **Victoria & Albert Museum,** and the **Science Museum** are all there. So is **Royal Albert Hall,** a landmark concert hall. **Kensington Gardens** is never more than a few minutes' walk from anywhere in South Ken. All in all, this is one of the best areas to stay in London. Here are some tips to help you decide whether to stay here:

✔ South Ken offers an abundance of reasonably priced hotels and B&Bs.

✔ The major museums are a short walk away, as are a number of restaurants and bars.

✔ Kensington Gardens and Kensington shopping are nearby.

Earl's Court

South of Kensington (and west of South Kensington) is Earl's Court, sometimes called Kangaroo Court for the preponderance of Australians who favor its budget hotels and nonswanky pubs and restaurants. Visitors pour in to the concerts and major exhibitions held at the **Earl's Court Exhibition Centre.** For decades the neighborhood has been home to a sizeable gay community, and though much of the action has moved to Soho, Earl's Court still has several gay pubs, restaurants, and hotels, such as the **Philbeach** and the **New York.** A bit tattered in places but undergoing gentrification, Earl's Court is still your best bet for truly inexpensive places to stay and eat. Earl's Court is the area's primary Tube station. If you stay in this neighborhood, you should know:

✔ Earl's Court is noted for its inexpensive lodgings and long-settled gay/lesbian ambience.

✔ Overall, Earl's Court is not the prettiest part of town, but it has some nice areas.

Paddington and Bayswater

Paddington Station is the focal point of the Paddington area, which is north of Kensington Gardens and Hyde Park. Inexpensive B&Bs, such as **Adare House,** cram Norfolk Square and Sussex Gardens. Quaint Paddington ain't; it's busy rather than lively, and no major tourist sites are located here. Bayswater, south of Paddington Station, is another area to look for B&Bs. Most are found in Victorian terrace houses around large squares. You find moderately priced establishments, such as the **Byron Hotel.** Like Paddington, Bayswater has no major tourist sites but is close to **Hyde Park.** The Tube stations are Paddington, Bayswater, Queensway, Lancaster Gate, and Marble Arch. If you stay in this area, you should know:

✔ Budget hotels are plentiful, but Paddington and Bayswater aren't very distinguished.

✔ Except to sleep, you won't end up spending a great deal of your precious time in either area.

Notting Hill

Notting Hill, with busy Bayswater Road to the north and Kensington to the west, has become a hot spot in recent years, particularly the neighborhood of Notting Hill Gate. Once a place to be avoided, now it's a place to be seen, drawing visitors to restaurants and clubs.

Portobello Road (the Hugh Grant/Julia Roberts film *Notting Hill* was shot here) is the site of one of London's most famous Saturday street markets and also the tiny **Gate Hotel** and its talkative parrot Bilko. The nicer parts of Notting Hill are filled with small late-Victorian houses and mansions sitting on quiet, leafy streets. The Tube station is Notting Hill Gate. Here are some things to know about staying in this area:

- ✔ The main streets have a youthful edge and energy.

- ✔ Notting Hill isn't really known for its hotel scene, but you can find some B&Bs and the quaint six-room Gate Hotel.

- ✔ Notting Hill is close to Portobello Market, but you won't spend more than a few hours there on Saturday.

- ✔ Getting to/from the West End at night requires extra time.

Getting the Most for Your Money

Every recommended hotel in Chapter 8 has a $ symbol to help you hone in on your price limit. These symbols reflect a hotel's high- and low-end rack rates for a double room. The following is what you can expect in terms of accommodation type, room size, and standard amenities in the five price categories:

- ✔ **$ ($150 and under).** This category covers many B&Bs and some small hotels. You get breakfast, served in a dining room, but no room service. Your room has a washbasin and perhaps a built-in shower, but you may have to share a bathroom down the hall. (More and more B&Bs are installing private baths, however miniscule, in their rooms.) Expect tight spaces and a basic no-frills approach to decorating. You may have to carry your own bags, and don't expect an elevator or air-conditioning. You may or may not have a TV and a direct-dial phone in your room.

- ✔ **$$ ($151–$225).** The B&Bs and hotels in this price range generally show a bit more flair than the ones in the $ category, but the rooms may still be small, and you may still not find an elevator. Most places include breakfast, usually served in a dining room; room service is unlikely. You probably won't have air-conditioning, but most likely will have a telephone and a TV in your room. And chances are you may have a private bathroom — although it may be small and have only a shower. You may find some amenities like hair dryers, trouser presses, and tea/coffeemakers.

- ✔ **$$$ ($226–$300).** The hotels in this category offer pretty lobbies, with elevators, and staff to carry your bags. Breakfast or afternoon tea may be included but generally isn't; the hotel will probably have an on-site restaurant with room service. The rooms are larger, with better furnishings than the previous categories, telephones, air-conditioning (usually), and double-glazed windows to cut down on noise (unless the hotel is on the Historic Register).

The TVs are likely hooked up to a satellite dish or cable network. The private bathrooms are generally roomy and comfortable, depending on the age of the hotel and how recently it's been refurbished. Amenities such as hair dryers, trouser presses, tea/coffeemakers, and special soaps and shampoos are standard.

✔ **$$$$ ($301–$400).** In this range, expect even fancier lobbies and elevators and more staff. Breakfast won't be included, but you can order whatever you want from a high-priced room service menu or eat in a good on-site restaurant. The rooms are large and well decorated, with minibars, satellite/cable TVs, telephones (perhaps two or more), air conditioning, double-glazed windows if possible, and even modem jacks for personal computers. A full range of amenities and entertainment options is in every room. The bathrooms are spacious and generally equipped with tubs *and* showers and deluxe toiletries. Security is monitored.

✔ **$$$$$ ($401 and up).** In this range, you pay for the name, the location, and the prestige. At these Rolls-Royce hotels, you find sumptuous lobbies and salons, an extensive staff at your beck and call, one or more bars, gourmet restaurants, 24-hour room service, and probably access to a spa or health club (if not on the premises, then nearby). You also encounter the rich and perhaps even the famous. The opulent rooms have everything you can imagine, from plush furniture to multiple phones (perhaps one in the bath) to modem jacks to full entertainment centers to heated towel racks and ultradeluxe toiletries in the oversized bathrooms. Security is tight.

Keeping Other Points in Mind

Brits, and Europeans in general, are not as committed to smoke-free environments as Americans are, although this opinion is beginning to change. More and more London hotels and B&Bs now have no-smoking rooms and sometimes reserve entire floors for nonsmokers. If you hate the smell of stale cigarette smoke, ask if no-smoking rooms are available. In the hotel descriptions in Chapter 8, I always note any hotels that are completely smoke-free.

All the hotels listed in Chapter 8 provide private bathrooms, unless I note otherwise in the description. Private bathrooms don't necessarily include both a shower and a tub, though; you may get one or the other (more often a shower). If having a tub is important to you, request one when you make your reservation. Don't expect American-sized bathrooms, especially in B&Bs; some of the baths are so compact you can almost fit them into your luggage.

Chapter 7

Booking Your Room

C hant this as a general mantra: "I will not arrive in London without a hotel reservation. I will not arrive in . . ." This point is especially important if you plan to be in London from mid-April to early October (high season). Hotels in the inexpensive-to-moderate range are always the first ones to be snapped up, but space can be tight everywhere, at any time of year, if a major trade show or convention is coming to the city.

Uncovering the Truth about Rack Rates

The maximum rate that a hotel charges for a type of room is the *rack rate*. If you walk in off the street and ask for a room for the night, the hotel may charge you this top rate. Sometimes the rate is posted on the fire/emergency exit diagrams on the back of your door.

Be aware that you don't have to pay the rack rate. Hardly anybody does. Just ask for a cheaper or discounted rate. The result is often favorable when savvy travelers make this request at larger hotels. However, prices aren't generally negotiable at smaller hotels and bed-and-breakfasts (B&Bs). Some of them do offer special rates for longer stays, however, or if you're there off-season. For more strategies on getting a good rate, see the next section.

Getting the Best Rate

The rate you pay for a room depends on many factors, and the way you make your reservation is the most important. The following strategies can help you get the best rate available:

✔ **Call around.** I recommend that you call both the U.S.toll-free number and the local London number for the prospective hotel. I know that calling both sources takes time and money, but the quoted rates can vary so widely you can save a bundle. (Smaller and less expensive B&Bs and hotels generally don't have toll-free numbers in the States, so you may have to call, fax, or e-mail those establishments directly.)

✔ **Ask about discounts.** If you make your reservation with a large chain hotel, be sure to mention membership in AARP, frequent-flyer programs, and any other corporate rewards program. Budget hotels and small B&Bs rarely offer these organization discounts, but you never know when the mention may be worth a few pounds off your room rate in larger hotels.

✔ **Travel off-season and on weekends.** Room rates change with the season and as occupancy rates rise and fall. You're less likely to receive discount rates if a hotel is close to full, but if it's close to empty, you may be able to negotiate a significant discount. Expensive hotels catering to business travelers are most crowded on weekdays and usually offer discounts for weekend stays.

You may be able to save 20% or more by traveling off-season, which is mid-October to mid-December and January to March (see Chapter 2).

✔ **Choose a package tour.** The best rates of all will probably be with an air/hotel package (see Chapter 5). With these packages, which are sometimes astonishingly cheap, you have to choose a hotel that's part of the package. Airline package hotels tend to be larger chains. So what? The money you save may amount to hundreds of dollars.

✔ **Use a travel agent.** Checking with travel agents is wise, too. A travel agent may be able to negotiate a better room rate than you could get by yourself. (The hotel gives the agent a discount in exchange for steering his or her business toward that hotel.)

Reserving the Best Room

After you know where you're staying, asking a few more questions can help you land the best possible room. For example:

✔ **Ask about staying in a corner room.** They're usually larger, quieter, and brighter, but they may cost a bit more.

✔ **Ask about staying in a room in the back of the building.** In London, especially, traffic noise can be loud and annoying. In the back you may get a room that looks over a quiet garden.

✔ **If your London hotel is a high-rise, request a room on a high floor.** Being farther away from the street means your room may

be quieter. Plus, a higher room may give you the added bonus of a
better view.

✔ **Ask whether the hotel is renovating.** If the answer is yes, request
a room away from the renovation work, and make sure you ask
again when you check in.

✔ **If you have any physical impairments, be sure to ask whether
the hotel has a lift (elevator).** Many small and older hotels in
London do not have elevators. If the hotel lacks a lift, ask whether
a *ground-floor* (first floor) room is available.

✔ **Inquire about the location of restaurants, bars, and meeting
facilities, which can be noisy.**

✔ **If you aren't happy with your room when you arrive, return to
the front desk right away.** If another room is available, the staff
should be able to accommodate within reason.

If you need a room where you can smoke, be sure to request one when
you reserve. If you can't bear the lingering smell of smoke, tell everyone who handles your reservation that you need a smoke-free room.
Hotels in London usually have nonsmoking rooms; some establishments are entirely smoke-free.

Private bathrooms in London don't necessarily include both a shower
and a tub; you may get one or the other (probably a shower). If having
a bathtub is important to you, request one when you make your reservation. But don't expect to get a large bathtub — they tend to be small
there.

Paying for Your Room

Hotels almost never consider a room reservation confirmed until they
receive partial or full payment (this policy varies from hotel to hotel).
You can almost always confirm your reservations immediately with a
credit card; otherwise, you must mail in your payment (generally using
an International Money Order available at most banks). Before booking,
always ask about the cancellation policy. If your plans change, you
don't want to pay for a room that you don't use. At some hotels you
can get your money back if you cancel a room with 24 hours notice; in
others, you must notify the hotel five or more days in advance. After
you've booked the room, request a written confirmation by fax, e-mail,
or post and be sure to take the confirmation with you on your trip.

Sorry, you can't escape that annoying **17.5% value-added tax (VAT).**
In general, the quoted room rate includes the VAT (except for rooms at
the upper end of the price scale). Be sure to ask, though, so you won't
get an unpleasant surprise when you're checking out. Unless I note otherwise (the listing will read "Rates don't include 17.5% VAT"), the VAT is
included in the rates for my recommended hotels.

Surfing the Web for Hotel Deals

Another great source for finding hotel deals is the Internet. Although the major travel-booking Web sites (Arthur Frommer's Budget Travel Online, Travelocity, Microsoft Expedia, Yahoo!, and Smarter Living; see Chapter 6 for details) offer hotel booking, you may be better off using a Web site devoted to lodging because more general sites don't list all types of properties. Some lodging sites specialize in a particular type of accommodation, such as bed-and-breakfast inns, which aren't on the more mainstream booking services. Other services, such as TravelWeb (see the following list), offer weekend deals on major chain properties that cater to business travelers and have more empty rooms on the weekends. Some good all-purpose Web sites that you can use to track down and make online reservations at hotels in London include:

✔ **All Hotels on the Web** (Internet: www.all-hotels.com) doesn't actually include *all* the hotels on the Web, but it does have tens of thousands of listings throughout the world, including London. Bear in mind that each hotel in the list has paid a small fee ($25 and up) for placement, so the list is not objective, but more like online brochures.

✔ **British Hotel Reservation Centre** (Internet: www.bhrc.co.uk) lists current and seasonal specials at selected London hotels.

✔ **Hotel Reservations Network** (Internet: www.180096hotel.com) lists bargain rates at hotels in U.S. and international cities, including London. If you click "London" and input your travel dates, the site provides a list of the best prices for a selection of hotels in various neighborhoods. Descriptions include an image of the property and a locator map. To book online, click "Book Now." The toll-free number is printed all over this site, so call if you want more options than the Web site lists online.

✔ **Hotel-U.K. Reservations Service** (Internet: www.demon.co.uk/hotel-uk) features Best Value hotels of the month and other money-saving promotions.

✔ **InnSite** (Internet: www.innsite.com) provides B&B listings for inns in dozens of countries around the globe, including the United Kingdom. You can find a B&B in London, look at images of the rooms, check prices and availability, and then e-mail the innkeeper if you have questions. This extensive directory includes listings only if the innkeeper submitted one (getting on the list is free).

✔ **London Tourist Board** (Internet: www.londontown.com) Web site has a long list of hotels to choose from, including some with special offers.

✔ **SeniorSearch U.K.** (Internet: www.wiredseniors.com/ageof reason/) is a site for seniors looking for special hotels and other forms of accommodation, including home and apartment exchanges.

✔ **TravelWeb** (Internet: www.travelweb.com) lists more than 16,000 hotels worldwide, focusing on chains, such as Hyatt and Hilton. You can book almost 90% of the properties online. Its Click-It Weekends, updated each Monday, offers weekend deals at many leading chains.

Arriving without a Reservation

Whatever your hotel choice in London, I want to remind you again: *Booking ahead is important*. However, if you do arrive without a reservation, your first option is to start calling the hotels directly — try to get into town in the morning, so you can begin your room search early.

You can also book rooms through the trustworthy agencies in the following list, but the first two don't have phone service so you must show up in person (in high season, expect long lines at both).

✔ The **Britain Visitor Centre,** 1 Regent St. (Tube: Piccadilly Circus), is open Monday through Friday 9:00 a.m. to 6:30 p.m. and Saturday and Sunday 10 a.m. to 4 p.m. (Saturdays June through September from 9 a.m. to 5 p.m.)

✔ The **Tourist Information Centre,** in the forecourt of Victoria Station (Tube: Victoria), is open January and February, Monday through Saturday from 8 a.m. to 7 p.m.; March through May, Monday through Saturday from 8 a.m. to 8 p.m.; June through September, Monday through Saturday from 8 a.m. to 9 p.m.; October through December, Monday through Saturday 8 a.m. to 8 p.m. and Sunday 10 a.m. to 4 p.m.

✔ The London Tourist Board's **Accommodation Bookings Hotline** at ☎ **020/7932-2020** or 020/7604-2890 is open Monday through Friday 9:30 a.m. to 5:30 p.m.; with this service you must book with a credit card.

The following private agencies can also help you find a room:

✔ **British Hotel Reservation Centre** (☎ **020/7828-2425;** E-mail: sales@bhrc.co.uk) offers a 24-hour phone line. The center provides free reservations and discounted rates at all the leading hotel groups and the major independents. This agency operates a reservations desk (open daily between 6 a.m. and midnight) at the Underground station of Heathrow Airport.

✔ **First Option Hotel Reservations** (☎ **0345/110-011;** Fax: 020/7945-6016) is another hotel booking service. This agency operates kiosks at the following Central London rail stations: Victoria, by Platform 9 (☎ **020/7828-4646**); Kings Cross, by Platform 8 (☎ **020/7837-5681**); Euston (☎ **020/7388-7435**); Paddington (☎ **020/7723-0184**); and Charing Cross (☎ **020/7976-1171**).

✔ The London office of **Worldwide Bed & Breakfast Association** (☎ **020/8742-9123**) can arrange a B&B room for you.

✔ **London Bed & Breakfast** (☎ **800/852-2632** in the United States or 020/8742-9123; Fax: 020/8749-7084 in the United Kingdom) can provide inexpensive accommodations in select private homes.

✔ **The London Bed and Breakfast Agency Limited** (☎ **020/ 7586-2768**) also offers inexpensive accommodations in private homes.

Of course, even if you find a room (which you probably will, somewhere), you can't be choosy about price or location when you literally arrive on the fly without a reservation. To keep all your options open, remember to book ahead.

Chapter 8

London's Best Hotels and B&Bs

In This Chapter
- ▶ Reviewing a list of London favorites
- ▶ Finding other neat places to stay
- ▶ Listing hotels by neighborhood and price

*W*hen you choose a London hotel or bed-and-breakfast (B&B), price and location are the key considerations. After you decide on a neighborhood and a price range (see Chapter 6 for descriptions of your options), you can begin your search for your perfect accommodations. (You may also want to check out the neighborhood and price indexes at the end of this chapter.)

The Kid Friendly icon in front of a hotel name indicates that the hotel is suitable for families with children. These hotels have rooms with three or four beds (called *triples* or *quads*) or adjoining rooms and/or include babysitting among their services.

Unless otherwise noted, the hotel prices in this chapter include value-added tax (VAT). For those listings that don't include VAT, you need to add another 17.5% to the quoted rate (generally, this addition is necessary only for luxury hotels).

To keep track of the hotels that interest you, use the worksheet at the end of this book called "Sweat Dreams: Choosing Your Hotel."

Reviews are alphabetical for easy reference. Listed immediately beneath the name of the hotel is the neighborhood of the hotel and the number of dollar signs corresponding to the hotel's rack rates, from the cheapest double room in low season to the most expensive in high season (see Chapter 6 for a key to the dollar signs).

I don't have room in this guide to describe more than a sampling of London's hotels. If my top recommendations are full, you can check out the section called, "Runner-Up Hotels" toward the latter part of this chapter. Or you can contact one of the hotel or B&B reservation services I list at the end of Chapter 7.

The story behind my recommendations

You may be wondering what critical yardsticks I use for recommending the hotels in this chapter. Here they are:

- ✔ First, I've stayed in my share of dumps over the years, and I sure didn't enjoy the experience. I don't think you would either. So I dumped the dumps. You won't find any on this list.

- ✔ Next criterion? Cleanliness. These hotels are well maintained; you won't find old cigarette butts on the floor or rings around the bathtubs.

- ✔ Next criterion? That old friend, location. All the hotels are in Central London and accessible to Underground station (Tube) stops.

- ✔ Finally, they all have a little something extra, so they stand out from the crowd of London hotels.

London's Top Hotels from A to Z

The Abbey Court
$$$ Notting Hill

This graceful small hotel is located in a renovated mid-Victorian town house near Kensington Gardens. With a flower-filled front patio and a rear conservatory where breakfast is served, this hotel has 22 charming guest rooms that feature 18th- and 19th-century country antiques and marble bathrooms equipped with Jacuzzi tubs, showers, and heated towel racks. You can take advantage of the services of the concierge, and you can arrange for babysitting.

20 Pembridge Gardens, London W2 4DU. ☎ *020/7221-7518. Fax: 020/7792-0858. Internet:* www.abbeycourthotel.co.uk. *Tube: Notting Hill Gate (then a 5-minute walk north on Pembridge Gardens Road) Rack rates: £155–£165 ($232–$237) double. AE, MC, V.*

Abbey House
$ Kensington

For tranquillity and affordability in a great location (next to Kensington Gardens and Palace), this small family-run B&B can't be beat. Although modernized, the 1860s-era building retains many original features. The 16 spacious guest rooms (some triples and quads suitable for families) have central heating and washbasins; every two units share a bathroom. The decor is cheerful and practical.

11 Vicarage Gate (off Kensington Church Street), London W8 4AG. ☎ *020/ 7727-2594. Internet:* www.abbeyhousekensington.com. *Tube: High Street*

Hotels in Westminster and Victoria

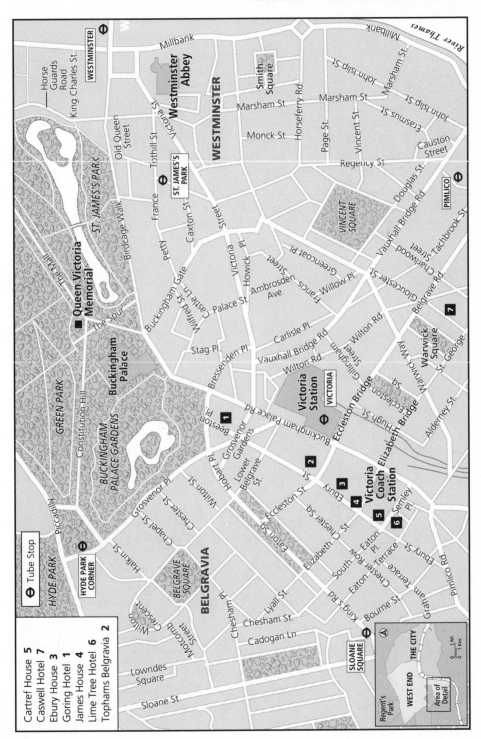

Cartref House **5**
Caswell Hotel **7**
Ebury House **3**
Goring Hotel **1**
James House **4**
Lime Tree Hotel **6**
Tophams Belgravia **2**

⊖ Tube Stop

WESTMINSTER

Horse Guards Road
King Charles St.
Millbank
Westminster Abbey
Smith Square
Millbank
River Thames

Old Queen Street
Marsham St.
Monck St.
Page St.
Horseferry Rd.
Marsham St.
Vincent St.
Erasmus St.
John Islip St.
John Islip St.
Marsham St.

WESTMINSTER

ST. JAMES'S PARK

France
Tothill St.
Victoria St.
Caxton St.
Regency St.
Causton Street
Douglas St.
PIMLICO

THE MALL
ST. JAMES'S PARK
Birdcage Walk
Petty France
Street
Victoria St.
Howick Pl.
Greencoat Pl.
VINCENT SQUARE
Vauxhall Bridge Rd.
Chaltwood Street
Tachbrook St.

Queen Victoria Memorial

The Spur

Buckingham Palace
Buckingham Gate
Stag Pl.
Wilfred St.
Castle Ln.
Palace St.
Francis Street
Ambrosden Ave.
Willow Pl.
Carlisle Pl.
Belgrave Rd.
Gloucester St.
St. George

GREEN PARK

Constitution Hill

BUCKINGHAM PALACE GARDENS

Bressenden Pl.
Beeston Pl.
Vauxhall Bridge Rd.
Wilton Rd.
Wilton Rd.
Gillingham Street
Warwick Way
Warwick Square

1

Victoria Station
VICTORIA

Eccleston Bridge
Elizabeth Bridge
Alderney St.

Piccadilly
HYDE PARK
HYDE PARK CORNER
Halkin St.
Chapel St.
Grosvenor St.
Chester St.
Wilton Pl.
Hobart Pl.
Grosvenor Gardens
Lower Belgrave St.
Buckingham Palace Rd.

2
3
4
5
6

Victoria Coach Station
Semley Pl.
Eccleston St.
Ebury St.
Chester St.
Hugh St.
Eccleston Sq.

BELGRAVIA
BELGRAVE SQUARE
Wilton Crescent
Motcomb Street
Chesham St.
Lyall St.
Eaton Sq.
Eaton Pl.
Chester Row
Eaton Terrace
Elizabeth St.
Chester Sq.
Eaton Pl.
South Eaton Pl.
Graham Terrace
King's Rd.
Bourne St.
Ebury St.
Pimlico Rd.

7

Lowndes Square
Cadogan Ln.
Chesham St.
Sloane St.
SLOANE SQUARE

Regent's Park
WEST END
THE CITY
Area of Detail
0   1 MI
0   1 km

Hotels in the West End

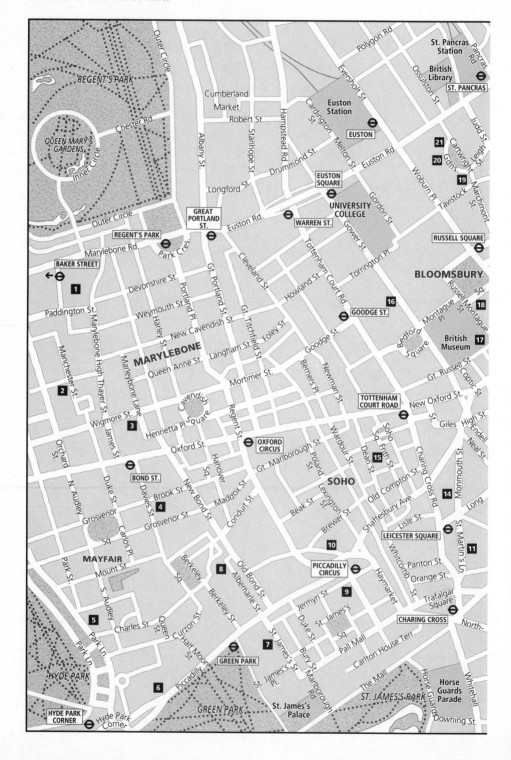

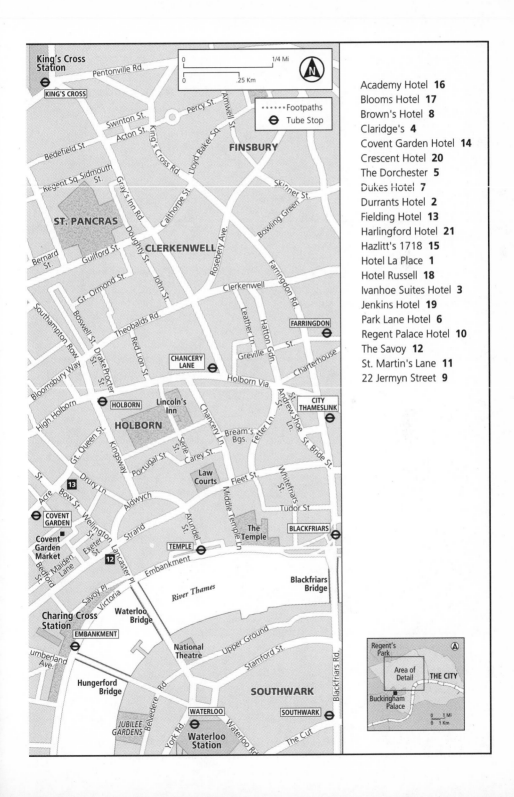

Academy Hotel **16**
Blooms Hotel **17**
Brown's Hotel **8**
Claridge's **4**
Covent Garden Hotel **14**
Crescent Hotel **20**
The Dorchester **5**
Dukes Hotel **7**
Durrants Hotel **2**
Fielding Hotel **13**
Harlingford Hotel **21**
Hazlitt's 1718 **15**
Hotel La Place **1**
Hotel Russell **18**
Ivanhoe Suites Hotel **3**
Jenkins Hotel **19**
Park Lane Hotel **6**
Regent Palace Hotel **10**
The Savoy **12**
St. Martin's Lane **11**
22 Jermyn Street **9**

Hotels from Knightsbridge to Earl's Court

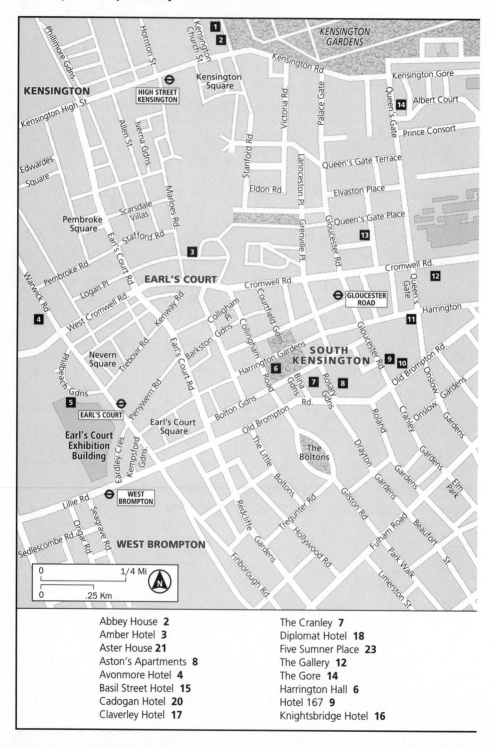

Abbey House **2**	The Cranley **7**
Amber Hotel **3**	Diplomat Hotel **18**
Aster House **21**	Five Sumner Place **23**
Aston's Apartments **8**	The Gallery **12**
Avonmore Hotel **4**	The Gore **14**
Basil Street Hotel **15**	Harrington Hall **6**
Cadogan Hotel **20**	Hotel 167 **9**
Claverley Hotel **17**	Knightsbridge Hotel **16**

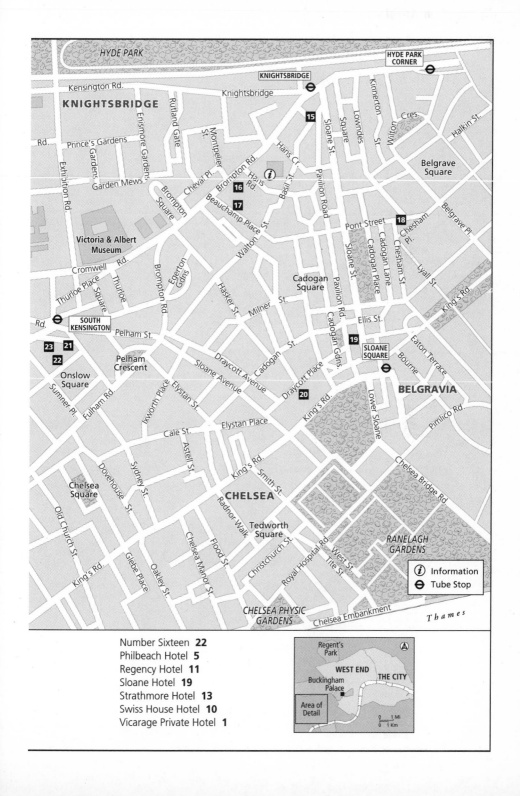

Number Sixteen **22**
Philbeach Hotel **5**
Regency Hotel **11**
Sloane Hotel **19**
Strathmore Hotel **13**
Swiss House Hotel **10**
Vicarage Private Hotel **1**

Hotels from Marylebone to Notting Hill

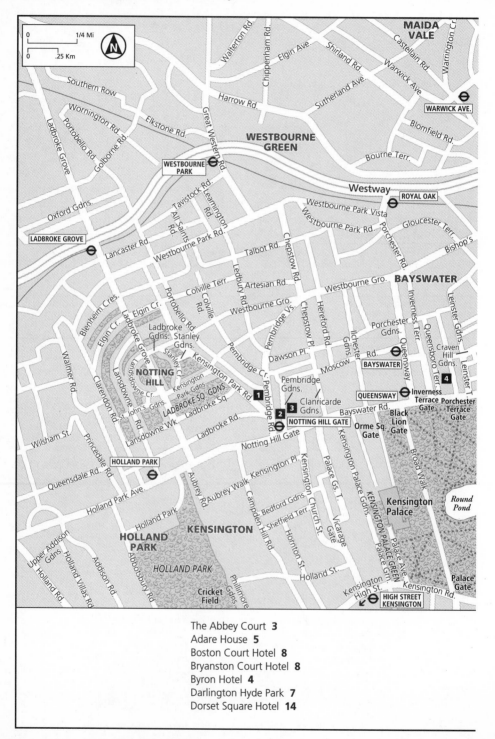

The Abbey Court **3**
Adare House **5**
Boston Court Hotel **8**
Bryanston Court Hotel **8**
Byron Hotel **4**
Darlington Hyde Park **7**
Dorset Square Hotel **14**

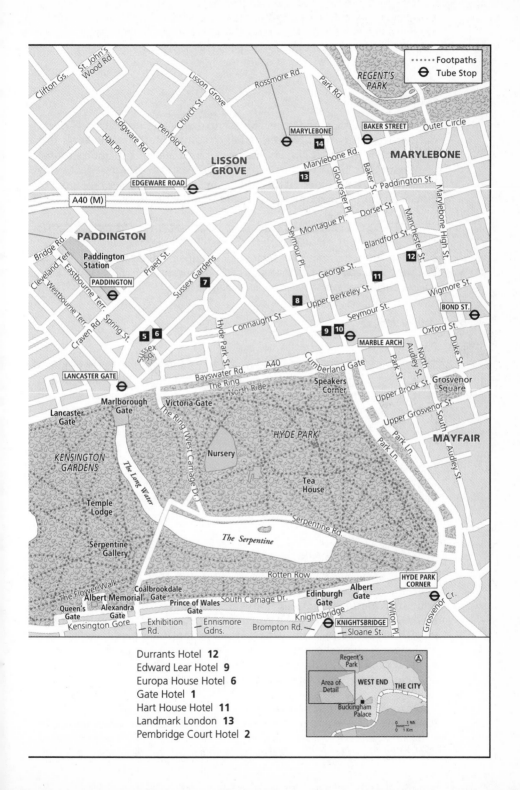

Durrants Hotel **12**
Edward Lear Hotel **9**
Europa House Hotel **6**
Gate Hotel **1**
Hart House Hotel **11**
Landmark London **13**
Pembridge Court Hotel **2**

Kensington (then a 5-minute walk east on Kensington High Street and north on Kensington Church Street). Rack rates: £68–£74 ($102–$111) double without bath-room. English breakfast included. No credit cards accepted.

Academy Hotel
$$$ Bloomsbury

You can easily walk to the British Museum, the theater district, and Covent Garden from this freshly refurbished 49-unit hotel that takes up five Georgian row houses. The abundance of nice features include original glass panels, colonnades, intricate exterior plasterwork, an elegant bar, a library room, a secluded patio garden, and a restaurant serving modern European food. The rooms are pleasant, but the bathrooms are small.

17–25 Gower St. (near the British Museum), London WC1E 6HG. ☎ *800/678-3096 in the United States or 020/7631-4115. Fax: 020/7636-3442. Internet:* www.etontownhouse.com. *Tube: Goodge Street (then a 10-minute walk east on Chenies Street and south on Gower Street). Rack rates: £152 – £185 ($228 – $277) double. English breakfast included. Rates don't include 17.5% VAT. AE, DC, MC, V.*

Adare House
$ Paddington

This well-maintained refurbished property retains a modest homey ambi-ence. Most of the 20 guest rooms are small, but immaculately clean and comfortably furnished; the bathrooms come with showers. Triple and quad rooms are suitable for families with children over two years old. Hyde Park is within easy walking distance.

153 Sussex Gardens (near Paddington Station), London W2 2RY. ☎ *020/7262-0633. Fax: 020/7706-1859. E-mail:* adare.hotel@virgin.net. *Tube: Paddington Station (then a 5-minute walk south on London Street and west on Sussex Gardens Road). Rack rates: £58–£76 ($87–$114) double. English breakfast included. MC, V.*

Aster House
$$–$$$ South Kensington

Found at the end of an early Victorian terrace, this 12-unit no-smoking charmer was named "Bed and Breakfast of the Year" by the London Tourism Awards 2001. Aster House reopened in April 2000 after a com-plete renovation. Each guest room is individually decorated in English country-house style, many with four-poster, half-canopied beds and silk wallpaper. The new bathrooms come with power showers. The break-fasts, served in the glassed-in garden conservatory, are more health-conscious than those served in most English B&Bs.

3 Sumner Place (near Onslow Square), London SW7 3EE. ☎ *020/7581-5888. Fax: 020/7584-4925. E-mail:* asterhouse@btinternet.com. *Tube: South Kensington (then a 5-minute walk west on Old Brompton Road and south on Sumner Place). Rack rates: £135–£175 ($202–$262) double. Continental breakfast included. MC, V.*

Aston's Apartments
$–$$ South Kensington

In three carefully restored Victorian redbrick townhouses, Aston's offers value-packed self-catering accommodations, some ideal for families. Each studio has a compact kitchenette, a small bathroom, and bright functional furnishings. The more expensive designer studios feature larger bathrooms, more living space, and extra pizzazz in the decor. If you like the idea of having your own cozy London apartment (with daily maid service), you can't do better. The owners have just added another property on nearby Queen's Gate; you can book a self-catering room there through the main Aston's number.

31 Rosary Gardens (off Hereford Square), London SW7 4NQ. ☎ *800/525-2810 in the United States or 020/7590-6000. Fax: 020/7590-6060. Internet:* www.astons-apartments.com. *Tube: Gloucester Road (then a 5-minute walk south on Gloucester Road and west on Hereford Square; Rosary Gardens is one block further west). Rack rates: £85–£120 ($125–$180) double. Rates don't include 17.5% VAT. AE, MC, V.*

Avonmore Hotel
$ Kensington

This small hotel is in a quiet neighborhood easily accessible to West End theaters and shops. You'd be hard-pressed to find more for your money: Each of the nine guest rooms offers a tasteful decor and an array of amenities not usually found in this price range. A few years ago this establishment was voted London's best private hotel by the Automobile Association (AA), and the high standards that earned that honor are still maintained. An English breakfast is served in a cheerful breakfast room; a bar and limited room service are also available, and the hotel can arrange for babysitting.

66 Avonmore Rd. (northwest of Earl's Court), London W14 8RS. ☎ *020/7603-4296. Fax: 020/7603-4035. Internet:* www.avonmorehotel.co.uk. *Tube: West Kensington (then a 5-minute walk north on North End Road and Mattheson Road to Avonmore Road). Rack rates: £90 ($135) double without bathroom, £100 ($150) double with bathroom. English breakfast included. AE, MC, V.*

Blooms Hotel
$$$–$$$$ Bloomsbury

With its cozy fireplace and period art, this 27-room hotel evokes a luxurious country-home atmosphere. Guests in this beautifully restored and tastefully furnished town house can enjoy morning coffee or light summer meals in a walled garden overlooking the British Museum. The guest rooms are good-size and individually designed with traditional elegance and muted colors; bathrooms are equally tasteful. Ground-floor rooms are available for the disabled. Specially priced rates in January, August, and weekends year-round are a real bargain.

7 Montague St. (next to the British Museum), London WC1B 5BP. ☎ *020/7323-1717. Fax: 020/7636-6498. E-mail:* blooms@mermaid.co.uk. *Tube: Russell Square (then a 5-minute walk west on Bernard Street and around Russell Square to Montague Place, at the northwest corner of the square). Rack rates: £170–£210 ($255–$315) double. AE, DC, MC, V.*

Boston Court Hotel
$ **Marylebone**

Within walking distance of Oxford Street shopping and Hyde Park, this 13-unit hotel on a street brimming with B&Bs offers affordable accommodations in a centrally located Victorian-era building. The guest rooms are on the small side and show a no-nonsense approach to decorating, but all have private showers and small refrigerators.

26 Upper Berkeley St. (near Marble Arch), London W1H 7PF. ☎ *020/7723-1445. Fax: 020/7262-8823. Internet:* www.bostoncourthotel.co.uk. *Tube: Marble Arch (then a 10-minute walk west on Bayswater Road, north on Edgware Road, and east on Upper Berkeley Street). Rack rates: £55–£59 ($93–$88) double with shower only, £75–£79 ($112–$118) double with bathroom. Continental breakfast included. MC, V.*

Bryanston Court Hotel
$$ **Marylebone**

Located in a neighborhood with many attractive squares, this 200-year-old hotel is one of Central London's finest in the moderate price range. The refurbished hotel has 54 small guest rooms (and equally small bathrooms) that are comfortably furnished and well maintained. You find a welcoming bar with a fireplace in the back of the lounge.

56–60 Great Cumberland Place (near Marble Arch), London W1H 7FD. ☎ *020/ 7262-3141. Fax: 020/7262-7248. Internet:* www.bryanston.com. *Tube: Marble Arch (then a 5-minute walk north on Great Cumberland Place to Bryanston Place). Rack rates: £110–£120 ($165–$180) double. Continental breakfast included. AE, DC, MC, V.*

Byron Hotel
$–$$ **Bayswater**

The family-run 45-room Byron occupies a Victorian house that's been thoroughly modernized but hasn't lost its traditional atmosphere. The guest rooms have ample closets, tile baths, and good lighting. Breakfast is served in a cheery dining room. The staff members are pleasant and helpful, and the hotel can provide child cots and help with special requirements for children's meals. Considering the amenities offered, this establishment offers an especially good value.

36–38 Queensborough Terrace (off Bayswater Road), London W2 3SH. ☎ *020/ 7243-0987. Fax: 020/7792-1957. E-mail:* byron@capricornhotels.co.uk. *Tube: Queensway (then a 5-minute walk east on Bayswater Road and north on*

Queensborough Terrace). Rack rates: £70–£120 ($105–$180) double. English or continental breakfast included. AE, DC, MC, V.

Cadogan Hotel
$$$–$$$$ Chelsea

You feel transported back to the Victorian era at this beautiful 69-room hotel, with a small wood-paneled lobby and sumptuous drawing room (good for afternoon tea), close to all the exclusive Knightsbridge shops. The Cadogan (pronounced Ca-*dug*-en) is the hotel where poet, playwright, and novelist Oscar Wilde was staying when he was arrested (room 118 is the Oscar Wilde Suite). The large guest rooms, many overlooking the Cadogan Place gardens, are quietly tasteful and splendidly comfortable, with large bathrooms. The sedate Edwardian restaurant is known for its excellent cuisine.

*75 Sloane St. (near Sloane Square), London SW1X 9SG. ☎ **800/260-8338** in the United States or 020/7235-7141. Fax: 020/7245-0994. Internet:* www.cadogan.com. *Tube: Sloane Square (then a 5-minute walk north on Sloane Street). Rack rates: £190–£240 ($285–$360) double. Rates don't include 17.5% VAT. AE, MC, V.*

Caswell Hotel
$ Westminster and Victoria

This 18-room hotel lies on a quiet cul-de-sac in an otherwise bustling area. The decor is understated, except for the abundance of chintz in the lobby. Four floors of nicely furnished guest rooms offer amenities usually found in higher-priced hotels; however, many are without bathrooms. The extremely thoughtful and considerate staff accounts for a great deal of repeat business.

*25 Gloucester St. (near Warwick Square), London SW1V 2DB. ☎ **020/7834-6345**. Internet:* www.hotellondon.co.uk. *Tube: Victoria Station (then a 10-minute walk southeast on Belgrave Road and southwest on Gloucester Street). Rack rates: £54 ($81) double without bathroom, £75 ($112) double with bathroom. English breakfast included. MC, V.*

Claverley Hotel
$$–$$$ Knightsbridge

On a quiet Knightsbridge cul-de-sac a few blocks from Harrods, this cozy place is considered one of London's best B&Bs. The public rooms feature Georgian-era accessories, 19th-century oil portraits, elegant antiques, and leather-covered sofas. Most of the 29 guest rooms have wall-to-wall carpeting, upholstered armchairs, and marble bathrooms with power showers. They offer an excellent English breakfast.

*13–14 Beaufort Gardens (off Brompton Road), London SW3 1PS. ☎ **800/747-0398** in the United States or 020/7589-8541. Fax: 020/7584-3410. E-mail:* claverleyhotel@ netscapeonline.co.uk. *Tube: Knightsbridge (then a 2-minute walk south past*

Harrods on Brompton Road to Beaufort Gardens). Rack rates: £130–£195 ($195–$292) double. English breakfast included. AE, DC, MC, V.

Covent Garden Hotel
$$$$–$$$$$ Covent Garden

Created from an 1850s French hospital and dispensary, this boutique hotel surrounds guests in luxury. No two of the 50 guest rooms are alike. Many rooms have large windows with rooftop views. The decor is a lush mix of antiques and fine contemporary furniture, and the granite-tiled bathrooms with glass-walled showers and heated towel racks are among the best in London. The wood-paneled public rooms are just as impressive. On-site **Brasserie Max** serves up eclectic bistro food and is a chic place to lunch. If you don't get enough exercise touring London, you can keep in shape at the small gym on the premises.

10 Monmouth St. (near Covent Garden Market), London WC2H 9BH. ☎ *800/ 553-6674* in the United States or 020/7806-1000. Fax: 020/7806-1100. Internet: www. firmdale.com. Tube: Leicester Square (then a 5-minute walk north on St. Martin's Lane, which becomes Monmouth Street). Rack rates: £220–£280 ($330–$420) double. Rates don't include 17.5% VAT. AE, DC, MC, V.

The Cranley
$$$–$$$$ South Kensington

On a quiet street near South Kensington's museums, the Cranley is housed in a trio of restored 1875 town houses. Luxuriously appointed public rooms and 37 high-ceilinged guest rooms with original plasterwork and concealed kitchens make this a standout. The white-tiled bathrooms are large and nicely finished, with tubs and showers. Suites on the ground (first) floor open onto a charming private garden and have Jacuzzis. Breakfast, available for £9.95 ($15), is served in a pleasantly stylish dining room.

10–12 Bina Gardens (off Brompton Road), London SW5 OLA. ☎ *800/448-8355* in the United States or 020/7373-0123. Fax: 020/7373-9497. Internet: www.thecranley. co.uk. Tube: Gloucester Road (then a 5-minute walk south on Gloucester Road, west on Brompton Road, and north on Bima Gardens). Rack rates: £180–£220 ($270–$330) double. AE, DC, MC, V.

Crescent Hotel
$ Bloomsbury

North of Russell Square in the heart of academic London, this comfortably elegant B&B hotel in a 200-year-old building has been in business for four decades. The 27 guest rooms include small singles with shared bathrooms in addition to more spacious twin, double, and family rooms that have private bathrooms (which tend toward the minuscule). The furnishings are simple but include many thoughtful extras, such as in-room telephones, cable television, and tea- and coffee-making facilities. Guests have access to the adjacent gardens with private tennis courts.

49–50 Cartwright Gardens (near Tavistock Square), London WC1H 9EL. ☎ 020/ 7387-1515. Fax: 020/7383-2054. Internet: www.crescenthoteloflondon.com. *Tube: Russell Square (then a 10-minute walk north on Marchmont St, which becomes Cartwright Gardens). Rack rates: £85 ($128) double with bathroom. English breakfast included. MC, V.*

Diplomat Hotel
$$–$$$ **Belgravia**

Belgravia is a very expensive area, and finding such a reasonably priced small hotel in this section of London is unusual. The lobby area features a partially gilded circular staircase and a cherub-studded Regency-era chandelier. The 27 high-ceilinged guest rooms feature tasteful Victorian decor, but are mostly on the small side, as are the bathrooms. The hotel isn't state-of-the-art but is very well maintained and a cut above the average for this price range.

2 Chesham St. (just south of Belgrave Square), London SW1X 8DT. ☎ 020/ 7235-1544. Fax: 020/7259-6153. Internet: www.btinternet.com/~diplomat. hotel. *Tube: Sloane Square (then a 5-minute walk northeast on Cliveden and north on Eaton Place, which becomes Chesham Street). Rack rates: £130–£140 ($195–$255) double. English breakfast included. AE, DC, MC, V.*

Dorset Square Hotel
$$–$$$$ **Marylebone**

This sophisticated 38-room luxury boutique hotel occupies a beautifully restored Regency townhouse overlooking Dorset Square, a private garden surrounded by graceful buildings. Inside and out, this hotel is the epitome of traditional English style. Each guest room is unique, filled with a superlative mix of antiques, original oils, fine furniture, fresh flowers, and richly textured fabrics. The bathrooms are marble and mahogany (just remember that some of those enticing little toiletries aren't free).

39–40 Dorset Sq. (just west of Regent's Park), London NW1 6QN. ☎ 800/553-6674 in the United States or 020/7723-7874. Fax: 020/7724-3328. Internet: www. firmdale.com. *Tube: Marylebone (then a 2-minute walk east on Melcombe to Dorset Square). Rack rates: £140–£240 ($210–$360) double. Rates don't include 17.5% VAT. AE, MC, V.*

Durrants Hotel
$$ **Marylebone**

Opened in 1789 off Manchester Square, this 92-room hotel provides an atmospheric London retreat. The pine- and mahogany-paneled public areas, including an 18th-century letter-writing room and a wonderful

Georgian room that serves as a restaurant, are quintessentially English. The wood-paneled guest rooms are generously proportioned (for the most part) and nicely furnished, with decent-size bathrooms.

George Street (across from the Wallace Collection), London W1H 6BJ. ☎ *020/ 7935-8131. Fax: 020/7487-3510. E-mail:* reservations@durrantshotel.com. *Tube: Bond Street (then a 5-minute walk west on Oxford Street and north on Duke Street and Manchester Street). Rack rates: £145–£150 ($217–$225) double. AE, MC, V.*

Edward Lear Hotel
$ Marylebone

One of the two 1780 brick town houses that make up this popular budget hotel was the home of the 19th-century artist/nonsense poet Edward Lear (famed for "The Owl and the Pussycat," among other delightful rhymes). His illustrated limericks decorate the walls of the sitting room. Steep stairs lead to the 31 guest rooms, which are small but comfortable. Fewer than half the rooms have private bathrooms, and the area — close to Marble Arch — has a lot of traffic noise. The rear rooms are quieter.

28–30 Seymour St. (near Marble Arch), London W1H 5WD. ☎ *020/7402-5401. Fax: 020/7706-3766. Internet:* www.edlear.com. *Tube: Marble Arch (then 1 block north to Seymour Street). Rack rates: £64.50 ($97) double without bathroom, £89.50 ($134) double with bathroom. English breakfast included. MC, V.*

Europa House Hotel
$ Paddington

If you want a private shower in your room but don't want to pay too much for the luxury, this family-run budget hotel may be your best choice. As in most B&Bs along Sussex Gardens, the guest rooms are small, but they're well kept and were refurbished in 1999. Some of the 18 rooms have three, four, or five beds, making them popular with families. A hearty English breakfast is served in the bright dining room.

151 Sussex Gardens (near Paddington Station), London W2 2RY. ☎ *020/7402-1923 or 020/7723-7343. Fax: 020/7224-9331. Internet:* www.europahousehotel.com. *Tube: Paddington Station (then a 5-minute walk south on London Street to Sussex Gardens). Rack rates: £57–£68 ($86–$102) double. English breakfast included. AE, MC, V.*

Fielding Hotel
$–$$ Covent Garden

The Fielding, named for author Henry Fielding (famous for *The History of Tom Jones*), is on a beautiful old street (now pedestrian only) lit by 19th-century gaslights and across from the Royal Opera House. The stairways are steep and narrow (the hotel has no elevator), and the 24 rather cramped guest rooms are undistinguished in decor, but they do have showers and toilets. Those quibbles aside, this quirky hotel is an excellent value. A small bar is on the premises, and the area is loaded with cafes, restaurants, and fabulous shopping.

4 Broad Court, Bow Street, London WC2B 5QZ. ☎ *020/7836-8305. Fax: 020/ 7497-0064. Internet:* www.the-fielding-hotel.co.uk. *Tube: Covent Garden (then a 5-minute walk north on Long Acre and south on Bow Street). Rack rates: £100–£130 ($150–$195) double. AE, DC, MC, V.*

Five Sumner Place
$$–$$$ South Kensington

This 14-room charmer — one of the best B&Bs in Kensington — occupies a landmark Victorian terrace house that has been completely restored in an elegant English style. The guest rooms are comfortably and traditionally furnished; all have bathrooms (a few have refrigerators as well). You can enjoy a full range of services, including breakfast in a Victorian-style conservatory.

5 Sumner Place (just east of Onslow Square), London SW7 3EE. ☎ *020/7584-7586. Fax: 020/7823-9962. Internet:* www.sumnerplace.com. *Tube: South Kensington (then a 3-minute walk west on Brompton Road and south on Sumner Place). Rack rates: £141–£151 ($211–$226) double. English breakfast included. AE, MC, V.*

The Gallery
$$ South Kensington

This relatively unknown 36-room hotel is near the cultural and retail attractions in South Kensington and Knightsbridge. The splendid hotel occupies two completely restored and converted Georgian residences. The elegant guest rooms are individually designed and include half-canopied beds and marble-tiled bathrooms. The lounge, with its rich mahogany paneling and moldings and deep colors, has the ambience of a private club. The overall decor is wonderfully Victorian, but every modern convenience is available. Two of the suites have their own roof terraces.

8–10 Queensberry Place (opposite the Natural History Museum), London SW7 2EA. ☎ *020/7915-0000. Fax: 020/7915-4400.* Internet: www.eeh.co.uk. *Tube: South Kensington (then a 5-minute walk west on Thurloe Street and Harrington Road and north on Queensberry Place). Rack rates: £120–£145 ($180–$217) double. Continental breakfast included. Rates don't include 17.5% VAT. AE, DC, MC, V.*

Gate Hotel
$ Notting Hill

This tiny three-story building dates from the 1820s (when people were much smaller), so the six color-coordinated guest rooms are cramped but atmospheric, and the stairs are steep. The Gate is the only hotel along the length of Portobello Road, with its antiques shops and Saturday bric-a-brac stalls. Kensington Gardens is a five-minute walk away.

6 Portobello Rd., London W11 3DG. ☎ *020/7221-0707. Fax: 020/7221-9128. Internet:* www.gatehotel.com. *Tube: Notting Hill Gate (then a 5-minute walk north on Pembridge Road and northwest on Portobello Road). Rack rates: £85–£95 ($127–$142) double. Continental breakfast included. MC, V.*

The Gore
$$$–$$$$ South Kensington

If you dream of the days of Queen Victoria, you can definitely appreciate the Victorian-era charm of the Gore, which has been in more or less continuous operation since 1892. On a busy road near Kensington Gardens and the Royal Albert Hall, the Gore is loaded with historic charm: walnut and mahogany paneling, oriental rugs, and 19th-century prints. Each of the 54 guest rooms is unique, filled with high-quality antiques and elegant furnishings. Even old commodes conceal the toilets.

189 Queen's Gate (south of Kensington Gardens), London SW7 5EX. ☎ *800/637-7200 in the United States or 020/7584-6601. Fax: 020/7589-8127. Internet:* www.gore hotel.com. *Tube: Gloucester Road (then a 10-minute walk east on Cromwell Road and north on Queen's Gate). Rack rates: £175–£265 ($262–$397) double. Rates don't include 17.5% VAT. AE, DC, MC, V.*

Harlingford Hotel
$ Bloomsbury

In the heart of Bloomsbury, this personable hotel occupies three 1820s town houses joined by a sometimes bewildering array of staircases (no elevators) and halls. The 44 guest rooms (all unique) are pleasantly comfy, some graced with floral prints and double-glazed windows to cut down on noise; the best rooms are on the second and third levels. The bathrooms are very small, however. The hotel has family rooms and can provide cots for children. Guests have use of the tennis courts in Cartwright Gardens.

61–63 Cartwright Gardens (north of Russell Square), London WC1H 9EL. ☎ *020/ 7387-1551. Fax: 020/7387-4616. E-mail:* book@harlingfordhotel.com. *Tube: Russell Square (then a 10-minute walk northwest on Woburn Place, east on Tavistock Square and north on Marchmont Street). Rack rates: £90 ($135) double. English breakfast included. AE, DC. MC, V.*

Harrington Hall
$$$–$$$$ South Kensington

Welcome to one of the most inviting addresses in the South Kensington area. This six-story terrace house is well represented by the beautifully designed classical lobby that sets the tone for the 200 stylish guest rooms (some much larger than others). Flowery fabrics and patterned carpets create a High English ambience. The bathrooms aren't particularly large, but they're nicely done. Amenities include a fitness center with a gym, a sauna, and showers.

5–25 Harrington Gardens (south of Kensington Gardens), London SW7 4JW. ☎ *800/ 44-UTELL in the United States or 020/7396-9696. Fax: 020/7396-9090. Internet:* www. harringtonhall.co.uk. *Tube: Gloucester Road (then a 2-minute walk south on Gloucester Road and west on Harrington Gardens). Rack rates: £180–£220 ($297–$363) double. AE, DC, MC, V.*

Hart House Hotel

$–$$ Marylebone

Cozy and well preserved, this Georgian-mansion-turned-hotel is within easy walking distance of West End theaters, shopping areas, and parks. The immaculately clean 16 guest rooms have recently been refurbished with traditional decor. Some very large rooms have big bathtubs and showers for families, and the staff can help you to arrange babysitting.

51 Gloucester Place, Portman Square (just north of Marble Arch), London W1U 8JF. ☎ *020/7935-2288. Fax: 020/7935-8516. Internet:* www.harthouse.co.uk. *Tube: Marble Arch (then a 5-minute walk north on Gloucester Place). Rack rates: £98–£105 ($147–$157) double. English breakfast included. AE, MC, V.*

Hazlitt's 1718

$$$ Soho

Built in 1718 (you may have guessed it from the name), this intimate 23-room gem offers old-fashioned atmosphere and a hip Soho location. Recent restoration exposed original wooden paneling and other features hidden for years, but the hotel still lacks an elevator. The charming Georgian-era guest rooms feature mahogany and pine furnishings and antiques as well as lovely bathrooms, many with clawfoot tubs. The back rooms are quieter; the front rooms are lighter, but without the quieting effect of double-glazed windows, you do hear the street noise. Continental breakfast is £7.25 ($12).

6 Frith St., Soho Square (just west of Charing Cross Road), London W1V 5TZ. ☎ *020/7434-1771. Fax: 020/7439-1524. Internet:* www.hazlitts.co.uk. *Tube: Tottenham Court Road (then a 10-minute walk west on Oxford Street and south on Soho Street to Frith Street at the south end of Soho Square). Rack rates: £175 ($262) double. Rates don't include 17.5% VAT. AE, DC, MC, V.*

Hotel La Place

$$–$$$ Marylebone

This desirable hotel, north of Oxford Street, caters to women traveling alone. The interior has been upgraded to boutique-hotel standards (although the exterior isn't especially impressive); the 21 moderately sized guest rooms are done in classic English style, with mahogany furnishings, brocades, TV armoires, and writing desks. The bathrooms are as nice as the rooms. The hotel's **Jardin** is a chic, intimate wine bar/ restaurant; you also find an Internet cafe on the premises. Madame Tussaud's wax museum is nearby.

17 Nottingham Place (near the southwest corner of Regent's Park), London W1M 3FF. ☎ *020/7486-2323. Fax: 020/7486-4335. Internet:* www.hotellaplace.com. *Tube: Baker Street (then a 5-minute walk east on Marylebone Road and south on Nottingham Place). Rack rates: £110–£165 ($165–$247) double. English breakfast included. AE, DC, MC, V.*

Hotel 167

$ **South Kensington**

Hotel 167 attracts hip young visitors drawn by the price and business people who like its central location. This hotel is bright and attractive, offering 16 comfortable guest rooms, each with a decent-size bathroom (some with showers, others with tubs). The rooms are furnished with a mix of fabrics and styles, mostly beiges and browns. Nearby Tube stations make the hotel convenient to the rest of London, and the busy neighborhood itself is fun to explore.

167 Old Brompton Rd., London SW5 OAN. ☎ *020/7373-0672. Fax: 020/7373-3360. Internet:* www.hotel167.com. *Tube: South Kensington (then a 10-minute walk west on Old Brompton Road). Rack rates: £90–£99 ($135–$148) double. Continental breakfast included. AE, DC, MC, V.*

Hotel Russell

$$–$$$ **Bloomsbury**

This huge, red brick hotel has been looking down on Russell Square in the heart of Bloomsbury for about a century. Built in the grand Victorian style, with a marble staircase, wood paneling, and crystal chandeliers, the hotel's multimillion-pound refurbishment, completed in 2000, restored a rich elegance to the 358 guest rooms. Bathrooms vary in size, but most are fairly roomy. The hotel is a bit impersonal, though, when it comes to service. Virginia Woolf would turn over in her grave if she knew the hotel had a restaurant serving burgers and grills named after her. In addition, **Fitzroy Doll's** is a fine-dining restaurant.

Russell Square, London WC1B 5BE. ☎ *020/7837-6470. Fax: 020/7837-2857. Internet:* www.principalhotels.co.uk. *Tube: Russell Square (the hotel is right on the square). Rack rates: £150–£198 ($225–$297) double. English breakfast included. AE, MC, V.*

Ivanhoe Suites Hotel

$ **Mayfair**

Located above a restaurant on a pedestrian street of boutiques and restaurants, and close to even more shopping on New and Old Bond

Streets, this town house hotel has eight stylishly furnished guest rooms with sitting areas and refrigerator/bars. The tiled bathrooms are fairly small; some have showers, some shower/bath combinations. You can enjoy an unusual number of services for a hotel this small and inexpensive, including breakfast served in your room. Hyde Park is five minutes away.

1 St. Christopher's Place, Barrett Street Piazza (just north of Oxford Street), London W1M 5HB. ☎ 020/7935-1047. Fax: 020/7224-0563. Tube: Bond Street (then a 5-minute walk north on Gees Court to Street Christopher's Place). Rack rates: £85 ($127) double. Continental breakfast included. AE, DC, MC, V.

James House and Cartref House
$ Westminster and Victoria

James House and Cartref House (across the street from each other, with a total of 11 rooms) deserve their reputations among the top B&Bs in London. Each guest room is individually designed; some of the large ones contain bunk beds, which makes them suitable for families. Fewer than half have private bathrooms. The English breakfast is hearty, and the place is remarkably well kept. Neither house has an elevator, but guests don't seem to mind. Both are completely smoke-free. It doesn't matter to which house you're assigned; both are winners.

108 and 129 Ebury St. (near Victoria Station), London SW1W 9QD; James House ☎ 020/7730-7338; Cartref House ☎ 020/7730-6176. Fax: 020/7730-7338. E-mail: jandchouse¢.com. Tube: Victoria Station (then a 10-minute walk south on Buckingham Palace Rd., west on Eccleston Street, and south on Ebury Street). Rack rates: £68 ($102) double without bathroom, £82 ($123) double with bathroom. English breakfast included. AE, MC, V.

Jenkins Hotel
$ Bloomsbury

This no-smoking hotel offers a bit of Georgian charm, a great location near the British Museum and West End theaters, a nice comfortable atmosphere, a full breakfast, and a wonderfully low price. The 15 guest rooms are small but all have private bathrooms. You don't find reception or sitting rooms, or even an elevator, but you can still settle in and feel at home. Although the hotel has no special facilities for kids, it welcomes children.

45 Cartwright Gardens (just south of Euston Station), London WC1H 9EH. ☎ 020/7387-2067. Fax: 020/7383-3139. Internet: www.jenkinshotel.demon.co.uk. Tube: Euston Station (then a 5-minute walk east on Euston Rd. and south on Mabledon Place to the south end of Cartwright Gardens). Rack rates: £88 ($132) double. English breakfast included. MC, V.

Knightsbridge Hotel

$$$ **Knightsbridge**

If you want a place convenient to many of the city's top theaters and museums, consider the Knightsbridge. This family-run hotel sits on a tree-lined, traffic-free square between fashionable Beauchamp Place and Harrods. The 40 comfortable, well-furnished guest rooms offer many amenities. The hotel was closed for a complete refurbishment in 2001 and is scheduled to reopen in late 2001; the new room rates were unavailable at press time and the rate shown below is the last one available.

12 Beaufort Gardens (just south of Harrods), London SW3 1PT. ☎ *020/7589-9271. Fax: 020/7823-9692. Internet:* www.knightsbridgehotel.co. *Tube: Knightsbridge (then a 5-minute walk west on Brompton Rd. and south on Beaufort Gardens). Rack rates: £150 ($248) double. English breakfast included. AE, MC, V.*

Landmark London

$$$$$ **Marylebone**

Millions of pounds have recently restored the Landmark to its former glory — it was the finest Victorian railway hotel in England when it opened in 1899. Awarded Best Hotel in London 2001 by The London Tourist Board, the hotel is built around the Winter Garden's eight-story atrium, home to the greatest jazz brunch in London. The Landmark sits in a great location, particularly if you're with kids, as Madame Tussaud's wax museum and Regents Park are only around the corner. The 299 rooms are among London's largest, with marble bathrooms, fax machines, and fast Internet access. The hotel offers every amenity, including babysitting, a large health club, and an indoor pool. Check the Web site for special offers.

222 Marylebone Rd. (half a block from Madame Tussaud's), London NW1 6JQ. ☎ *800/323-7500 in the United States or 020/7631-8000. Fax: 020/7631-8080. Internet:* www.landmarklondon.co.uk. *Tube: Marylebone (the hotel is just a few steps away). Rack rates: £350–£415 ($525–$622) double. Rates don't include 17.5% VAT. AE, DC, MC, V.*

Lime Tree Hotel

$–$$$ **Westminster and Victoria**

This cozy brick-fronted town house is near Buckingham Palace, Westminster Abbey, and the Houses of Parliament. The 26 guest rooms are simply furnished but generally larger and with more amenities than are usually available in this price range, making this hotel a wise choice for travelers on a budget. The bathrooms are small. The front rooms have small balconies overlooking Ebury Street; the rear rooms are quieter and look out over a small garden.

135–137 Ebury St. (near Victoria Station), London SW1W 9RA. ☎ *020/7730-8191. Fax: 020/7730-7865. Internet:* www.limetreehotel.co.uk. *Tube: Victoria*

Station (then a 5-minute walk north on Grosvenor Gardens and south on Ebury Street). Rack rates: £105–£115 ($107–$172) double. English breakfast included. AE, DC, MC, V.

Number Sixteen
$$ South Kensington

Gardeners will appreciate the award-winning gardens at this luxuriously appointed B&B in four early-Victorian town houses. The 40 guest rooms feature an eclectic mix of English antiques and modern paintings, and the bathrooms are large by London standards. The rooms look out over the private gardens of Sumner Place. On chilly days, you find a fire crackling in the drawing-room fireplace. Breakfast is served in the rooms, but if the weather's fine, you can have it in the garden and enjoy the fish pond and the bubbling fountain.

16 Sumner Place (north of Onslow Square), London SW7 3EG. ☎ 800/592-5387 in the United States or 020/7589-5232. Fax: 020/7584-8615. Internet: www.number sixteenhotel.co.uk. *Tube: South Kensington (then a 5-minute walk west on Brompton Rd. and south on Sumner Place). Rack rates: £120–£140 ($180–$210) double. Continental breakfast included. Rates don't include 17.5% VAT. AE, DC, MC, V.*

Park Lane Sheraton Hotel
$$$$$ Mayfair

Sometimes called the "Iron Lady of Piccadilly" because it's so well built, this landmark hotel opened in 1927. The cheapest of the 305 guest rooms are fairly spacious but old-fashioned and lack air conditioning. You may prefer the recently renovated executive rooms and suites, all of which are decorated with a warm mix of classic English furnishings and have beautiful marble bathrooms. The price goes up according to location (particularly if it's a suite overlooking Green Park), size, and decor. Every conceivable amenity is available. The **Palm Court Lounge** is a swank place for afternoon tea (see Chapter 15), and two restaurants are on the premises.

Piccadilly (across from Green Park), London W1Y 8BX. ☎ 800/325-3535 in the United States or 020/7499-6321. Fax: 020/7499-1965. Internet: www.sheraton. com/parklane. *Tube: Green Park (then a 3-minute walk southwest along Piccadilly). Rack rates: £275–£355 ($412–$472) double. AE, DC, MC, V.*

Philbeach Hotel
$ Earl's Court

The Philbeach is the largest and most established of the Earl's Court gay-friendly hotels. A large house in a Victorian *crescent* (row houses built in a long curving line), the hotel has a more relaxed (some would say raunchy) atmosphere than the gay-friendly **New York Hotel (☎ 020/7244-6884)** next door. The decor is slightly baroque, bringing together an eclectic mix of paintings and furniture. About half the 40 rooms have bathrooms that include tiny showers. Guests can enjoy a TV lounge, an intimate basement bar, and a glass-walled dining room off the garden for breakfast; in the evening, the last becomes a good French restaurant called Wilde About Oscar. Men will probably be more comfortable here than women. A two-night minimum is required on weekends.

30–31 Philbeach Gardens (near the Earl's Court Exhibition Centre), London SW5 9EB. ☎ *020/7373-1244. Fax: 020/7244-0149. Internet:* www.philbeachhotel. freeserve.co.uk. *Tube: Earl's Court (take the Warwick Rd. exit; the hotel is a 5-minute walk north on Warwick Street and west on Philbeach Gardens). Rack rates: £69 ($103) double without bathrom, £90 ($135) double with bathroom. Continental breakfast included. AE, DC, MC, V.*

Regency Hotel
$$$ South Kensington

This hotel occupies six, refitted, Victorian terrace houses. A Chippendale fireplace graces the lobby and five Empire chandeliers suspended vertically, one on top of the other, hangs in one of the stairwells. The 210 modern guest rooms are subdued and attractive, with good-size bathrooms. The one downside is that the air-conditioning system on the west side of the building can be pretty loud on hot summer nights. Guests can use the health club with steam rooms and saunas.

100 Queen's Gate (near Royal Albert Hall), London SW7 5AG. ☎ *800/223-5652 in the United States or 020/7373-7878. Fax: 020/7370-9700. Internet:* www.regency-london.co.uk. *Tube: South Kensington (then a 3-minute walk west on Old Brompton Rd. to Queen's Gate). Rack rates: £160 ($240) double. English breakfast included. Rates don't include 17.5% VAT. AE, DC, MC, V.*

Regent Palace Hotel
$–$$$ Piccadilly Circus

One of Europe's largest hotels, the 920-room Regent Palace sits at the edge of Piccadilly Circus. The hotel has finally upgraded its utilitarian 1915 design. About a quarter of the guest rooms now contain toilets and showers; the others have sinks in the rooms and shared facilities in the halls (an attendant provides you with soap and towel). With a lobby that looks like an airport ticket counter (expect lines) and an endless flow of tourists, feeling anonymous here is easy. But step out the door and you're in the exciting heart of the West End. A theater booking service is on the premises. Rates are lower Sunday through Thursday.

Glasshouse Street, Piccadilly Circus, London W1B 5DN. ☎ *0870/400-8703. Fax: 020/7287-0238. Internet:* www.forte-hotels.com. *Tube: Piccadilly Circus (then a 2-minute walk north; the hotel sits at the fork of Glasshouse Street and Sherwood Street). Rack rates: £69–£89 ($103–$133) double without bathroom; £119–£129 ($178–$193) double with bathroom. AE, DC, MC, V.*

The Savoy
$$$$$ The Strand

An opulent eight-story landmark from 1889, the Savoy boasts 15 types of guest rooms (233 rooms in all), including some famous art deco ones with their original features. They're all spacious and splendidly decorated. The bathrooms, as large as some hotel rooms, are clad in red-and-white marble and have enormous glass-walled showers and heated towel racks. The most expensive rooms offer river views; others look out over the hotel courtyard. The **Savoy Grill** is one of London's most famous restaurants (see Chapter 14), and in the Thames Foyer you can get a superlative English tea (see Chapter 15); the **Savoy Theatre** is connected to the hotel.

The Strand (just north of Waterloo Bridge), London WC2R 0EU. ☎ *800/63-SAVOY in the U.S. or 0800/7671-7671. Fax: 0171/240-6040. Internet:* www.savoy-group. co.uk. *Tube: Charing Cross (then a 5-minute walk east along The Strand). Rack rates: £290–£425 ($435–$637) double. Rates don't include 17.5% VAT. AE, DC, MC, V.*

Sloane Hotel
$$–$$$ Chelsea

This captivating full-service hotel makes an ideal spot for a luxurious, romantic hideaway. The 12 individually decorated guest rooms feature antique treasures and rich fabrics; the larger rooms have sitting areas and the bathrooms are marble. On the rooftop terrace you can have breakfast (£9 to £12/$13 to $18), afternoon tea, or evening cocktails.

29 Draycott Place (west of Sloane Square), London SW3 2SH. ☎ *800/324-9960 in the United States or 020/7581-5757. Fax: 020/7584-1348. Internet:* www. premierhotels.com. *Tube: Sloane Square (then a 5-minute walk west on Symons Street, at the northwest corner of the square, to Draycott Place). Rack rates: £150–£195 ($225–$292) double. Rates don't include 17.5% VAT. AE, DC, MC, V.*

St. Martin's Lane
$$$$ Piccadilly Circus

Developed by hotelier Ian Schrager, St. Martin's Lane opened in 1999 and is *the* place to stay if you have the bucks and are into trendy high design. This once-nondescript office block has become a haven for the hip, now boasting an ultracool, almost surreal lobby; 3 restaurants; and 204 beautifully minimalist all-white guest rooms designed by trendy Philippe Starck. The bathrooms are roomy and luxurious and the windows floor-to-ceiling; every room has its own color-lighting panel, so you can control the mood. Weekend rates are available.

45 St. Martin's Lane (next to the English National Opera), London WC2N 4HX. ☎ *020/7300-5500. Fax: 020/7300-5501. Tube: Leicester Square (then a 2-minute walk east on Court to St. Martin's Lane). Rack rates: £235–£255 ($352–$382) double. Rates don't include 17.5% VAT. AE, DC, MC, V.*

Strathmore Hotel

$$$ South Kensington

Formerly the residence of the 14th earl of Strathmore, the Queen Mum's father, this hotel overlooks a private garden square just minutes from the South Ken museums. Many of the guest rooms feature a high-ceilinged spaciousness rare in London hotels, and bathrooms with tubs and showers. Plenty of handcarved rosewood furniture and well-chosen fabrics decorate the rooms. One drawback is that on weekends, no general manager is on duty; also, service can sometimes be rather impersonal.

41 Queen's Gate Gardens (at the southeast corner of the gardens), London SW7 5NB. ☎ *020/7584-0512. Fax: 020/7584-0246. Internet:* www.grangehotels.co.uk. *Tube: Gloucester Rd. (then a 2-minute walk north on Gloucester Rd. and east on Queen's Gate Gardens). Rack rates: £155–£169 ($232–$253) double. AE, MC, V.*

Swiss House Hotel

$ South Kensington

Swiss House is a comfortable bargain B&B. It lacks an elevator and isn't stylish, but the 16 guest rooms are clean and nice, with pale walls, floral-print bedspreads, and small but serviceable bathrooms. The rear rooms are quieter and have views out into a garden. Located in the heart of South Ken (next door to Hotel 167), this hotel is well known to budget travelers, so book your reservations early. The hotel staff can arrange for babysitting.

171 Old Brompton Rd. (south of the Gloucester Rd. Tube station), London SW5 0AN. ☎ *020/7373-2769. Fax: 020/7373-4983. Internet:* www.swiss-hs.demon.co.uk. *Tube: Gloucester Rd. (then a 5-minute walk south on Gloucester Rd. and west on Old Brompton Rd.). Rack rates: £85–£99 ($127–$149) double. Continental breakfast included. AE, DC, MC, V.*

Tophams Belgravia

$$ Westminster and Victoria

Completely renovated in 1997, Tophams includes five small, interconnected row houses. The flower-filled window boxes in the front add charm and color. The best of the 40 guest rooms are comfortably appointed, with private bathrooms and four-poster beds. The restaurant offers both traditional and modern English cooking for lunch and dinner. The location is convenient for travelers planning to explore London by Tube or train. They offer a 10% discount to seniors over 60.

28 Ebury St. (around the corner from Victoria Station), London SW1W 0LU. ☎ *020/ 7730-8147. Fax: 020/7823-5966. Internet:* www.tophams.co.uk. *Tube: Victoria Station (then a 5-minute walk north on Grosvenor Gardens and south on Ebury Street). Rack rates: £130–£150 ($195–$225) double. English breakfast included. AE, DC, MC, V.*

22 Jermyn Street
$$$$ St. James's

This chic 18-room boutique hotel near Piccadilly Circus is an Edwardian town house on an exclusive street where almost every shop has a *royal warrant* (the sign of official royal patronage). In the richly appointed guest rooms, contemporary decor and fabrics mix with antique furnishings to create a stylish and comfortable ambience. The granite bathrooms are just as nice. Many amenities and 24-hour room service are available.

22 Jermyn St. (just south of Piccadilly Circus), London SW1Y 6HL. ☎ *800/682-7808 in the United States or 020/7734-2353. Fax: 020/7734-0750. Internet:* www. 22jermyn.com. *Tube: Piccadilly Circus (take Lower Regent Street exit; Jermyn Street is the first right outside the station). Rack rates: £210 ($315) double. AE, DC, MC, V.*

Vicarage Private Hotel
$ Kensington

The family-run Vicarage offers old-world English charm, hospitality, and a good value. The hotel is on a residential garden square close to High Street Kensington and Kensington Palace. The 18 guest rooms, individually furnished in Victorian style, can accommodate up to four; room 19 on the top floor is particularly charming. Some of the double and twin rooms have small bathrooms. The hotel welcomes children and will arrange for babysitting; however, the hotel isn't really equipped to deal with the needs of the under-3 set. Many guests return here year after year.

10 Vicarage Gate (west of Kensington Gardens), London W8 4AG. ☎ *020/7229-4030. Fax: 020/7792-5989. Internet:* www.londonvicaragehotel.com. *Tube: Kensington High Street (then a 10-minute walk east on Kensington High Street and north on Kensington Church Street). Rack rate: £76 ($114) double without bathroom, £100 ($150) double with bathroom. English breakfast included. No credit cards.*

The big splurge

In this chapter I supply entries for several deluxe **$$$$$** hotels, among them the **Park Lane, The Savoy,** and the **St. Martin's.** If you're looking for the plushest of the plush, here are a few more suggestions:

✔ **Brown's Hotel** (29–34 Albemarle St. [near Berkeley Square], W1A WIS40; ☎ **020/7493-6020;** Fax: 020/7493-9381; Internet: www.brownshotel.com)

✔ **Claridge's** (Brook Street [near Grosvenor Square], W1A 2JQ. ☎ **800/223-6800** in the United States or 020/7629-8860; Fax: 020/7499-2210; Internet: www.savoy-group.co.uk)

✔ **The Dorchester** (53 Park Lane [at the east side of Hyde Park], W1A 2HJ. ☎ **800/727-9820** in the United States or 020/7629-8888; Fax: 020/7409-0114; Internet: www.dorchesterhotel.com)

Runner-Up Hotels

Amber Hotel

$$ Earl's Court The Amber is a Victorian charmer in Earl's Court with a private garden in back. *101 Lexham Gardens, London W8 6JN.* ☎ *020/7373-8666. Fax: 020/7835-1194.*

Basil Street Hotel

$$$$ Knightsbridge This Edwardian hotel is practically on Harrods doorstep and offers babysitting services. *8 Basil St., London SW3 1AH.* ☎ *020/7581-3311. Fax: 020/7581-3693. E-mail:* thebasil@aol.com.

Darlington Hyde Park

$$ Paddington This Paddington area hotel is a bit short on style but a good value. *111–117 Sussex Gardens, London W2 2RU.* ☎ *020/7460-8800. Fax: 020/7460-8828. Internet:* www.hydeparkhotels-uk.com.

Dukes Hotel

$$$$$ St. James's Dukes provides charm, style, and tradition in a 1908 town house; babysitting is just one of its many amenities. *35 St. James's Place, London SW1A 1NY.* ☎ *800/381-4702 in the United States or 020/7491-4840. Fax: 020/7493-1264. Internet:* www.dukeshotel.co.uk.

Ebury House

$ Westminster and Victoria This B&B near Victoria Station is known for the warmth of its hospitality. *102 Ebury St., London SW1W 9QD.* ☎ *020/7730-1350. Fax: 020/7259-0400.*

Fairways Hotel

$ Paddington This B&B has a homelike atmosphere and bargain rates. *186 Sussex Gardens, London W2 1TU.* ☎ *020/7723-4871. Fax: 020/7723-4871. Internet:* www.scoot.co.uk/fairways_hotel.

Goring Hotel

$$$$ Westminster and Victoria The Goring has a great location just behind Buckingham Palace and top-notch service. *This family-run property offers a particularly warm welcome to families. 15 Beeston Place, Grosvenor Gardens, London SW1W OJW.* ☎ *020/7396-9000. Fax: 020/7834-4393. Internet:* www.goringhotel.co.uk.

Pembridge Court Hotel

$$$ Notting Hill Antiques furnish this lovely hotel located in Notting Hill Gate. Nearby parks and fun gifts for children make this a good choice for families. *34 Pembridge Gardens, London W2 4DX.* ☎ *020/7229-9977. Fax: 020/7727-4982. Internet:* www.pemct.co.uk.

Index of Accommodations by Neighborhood

Bayswater
Byron Hotel ($–$$)

Belgravia
Diplomat Hotel ($$–$$$)

Bloomsbury
Academy Hotel ($$)
Blooms Hotel ($$$–$$$$)
Crescent Hotel ($)
Harlingford Hotel ($)
Hotel Russell ($$–$$$)
Jenkins Hotel ($)

Chelsea
Cadogan Hotel ($$$–$$$$)
Sloane Hotel ($$–$$$)

Covent Garden
Covent Garden Hotel ($$$$–$$$$$)
Fielding Hotel ($–$$)

Earl's Court
Amber Hotel ($$)
Philbeach Hotel ($)

Kensington
Abbey House ($)
Avonmore Hotel ($)
Vicarage Private Hotel ($)

Knightsbridge
Basil Street Hotel ($$$$)
Claverley Hotel ($$–$$$)
Knightsbridge Hotel ($$$)

Marylebone
Boston Court Hotel ($)
Bryanston Court Hotel ($$)
Dorset Square Hotel ($$–$$$$)
Durrants Hotel ($$)
Edward Lear Hotel ($)

Hart House Hotel ($–$$)
Hotel La Place ($$–$$$)
Landmark London ($$$$$)

Mayfair
Ivanhoe Suites Hotel ($)
Park Lane Hotel ($$$$$)

Notting Hill
The Abbey Court ($$$)
Gate Hotel ($)
Pembridge Court Hotel ($$$)

Paddington
Adare House ($)
Darlington Hyde Park ($$)
Europa House Hotel ($)
Fairways Hotel ($)

Piccadilly Circus
Regent Palace Hotel ($–$$$)
St. Martin's Lane ($$$$$)

Soho
Hazlitt's 1718 ($$$)

South Kensington
Aster House ($$–$$$)
Aston's Apartments ($–$$)
The Cranley ($$$–$$$$)
Five Sumner Place ($$–$$$)
The Gallery ($$)
The Gore ($$$–$$$$)
Harrington Hall ($$$–$$$$)
Hotel 167 ($)
Number Sixteen ($$$)
Regency Hotel ($$$)
Strathmore Hotel ($$$)
Swiss House Hotel ($)

St. James's
Dukes Hotel ($$$$)
22 Jermyn Street ($$$$)

The Strand
The Savoy ($$$$$)

Westminster and Victoria
Caswell Hotel ($)
Ebury House ($)

Goring Hotel ($$$$)
James House and Cartrel House ($)
Lime Tree Hotel ($–$$$)
Tophams Belgravia ($$)

Index of Accommodations by Price

$

Abbey House (Kensington)
Adare House (Paddington)
Aston's Apartments (South Kensington)
Avalon Hotel (Bloomsbury)
Avonmore Hotel (Kensington)
Boston Court (Marylebone)
Byron Hotel (Paddington and Bayswater)
Caswell Hotel (Westminster and Victoria)
Crescent Hotel (Bloomsbury)
Ebury House (Westminster and Victoria)
Edward Lear Hotel (Marylebone)
Europa House Hotel (Paddington)
Fairways Hotel (Paddington)
Fielding Hotel (Covent Garden)
The Gate (Notting Hill)
Harlingford Hotel (Bloomsbury)
Hart House Hotel (Marylebone)
Hotel 167 (South Kensington)
Ivanhoe Suites Hotel (Mayfair)
James House and Cartrel House (Westminster and Victoria)
Jenkins Hotel (Bloomsbury)
Lime Tree Hotel (Westminster and Victoria)
Philbeach Hotel (Earl's Court)
Regent Palace Hotel (Piccadilly Circus)
Swiss House (South Kensington)
Vicarage Private Hotel (Kensington)

$$

Academy Hotel (Bloomsbury)
Amber Hotel (Earl's Court)
Aster House (South Kensington)
Aston's Apartments (South Kensington)
Bryanston Court Hotel (Marylebone)
Byron Hotel (Paddington and Bayswater)
Claverley Hotel (Knightsbridge)
Darlington Hyde Park (Paddington)
Diplomat Hotel (Belgravia)
Dorset Square Hotel (Marylebone)
Durrants Hotel (Marylebone)
Fielding Hotel (Covent Garden)
Five Sumner Place (South Kensington)
The Gallery (South Kensington)
Hart House Hotel (Marylebone)
Hotel La Place (Marylebone)
Hotel Russell (Bloomsbury)
Lime Tree Hotel (Westminster and Victoria)
Regent Palace Hotel (Piccadilly Circus)
Sloane Hotel (Chelsea)
Tophams Belgravia (Westminster and Victoria)

$$$

The Abbey Court (Notting Hill)
Aster House (South Kensington)
Blooms Hotel (Bloomsbury)
Cadogan Hotel (Chelsea)
Claverley Hotel (Knightsbridge)
The Cranley (South Kensington)
Diplomat Hotel (Belgravia)
Dorset Square Hotel (Marylebone)
Five Sumner Place (South Kensington)
The Gore (South Kensington)
Harrington Hall (South Kensington)
Hotel La Place (Marylebone)
Hazlitt's 1718 (Soho)
Hotel Russell (Bloomsbury)

Knightsbridge Hotel (Knightsbridge)
Lime Tree Hotel (Westminster and
    Victoria)
Number Sixteen (South Kensington)
Pembridge Court (Notting Hill)
Regency Hotel (South Kensington)
Regent Palace Hotel (Piccadilly Circus)
Sloane Hotel (Chelsea)
Strathmore Hotel (South Kensington)

$$$$
22 Jermyn Street (St. James's)
Basil Street Hotel (Knightsbridge)
Blooms Hotel (Bloomsbury)
Cadogan Hotel (Chelsea)

Covent Garden Hotel (Covent Garden)
The Cranley (South Kensington)
Dorset Square Hotel (Marylebone)
Dukes Hotel (St. James)
The Gore (South Kensington)
Goring Hotel (Westminster and
    Victoria)
Harrington Hall (South Kensington)

$$$$$
Covent Garden Hotel (Covent Garden)
Landmark London (Marylebone)
Park Lane Hotel (Mayfair)
The Savoy (The Strand)
St. Martin's Lane (Piccadilly Circus)

Chapter 9

Taking Care of the Remaining Details

● ●

In This Chapter

▶ Crossing borders: Passports

▶ Taking care of your health: Medications and emergencies

▶ Making reservations: Restaurants and theater

▶ Packing light: What to take and what to leave

● ●

*B*efore you depart for London to take that boat ride on the river Thames or visit the Old Royal Observatory ("the center of time and space"), you have some loose ends to tie up. Do you have an up-to-date passport? Have you taken steps to meet your health needs while you're on your trip? Have you made reservations for the restaurant you have to try, and do you have your tickets for the play you just can't miss? Do you know what to pack for a trip to London? This chapter helps you wrap up these and other last-minute details.

At press time, travel to London is safe. However, in the wake of the terrorist attacks in the United States on September 11, 2001, international travelers should take the following precautions:

✔ Check the Web site of the U.S. State Department at `http://travel.state.gov/travel_warnings.html` for any possible travel advisories.

✔ The airline you fly may have restrictions on items you can and cannot carry on board. Call ahead to avoid delays in screening.

✔ Arrive at the airport at least two hours before your scheduled flight, maybe earlier. Call your airline for specific recommendations.

✔ Have the address and phone number of your country's embassy with you. See the Appendix for this information.

✔ Maintain a low profile, if possible. Prominently displaying American flags or American company decals on your luggage may not be a good idea.

Dealing with Passports

A valid passport is the only legal form of identification accepted around the world. Except in rare instances, you can't cross an international border without it. Getting a passport is easy, but the process takes some time.

The *U.S. Department of State's Bureau of Consular Affairs* maintains www.travel.state.gov, a Web site that provides everything you ever wanted to know about passports (including a downloadable application), customs, and other government-regulated aspects of travel.

Applying for a U.S. passport

Apply for your passport at least a month, preferably two, before you plan to leave on your trip. The processing takes an average of three weeks, but can run longer during busy periods (especially in spring). For people over age 15, a passport is valid for ten years; for those 15 and under, a passport is valid for five years.

If you're a U.S. citizen applying for a first-time passport and are 14 years of age or older, you need to apply in person at one of the following locations (see "Applying for Canadian, Australian, and New Zealand passports" later in this chapter for info on how to apply in other countries):

✔ One of the 13 passport offices throughout the United States — in Boston, Chicago, Honolulu, Houston, Los Angeles, Miami, New Orleans, New York City, Philadelphia, San Francisco, Seattle, Stamford (Connecticut), and Washington, D.C. Check the telephone directory or call the *National Passport Information Center* at ☎ 900/225-5674 (35¢ per minute) or 888/362-8668 ($4.95 per call) for the addresses of these offices.

✔ A federal, state, or probate court.

✔ A major post office. (Not all accept applications; call the phone number in the previous paragraph to find the post offices that do.)

To apply for your first passport, fill out form *DS-11*. To renew your passport, you need form *DS-82* or *DS-19*. You can obtain these applications at the locations in the preceding list or by mail from Passport Services, Office of Correspondence, Department of State, 1111 19th St. NW, Washington, DC 20522-1705.

For first-time passports, travelers 14 to 18 years of age must apply in person and fill out form DS-11. Parents or guardians of children under 13 can obtain passports for them by presenting two photos of each child. Children's passports are valid for five years.

Bring the following when you apply for your first passport or to renew an old one:

- ✔ **Application fee.** For people over age 15, a passport costs $60 total ($45 plus a $15 handling fee); for those 15 and under, a passport costs $40 total.

- ✔ **Completed passport application (form DS-11 or form DS-82).** You can fill out this form in advance to save time. However, do not sign the application until you present it in person at the passport agency, court, or post office.

- ✔ **Proof of identity.** Among the accepted documents are a valid driver's license, a state or military ID, a student ID (if you're currently enrolled), an old passport, or a naturalization certificate.

- ✔ **Proof of U.S. citizenship.** Bring your old passport if you're renewing; otherwise, bring a certified copy of your birth certificate with registrar's seal, a report of your birth abroad, or your naturalized citizenship documents.

- ✔ **Two identical 2-x- 2-inch photographs with a white or off-white background.** You can get these taken in just about any corner photo shop; these places have a special camera to make the photos identical. Expect to pay up to $10 for them. **Note:** You can't use the strip photos from one of those photo vending machines.

If you're 18 or older and renewing a passport issued no more than 12 years ago, you don't have to apply in person; you can renew the passport by mail. Include your expired passport, pink renewal form DS-82, two identical photos (see the preceding bulleted list), and a check or money order for $45 (no extra handling fee). Send the package (registered, just to be safe) to one of the agencies listed on the back of the application form. Allow at least four to six weeks for your application to be processed and your new passport to be sent.

If your name has changed, you can renew your passport by mail using form *DS-19*. Send a copy of the completed form, a certified copy of your marriage certificate or your name change court decree, and your valid U.S. passport to the address listed on the back of the form. Allow at least four to six weeks to receive your new passport. This service is free.

Need your passport in a hurry, perhaps to take advantage of that incredibly low airline fare to London? To expedite your passport (for receipt in five business days), visit an agency directly or go through the court or post office and have them send the application via overnight mail. This process costs an extra $35. For more information, call the National Passport Information Center at ☎ **900/225-5674** (35¢ per minute) or 888/362/8668 ($4.95 per call).

When you have your passport photos taken, get an additional set (of you and your children) to take along with you. You need a photo to buy a seven-day or longer London Travelcard. And your child needs one to apply for a Child Photocard, which qualifies children to pay reduced prices on buses (see Chapter 11 for more details). Having extra photos on hand saves you the time, bother, and expense of having them taken in London.

Applying for Canadian, Australian, and New Zealand passports

The following list offers more information for citizens of Canada, Australia, and New Zealand:

- ✔ **Australians** can visit a local post office or passport office; call toll-free ☎ 131-232 (from Australia), or log on to www.dfat.gov.au/passports for details on how and where to apply. Adult passports cost AUS$128, and passports for travelers under 18 are AUS$64. Applicants must provide two, identical, color photographs (no smaller than 35 x 45 mm and not larger than 40 x 50 mm) and proof of identity.

- ✔ **Canadians** can pick up passport applications at the central Passport Office (Department of Foreign Affairs and International Trade, Ottawa, ON K1A 0G3; ☎ 800/567-6868), one of the 28 regional passport offices, most travel agencies, or from www.dfait-maeci.gc.ca/passport (which has downloadable forms). Children under 16 may be included on a parent's passport, but they need their own passport to travel unaccompanied. Applications must include two identical 2-x-2-inch photos and a birth certificate or Certificate of Canadian Citizenship. Passports are valid for five years and cost C$60. Processing takes five to ten days if you apply in person or ten days to three weeks by mail.

- ✔ **New Zealanders** can pick up passport applications at any travel agency, online at www.passports.govt.nz, or at the Passport Office, P.O. Box 10–526, Wellington (☎ 0800/225-050). Adult passports cost NZ$80, and passports for travelers under 16 are NZ$40. Mail the completed form, along with a pair of identical 50-x-40-mm photos and proof of citizenship, to the Wellington office.

Understanding passport rules

If you're a citizen of the United States, Canada, Australia, or New Zealand, you must have a passport with at least two months remaining validity to enter the United Kingdom. Citizens of European Union (EU) countries supposedly do not need a passport to visit other EU countries, but in reality they do need one if their country doesn't issue identity cards. You need to show your passport at the customs and immigration area when you arrive at a London airport. After your passport is stamped, you can remain in the United Kingdom as a tourist for up to three months.

Keep your passport with you at all times. You need to show it only when you're converting traveler's checks or foreign currency at a bank or currency exchange. However, you may be asked to present your passport to the hotel clerk when you check in; after examining it, the clerk will return the passport to you. If you're not going to need your passport for currency exchanges, ask whether the hotel has a safe where you can keep it locked up.

Dealing with a (gulp) lost passport

Don't worry; if you lose your passport in England, you won't be sent to the Tower of London, but you need to take steps to replace it *immediately.* First, notify the police. Then go to your consulate or high commission office (they are all located in London). Bring all available forms of identification, and the staff will get started on generating your new passport. For the addresses of consulates and high commissions, see the Appendix. Always call first to verify open hours.

Playing It Safe with Travel and Medical Insurance

I want to give you some advice on the three kinds of travel insurance — trip-cancellation insurance, medical insurance, and lost luggage insurance.

- ✔ **Trip-cancellation insurance** is a good idea if you signed up for an escorted tour and paid a large portion of your vacation expenses up front (for information on escorted tours, see Chapter 5). Trip cancellation insurance covers three emergencies — if a death or sickness prevents you from traveling, if a tour operator or airline goes out of business, or if some kind of disaster prevents you from getting to your destination.

- ✔ **Medical insurance** doesn't make sense for most travelers. Your existing health insurance should cover you if you get sick while on vacation (although if you belong to an HMO, check to see whether you're fully covered while in the United Kingdom).

- ✔ **Lost luggage insurance** is not necessary for most travelers. Your homeowner's or renter's insurance should cover stolen luggage if you have off-premises theft coverage. Check your existing policies before you buy any additional coverage. If an airline loses your luggage, the airline is responsible for paying $1,250 per bag on domestic flights and $635 per bag (maximum of two bags) on international flights. If you plan to carry anything more valuable than that, keep it in your carry-on bag.

Some credit cards (American Express and some gold and platinum Visa and MasterCards, for example) offer automatic flight insurance against death or dismemberment in case of an airplane crash. If you feel you still need more insurance, try one of the following companies:

- ✔ **Access America,** 6600 W. Broad St., Richmond, VA 23230 (☎ **800/284-8300**).

- ✔ **Travelex Insurance Services,** P.O. Box 641070, Omaha, NE 68164-7070 (☎ **800/228-9792**).

- ✔ **Travel Guard International,** 1145 Clark St., Stevens Point, WI 54481 (☎ **800/826-1300;** Internet: www.travelguard.com).

- ✔ **Travel Insured International, Inc.,** P.O. Box 280568, East Hartford, CT 06128 (☎ **800/243-3174;** Internet: www.travelinsured.com).

 Don't pay for more insurance than you need. For example, if you need only trip-cancellation insurance, don't buy coverage for lost or stolen property. Trip-cancellation insurance costs about 6% to 8% of the total value of your vacation.

Staying Healthy When You Travel

Getting sick may ruin your vacation, so I strongly advise against it (of course, the last time I checked, the influenza bugs weren't listening to me any more than they probably listen to you).

Talk to your doctor before leaving on a trip if you have a serious and/or chronic illness. If you have a serious condition, such as heart disease, epilepsy, or diabetes, wear a MedicAlert identification tag, which immediately alerts any doctor to your condition and gives him or her access to your medical records through MedicAlert's 24-hour hot line (a worldwide toll-free emergency response number is on the tag). Membership is $35, plus a $20 annual renewal fee. Contact the *MedicAlert Foundation,* P.O. Box 1009, Turlock, CA 95381-1009 (☎ **800/863-2427;** Internet: www.medicalert.org).

Bring all your medications with you, as well as prescriptions for more medications (in generic, not brand name, form) if you worry that you may run out. Also, pack your medications in a carry-on that you always keep with you. If you have health insurance, be sure to carry your insurance card in your wallet. If you worry about getting sick away from home, buy medical insurance (see the preceding section on insurance), which may cover you more completely than your existing health insurance.

If you fall ill while traveling, ask the concierge at your hotel to recommend a local doctor. If you can't locate a doctor, contact your country's embassy or consulate (see the Appendix for addresses and phone numbers). If the situation is serious, dial ☎ 999 (no coins required), the number for police and medical emergencies in London. If the situation is life threatening, go to the emergency or accident department at the local hospital. Any taxi driver can take you there.

Under the United Kingdom's nationalized health care system, you're eligible only for free *emergency* care. If you're admitted to a hospital as an *in-patient,* even from an accident and an emergency department, you must pay unless you're a U.K. resident or a citizen of the European Union. This financial obligation is true for follow-up care as well. See the Appendix for the names, addresses, and phone numbers of hospitals offering 24-hour emergency care in London.

Most U.S. health insurance plans and HMOs cover at least part of the out-of-country hospital visits and procedures if insurees become ill or are injured while out of the country. Most require that you pay the bills up front at the time of care, issuing a refund after you return and file all the paperwork.

Before leaving home, you can obtain a directory of U.K. doctors from the *International Association of Medical Assistance to Travelers* (IAMAT). Its address in the United States is 417 Center St., Lewiston, NY 14092 (☎ 716/754-4883); in Canada, 40 Regal Rd., Guelph, Ontario N1K 1B5 (☎ 519/836-0102); and in New Zealand, P.O. Box 5049, Christchurch 5 (no phone). IAMAT is on the Web at www.sentex.net/~iamat.

Not Renting a Car in London

Having a car in London is far more a hassle than a help for the following reasons:

- ✔ Maneuvering through London's congested and complicated maze of streets can be an endurance test even for Londoners.

- ✔ Finding your way through the city in heavy traffic while driving on the *left-hand side* of the road can turn even the best American driver into a gibbering nut case.

- ✔ Parking is difficult to find and expensive (street meters cost £1/$1.65 for 20 minutes).

- ✔ Gas (*petrol* in Britspeak) costs about $4 a gallon.

- ✔ Public transportation — especially the Tube — will get you everywhere you want to go at a fraction of the cost.Do yourself a favor: Forget about renting a car. If you want to be with Londoners on their own turf (or in their own tunnels), the Tube (Underground) is a great way to do it. Even if you're planning excursions outside London, the trains are a better option. (However, see Chapter 21 for details on renting a car for day-tripping.)

Getting Reservations and Tickets before You Leave Home

If your time in London is limited and you don't want to miss specific plays, concerts, or top restaurants, make your reservations or buy your tickets in advance.

Your finest table, please: Dinner reservations

For dinner reservations, call the restaurant directly from home (the restaurant listings in Chapters 14 and 15 include phone numbers), but keep in mind the time change (London is five hours later than eastern standard time, so when it's noon in New York, it's 5 p.m. in London). You can also ask your hotel concierge to make the reservation for you after you arrive, but be sure to do so far enough ahead — you may have to reserve a couple of days or even a week or two in advance for some trendy places. For a list of hot restaurants in London that require advance booking, see Chapter 13.

If you plan on enjoying high tea at the Ritz or one of the other elegant London hotels that serve legendary afternoon teas (I list them in Chapter 15), you may have to book that reservation in advance as well.

Two on the aisle: Theater tickets

Every London theater has a row (or more) of house seats that are kept until the last possible moment. Those seats as well as any returns generally go on sale the day of the performance — in the morning or an hour before curtain time. You have a good chance of getting a seat to a sold-out show if you go directly to the box office.

You may be looking forward to a specific event, and missing it would ruin your trip. On my last trip, my must-see was Dame Maggie Smith in Alan Bennett's new play, *The Lady in the Van*. Every day in front of the box office, a long queue of theater lovers desperately hoped to snag a return ticket. Dame Maggie, as they say, was the hottest show in town. So I was glad that I'd booked a seat in advance.

To book (and pay an additional commission) before you leave home, contact one of the following:

✔ **Albemarle.** This respected booking agency (at 74 Mortimer St., London, W1N 8HL; ☎ **020/7637-9041** in the U.K.; Fax: 020/ 7631-0375; E-mail: sales@albemarle-london.com; Internet: www.albemarle-london.com) maintains a definitive London Theatre Web site with listings of all current West End shows, opera, ballet, and rock and pop concerts. If you find a performance you want to attend, you can purchase a ticket via e-mail. The prices include a booking fee of 23% plus tax. Albemarle sells the best seats to most shows for £44.10 ($66); the face value of the ticket is £35 ($52). Time permitting, the company will mail tickets worldwide; otherwise, you can pick them up at the theater or have them delivered to your hotel.

✔ **Keith Prowse.** The New York office of this London-based ticket agency (☎ **800/669-7469** or 914/328-2357; Internet: www.keith prowse.com) handles West End (commercial) shows, the English National and Royal Opera, pop concerts, and events such as the Chelsea Flower Show and the British Open (see Chapter 2 for more on these last two). After payment is received, the agency sends you a voucher to be exchanged for tickets at the box office.

If you want to attend an opera or a ballet at the **Royal Opera House,** prebook months, not days, in advance. Check out the major performing-arts venues in Chapter 23; if the group has a Web site, I list it. Usually you can book directly online.

In the know: What's playing and where

The ticket-booking agencies in the preceding section can tell you what's currently on. The following Web sites are also useful for finding out what's playing in London:

✔ **Electronic Telegraph** (Internet: www.telegraph.co.uk), the online version of the *Daily Telegraph,* reviews theater and other performance events in its "Arts & Books" section.

✔ The online version of the **Evening Standard** newspaper (Internet: www.thisislondon.co.uk) has listings of current theater and music events.

✔ **The Society of London Theatre** (Internet: www.officiallondon theatre.co.uk) offers a comprehensive listing of plays, opera, and dance.

✔ The Net edition of the **Sunday Times** (Internet: www.sunday-times.co.uk) offers reviews and listings of West End shows and other events. Look under "Arts" and "Culture."

✔ **Time Out** (www.timeout.com), a weekly entertainment magazine, provides online theater, music, dance, and other events listings. You can browse through and find everything that's currently playing, including smaller venues.

Packing It Up and Taking It on the Road

Before you start packing, think realistically about what you need for the length of time you'll be gone. And think practically. A sauce stain makes a white silk dress or dress shirt unwearable (I hope). In general, plan to dress in *layers*. Pack *nonwhite* clothing. And unless you're going to London in the height of summer (perhaps even then), consider that the temperature will probably be between *45 and 70 degrees Fahrenheit, and the climate is often damp.*

Before you choose a suitcase for your trip, decide what kind of traveling you intend to do. A bag with wheels makes sense for walking with luggage on hard floors. Wheels won't help you carry baggage on uneven roads or up and down stairs. A fold-over garment bag is a nuisance if you pack and unpack often, but it can help keep dressy clothing wrinkle-free. Hard-sided luggage protects breakable items better but weighs more than soft-sided bags.

Deciding what to bring

To start packing compile everything that you think you'll need on your trip. Then get rid of half of it. You don't want to injure yourself by lugging half your house around with you. Getting from the airport and your hotel can be difficult; but if you're staying in a B&B without an elevator, lugging a heavy load of suitcases up and down narrow London stairways can be a royal pain in the gluteus max.

Some essentials for your trip include:

- ✔ Comfortable walking shoes
- ✔ A versatile sweater (gray or dark colored); make it a heavy sweater if visiting in late fall or winter
- ✔ A waterproof jacket or coat (preferably one with a hood); select outerwear that's lined if visiting in late fall or winter
- ✔ Something to sleep in (London thermostats are often set rather low)
- ✔ A collapsible umbrella (or *brolly* as the Brits call them)
- ✔ Gloves and a scarf if visiting in late fall or winter

You need a formal suit or fancy dress only if you plan to attend a board meeting, a funeral, a wedding, or some similar occasion, or you want to dine in one of the city's finest restaurants. For daily wear around the city, a pair of jeans or khakis will do. You may want to consider a couple of cotton pullovers you can wear under a sweater or sweatshirt.

Weather patterns

According to 18th-century writer Dr. Samuel Johnson (1709–1784), "When two Englishmen meet, their first talk is of the weather." Things haven't changed much since then. The unpredictability of the English climate has led to another sound British maxim: There is no such thing as bad weather, there is only inappropriate clothing. For an Englishman, appropriate foul-weather gear includes a *mac* (short for mackintosh, a raincoat), a *brolly* (umbrella), and *Wellingtons* (rubber boots).

The English favor woolens because the fabric is warm and practical, and it holds its shape even after a drenching downpour.

Many hotel rooms are equipped with trouser presses, which get out the wrinkles and save you the hassle of toting along a travel iron.

Dressing like a Londoner

London — like Paris, Milan, and New York — is a fashion-conscious city. This doesn't mean that you *must* be fashionable, only that you *can* be, and that if you are, other fashionable people may notice you. If you plan to eat in any upscale restaurants, you'll encounter a smart-but-casual dress code. You won't be let in if you try to enter the dining room wearing jogging shoes, sweatpants, or blue jeans.

Smart-but-casual men need to bring along a pair of dressy but comfortable trousers and a sports jacket (or a suit if you like), a shirt and tie (or dressy sweater), and leather shoes (preferably with a nice shine). Smart-but-casual women can wear a dress, a skirt and blouse, a suit with skirt and jacket, or a pantsuit. One thing you may want to know: As in New York, the big color in London is black. So if you're wondering what color is in this and every season, it's *noir, noir,* Nanette.

Traveling with carry-on bags

In the wake of the September 2001 terrorist attacks, the Federal Aviation Administration (FAA) has devised new guidelines for carry-on baggage. At press time, passengers are limited to bringing just one carry-on bag and one personal item onto the aircraft (previous regulations allowed two carry-on bags and one personal item, such as a briefcase or a purse). These items must fit in the overhead compartment or beneath the seat in front of you. For more information on restrictions, check the FAA Web site at www.faa.gov.apa/pr/index.cfm or contact your airline.

As one of your carry-ons, select a backpack or shoulder bag that can double as an all-purpose bag for your guidebooks, maps, and camera while you're exploring in London.

Your carry-on should contain a book (this one, of course), any medications you use, any breakable items that you don't want to put in your suitcase, a snack in case you don't like the airline food (the flight will be at least six hours), and your vital documents (such as return tickets and passport).

Leaving electronics at home

Some electronic items may be necessary — a laptop, for example, if you have to work while in London. However, except for the absolute necessities, leave all the other electronic devices at home.

If you think that you won't enjoy your trip without a few electrical gadgets, here's what you need to know if you're coming from North America: You can't plug an appliance from the United States or Canada into a British outlet without frying your appliance and/or blowing a fuse. North American current runs 110V, 60 cycles; the standard voltage throughout Britain is 240V AC, 50 cycles. You need a current converter or transformer to bring the voltage down and the cycles up. Two-pronged North American plugs won't fit into the three-pronged square British wall sockets, so you also need a three-pronged square adapter and/or converter if you use North American appliances in Britain. Plug adapters and converters are available at most travel, luggage, electronics, and hardware stores. Some plug adapters are also current converters. Most contemporary laptop computers automatically sense the current and adapt accordingly (check the manual, bottom of the machine, or manufacturer first to make sure that you don't destroy your data and/or equipment).

Travel-size versions of hair dryers, irons, shavers, and so on are dual voltage, which means that they have built-in converters (usually you have to turn a switch to go back and forth). If you insist on lugging your own hair dryer or electric shaver to London, make sure that it's dual voltage or that you carry along a converter. Hotels black out on a regular basis when someone from North America plugs in a 110V hair dryer, and the appliance explodes in an impressive shower of sparks or melts in his or her hands. To avoid voltage issues, use a straight-edge razor for shaving, unless you have a battery-operated electric shaver. However, most hotels have a special plug for low-wattage shavers *and shavers only.*

Part III
Settling into London

WHILE ON VACATION IN LONDON, BILL AND DENISE WATCH A LOCAL FAMILY WORKING ON THE TRADITIONAL THATCHED ROOF COTTAGE, THATCHED ROOF SATELLITE DISH, AND THATCHED ROOF JEEP CHEROKEE.

In this part...

Daydreaming about going to a place is cheap, convenient, and lots of fun: You don't have to concern
yourself with how to get from point A to point B without
wasting time and money. But when you actually reach
London, reality sets in. You won't be familiar with how
the Underground runs, how the bus system works,
when the trains run, or how to get a taxi. But don't worry.
In this part, I help you settle into London. In Chapter 10,
I guide you from the airport into the city and introduce
you to London's neighborhoods. In Chapter 11, I tell you
everything you need to know about public transportation,
including ways to save a bundle on bus and Tube tickets.
A quick and easy primer on U.K. currency follows in
Chapter 12.

Chapter 10

Arriving and Getting Oriented

In This Chapter

▶ Traveling from the airport (or train station) to your hotel

▶ Getting yourself oriented to the London neighborhoods

▶ Finding help and information after you arrive

Although London is among the world's largest cities, in both size and population, many of its neighborhoods were once small villages. With urban roots (and routes) that hark back to Roman times, London's not always the easiest city to navigate. Streets aren't organized in a grid, and some have cobblestones, although most have been paved and modernized. This quaint, village-like quality is one reason for London's enduring charm, but charm is little comfort when you're lost in a strange place, so let me help you get your bearings. Neighborhood boundaries come later in this chapter. First, you need to get from the airport (or train station) into Central London.

Arriving by Plane and Getting to Central London

Heathrow and Gatwick airports handle the bulk of London's international flights. The airports are accustomed to handling thousands of customers every day, so you needn't fear any unpleasant surprises.

Proceeding through passport control and customs

Have your passport ready because your first stop after deplaning is passport control (for details on getting a passport, see Chapter 9). The procedure is fairly routine. On the plane you fill out a *landing card* that asks for your name, home address, passport number, and the address where you'll be staying in London. Present the completed card with your passport to the official at passport control. The official may ask for the following information:

✔ How long you'll be staying (you must stay less than three months if you don't have a visa)

✔ Where you plan to stay

✔ Whether the trip is for business or pleasure (don't be afraid to say pleasure)

✔ What your next destination will be

✔ How much money you have with you

Although you may think that the question about your finances is snoopy impertinence, officials have good reason to ask. They want to verify that people entering England won't apply for some kind of welfare or National Health insurance benefits and become a burden on the country.

Officials may stamp your passport without asking a thing. After your passport is stamped, proceed to pick up your luggage. From there, you wind your way out through the Customs Hall.

At the customs area, you get two choices: "Nothing to Declare" and "Goods to Declare." Chances are you won't be declaring anything, in which case you walk right through. Limits on imports for visitors 17 and older entering England include the following:

✔ 200 cigarettes, 50 cigars, or 250 grams (8.8 oz.) of loose tobacco

✔ 2 liters (2.1 qt.) of still table wine

✔ 1 liter of liquor over 22% alcohol content or 2 liters of liquor under 22%

✔ 2 fluid ounces of perfume

If you fall within these limits, go through the "Nothing to Declare" area at customs. You may, however, be stopped for a random luggage search. Don't take it personally if this happens. Unless you're smuggling in contraband, you have nothing to worry about. For details on duty-free shopping and limits on what you can bring back home, see Chapter 19.

Landing at busy Heathrow

About 15 miles west of Central London, Heathrow (☎ 020/8759-4321) is the largest of London's airports as well as the world's busiest, with four passenger terminals serving flights from around the globe. Moving walkways and signposts that mark just about everything make the trek through the long corridors easy. You'll probably arrive at Terminal 3 or 4:

✔ Terminal 3 is for non-British, long-haul flights.

✔ Terminal 4 is for British Airways intercontinental flights and the superfast Concorde.

After clearing customs (see the preceding section), you enter the main concourse of your terminal. You can pick up a free map and general info from the *Tourist Information Centre* in the Terminal 3 Arrivals Concourse (open daily 6 a.m. to 11 p.m.) or in the Underground concourse of Terminals 1, 2, and 3 (open daily 8 a.m. to 6 p.m.). Other available services include ATMs, hotel booking agencies (see Chapter 7), theater booking services, and several banks and bureaux de change (where you can swap your dollars or traveler's checks for pounds and pence).

You have several options for getting into the city. The **London Underground** (☎ 020/7222-1234), called the *Underground* or the *Tube,* is the London subway system and the cheapest mode of public transportation for most Central London destinations (see the inside back cover of this book for a map of the Underground system). All terminals at Heathrow link up with the Tube system. Follow the Underground signs to the ticket booth. The Piccadilly Line gets you into Central London in about 45 minutes for a fare of £3.60 ($5). Underground trains run from all four Heathrow terminals every 5 to 9 minutes Monday through Saturday 5:30 a.m. to 11:30 p.m. and Sunday 6 a.m. to 11 p.m.

The one potential hassle with the Underground is that the Tube trains don't have luggage racks. Stash your bags as best you can — behind your legs, on your lap, or near the center doors where there's more space. Keep in mind that during rush hour, the trains become increasingly packed as you get closer to London. To reach your hotel on the Underground, you may have to change trains or take a cab from the Underground station closest to your destination.

For more information on the Underground, including discount passes (called *Travelcards*), check out Chapter 11.

If the Underground is closed, you can ride the **N97 night bus** from Heathrow to Central London. Buses (located in front of the terminals) run every 30 minutes Monday through Saturday midnight to 5 a.m. and Sunday 11:00 p.m. to 5:30 a.m. The trip takes about an hour; a one-way fare is £1.50 ($2.25) before 4:30 a.m. or £1 ($1.50) after 4:30 a.m.

The **Airbus Heathrow Shuttle** (☎ 020/8400-6655) may be a better alternative to the Underground if you have lots of heavy luggage. Two routes are available: The A1 goes from Heathrow to Victoria Station via Cromwell Road, Knightsbridge, and Hyde Park Corner; the A2 goes to Kings Cross Station via Bayswater, Marble Arch, Euston, and Russell Square. Travel time for both is about 75 minutes, and the fare is £7 ($11), payable on the bus. Up to three buses an hour depart daily 4:00 a.m. to 11:23 p.m. from the front of Heathrow's terminals.

The **Heathrow Express** (☎ 0845/600-1515; Internet: www. heathrowexpress.co.uk) is a dedicated train line running from all four Heathrow terminals to London's Paddington Station in only 15 minutes. The trains have air conditioning, ergonomically designed seating, and plenty of luggage space. The fare is £12 ($18) Express class or

£20 ($30) first class. First class offers larger, more comfortable seats and a bit more room than Express class; for most travelers, the extra expense isn't worth it. You can buy tickets at the airport or on board the train. Service runs Monday through Saturday 5:07 a.m. to 11:47 p.m. and Sunday 5:03 a.m. to 11:48 p.m. All the major airlines have check-in counters right at Paddington, so when you're returning from London to the airport you can conveniently check your luggage *before* boarding the train; then when you arrive at Heathrow, you can go directly to your departure gate without further check-in.

If you're travel-weary, you may want the luxury of taking a **taxi** (☎ 020/8745-7487) directly to your hotel. Taxis are especially cost effective if four or five people are traveling together. You can order one at the Taxi Information booths in all four terminals. Expect to pay about £35 ($52) plus tip (15% of the total fare) for a trip of about 45 minutes. Cabs are available 24 hours a day. Wheelchair facilities are available at all times for the disabled.

Flying to calmer Gatwick

Gatwick (☎ 01293/535-353) is considerably smaller than Heathrow but provides the same services, except that the British Tourist Authority doesn't have an office there. Gatwick is about 28 miles south of Central London. Once used only for charters, Gatwick now handles international flights from some U.S. airlines; international flights come in at the South Terminal. Gatwick also has a North Terminal.

 If you land at Gatwick instead of Heathrow, you have fewer means of transportation into Central London. The highway system from Gatwick into London is far less efficient than from Heathrow, so buses, minivans, or cabs can end up taking two to three hours in heavy traffic.

Your quickest way of getting into Central London from Gatwick is the convenient **Gatwick Express train** (☎ 0990/301-530). You can board the train right in the South Terminal, and in about 30 minutes, you'll be at Victoria Station. Cost is £10.20 ($15) Express class, £16 ($24) first class. As with the Heathrow Express, first class is roomier than Express class and features larger, more comfortable seats. Trains run daily every 15 minutes from 5 a.m. to midnight; they run hourly throughout the night.

Slightly less expensive is the local **Connex South-Central train** (☎ 01332/387-601), which also runs to Victoria Station and usually takes about 5 minutes longer; its fare is £8.20 ($12). Four trains run each hour during the day; from midnight to 5 a.m., they run every half-hour.

Another train service, the **Thameslink** (☎ 0845/748-4950), runs between Gatwick and King's Cross Station for £9.50 ($14). Service is every 15 minutes daily 3:45 a.m. to 12:15 a.m.; trip time is about 45 minutes.

For 24-hour taxi service between Gatwick and Central London, call

> ✔ Gatwick Airport Cars (☎ **01293/562-291**)
>
> ✔ Gatwick Goldlines Cars (☎ **01293/568-368**)

You can order a taxi at the Taxi Information booth when you arrive at Gatwick Airport. Fares for both companies are the same: £60 ($90) plus tip for the journey that takes about 90 minutes.

Touching down at another airport

If you fly into London from elsewhere in Europe, you may arrive at airports other than Heathrow and Gatwick. The following sections help you navigate from these less-used facilities.

Stansted: For national and European flights

Stansted (☎ **01279/680-500**) is a single-terminal airport used for national and European flights. The airport is about 33 miles northeast of Central London. The **Stansted Skytrain** (☎ **01332/387-601**) to Liverpool Street Station takes 45 minutes and costs £10.70 ($16). Trains run every half-hour daily 6:00 a.m. to 11:59 p.m. Taxi fare into the city averages about £60 ($90) plus tip.

London City Airport: European destinations only

London City Airport (☎ **020/7646-000**) is a mere 6 miles east of the city center, but it services only European destinations. A **Red Route shuttle bus** (☎ **020/7646-0000**) takes passengers from the airport to Liverpool Street Station in 25 minutes for £5 ($8). The buses run every 10 minutes daily 6:00 a.m. to 9:30 p.m. A taxi to the vicinity of Marble Arch costs about £25 ($41) plus tip.

Luton: Serving European charters

Luton (☎ **01582/405-100**) services European charter flights. This small, independent airport is about 33 miles northwest of the city. The **Greenline 757 Bus** (☎ **0990/808-080**) runs from the airport to the Victoria Coach Station on Buckingham Palace Road daily every hour 5:30 a.m. to midnight; the trip takes about 75 minutes and costs £7 ($11).

You can also take the 24-hour **Railair Coach Link** to Luton Station (3 miles away), which connects with the Luton Flyer train to King's Cross Station in Central London. The fare is £10 ($17); trip time is one hour.

Taxis into the city cost about £50 ($75) plus tip.

Disembarking at a Channel Port

If coming from the Continent by train and ferry or *hovercraft* (a high-speed ferry), you cross the English Channel and disembark at one of the United Kingdom's Channel ports. The ports closest to London are *Dover, Ramsgate,* and *Folkestone* to the east and *Southampton, Portsmouth,* and *Newhaven* to the south. The *QEII* cruise ship also docks at Southampton.

Trains connecting with ferries on the U.K. side of the Channel generally go to Liverpool Street Station, Victoria Station, or Waterloo International. Waterloo International (part of Waterloo Station) is also where the Eurostar Chunnel trains arrive from Paris and Brussels. On the Eurostar, you don't have to make any train-to-boat-to-train transfers along the way. For more on the Eurostar, see Chapter 5.

All London stations link to the Underground system. Just look for the Underground symbol (a circle with a line through it). The stations connect to the Underground as follows:

- ✓ **Waterloo** is linked to the Northern and Bakerloo lines.

- ✓ **Victoria** is on the District, Circle, and Victoria lines.

- ✓ **Liverpool Street** is on the Circle, East London, Metropolitan, and Central Lines.

Taxis wait outside all train stations. See Chapter 11 for more information on the London Underground and taxis.

London's train stations are swarming with activity. You find bookstores, *bureaux de change* (currency exchange facilities), restaurants, newsstands, and many of the services airports traditionally offer. While passing through, you can stock up on maps and brochures and, if you arrived in London without a hotel reservation, you can book a room from Victoria and several other train stations (see Chapter 7 for details). Also see the section "Finding Information after You Arrive" later in this chapter for information about the tourist information centers that you find in several London train stations.

Keep in mind that the United Kingdom, like the rest of Europe, uses the 24-hour clock for rail and other timetables, which means that 0530 is 5:30 a.m., 1200 is noon, and 1830 is 6:30 p.m. Don't be confused: Just continue counting up from noon: 1300 = 1 p.m., 1400 = 2 p.m., 1500 = 3 p.m., and so on up to 2400 (midnight). In this guide, I stick to the American a.m. and p.m. system. Like most of the rest of the world, London goes on daylight saving time from April through October.

Resetting your internal clock

Passengers flying to London generally experience *jet lag,* so you need to try to reset your internal clock. On a six-hour flight from the East Coast of the United States, for example, you move through five hours of time change. When you arrive at 7 a.m. *your* time, it'll be noon *London* time. My best advice is to try to get acclimated to London time immediately. Reset your watch before you get off the plane. Don't keep looking for a clock, trying to figure out what time it is back home.

Stay up as long as you can your first day in London and then wake up at a normal time (well, try to, anyway) the second day. Drink plenty of water both days, as well as on the plane, to avoid dehydration and to help keep you regular. Try to eat at usual London meal times. I always find that walking a lot on my first day in London helps me to beat jet lag and gets me in synch with the city.

Figuring Out the Neighborhoods

Londoners orient themselves by neighborhood (see the map "London's Neighborhoods"). Sounds simple enough, but with London's confusing and sometimes oddly named streets and its seemingly endless plethora of neighborhoods, you may have a hard time telling where one neighborhood begins and another leaves off. For orientation purposes, I give you major streets as boundary markers. But be aware that the neighborhoods frequently bleed beyond these principal arteries.

To help you find your way around, I strongly suggest that you buy a copy of *London A to Z* (ask for *London A to Zed,* because *z* is pronounced *zed*). You can pick up this indexed London street map at just about any bookstore or newsstands (you may want to get it while you're at the airport).

Although **Greater London** encompasses a whopping 622 square miles, the main tourist portion is only a fraction (25 square miles at the most) of that distance. Most sites within this 25-mile range are convenient to the Underground system (the Tube). You may have a short (10 minute or less) walk from the Tube stop to your destination) but London is flat, and for walkers it's a dream.

London is divided into **postal districts,** like ZIP codes in the United States. All London street addresses include a designation such as SW1 or EC3. (In London, the postal districts are related to where they lie geographically from the original post office, which was at St. Martin-le-Grand in The City.) Addresses in the City of London, the easternmost portion of Central London, have designations such as EC2, EC3, or EC4. As you move west, the codes change to W, WC, SW, NW, and so on.

London's Neighborhoods

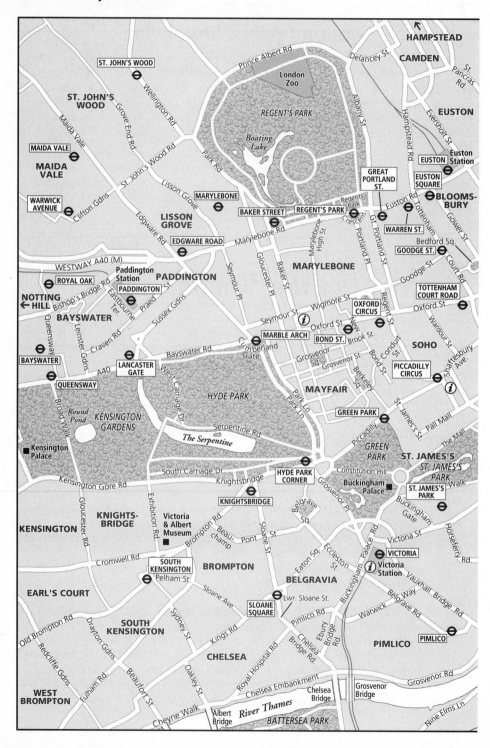

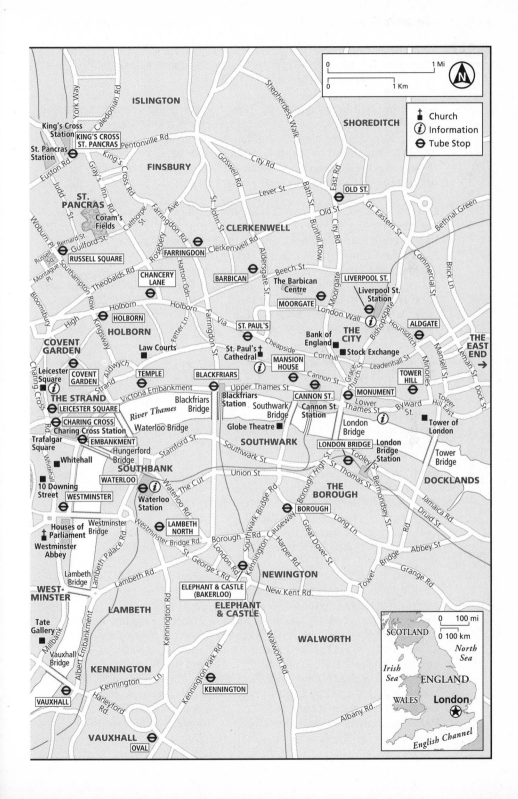

You don't need to bother yourself with postal districts except when you're looking up streets in *London A to Z* (many streets in different parts of London have the same name) or sending something by mail. When you actually hit the streets, the postal district designations aren't as important as the nearest Tube stop.

Remember that London grew up along the north and south banks of the river **Thames,** which snakes through the city in a long, loose S curve. This great tidal river played a fundamental role in London's growth, development, and prosperity. London's major tourist sights, hotels, and restaurants are on the river's north bank, and many of the city's famous performing-arts venues are on the South Bank.

Central London, on the north bank of the Thames, is considered to be the city center, the area covered by the Circle Line Underground route. Paddington Station anchors the northwestern corner, Earl's Court marks the southwestern corner, Tower Hill sits at the southeastern corner, and Liverpool Street Station anchors the northeastern corner. Central London is divided into three areas: **The City,** the **West End,** and **West London**. In the descriptions that follow, I start at The City and move west from there. Check out Chapter 6 if you think that you'd like to stay in one of these neighborhoods, and you need more information.

The City of London: The heart of it all

A self-governing entity that extends south from Chiswell Street to the river Thames, the City of London is bounded on the west by Chancery Lane and to the east by the **Tower of London,** the city's most important historic monument.

Fleet Street, associated with printing and publishing since the 1500s but now a little forlorn since the departure of most of its newspaper offices, cuts through the center of the district to Ludgate Circus, where it becomes Ludgate. Follow that road and you get to **St. Paul's Cathedral,** its massive dome beautifully illuminated at night. St. Paul's is just one of the buildings built atop the ancient area known as *The City.*

Covering the original 1 square mile that the Romans called Londinium, The City encompasses the territory between Moorfields to the north and the Thames to the south and from Aldgate to the east and Temple Bar to the west. Today this area is the Wall Street of England, home to the **Bank of England,** the **Royal Exchange,** and the **Stock Exchange,** as well as the new **Lloyds of London** building and the **NatWest Tower,** London's second tallest building. You also find the **Museum of London,** the remains of the **Roman Temple of Mithras,** the church of **St. Stephen Walbrook** (designed by Christopher Wren), the Wren-designed **Monument** that commemorates the Great Fire of London in 1666, and the **Barbican Centre,** a mega-arts complex of theaters and concert halls.

Liverpool Street Station is the main rail terminus in this area. The major Tube stops are Blackfriars, Tower Hill, St. Paul's, Liverpool Street Station, Bank, Barbican, and Moorgate.

The West End: Downtown London

The West End (that is, west of The City) is "downtown" London. The West End is known for the theater, entertainment, and shopping areas around Piccadilly Circus and Leicester Square. But a host of neighborhoods make up the West End. I describe them briefly in sections that follow.

Holborn

Abutting the City of London to the west is the old borough of Holborn, the legal heart of London and home to the **Inns of Court, Lincoln's Inn Fields, Royal Courts of Justice,** and **Old Bailey.**

This "in-between" district is bounded roughly by Theobald's Road to the north, Farringdon Road to the east, the Thames to the south, and Kingsway, Aldwych, and Lancaster Place to the west. The major Tube stops are Holborn, Temple, Blackfriars, and Aldwych.

The Strand and Covent Garden

The northern section of The Strand, the area west of Holborn, is Covent Garden, with Shaftesbury Avenue as its northern boundary. Covent Garden has many theaters, eateries, and shops and is home to the **Royal Opera House** and **Covent Garden Market,** one of the busiest shopping areas in London. Covent Garden is an area for strolling, shopping, and stopping for tea or a meal.

Formerly one of the premier streets in England, The Strand (the same name as the neighborhood) runs from Trafalgar Square to Fleet Street; The Strand is the principal thoroughfare along the southern edge, with Charing Cross Road to the west and Kingsway, Aldwych, and Lancaster Place to the east. **Cleopatra's Needle,** an Egyptian obelisk dating from about 1475 B.C. and moved to England in 1878, is located in the Victoria Embankment on the north side of the Hungerford Bridge. The major Tube stops are Covent Garden, Leicester Square, and Charing Cross.

Bloomsbury

Just north of Covent Garden, New Oxford Street and Bloomsbury Way mark the beginnings of the Bloomsbury district, home of the **British Museum** and several colleges and universities, as well as the only surviving London home of novelist Charles Dickens.

This intellectual pocket of Central London was home to the famed Bloomsbury Group, whose members included novelist Virginia Woolf and historian Lytton Strachey. Bloomsbury is bounded to the east by Woburn Place and Southampton Row, to the north by Euston Road, and to the west by Tottenham Court Road. The major Tube stops are Euston Square, Russell Square, Goodge Street, and Tottenham Court Road.

Soho

This lively area is full of restaurants, cafes, bars, pubs, and nightclubs and is popular with the gay community. London's **Gay Village** is centered around Old Compton Street. Gerrard Street is one of the main streets of **Chinatown.** Much of Soho used to be a down-to-earth Italian neighborhood, but the area later became known for its strip joints and porn palaces. You still see remnants of the sex 'n' sleaze era, but most of it is now gone, and things are going upscale.

The Soho neighborhood occupies the maze of densely packed streets north of Shaftesbury Avenue, west of Charing Cross Road, east of Regent Street, and south of Oxford Street. The major Tube stops are Leicester Square, Covent Garden, and Tottenham Court Road.

Piccadilly Circus, Leicester Square, and Charing Cross

This area, just west of The Strand, is "downtown" London or Theatre-land. Piccadilly Circus, with its landmark statue of Eros, is the area's major traffic hub and best-known tourist destination, feeding into Regent Street and Piccadilly. The **Royal Academy of Arts** is just west of Piccadilly Circus. A few minutes' walk to the east puts you at Leicester Square and Shaftesbury Avenue, where you find most of the West End theaters. From Leicester Square, Charing Cross Road runs south to **Trafalgar Square** with its delightful fountains and four immense bronze lions guarding its corners. Around the square, you see the **National Gallery. Charing Cross Road** is well known for its bookshops. The Tube stops are Piccadilly Circus, Leicester Square, and Charing Cross.

Mayfair

Elegant and exclusive, Mayfair is luxury-hotel and luxury-shopping land. The area is nestled in among Regent Street on the west, Oxford Street on the north, Piccadilly on the south, and Hyde Park on the west. The major Tube stops are Piccadilly Circus, Bond Street, Marble Arch, and Hyde Park Corner.

Marylebone

In a sense, Marylebone (pronounced *Mar*-lee-bone) is "Medical London" because the area has several hospitals and the famous **Harley Street Clinic.** But perhaps the most famous street is Baker Street, home of the fictional Sherlock Holmes. **Madame Tussaud's** wax museum is on Marylebone Road.

Marylebone is the neighborhood north of Mayfair and Bloomsbury and is capped to the north by giant **Regent's Park** (Marylebone Road runs south of the park). Great Portland Street is the area's eastern boundary and Edgware Road the western. The major Tube stops are Baker Street, Marylebone, and Regent's Park.

St. James's

St. James's is "Royal London," a posh green haven beginning at Piccadilly and moving southwest to include **Green Park** and **St. James's Park,** with **Buckingham Palace** between them and **St. James's Palace** across from St. James's Park.

Pall Mall (pronounced *Pell Mell*), lined with exclusive "gentlemen's clubs," runs roughly east-west into the area and meets the north-south St. James's Street. Regent Street is the eastern boundary. The Tube stops are St. James's Park and Green Park.

Westminster

East and south of St. James's, Westminster draws visitors to **Westminster Abbey** and the **Houses of Parliament,** the seat of British government.

Westminster extends from Northumberland Avenue just south of Charing Cross to Vauxhall Bridge Road, with the Thames to the east and **St. James's Park** to the west. Victoria Station, on the northwestern perimeter, is a kind of axis for Westminster, Belgravia, and Pimlico. The Tube stops are Westminster, St. James's Park, and Victoria.

Pimlico

The pie-shaped wedge of London extending west from Vauxhall Bridge Road to Buckingham Palace Road is Pimlico. Crowning the area to the north is Victoria Station. Near the Vauxhall Bridge is the **Tate Britain** gallery. The Tube stops are Pimlico and Victoria.

Belgravia

A posh quarter long favored by aristocrats, Belgravia is where many foreign embassies are located. Beginning west of Victoria Station and Green Park, Belgravia extends south to the river and west to Sloane Street; **Hyde Park** is its northern boundary. The Tube stops are Victoria, Hyde Park Corner, and Sloane Square.

Central London: Parks, museums, and more

Beyond the West End, you discover Central London's residential, cultural, and shopping attractions, including beautiful gardens, and popular museums.

Knightsbridge

West of Belgravia is the fashionable residential and shopping district of Knightsbridge, bounded to the north by **Hyde Park** and to the west by

Brompton Road. Here you find **Harrods,** the famed department store that has been a London shopping staple for a century and a half. Running through the neighborhood is pretty Beauchamp (pronounced *Beech*-um) Place with its expensive boutiques. The Tube stops are Knightsbridge and Sloane Square.

Chelsea

South of Knightsbridge and west of Belgravia, artsy, trendy Chelsea begins at Sloane Square and runs south to Cheyne Walk and Chelsea Embankment along the Thames. The famous King's Road acts as its northern boundary and Chelsea Bridge Road its eastern border. To the west the area extends as far as Earl's Court Road, Redcliffe Gardens, and Edith Grove. In Chelsea you find **Carlyle's House** and the lovely and historic **Chelsea Physic Garden.** The annual Chelsea Flower Show is held on the grounds of Chelsea Royal Hospital. The Tube stop is Sloane Square.

South Kensington

Forming the green northern boundary of South Kensington are **Kensington Gardens** and **Hyde Park.** South Ken is London's museum capital and is packed with hotels and restaurants. Tourists enjoy the attractions of the **Natural History Museum, Science Museum,** and **Victoria & Albert Museum.**

South Kensington is bounded to the south by Brompton Road, to the west by Gloucester (pronounced *Glos*-ter) Road and to the east by Fulham Road. The Tube stops are Gloucester Road and South Kensington.

Kensington

The residential neighborhood of Kensington fills in the gap between **Kensington Gardens** and **Holland Park,** with Notting Hill Gate and Bayswater Road marking the northern boundary. Kensington Church Street runs north-south between Notting Hill Gate and Kensington High Street. The Tube stop is High Street Kensington.

Earl's Court

This down-to-earth neighborhood has long been a haven for budget travelers (particularly Australians, hence its nickname Kangaroo Court) and for gays and lesbians. Earl's Court is gradually being renovated, but many streets still look a bit down at the heels. This area offers no major tourist attractions.

The area begins south of West Cromwell Road and extends south to Lillie Road and Brompton Road. Its western boundary is North End Road and its eastern boundary Earl's Court Road. The Tube stop is Earl's Court.

Notting Hill

Beginning north of Holland Park, Kensington Gardens, and Hyde Park (Holland Park Avenue and Bayswater Road run along the northern perimeter of the parks) you find the antiques shops of Notting Hill and the rising subneighborhood of Notting Hill Gate.

The area is bounded by Clarendon Road to the west, Queensway to the east, and Wesbourne Grove to the north. The most famous street, Portobello Road, runs north-south through the center. The neighborhood served as a backdrop for the 1999 movie *Notting Hill,* starring Julia Roberts and Hugh Grant. The Tube stops are Notting Hill Gate, Bayswater, and Queensway.

Bayswater and Paddington

Picking up where Notting Hill ends, Bayswater runs east to meet Marylebone at Edgware Road. The roaring A40 (Westway) highway acts as its northern boundary. Paddington Station is in the northwestern corner of Bayswater.

This commercial area is not much to look at. The neighborhood offers no major tourist attractions but many budget B&Bs. The Tube stops are Paddington, Lancaster Gate, Marble Arch, and Edgware Road.

The South Bank

You most likely won't be staying on the South Bank, but you may go there for a play, an exhibition, or a concert at one its internationally known arts and performance venues or museums. The Tube stops are Waterloo, London Bridge, and Southwark.

The **Royal National Theatre,** the **South Bank Centre** (which contains the **Royal Festival Hall** and two smaller concert halls), the **Hayward Gallery,** and the **National Film Theatre** are all clustered beside the river within easy walking distance of Waterloo Station. Closer to Westminster Bridge is the city's newest high-rise attraction: the **British Airways London Eye observation wheel**.

For a scenic route to the South Bank, take the Tube to Embankment, on the north bank, and walk across the Thames on the Hungerford pedestrian bridge. The **Jubilee Walkway,** a breezy riverside path, extends south from the arts complexes to the **London Aquarium** and north to the new **Tate Modern** and the **Globe Theatre** (a re-creation of the Elizabethan outdoor theater used by William Shakespeare), **Southwark Cathedral,** and **Tower Bridge.** The new pedestrian-only **Millennium Bridge** spans the Thames from the **Tate Modern** to **St. Paul's.**

Finding Information after You Arrive

You can find hotel- and theater-booking agencies, a currency exchange, and lots of free brochures on river trips, walking tours, and day trips from London at the **Britain Visitor Centre,** 1 Regent St., Piccadilly Circus, SW1 (Tube: Piccadilly Circus), which provides tourist information to walk-in visitors (no phone assistance is available). The center is open Monday through Friday 9:00 a.m. to 6:30 p.m. and Saturday and Sunday 10 a.m. to 4 p.m. (Saturdays June through October 9 a.m. to 5 p.m.)

An excellent bookshop is among the features of the main **Tourist Information Centre,** run by the London Tourist Board and located in the forecourt of Victoria Station (Tube: Victoria). The office opens at 8 a.m. Monday to Saturday throughout the year but has different closing hours: January and February at 7 p.m., March through May at 8 p.m., June through September at 9 p.m., and October through December at 8 p.m. October through December the center is also open on Sundays 8:00 a.m. to 6:15 p.m. This office also offers booking services and free literature on London attractions and entertainment. You can find other Tourist Information Centres in the Liverpool Street Underground Station (open Monday through Friday 8 a.m. to 6 p.m., Saturday 8:00 a.m. to 5:30 p.m., and Sunday 9:00 a.m. to 5:30 p.m.), the Arrivals Hall of the Waterloo International Terminal (open daily 8:30 a.m. to 10:30 p.m.), the Terminal 1, 2, and 3 Underground station (open daily 8 a.m. to 6 p.m.), and the Terminal 3 Arrivals concourse (open daily 6 a.m. to 11 p.m.) at Heathrow Airport.

The **London Line** at ☎ **09068/663-344** provides 24-hour information, updated daily, on scheduled events. At 60p (80¢) per minute, this service isn't cheap, but it's reliable.

A London Underground map is as indispensable as the *London A to Z* (which includes an Underground map). You can pick up a free Tube and bus map at any Underground ticket office. For current listings and reviews of plays and other events, consider buying a copy of *Time Out.* This magazine hits the newsstands each Wednesday and costs £1.95 ($3).

If you're traveling with kids, you may find **Kidsline** helpful; call ☎ **020/ 7222-8070** (Monday through Friday 4 to 6 p.m. and summer holidays 9 a.m. to 4 p.m.) for tips on kid-friendly places to go and things to see. The London Tourist Board's children's information line at ☎ **0839/ 123-404** is a recorded service that provides details about events and exhibitions that children will enjoy; the line costs 39p to 49p (65¢ to 80¢) per minute.

Chapter 11

Getting around London

* *

In This Chapter

▶ Going with the flow: Mass transit

▶ Hailing your driver: Taxis

▶ Hitting the pavement: Walking

* *

*W*hether you're grinding through rush-hour traffic on top of a double-decker bus, whizzing along in an Underground (subway) train, or nervously eyeing the meter in a cab, making your way around London is part of the overall London experience. I always use the Underground because it's fast and relatively inexpensive. The Underground and the buses put you in close contact with Londoners going about their daily routines, which means that public transportation is a great place to people watch. Plus, trains and buses are safe.

Take it from me, driving in London is a sport best played by the locals, so don't even think about renting a car when you're in the city. (See Chapter 21 for information about renting a car for day trips outside the city.) Even more difficult than driving in London is finding a place to park; if you park illegally, you'll be fined, and you may even have your car immobilized by a wheel clamp or towed away and impounded. Do your nerves a favor and take the bus, Underground, or taxi. Or take a leisurely stroll and enjoy the sights from the pavement. This chapter provides the information that you need to get around London by public transportation or on foot.

 For general London travel information, call ☎ 020/7222-1234. You can get free bus and Underground maps and buy Travelcards and bus passes (see the next section) at any major Underground station or at the **London Travel Information Centres** in the stations at King's Cross, Liverpool Street, Oxford Circus, Piccadilly Circus, St. James's Park, Victoria, and Heathrow Terminals 1, 2, and 3.

Going Underground: The Tube

The London subway system — always referred to as the **Tube** or the **Underground** — is fast and convenient, and nearly everyone but the royals uses it. Millions of residents and visitors ride the Tube daily. Thirteen Tube lines crisscross the city and intersect at various stations where passengers can change from one train to the next. On Underground maps, every line is color-coded (Bakerloo is brown, Piccadilly dark blue, and so on). Each Tube stop is marked by a red circle with a horizontal line through it. (For a map of the Underground, see the inside back cover of this book.) Nearly every place in London is near a Tube stop. The system is simple and comprehensive, so planning your route is easy.

All you need to know is the name of your stop and the direction you're heading. After you figure out which line you need to take, look on the map for the name of the last stop in the direction you need to go. The name of the last stop on the line is marked on the front of the train (it's easy to read) and sometimes on electronic signboards that display which train is arriving. Inside all but the oldest trains are electronic signs and/or recorded voices that announce the name of each approaching stop. London's Underground stations often have newspaper kiosks and small shops in them or directly outside. You rarely encounter a panhandler in a Tube station.

The Tube stations vary considerably. Some, such as Covent Garden and Gloucester Road, have elevators to the trains (and optional stairways). Others, such as Leicester Square and Piccadilly Circus, provide very long escalators. Some offer stairways only. In major stations handling more than one line, long (but clearly marked) tunnels extend from one line to another. Most of the trains are new or have been updated.

The trains aren't air-conditioned, however, so during packed weekday rush hours (8:00 to 9:30 a.m. and 5 to 7 p.m.), they can be stuffy. Smoking isn't permitted. As with any transit system, occasional glitches and delays occur. The only time to think twice about taking the Tube is Friday and Saturday after 10:30 p.m., when drinkers are leaving pubs. Inebriated louts can be obnoxious. The Underground service ends around midnight (a little earlier on less used lines). Keep this in mind when you're out painting the town red. If you stay out into the wee hours, you'll have to take a taxi or one of the night buses back to your hotel.

Most of the Underground system operates with automated entry and exit gates. You feed your ticket into the slot, the ticket disappears and pops up again like a piece of toast, the gate bangs open, you remove the ticket, and you pass through the gate. You go through the same process to get out, but the machine keeps the ticket (unless your ticket is a Travelcard, which is returned). Some stations outside Central London employ ticket collectors.

The Tube: Past and present

Opened in 1999, the Jubilee Line is the newest Tube line. Architecture buffs may want to check out some of the new stations (such as London Bridge and Southwark) on this line. And London's oldest Underground line? The system's first Tube train began operating almost 150 years ago. You can see one of the first (dark, primitive) Underground cars and a fantastic collection of original horse-drawn omnibuses at the **London Transport Museum** (see Chapter 17 for details).

You've got a ticket to ride

You can get tickets for the Underground at the ticket window or from one of the automated machines found in most stations (machines can change £5, £10, and £20 notes). Fares to every station are posted.

The city is divided into **zones** for purposes of setting fares. Zone 1 covers all of Central London. Zone 6 extends as far as Heathrow to the west and Upminster to the east. Make sure that your ticket covers all the zones you'll be traveling through (no problem if you're staying in Central London, the location of the main tourist sights). If you're caught riding in a zone without the proper ticket, you have to pay a £10 ($15) penalty fare.

A **single-fare one-way ticket** within one zone costs £1.50 ($2.25) for an adult and 60p (90¢) for a child 5 to 15. This amount is the maximum that passengers must pay to travel within Central London. Tickets are valid on the day of issue only.

If you plan to travel by Underground, you can save time and money by buying a book of ten tickets, called a **carnet.** Carnet tickets are valid in one zone only; one ticket is good for one ride on any day. The price is £11.50 ($18) for an adult and £5 ($7) for a child. With a carnet, you can save £3.50 ($5) over single fares and won't have to wait in line to buy tickets. With a Travelcard, you can save even more.

Travelcards: The best fare going (and coming)

For the best rate — if you plan on using London's public transportation system extensively — consider buying the one-day, weekend, seven-day, or one-month **Travelcard,** which allows unlimited travel by Underground *and* bus.

✔ A **one-day Travelcard for Zones 1 and 2** (everything in Central London) costs £4 ($6) for an adult and £2 ($3) for a child; this card is valid after 9:30 a.m. weekdays and all day Saturday and Sunday.

✔ The **weekend Travelcard for Zones 1 and 2** costs £6 ($9) for an adult and £3 ($5) for a child; this card is not valid after midnight.

✔ A **seven-day Travelcard for Zone 1** is useful if you're going to be in London for a week and don't plan to travel outside Central London; the card costs £15.90 ($25) for an adult and £6.60 ($11) for a child. This card is valid all day, every day, but it must be used before 4:30 a.m. on the day of expiration.

 The **Family Travelcard** is a good deal for families or groups of one or two adults traveling with one to four children; the card is valid from 9:30 a.m. to midnight Monday through Friday and all day Saturday and Sunday before midnight. Rates for one day of travel in Zones 1 and 2 are £2.60 ($3.90) for an adult and 80p ($1.20) for a child.

 You and your children will need passport-sized photos to buy seven-day Travelcards in London. The photo is affixed to a separate ID card. No photos are required for **Visitor Travelcards** purchased in the States, however (see Chapter 3).

Hopping a Double-Decker: Buses

Taking a bus in London is a good-news, bad-news proposition. The bad news is that you'll arrive at your destination faster by taking the Tube or walking (during rush hour, buses creep along at about the same pace as a pedestrian). Also, you need to know the streets of London in order to exit the bus at the correct stop. So you don't overshoot your destination, get a free bus map at one of the Travel Information Centres (see the introduction to this chapter).

The good news is that riding the bus is cheaper than taking the Tube; you don't need to use escalators, elevators, or tunnels; and you get to see the sights as you travel. London is known for its big, red double-decker buses, and most tourists want to ride on top of one at least once; it's just plain fun.

Each bus stop is clearly marked by a concrete post with a red or white sign on top reading "London Transport Bus Service." Another sign shows the routes of the buses that stop there. If the sign on the post is

✔ **Red:** It's a *request stop,* and you must hail the approaching bus as you would a taxi (don't whistle, just put up your hand).

✔ **White:** The bus stops automatically. Be sure to check the destination sign in front of the bus to make certain that it's going the entire route.

Playing the fare game

The bus network was recently divided into two fare zones to simplify cash transactions:

> ✔ **Zone 1** covers all of Central London, including all the main tourist sites.
>
> ✔ **Zone 2** is everything beyond Zone 1.

If you're traveling by bus into, from, within, and across Central London (Zone 1), the bus fare for adults is £1 ($1.50). For any bus journey you take in outer London (Zone 2), the fare is 70p ($1.05). Children pay a 40p (60¢) flat rate good for both zones. **Note:** No child fares are in effect between 10 p.m. and 4:30 a.m. Children 14 and 15 years old must have a Child Photocard to get the child rate; this free ID card is available at Tube stations or Travel Information Centres (see the introduction to this chapter) and requires a passport-sized photo.

In the past, a conductor on board went around and collected fares with a polite "'kew" (thank you). Today, the driver often doubles as the conductor. Have some coins with you because the driver does not change bank notes.

If you plan to travel extensively by bus, purchase a one-day bus pass. You can use it all day (before 9:30 a.m., even on weekdays, unlike the Travelcard), but the pass is not valid on *N-prefixed night buses,* discussed in the next section. You can purchase one-day and longer bus passes at most Underground stations, selected newsstands, and the Travel Information Centres. A one-day bus pass for all of Central London costs £3 ($5) for an adult and £1 ($1.50) for a child 5 to 15. A seven-day bus pass for Central London costs £11.50 ($17) for an adult and £4 ($6) for a child 5 to 15. **Note:** Children must have a Child Photocard ID in order to buy and use any of these tickets; the card is free at major Tube stations and Travel Information Centres but requires a passport-size photograph.

Cruising on the night buses

The bars where you live may stay open until near dawn. However, in London, the pubs close at 11 p.m., the Tube stops running about 11:30 p.m., and at midnight the buses become **night buses** (marked with an *N*), changing their routes and increasing their Central London fares to £1.50 ($2.25). You can't use a one-day bus pass, family Travelcard, or weekend Travelcard on a night bus; you can, however, use a Visitor Travelcard (see Chapter 3) or a seven-day or longer Travelcard. Nearly all night buses pass through Trafalgar Square, Central London's late-night mecca for insomniacs.

Hailing Your Ride: Taxis

Taking a taxi in London is a safe and comfortable way to get around the city. In fact, riding in the old-fashioned, roomy black taxis is a pleasure, although today you find many smaller and newer models. Whatever their size or color, London cabs aren't cheap. The fare starts at £1.40 ($2.10) for one person, with 40p (60¢) for each additional passenger. The meter leaps 20p (30¢) every 111 yards or 90 seconds. You may also need to pay surcharges: 10p (15¢) per item of luggage; 60p (90¢) weeknights 8 p.m. to midnight; 90p ($1.40) from midnight until 7 a.m.; 60p (90¢) Saturdays and Sundays until 8 p.m. and 90p ($1.40) after 8 p.m. Tipping the cabbie 15% of the total fare is customary.

You can hail a cab on the street. If a cab is available, its yellow or white "For Hire" sign on the roof is lit. You can order a radio cab to pick you up by calling ☎ **020/7272-0272** or ☎ **020/7253-5000,** two different companies. Just remember that if you do order a radio cab, the meter starts ticking when the taxi receives notification from the dispatcher.

London is one city where you don't have to worry whether the cabdriver knows how to reach your destination. Extensive training, which includes an exhaustive street test called "The Knowledge," makes London cabbies among the most adept in the world at finding a street address.

Pounding the Pavement: Walkies

You're cheating yourself out of experiencing the true essence of London if you don't take some time to explore on foot the city's side streets, country lanes, little *mews dwellings* (former stables converted into homes), and garden squares.

London architecture spans some 2,000 years. As you walk through its streets, you see building styles that incorporate everything from remnants of the original brick-and-mortar walls erected by the Romans to the postmodern **Canary Wharf Tower,** at 800 feet the city's tallest building. Wedged into this dense urban landscape you find ancient bastions of power such as the **Tower of London,** Gothic glories such as 900-year-old **Westminster Abbey,** tidily elegant Regency terraces in Mayfair, private palaces in St. James's, and Victorian town houses in Kensington.

If you want to take a detailed stroll or two around the city, focusing on your own interests, such as Dickens's London or Westminster and Whitehall, check out the 11 tours in *Frommer's Memorable Walks in London,* published by Hungry Minds, Inc.

What walkers need to know

When you're walking in London (or anywhere in the United Kingdom) remember that:

- ✔ **When you cross any street, look in the direction opposite from the one you're accustomed to.** That is, look right as you cross most streets, instead of left (as you would automatically do in the States or elsewhere in the world). This advice sounds simple enough on paper, but in practice you need to keep reminding yourself. At many busy London intersections you are reminded to "Look right" or "Look left" by signs painted on the street.
- ✔ **Pedestrian crossings are marked by striped lines (called zebra crossings) on the road.** Flashing lights near the curb indicate that drivers must stop and yield the right of way if a pedestrian has stepped into the zebra crossing to cross the street.

Although London is a walker's paradise, Central London is much too large to cover on foot. However, parts of this area are wonderfully compact and intimate.

Walkers' sites in Central London

One place you can best explore on foot is **Chelsea:** Start at Sloane Square or busy King's Road and meander southwest toward Cheyne Walk along the river.

You can also meander through cafe-laden **Soho,** just north of Shaftesbury Avenue, or the pedestrian-only precincts of the **Covent Garden** area just south of Shaftesbury. And **South Kensington,** with its great museums, is full of charming side streets and squares.

Even more atmospheric is the area in and around **Lincoln's Inn Fields** in Holborn, where the traditions of old London pervade the beautiful 17th-century courts of law. At night, the **Houses of Parliament,** the clock tower containing the bell known as **Big Ben,** and **Westminster Abbey** are all floodlit, creating an impressive sight. To get there, walk down Whitehall from Charing Cross.

Parks and other scenic walks

London is home to some of the world's most beautiful parks, which are best experienced on foot. (That's why they're there.)

The Green Park Tube stop provides convenient access to **Green Park** from the north; from the Tube stop you can walk down to Constitution Hill, a major thoroughfare closed to traffic on Sundays, and on to

Buckingham Palace. Continue east into **St. James's Park** via Pall Mall (also traffic free on Sundays), passing **Clarence House** (home of the Queen Mum) and **St. James's Palace** (London home of Prince Charles and the boys, Prince William and Prince Harry), or stroll along the shores of **St. James's Park Lake.**

You can enter **Hyde Park** from the Hyde Park Corner Tube stop; head west into this massive green lung via the paths paralleling the north and south banks of the Serpentine, Hyde Park's lake. After you cross the Serpentine Bridge, you're in **Kensington Gardens;** the famous statue of Peter Pan is to the north. **Kensington Palace** (home to Princess Margaret and other royals) is on the western perimeter, beyond the Round Pond. You can find **Regent's Park** to the north in Marylebone, which houses the **London Zoo** in its northern section and **Queen Mary's Gardens** roughly in its center.

In July 2000, a 7-mile walk commemorating the life of Princess Diana opened. The walk passes through four of London's royal parks: **St. James's Park, Green Park, Hyde Park,** and **Kensington Gardens.** Along the way are 70 plaques pointing out sites associated with Diana, including **Kensington Palace** (her home for 15 years), **Buckingham Palace, St. James's Palace** (where she once shared an office with Prince Charles), and **Spencer House** (once her family's mansion and now a museum — see Chapter 17).

One of the best scenic walks in London is the **Jubilee Walkway,** marked on the London map distributed free by the British Tourist Authority. The walkway runs along the South Bank from Lambeth Bridge to Tower Bridge, offering great Thameside views of the north bank along the way, and it continues on the north bank from the **Tower of London** all the way down to the **Houses of Parliament.** The walk will take you a good half-day, but it provides an opportunity to see a large and important area of London.

Chapter 12

Managing Your Money

- -

In This Chapter

▶ Getting a primer on pounds and pence

▶ Changing your dollars into pounds after you arrive

▶ Finding and using ATMs

▶ Dealing with theft and loss

- -

*T*ravelers to foreign destinations, especially first-time travelers, have big money worries — they don't worry so much about having enough money as they do about the difference between money in their home countries and money abroad. What are the conversion rates? Where can they change one currency into another for the best rate? Are traveler's checks better than credit cards or ATM cards? Will their home PIN work in a foreign country? Travelers have a seemingly endless list of money matters to consider.

You can't avoid these questions because you'll spend money every day of your trip, often in ways that you don't spend it at home. British currency is different, I'll grant you that, but you can certainly get the hang of it. In this chapter, I explain the basic money matters you'll encounter. You can also check out Chapter 3 for information on purchasing traveler's checks before you go and using credit cards and ATMs in London.

 When you arrive at the airport in London, the immigration authorities may want to know how much money you're carrying. In order to enter the United Kingdom, you must have sufficient means (cash, traveler's checks, credit cards) to maintain and accommodate yourself and any dependents without resorting to public funds (of course, you may not be asked this either; see Chapter 10 for more information on the requirements to enter the United Kingdom).

Making Sense of Pounds and Pence

Britain's unit of currency is the **pound sterling (£)**. Every pound is divided into **100 pence (p)**. Coins come in denominations of 1p, 2p, 5p, 10p, 20p, 50p, £1, and £2. Notes are available in £5, £10, £20, and £50 denominations. As with any unfamiliar currency, British pounds and

Euro free zone, for now

The fate of British currency in its pounds-and-pence form is one of the most hotly debated topics in the United Kingdom today. Eleven European countries adopted a single European currency, called the *euro,* on January 1, 1999. Cautious, contentious Britain has opted out of switching over to the euro just yet. The various national currencies in European Union countries will be homogenized into euros (or *ecus,* European Currency Units) in mid-2002. Britain, however, has not yet adopted the plan. If you visit London in 2002, you won't have to worry about the euro.

pence take a bit of getting used to. The coins have different sizes, shapes, and weights according to value. Each bank note denomination has its own color and bears a likeness of the Queen. All currency is drawn on the Bank of England.

Exchanging Your Currency

The **exchange rate,** which fluctuates every day, is the rate you get when you use your own currency to buy pounds sterling (see Table 12-1). In general, $1 = 66p (or £1 = $1.50). These are *approximate* figures, but they're what I use for all prices in this guide (rounded off to the nearest dollar). When you're about to leave on your trip, check with your bank or look in the newspaper to find out the current rate.

Table 12-1		Simple Currency Conversions	
U.S. Dollars to U.K. Pounds		*U.K. Pounds to U.S. Dollars*	
U.S.	*U.K.*	*U.K.*	*U.S.*
$1	66p	£1	$1.50
$5	£3.30	£2	$3.00
$10	£6.60	£5	$7.50
$20	£13.20	£10	$15.00
$50	£33.00	£20	$30
$100	£66	£50	$75.00

Changing money (either cash or traveler's checks) into a foreign currency makes many people nervous, especially if they're changing money for the first time. You needn't fear. Changing money is really a fairly simple operation. Just remember that every time you exchange money, you need to show your passport.

Visiting a bureau de change or a British bank

If you want some pounds in hand when you arrive at the airport (to pay for a taxi perhaps), you can exchange currency before you leave home at many banks and at foreign exchange services at international airports (see Chapter 3). Otherwise, you can easily change cash or traveler's checks in London by using a currency-exchange service called a **bureau de change.** These services are available at major London airports, any branch of a major bank, all major rail and Underground stations in Central London, post offices, and American Express or Thomas Cook offices. Unless located in a bank or travel agency, most bureaux de change are open daily from 8 a.m. to 9 p.m.

Every major bank in Central London has a foreign currency window where you can exchange traveler's checks or cash. Weekday hours for banks are generally 9:30 a.m. to 4:30 p.m., but a few open earlier. Some banks (usually based in busy shopping areas) are open all day Saturday. All banks are closed on public holidays, but many branches have 24-hour banking lobbies with ATMs and/or ATMs on the street outside. Banking is a volatile business, with mergers, acquisitions, and name changes occurring all the time. The big names in London include **Barclays Bank** (☎ 020/7441-3200), **Midland Bank** (☎ 020/7599-3232), and **NatWest** (☎ 020/7395-5500). These banking companies all have branches throughout the city.

Reputable London banks and bureaux de change exchange money at a competitive rate but charge a commission (typically 1% to 3% of the total transaction) and a small additional fee (usually £3[$4.50]). Some currency-exchange services now guarantee you the same exchange rate when you return pounds for dollars (keep your receipt if you want to use this service).

All U.K. bureaux de change and other money-changing establishments are required to display exchange rates and full details of any fees and rates of commission with clarity and equal prominence. Rates must be displayed at or near the entrance to the premises. Rates fluctuate from place to place, and so do fees, so shopping around sometimes pays.

Steer clear of bureaux de change that offer good exchange rates but charge a heavy commission (up to 8%). You find them in major tourist sections of London (some are open 24 hours). Some hotels also cash traveler's checks, but their commission is often considerably higher than at a bank or bureaux de change. Before exchanging your money, always check to see the exchange rate, how much commission you'll have to pay, and whether additional fees apply.

You can avoid paying a second commission fee by using American Express traveler's checks and cashing them at an **American Express** office. The main office is in London at 6 Haymarket, SW1 (☎ **020/ 7930-4411;** Tube: Piccadilly). Its foreign exchange bureau is open Monday through Friday from 9:00 a.m. to 5:30 p.m., on Saturday from 9 a.m. to 6 p.m., and on Sunday from 10 a.m. to 5 p.m. For the addresses of other American Express offices in London, see the Appendix.

Gaining pounds from ATMs

You can find ATMs all over London, strategically located at every commercial juncture and byway: inside and/or outside banks, in large supermarkets and department stores, and even in some Underground stations. For convenience, they can't be beat. Using your bank or credit card and a PIN (check with your bank to determine if your PIN works in Europe; you may need to get a new one), you can immediately access British pounds and avoid a visit to a bureau de change. U.S. banks in London tend to be for corporate business accounts rather than personal banking, so be prepared to use another bank's ATM and pay a fee. See Chapter 3 for more detailed information on using your bank or credit card in London's ATMs.

Citibank customers who use ATMs at **Citibank International** (☎ **020/ 7234-5678**) — with branches at 332 Oxford St., W1 (Tube: Marble Arch), and 336 Strand, WC2 (Tube: Charing Cross) — pay no transaction fee.

Traveling Smart: Handling Loss or Theft

Horrors! You reach for your money and find that it's missing. You left your wallet on the table at the pub last night. Or you've fallen afoul of a thief. London is a pretty safe city, but crime happens.

If you follow four basic rules, you can minimize the risk of a crime happening to you:

- ✔ Don't keep your wallet in your back pocket or in your backpack, but do keep it out of sight.

- ✔ Don't leave your purse, briefcase, backpack, or coat unattended in any public place.

- ✔ Ladies: Don't hang your purse over the back of your chair in crowded or outdoor cafes or restaurants.

- ✔ Don't flash your money or credit cards around.

In the unlikely event that someone steals your wallet or purse, you need to cancel all your credit cards. You should probably cancel your cards even before you call the police (call directory assistance at ☎ **192,** free from public payphones, for the police station nearest you). If you lose a credit card, think back to where you had the card last and call that place. Some good soul may have found it and turned it in. If it's a lost cause, however, cancel your card, so no one else can use it.

Almost every credit card company has an emergency toll-free number that you can call if your card is lost or stolen. The company will cancel the card immediately, and may also be able to wire you a cash advance; in many places, you can get an emergency replacement card in a day or two. See the Appendix for the U.K. numbers to call if your credit card gets lost or stolen while you're in London.

If you carry traveler's checks (see Chapter 3), be sure to keep a record of their serial numbers (keep the record separate from the checks, of course). Write down the numbers of the checks as you cash them. If the checks are stolen, you need to be able to report exactly which checks are gone in order to get them replaced. The check issuer can tell you where to pick up the new checks.

If your purse or wallet is gone, the police aren't likely to recover it for you. However, after you cancel your credit cards, call to inform the police. You may need the police report number for credit card or insurance purposes later.

Taxing Matters: So Just Where Is This Added Value?

No discussion of money matters in London is complete without a reference to the dreaded **value-added tax (VAT),** Britain's version of a sales tax. The VAT amounts to 17.5% and is added to the total price of all consumer goods (the price tag already includes it) as well as hotel and restaurant bills. If you're not a resident of the European Union, you can get your VAT refunded on purchases made in the United Kingdom (but not the VAT paid at hotels and restaurants). See Chapter 19 for details.

Part IV
Dining in London

"Now THAT was a great meal! Beautiful presentation, an imaginative use of ingredients, and a sauce with nuance and depth. The British really know how to make a 'Happy Meal'."

In this part...

Sometimes I wonder if I love to travel so much because I like to eat but hate to cook. Traveling, after all, is the perfect excuse to eat out all the time. But even though dining out is one of the great pleasures of any trip, it can also be a big hassle if you don't know where to go or what to order. (Kippers may sound cute and delicious, but do you really like smoked fish?) In this part, I invite you to sit down and raise your fork for some delicious victuals.

In Chapter 13, I introduce you to London's dining scene. I cover the kinds of restaurants you'll find (from pubs and fish-and-chips joints to the hottest haute havens) and the variety of cuisine you'll encounter. My A-to-Z list of recommended London restaurants is in Chapter 14. I include several low- to moderate-priced places, but if you're a real "foodie," you'll also find some fabulous places to sink your choppers and curl your tongue around a truly great gourmet meal. In Chapter 15, I provide still more options: places for a spot of tea, for quick(er) bits, and for something to satisfy your sweet tooth.

Chapter 13

Getting the Lowdown on London's Dining Scene

*Y*ou can still find traditional English dishes in London: Yorkshire pudding, fish-and-chips, or *bangers and mash* (sausages and mashed potatoes). So if you want to sample the old cuisine, you won't be disappointed. But London now offers a vast array of culinary choices; more than 5,700 restaurants prepare the cuisines of more than 60 countries. This chapter explains what you need to know about new trends; traditional, modern, and ethnic cuisines; spots favored by locals; finding a bargain; and more. For a glossary of English food terms, see the Cheat Sheet at the beginning of this book.

Finding Out What's Cooking in London

Multi-cultural London is always in the midst of culinary evolution. The local food horizon expanded as the postwar generation began to travel outside England, experiencing new cuisines, and as "exotic" foods became more readily available in the markets.

Traditional "plain English cooking" — undeniably hearty but sometimes thought of as dull — is certainly still prevalent in London, and the style is even enjoying renewed interest and respect. Londoners still enjoy their fish-and-chips, steak-and-kidney pies, and bangers and mash. And the best dishes — game, lamb, meat and fish pies, and roast beef with Yorkshire pudding — are readily available. But Modern British cuisine takes old standards and deliciously reinvents them with foreign influences and ingredients, mostly from France (sauces), the Mediterranean (olive oil, oregano, and garlic), and northern Italy (pasta, polenta, and risotto). Besides Modern British, London foodies continue to favor classic French and Italian cuisines in their own right.

Other new influences making their way into Modern British cooking come from Thailand and Morocco (couscous). Indian cooking, one of the more pleasant reminders of the Empire, has been a favorite ethnic food for some time. London is filled with Indian restaurants (about 1,500 of them) serving curries and dishes cooked in clay tandoori pots. *Balti,* a thick curry from Pakistan, is the one of the more recent ethnic must-try dishes in London.

Eating Trendy: Some Like It Haute

To be trendy and talked about, a London restaurant must have a celebrity owner, a celebrity chef, a solid reputation, a great view, a chic location, and/or unmistakable ambience — and, of course, memorable food helps, too. In this section I point out the hot spots of the moment. Keep in mind that the restaurant scene changes all the time; this information was current when this book went to press.

Sir Terence Conran is a proven leader at creating hot London restaurants. His **Oxo Tower Restaurant** and the adjacent **Oxo Tower Brasserie** perch above the Thames on the South Bank. Sir Terence is also the name behind **Le Pont de la Tour** overlooking Tower Bridge; the bright **Bluebird** in Chelsea; and the showy below-ground **Quaglino's** in St. James's (when I last ate there, the five diners at the table across from me were all on their cell phones at the same time).

Other hot haute spots include the super-trendy **Asia de Cuba** in Ian Schrager's new St. Martin's Lane hotel; Chelsea's **Aubergine,** where the classic French cooking has earned two Michelin stars; the **Savoy Grill,** a downplayed power-player hangout in the Savoy hotel; **Zafferano,** a superlative Italian restaurant in tony Knightsbridge; **Vong,** a French-Thai fave, also in Knightsbridge; the stylish **L'Odeon,** where window tables provide a bird's-eye view of Piccadilly Circus; and **The Ivy,** a long-time Soho favorite for chic-seekers.

The preceding restaurants require booking at least a week or more in advance. You can find their telephone numbers and full descriptions in Chapter 14.

Discovering the Top Dining Areas

London offers a mouth-watering mix of restaurants; you can enjoy a wide variety of foods throughout the city. Soho and neighboring Covent Garden offer the most choices in the West End, with British, African, Caribbean, Mongolian, American (North and South), French, Italian, Spanish, Thai, Korean, Japanese, Middle Eastern, Eastern European, Modern European, Turkish, and vegetarian all represented. South Kensington makes up another eclectic grab bag of culinary choices.

Unlike some other large cities, ethnic restaurants aren't grouped together within specific areas of London. However, several Chinese restaurants are clustered along Lisle, Wardour, and Gerrard streets in Soho's Chinatown. And Notting Hill has long been a standby for low-price Indian and Caribbean restaurants.

Searching Out Where the Locals Eat

Londoners, like the residents in any large city, have their favorite neighborhood eateries. Pubs, cafes, and wine bars are places where locals go for casual meals that aren't as expensive as restaurants.

Ordering up pub grub

Pubs are your best bet for getting a good meal for a low price. The food is generally traditional and down-to-earth: meat pies and *mash* (mashed potatoes), fish-and-chips, *mixed grills* (sausages and a chop or cutlet), salads, sandwiches, and the famous *ploughman's lunch* (bread and cheese or pâté). Pub food may be prepackaged and frozen and then microwaved. However, more and more pubs resemble casual restaurants — except that people are drinking. The food may be fresh, more adventurous, and better prepared at the better pubs.

Pubs are drop-in places, and finding a table at lunchtime isn't always easy. Pubs don't accept reservations. Order your food from the serving counter and your drinks from the bar, and then seat yourself. Pub grub is generally washed down with beer, the British national drink. Draft beer in Britain is served at room temperature, as are most soft drinks. Bottled imported beer, served cold, is generally available but more expensive. For more on Britain's beers, see the sidebar in Chapter 24, "A beer primer: Are you bitter or stout?"

Unless a pub has a special *children's certificate,* kids under 14 are allowed only into the gardens and separate family rooms. The legal drinking age in the United Kingdom is 18, although restaurants can serve beer or cider to kids over 16 who order a meal. Pubs tend to be smoky.

Which pubs are my favorites? When I'm in Kensington, I often drop in at the **Devonshire Arms** for lunch. If I'm exploring the South Bank, I sometimes stop at **The Founder's Arms,** which overlooks the Thames and has outside tables. Two pubs that I like in The City are **The Fox & Anchor,** famous for its huge breakfasts, and **The George & Vulture,** a 17th-century pub that serves good traditional lunches. I describe all these pubs in Chapter 14. See also Chapter 27 for descriptions of my favorite historical pubs.

Sipping and eating at wine bars

Wine bars are more upscale than pubs and usually less smoky. Like pubs, wine bars don't permit children under 14, except in gardens or family rooms. Be aware that a meal in a wine bar costs more than a similar meal in a pub. Of course, you can order wine instead of beer.

I particularly like two wine bars in London: **Café Suze,** in Marylebone, serves up great Pacific Rim-influenced dishes and wines from New Zealand and Australia; **Ebury Wine Bar,** in the Westminster and Victoria neighborhood, features many mouth-watering traditional dishes to accompany its great wine list. I describe both of these wine bars in greater detail in Chapter 14.

Kicking back at cafes

London's cafes generally serve light, inexpensive food and offer limited menus. Most people enjoy a cup of coffee or pot of tea and a sandwich. The cakes and other sweets may tempt you too.

One of my favorite cafes is the always-crowded **Pâtisserie Valerie** on Old Compton Street in Soho. I also enjoy the old-fashioned **Richoux** tearoom-cafes found in Knightsbridge, Mayfair, and Piccadilly. You find addresses for these places in Chapter 15.

Gays and lesbians on the lookout for low-priced meals in groovy gay-friendly environments flock to Soho's newest phenomenon: the gay cafe/bar. These trendy hangouts serve good, low-priced meals and pay serious attention to decor.

Eating Out without Losing Your Shirt: Tips for Cutting Costs

If the thought of paying $50 dinner tabs gives you heartburn, you can visit pubs, cafes, sandwich bars, pizza places, and fast-food restaurants to get edible, economical food. See the preceding section and Chapter 15 for my recommendations for budget bites. Another alternative: Many of London's top restaurants offer *fixed-price meals* (also called *set-price* or *prix-fixe* meals), which allow you to order two to three courses from a limited menu for a set price that is cheaper than ordering the courses individually. Sometimes these bargains are called pre- or post-theater menus and they're served only from about 5:30 to 7:00 p.m. and after 9:30 p.m. Wine is generally fairly expensive, so forgo that if price is an issue. And try your splurge dining at lunch, when prices are often one-third less than those at dinner, and the food is the same.

Restaurants automatically add that annoying 17.5% VAT (value-added tax) to your tab. They may tack on a moderate cover charge for bread (even if you don't eat it) as well.

Be aware that the words "service charge" on a bill mean a gratuity has already been added. (The menu should say, "service charge included.") If so, you're not expected to leave any additional tip. Plenty of unwary tourists double tip without realizing it. Some restaurants add a service charge to your bill and also have a tip area on the credit-card receipt that you sign. If you've already paid a service charge, don't leave an additional tip. If the menu says "service not included," however, then leave a tip of at least 15% for acceptable service.

Dining Details

Don't worry: Unless you eat with your fingers and literally lick your plate clean, you'll fit in at any London restaurant. But keep in mind the degrees of dining finesse. The following sections tell you about reserving a table, dressing appropriately, paying the bill (check), and other dining details.

At the end of a meal, Americans ask for a "check," whereas Brits ask for the "bill."

Making reservations

London's trendiest restaurants (see "Eating Trendy: Some Like It Haute," earlier in this chapter) require booking more than a week in advance. At all but the "smartest" London restaurants, you can usually get a table on fairly short notice during the week, especially if you're willing to dine before 7 p.m. or after 9 p.m. Some of the mega-eateries hold up to several hundred diners at one time.

If you can't get a dinner reservation, try for lunch instead (lunch will probably be less expensive anyway).

Dressing to dine

Fashion-conscious Londoners are quick to spot the gauche and the gaudy. They tend to play down garish Hollywood-style glamour in favor of sedate stylishness. But London is becoming a bit more casual. You can wear what's comfortable for you at most restaurants. However, at a hot spot or any $$$ and $$$$ restaurant (see Chapter 14 for a key to the dollar symbols), I suggest that you dress up rather than down. Assume that a "smart but casual" dress code is in effect in these places and leave the running shoes and blue jeans back at the hotel. Here are my recommendations:

- ✔ **Men:** Wear a sports jacket and dress trousers (or a suit) with a shirt and tie.

- ✔ **Women:** A basic black dress or tailored suit is appropriate if you're going to "swan about" in stylish eateries.

Lighting up

Non-smoking sections are becoming more common in London's restaurants (not in pubs), but the sections aren't always effectively smoke-free. You may be in the same room as the smokers, just in a different area. If smoking bothers you, ask about the restaurant's non-smoking section when you call to reserve your table.

Dining hours

As a general rule, breakfast is served 7:30 to 9:30 a.m., lunch (often called dinner) is 12:30 to 2:30 p.m., and dinner (often called supper) is served 7:00 to 9:30 p.m. Afternoon tea is served 3:30 to 5:30 or 6:00 p.m. Brunch is generally served 11 a.m. to 4 p.m. on weekends.

Chapter 14

London's Best Restaurants

● ●

In This Chapter

▶ Reviewing my favorite restaurants in London

▶ Listing restaurants by neighborhood, cuisine, and price

● ●

*L*ondon is home to more than 5,700 restaurants. As you can imagine, choosing which establishments to include in this chapter of my favorites is a monumental task. I try to cover as much of Central London as possible. For those of you who want to get the flavor of merry old England, I include some of the oldest and most respected London restaurants serving traditional English food. For the more chic and trendy among you, I include restaurants that serve the best of Modern British cuisine as well as hybrids of British/French and British/ Continental. For people on a budget — or who just want to eat in a down-to-earth, amiable environment — I also review some of the best London pubs. All the establishments are easy to get to, and you can reach all of them by taking the Underground (Tube) system and perhaps walking a bit. For indexes of the restaurants by neighborhood, cuisine, and price, see the end of this chapter. For locations, see the maps in this chapter.

The Kid Friendly icon in front of a restaurant name indicates that the place is suitable for families with children. These restaurants welcome families and may offer a children's menu.

Note that restaurant prices in this chapter do not include the 17.5% VAT (value-added tax). Unfortunately, you can't avoid paying this extra expense.

What the $ Symbols Mean

Reviews are alphabetical for easy reference. Listed immediately beneath the name of the restaurant is its neighborhood and from one to four dollar signs. The dollar signs denote the *average* cost of dinner for one person, including an appetizer (a *starter*), a main course (a *main*), a dessert (an *after* or a *pudding*), a nonalcoholic drink, tax, and a tip. Estimating what an average meal will cost is difficult, because everyone

The skinny on the beef

Sirloin, so the story goes, got its name from James I when he was a guest at Houghton Tower in Lancashire. When a succulent leg of beef was placed before him, he knighted it with his dagger, crying, "Arise, Sir Loin!"

eats differently. In addition, many places have fixed-price meals that include two or three courses for a price that's less than ordering the courses individually. But I indicate general price ranges with these symbols:

$	$25 or under
$$	$26 to $35
$$$	$36 to $50
$$$$	$51 and up

Please bear in mind that if you order the most expensive entree and a bottle of wine, a $$ restaurant can easily become a $$$$ restaurant. On the other hand, if you order from a set-price menu, a $$$$ restaurant tab may dip down to $$.

My Faves: London Restaurants from A to Z

Asia de Cuba

$$$ Piccadilly Circus and Leicester Square   CUBAN/ASIAN

If you're dying to check out the scene at one of London's ultracool hot spots, pack your chic black clothes and call now to reserve a place at Asia de Cuba in Ian Schrager's new St. Martin's Lane hotel. The Asia de Cuba in New York City was so popular that they exported the place to London. For starters, try the Cuban black-bean dumplings or the Chinese five-spice foie gras. Then move on to Szechuan peppercorn-crusted tuna or Chino Latino spiced baby chicken. At places like this, one always feels more comfortable receiving at least one call on a cellular phone while dining.

45 St. Martin's Lane, WC2 (in the St. Martin's Lane hotel). ☎ *020/7300-5500. Reservations recommended at least 2 to 3 weeks in advance. Tube: Leicester Square (then a 2-minute walk east on St. Martin's Court to St. Martin's Lane). Main courses: £14.50–£34 ($22–$51). AE, DC, MC, V. Open: Mon–Sat 11:30 a.m.–2:30 p.m., Mon–Wed 6 p.m. to midnight, Thurs–Sat 6 p.m.–1 a.m.; Sun 6:00 p.m.–10:30 p.m.*

Restaurants in and around The City

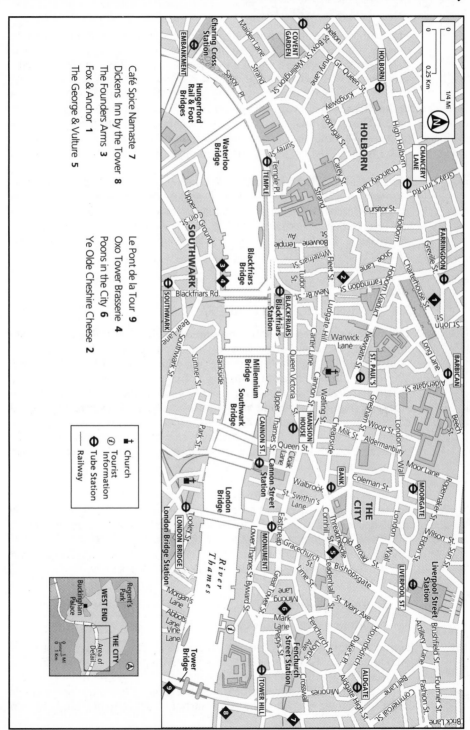

Café Spice Namaste **7**
Dickens Inn by the Tower **8**
The Founders Arms **3**
Fox & Anchor **1**
The George & Vulture **5**

Le Pont de la Tour **9**
Oxo Tower Brasserie **4**
Poons in the City **6**
Ye Olde Cheshire Cheese **2**

✚ Church
ⓘ Tourist Information
Ⓞ Tube Station
— Railway

Aubergine

$$$$ Chelsea FRENCH

This top-name restaurant has only 14 tables, and you compete with its rich-and-famous clientele of celebrities, royalty, and commoners for the privilege of dining there. But it's well worth the try. If you do get in, make sure you look reasonably chic (this restaurant isn't the place for tourist togs). Every dish, from the fish and lighter Mediterranean-style choices to the Bresse pigeon with wild-mushroom ravioli and the venison filet with braised baby turnips, is a culinary achievement of the highest order, winning two Michelin stars. And the celebrated cappuccino of white beans with grated truffle makes a perfect ending to a superb dining experience.

11 Park Walk, SW10. ☎ 020/7352-3449. Reservations recommended 2 months in advance. Tube: Sloane Square (then a 10-minute walk southwest on King's Road to Park Walk; or bus 11, 19, 22, or 211 southwest on King's Road from the Tube station). Fixed-price menus: lunch £18 ($27) for 2 courses, £22.50 ($34) for 3 courses; dinner £45.50 ($68) for 3 courses. AE, DC, MC, V. Open: Mon–Fri noon to 2:15 p.m., Mon–Sat 7:00–10:30 p.m.

Bluebird

$$$ Chelsea MODERN EUROPEAN

This establishment is definitely upscale but still comfortable and refreshingly unpretentious. Formerly a car-repair garage, this sleek white-and-blue place with a gleaming chrome bar, central skylights, and an open kitchen with a wood-burning stove was the creation of restauranteur Sir Terence Conran. The menu emphasizes hearty, cooked-to-the-minute cuisine, and highlights include fish and fresh shellfish (oysters, clams) and crustaceans (lobster, crab), as well as grilled meats (veal, lamb, pigeon, and organic chicken). On my last visit, the white gazpacho was overly olive-oiled but the roast pork was delicious. A cafe and food store are on the first floor.

350 King's Rd., SW3. ☎ 020/7559-1000. Reservations recommended. Tube: Sloane Square (then a 10-minute walk south on King's Road; or bus 19, 22 or 49 from the Tube station). Main courses: £9.75–£30 ($15–$45). Fixed-price menus: lunch (12:30–3:00 p.m.), pretheater (6–7 p.m.) £12.75–£15.75 ($19–$24). AE, DC, MC, V. Open: Mon–Fri noon to 3:30 p.m. and 6:00–11:30 p.m., Sat 11:00 a.m.–3:30 p.m. and 6:00–11:30 p.m., Sun 11:00 a.m.–3:30 p.m. and 6:00–10:30 p.m.

Brasserie St. Quentin

$$ South Kensington FRENCH

London's most authentic-looking French brasserie, St. Quentin attracts many people in the city's French community (a positive sign for a French restaurant outside of France). Mirrors and crystal chandeliers add a touch of elegance. You can dine on grilled tuna with tomato and pepper salsa, stuffed leg of rabbit, breast of Barbary duck, and corn-fed chicken

Restaurants in Westminster and Victoria

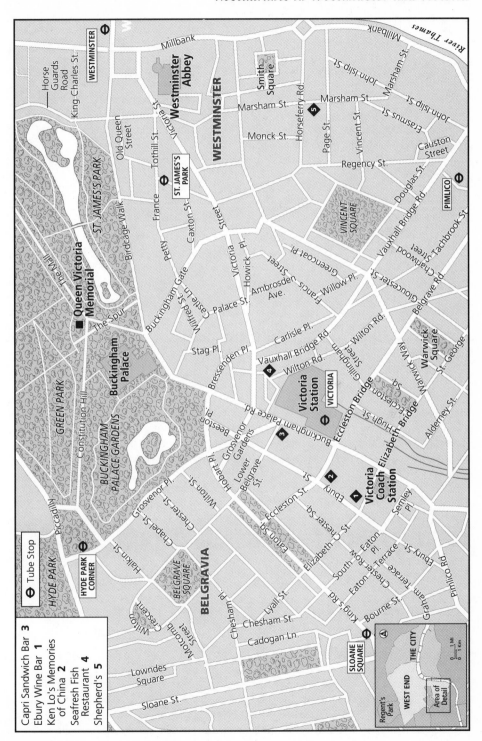

Restaurants in the West End

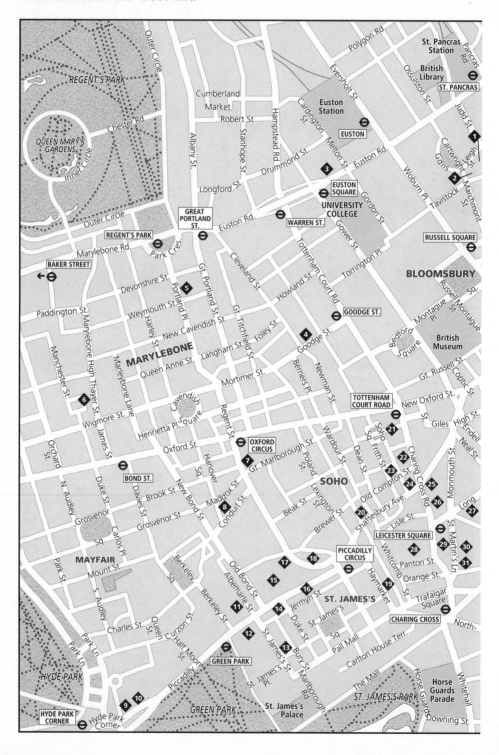

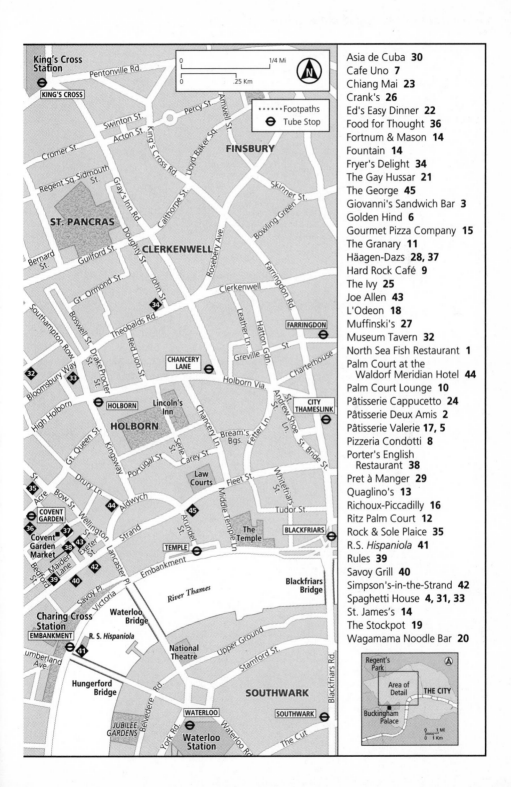

Asia de Cuba **30**
Cafe Uno **7**
Chiang Mai **23**
Crank's **26**
Ed's Easy Dinner **22**
Food for Thought **36**
Fortnum & Mason **14**
Fountain **14**
Fryer's Delight **34**
The Gay Hussar **21**
The George **45**
Giovanni's Sandwich Bar **3**
Golden Hind **6**
Gourmet Pizza Company **15**
The Granary **11**
Häagen-Dazs **28, 37**
Hard Rock Café **9**
The Ivy **25**
Joe Allen **43**
L'Odeon **18**
Muffinski's **27**
Museum Tavern **32**
North Sea Fish Restaurant **1**
Palm Court at the
    Waldorf Meridian Hotel **44**
Palm Court Lounge **10**
Pâtisserie Cappucetto **24**
Pâtisserie Deux Amis **2**
Pâtisserie Valerie **17, 5**
Pizzeria Condotti **8**
Porter's English
    Restaurant **38**
Pret à Manger **29**
Quaglino's **13**
Richoux-Piccadilly **16**
Ritz Palm Court **12**
Rock & Sole Plaice **35**
R.S. *Hispaniola* **41**
Rules **39**
Savoy Grill **40**
Simpson's-in-the-Strand **42**
Spaghetti House **4, 31, 33**
St. James's **14**
The Stockpot **19**
Wagamama Noodle Bar **20**

Map details:

King's Cross Station
Pentonville Rd.
KING'S CROSS
Swinton St.
Acton St.
Percy St.
Amwell St.
Lloyd Baker St.
King's Cross Rd.
FINSBURY
Cromer St.
Regent Sq. Sidmouth St.
Gray's Inn Rd.
Calthorpe St.
Skinner St.
Bowling Green
ST. PANCRAS
Bernard St.
Guilford St.
Doughty St.
John St.
Rosebery Ave.
CLERKENWELL
Clerkenwell
Farringdon Rd.
Gt. Ormond St.
Theobalds Rd.
Red Lion St.
Leather Ln.
Hatton Gdn.
Greville St.
Charterhouse
FARRINGDON
Southampton Row
Boswell St. Drake
Procter St.
Bloomsbury Way
Holborn Via.
CHANCERY LANE
CITY THAMESLINK
High Holborn
HOLBORN
Lincoln's Inn
Chancery Ln.
Bream's Bgs.
St. Andrew
Shoe Ln.
St. Bride St.
Gt. Queen St.
Kingsway
Serle St.
Letter Ln.
Carey St.
Portugal St.
Drury Ln.
Law Courts
Fleet St.
Whitefriars St.
Tudor St.
BLACKFRIARS
COVENT GARDEN
Acre
Bow St.
Wellington St.
Aldwych
Strand
Arundel St.
Middle Temple Ln.
The Temple
Covent Garden Market
Exeter St.
Maiden Lane
Bedford St.
Savoy Pl.
Embankment
Lancaster Pl.
TEMPLE
Charing Cross Station
EMBANKMENT
Victoria Embankment
R. S. Hispaniola
Waterloo Bridge
Blackfriars Bridge
River Thames
umberland Ave.
Hungerford Bridge
National Theatre
Upper Ground
Stamford St.
Blackfriars Rd.
SOUTHWARK
JUBILEE GARDENS
Belvedere Rd.
York Rd.
WATERLOO
Waterloo Rd.
SOUTHWARK
Waterloo Station
The Cut

0 ····· 1/4 Mi
0 ····· .25 Km
N

····· Footpaths
⊖ Tube Stop

Regent's Park
Area of Detail
THE CITY
Buckingham Palace
0 — 1 Mi
0 — 1 Km

Restaurants from Knightsbridge to Earl's Court

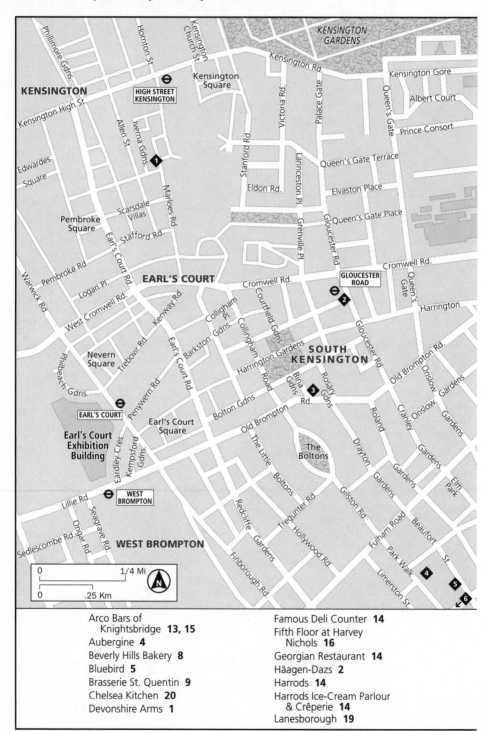

Arco Bars of
   Knightsbridge **13, 15**
Aubergine **4**
Beverly Hills Bakery **8**
Bluebird **5**
Brasserie St. Quentin **9**
Chelsea Kitchen **20**
Devonshire Arms **1**

Famous Deli Counter **14**
Fifth Floor at Harvey
   Nichols **16**
Georgian Restaurant **14**
Häagen-Dazs **2**
Harrods **14**
Harrods Ice-Cream Parlour
   & Crêperie **14**
Lanesborough **19**

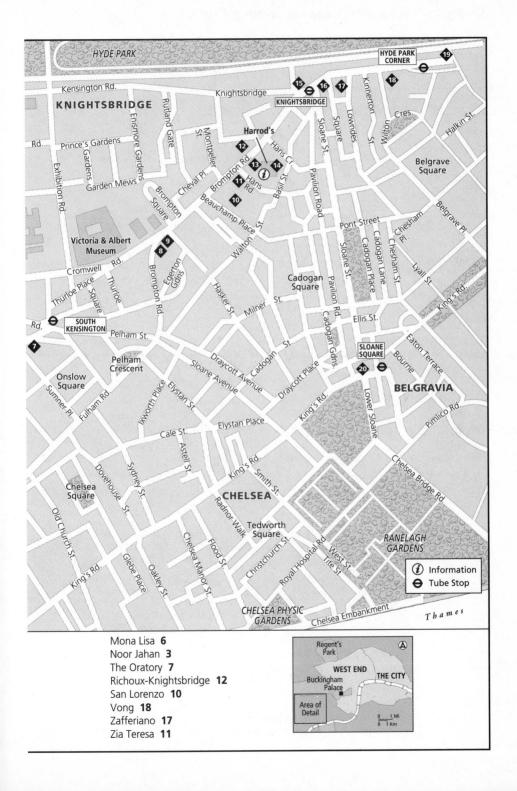

Mona Lisa **6**
Noor Jahan **3**
The Oratory **7**
Richoux-Knightsbridge **12**
San Lorenzo **10**
Vong **18**
Zafferiano **17**
Zia Teresa **11**

Restaurants from Marylebone to Notting Hill

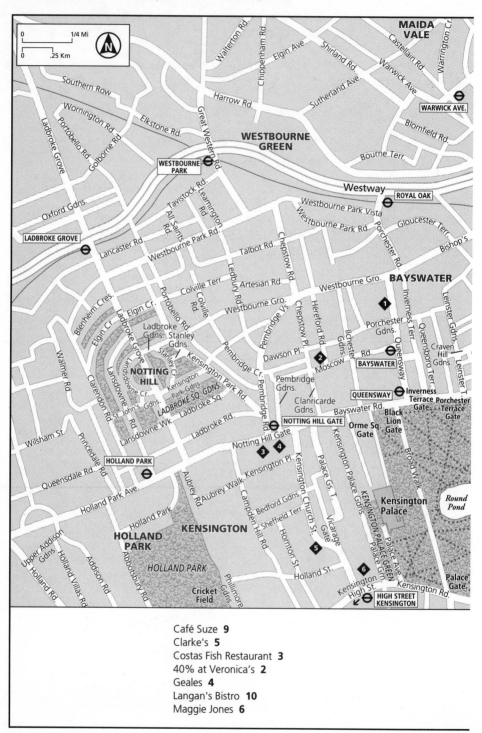

Café Suze **9**
Clarke's **5**
Costas Fish Restaurant **3**
40% at Veronica's **2**
Geales **4**
Langan's Bistro **10**
Maggie Jones **6**

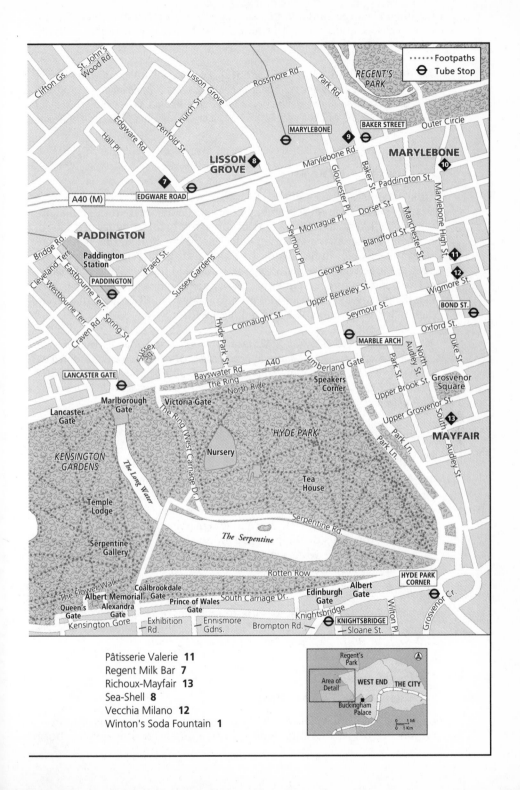

Pâtisserie Valerie **11**
Regent Milk Bar **7**
Richoux-Mayfair **13**
Sea-Shell **8**
Vecchia Milano **12**
Winton's Soda Fountain **1**

with leeks, morels, and chablis sauce. Cornish crab with crème fraîche and terrine of duck liver with walnut dressing are among hors d'oeuvres you may enjoy trying.

243 Brompton Rd., SW3. ☎ 020/7581-5131. Reservations required. Tube: South Kensington (then a 5-minute walk east on Brompton Road). Main courses: £9.50–£22 ($14–$33). Fixed-price menus: 2-course lunch or 2-course dinner (6:30–7:30 p.m.) £11.50 ($17). AE, DC, MC, V. Open: Mon–Sat 11 a.m.–11 p.m., Sun 11:00 a.m.–10:30 p.m.

Café Spice Namaste
$$ The City   INDIAN

This establishment's homemade chutneys alone are worth the trip. Despite fierce competition among London's Indian restaurants, this one remains a perennial favorite for the consistently high quality of its food. Housed in a landmark Victorian hall near Tower Bridge, this place concentrates on spicy Indian dishes that have a strong Portuguese influence, such as Goa's signature dish, *sorpotel* (diced kidney, liver, and pork slow-cooked and served in an oniony stew). Superb chicken, duck, lamb, and fish dishes are available served mild to spicy-hot. All dishes are accompanied by fresh vegetables and Indian bread.

16 Prescot St., E1. ☎ 020/7488-9242. Reservations required. Tube: Tower Hill (then a 5-minute walk north on Minories Street and east on Goodman's Yard, which becomes Prescot Street after you cross Mansell Street). Main courses: £8–£12 ($12–$18). AE, DC, MC, V. Open: Mon–Fri noon to 3 p.m. and 6:15–10:30 p.m., Sat 6:30–10:30 p.m.

Café Suze
$$ Marylebone   PACIFIC RIM/INTERNATIONAL

At this intimate wine bar a couple of blocks from Madame Tussaud's, ingredients from the Pacific Rim are served in all kinds of deliciously inventive ways. The menu changes every two or three weeks. Offerings may include such delicacies as huge New Zealand greenshell mussels, Australian beef medallions on spiced pumpkin mash, and Australian swordfish with cashew butter. The wine list is heavily accented with vintages from Australia and New Zealand. After ten years, this successful bistro has opened another location at 41 North Audley St., W1 (☎ 020/7491-3237).

1 Glentworth St., NW1. ☎ 020/7486-8216. Reservations recommended. Tube: Baker Street (then a 2-minute walk west on Marylebone Road). Main courses: £8.95–£9.95 ($13–$15). AE, DC, MC, V. Open: Mon–Fri 11 a.m.–11 p.m.

Chelsea Kitchen
$ Chelsea   INTERNATIONAL

A London institution, Chelsea Kitchen has been feeding locals and drop-ins since 1961. At this simple place with a diner-like atmosphere, both the plates and the crowds move fast. Menu staples include leek-and-potato soup, chicken Kiev, chicken parmigiana, burgers, and steaks. Kids enjoy the casual atmosphere and simple foods.

98 King's Rd. (off Sloane Square), SW3. ☎ 020/7589-1330. Reservations recommended. Tube: Sloane Square (the restaurant is at the beginning of King's Road just west of the square). Main courses: £3–£5.50 ($4.50–$8). Fixed-price menu: 2-course lunch or dinner £6 ($9). No credit cards. Open: Daily 8:00 a.m.–11:45 p.m.

Chiang Mai
$$ Soho   THAI

Chiang Mai is next door to Ronnie Scott's, the most famous jazz club in England (see Chapter 24), so it's a good stop for an early dinner before a night on the town. Named after the ancient northern capital of Thailand (known for its rich, spicy foods), this unpretentious but pleasant place is good for hot-and-sour beef and chicken dishes, pad thai noodles with various toppings, and vegetarian meals. I suggest that you order a couple of different courses and share. Children's specials are available.

48 Frith St. (off Soho Square), W1. ☎ 020/7437-7444. Tube: Tottenham Court Road (then a 5-minute walk west on Oxford Street and south on Soho Street; Frith Street is at the southwest corner of Soho Square). Main courses: £6–£9 ($9–$15). AE, MC, V. Open: Mon–Sat noon to 3 p.m. and 6–11 p.m., Sun 6:00–10:30 p.m.

Clarke's
$$$ Notting Hill   MODERN EUROPEAN

This bright modern restaurant owned by chef Sally Clarke is among the hottest in town. Its fixed-price menu offers no choices, but you won't mind when you taste the food. The menu changes daily but emphasizes British produce and Mediterranean-style charcoal-grilled foods with herbs and organically grown vegetables. A typical meal may include an appetizer of poached cod with anchovy-and-basil mayonnaise; grilled chicken breast with black truffle, crisp polenta, and arugula; and warm pear-and-raisin puff pastry with maple-syrup ice cream.

124 Kensington Church St., W8. ☎ 020/7221-9225. Reservations recommended. Tube: Notting Hill Gate (then a 5-minute walk south on Kensington Church Street). Fixed-price menus: 2-course lunch £8.50–£14 ($13–$21); 4-course dinner £44 ($66). AE, DC, MC, V. Open: Mon–Fri 12:30–2:00 p.m. and 7–10 p.m.

Crank's
$ Soho   VEGETARIAN

The wood floors and vibrant colors of this restaurant are appropriate for its all-natural cuisine. This self-service vegetarian restaurant is part of a chain, with four other branches in London. Organic-white and stone-ground flours are used for breads and rolls. The raw vegetable salad is especially good, and a hot stew of savory vegetables served with a salad is always a good choice. Homemade honey cake, cheesecake, tarts, and crumbles are featured.

17 Great Newport St., WC2 ☎ *020/7836-5226. Tube: Leicester Square (then a 2-minute walk north on Charing Cross Road to Great Newport Street). Main courses: £5–£9 ($7–$14). AE, DC, MC, V. Open: Mon–Sat 10 a.m.–8 p.m.*

Devonshire Arms

$ Kensington   TRADITIONAL BRITISH

This mid-19th-century pub is a good place to stop when shopping on Kensington High Street. The pub is large enough that you can always get a seat, and the food is above average. You can get a daily special or order à la carte from the menu. Pub staples include beef-and-onion pie, fish-and-chips, and steak-and-kidney pudding. Two good choices are the club sandwich and the vegetarian lasagne verdi.

37 Marloes Rd., W8. ☎ *020/7937-0710. Tube: High Street Kensington (then a 5-minute walk west on Kensington High Street and south on Wright's Lane to Marloes Road). Main courses: £5.50–£6.50 ($8–$10). AE, MC, V. Open: Pub Mon–Sat 11 a.m.–11 p.m.; Sun noon to 10:30 p.m.; food served daily to 2:45 p.m.*

Dickens Inn by the Tower

$ The City   TRADITIONAL/MODERN BRITISH

This former spice warehouse is now a three-story restaurant with sweeping Thames and Tower Bridge views. The ground-floor Tavern Room serves lasagne, soup, sandwiches, and chili. Pizza on the Dock, a floor above and a good spot for families, offers four sizes of pizzas. Dickens Restaurant, on the top floor, is a relatively formal (geared more toward adults) dining room serving Modern British cuisine; specials include steaks, charcoal-grilled brochette of wild mushrooms, and baked cod filet.

St. Katharine's Way (near the Tower of London), E1. ☎ *020/7488-2208. Reservations recommended. Tube: Tower Hill (then a 10-minute walk east on Tower Hill East and south on St. Katherine's Street to St. Katherine's Way). Main courses: Dickens Restaurant, £12.95–£19 ($19–$29); Tavern Room, £2.99–£5.50 ($4.50–$8); Pizza on the Dock, £7–£29 ($10–$44). AE, DC, MC, V. Open: Dickens Restaurant, daily noon to 3 p.m. and 6:30–10:30 p.m.; Tavern Room, daily 11 a.m.–3 p.m.; Pizza on the Dock, daily noon to 10 p.m.*

Ebury Wine Bar

$$ Westminster and Victoria   BRITISH/INTERNATIONAL

This popular wine bar offers a surprisingly good and varied menu and excellent wines. The narrow, woodsy attractive interior is reminiscent of a Paris bistro. In addition to steaks, the oft-changing menu features traditional dishes like Cumberland sausages, meatloaf, and roast pork, but you may find something with a Pacific Rim influence as well (like Thai fish balls).

139 Ebury St., SW1. ☎ 020/7730-5447. Reservations recommended. Tube: Victoria (then a 10-minute walk west on Belgrave Street and south on Ebury Street). Main courses: £10–£17 ($15–$25). AE, DC, MC, V. Open: Daily 11 a.m.–11 p.m.

Ed's Easy Diner
$ Soho   NORTH AMERICAN

It may seem strange to go to London to visit this replica of an old American diner, where customers perch on stools at a wraparound counter and listen to old songs blaring from the jukebox, but it's a safe bet for the kids. A bit more authentic than the version at the Pepsi Trocadero in Piccadilly Circus, this Ed's still attracts a fair share of teens. If you've a yen for the cholesterol-laden food you're supposed to avoid, chow down with Ed's big burgers with fries or onion rings, giant Kosher weenies slathered with cheddar cheese, chili, tuna melts, and grilled cheese.

12 Moor St. (off Cambridge Circus), W1. ☎ 020/7439-1955. Tube: Leicester Square (then a 5-minute walk north on Charing Cross Road and west on Moor Street). Main courses: £4.20–£5.75 ($6–$9). MC, V. Open: Mon–Thurs 11:30 a.m. to midnight, Fri 11:30 a.m.–1:00 a.m., Sat 9 a.m.–1 a.m., Sun 9 a.m.–11 p.m.

Food For Thought
$ Covent Garden   VEGETARIAN

Covent Garden offers a plethora of expensive restaurants for meat-eaters, so this basement hole-in-the-wall with cafeteria-style service is a pleasant and welcome alternative. The menu changes constantly, but the daily soup is always a treat (such as carrot and fresh coriander) and the main courses can include a sweet and tangy Jamaican curry, Italian bean casserole, and cannelloni *ripieni* (stuffed with eggplant), as well as daily quiche and salad specials. The desserts generally include simple fare such as apple-and-rhubarb crumble and fruit with yogurt.

31 Neal St., WC2. ☎ 020/7836-0239. Reservations not accepted. Tube: Covent Garden (then a 2-minute walk north on Neal Street). Main courses: £3.50–£5.70 ($5–$9). No credit cards. Open: Mon–Sat noon to 8:30 p.m., Sun noon to 4:30 p.m.

Fortnum & Mason
$$ St. James's   TRADITIONAL BRITISH

Fortnum & Mason, a posh, legendary London store that's a "purveyor to the Queen" and famous for its food section (see Chapter 19), also has three restaurants. You can choose the mezzanine-level Patio for lunch and tea. The Patio's lunch menu offers an assortment of pricey sandwiches and main courses, especially hot and cold pies (steak and kidney, curried fish and banana, chicken, and game) and *Welsh rarebit* (thick melted cheese poured over toast) prepared with Guinness stout. The lower-level Fountain offers breakfast, lunch, tea, and dinner. The fourth-floor St. James's serves lunch and afternoon tea. The more well heeled dine at St. James's, where the menu is even more traditionally British: For starters, try the *kipper* (smoked herring) mousse or potato and Stilton brûlée; main courses include pies and roast rib of Scottish beef. Although crowded with tourists, these three establishments remain pleasant places where you can get a good meal and a glimpse of the fading empire. The Fountain and Patio are good places to dine with a family, although St. James's also welcomes children.

181 Piccadilly, W1. ☎ *020/7734-8040. Reservations accepted for St. James's only. Tube: Piccadilly Circus (then a 5-minute walk west on Piccadilly). Main courses: lunch £7.50–£15.95 ($11–$24); fixed-price dinners £14.95–£19.95 ($22–$30). AE, DC, MC, V. Open: St. James's and the Patio, Mon–Sat 9:30 a.m.–5:30 p.m.; the Fountain, Mon–Sat 9 a.m.–8 p.m.*

40% at Veronica's

$$ Bayswater TRADITIONAL/MODERN BRITISH

The food here is an intriguing mixture of historical and modern British cuisine. One dining room is Victorian in theme, the other avant-garde. I suggest you stick to the Victorian room, which offers dishes based on medieval, Tudor, and Victorian recipes given a creative twist. Your appetizer may be an Elizabethan salad called salmagundy, made with crunchy pickled vegetables, or Tweed Kettle, a 19th-century recipe to improve the taste of salmon. Many dishes are vegetarian, and everything tastes better when followed with an English farmhouse cheese or a pudding.

3 Hereford Rd., W2. ☎ *020/7229-5079. Reservations required. Tube: Bayswater (then a 5-minute walk west on Moscow Road and north on Hereford Road). Main courses: £11.50–£16.50 ($17–$25). Fixed-price menus: £13.50–£18 ($20–$27). AE, DC, MC, V. Open: Daily 6:30–10:30 p.m.*

The Founders Arms

$ South Bank MODERN BRITISH

This modern pub/restaurant sits right on the Thames, a few minutes walk east from the South Bank Centre or west from the new Tate Modern and Shakespeare's Globe. You can sit inside or out by the water. Although some British pub favorites — such as *bangers and mash* (sausages and mashed potatoes), steak and ale pie, and lamb's liver and bacon on *bubble and squeak* (mashed potatoes mixed with cabbage or meat and then fried) — are available, other dishes are more ambitious. Pasta, fresh fish, and other daily specials are listed on a chalkboard. Or you can just get a sandwich.

52 Hopton St., SE1. ☎ *020/7928-1899. Tube: Waterloo (then a 10-minute walk north along the Thames Path in front of the National Theatre). Main courses: £4.95–£9.95 ($7–$15). AE, MC, V. Open: Mon–Sat 9 a.m.–8:30 p.m., Sun 10 a.m.–8 p.m.; hot food served daily noon to close.*

Fox & Anchor

$ The City   TRADITIONAL BRITISH

This unique pub is one of the best places in town for a big English breakfast. Butchers from the nearby Smithfield meat market, nurses coming off their night shifts, clerks from The City, and tycoons have been eating enormous breakfasts here since 1898. The full house breakfast plate comes with at least eight items, including sausage, bacon, kidneys, eggs, beans, black pudding, and a fried slice of bread, along with unlimited tea or coffee, toast, and jam. If you're feeling festive, order a *Black Velvet* (champagne with Guinness) or a *Bucks fizz* (orange juice and champagne — what Americans call a mimosa). You can order breakfast until 3 p.m., and breakfast is the meal to go for. If you'd rather have lunch, try a steak or the steak-and-kidney pie. Meat is what the Fox & Anchor does best.

115 Charterhouse St., EC1. ☎ *020/7253-5075. Reservations recommended. Tube: Barbican (then a 5-minute walk north on Aldersgate and west on Charterhouse Street). Breakfasts: full house £7 ($11); steak £6.50–£10.95 ($10–$17). Lunch: £5–£15 ($8–$23). AE, DC, MC, V. Open: Mon–Fri 7 a.m.–9 p.m., food served 7 a.m.–3 p.m.*

The Gay Hussar

$$$$ Soho   HUNGARIAN

The Gay Hussar is thought to be the best Hungarian restaurant outside Hungary. Gay in the cheery old ha-ha sense of the word, the restaurant serves undeniably authentic Hungarian cuisine: chilled wild-cherry soup, caraway potatoes, cabbage stuffed with minced veal and rice, tender chicken served in mild paprika sauce with cucumber salad and noodles, and of course veal goulash with egg dumplings. The portions are immoderately large, but try to save room for the poppyseed strudel or the walnut pancakes for dessert.

2 Greek St. (off Soho Square), W1. ☎ *020/7437-0973. Reservations recommended. Tube: Tottenham Court (then a 2-minute walk west on Oxford Street and south on Soho Street; Greek Street is at the southeast corner of Soho Square). Main courses: £12–£16.75 ($18–$25). Fixed-price menus: lunch £15.50 ($23) for 2 courses, £18.50 ($28) for 3 courses. AE, DC, MC, V. Open: Mon–Sat 12:15–2:30 p.m. and 5:30–10:45 p.m.*

The George

$ The Strand   TRADITIONAL BRITISH

Beware: A headless cavalier is rumored to haunt these premises, evidently looking for his head *and* a drink. A favorite pub for barristers, the

George is opposite the Royal Courts of Justice and dates back to 1723, with much of the original structure still standing. Hot and cold meals, including bangers and mash, fish-and-chips, and steak-and-kidney pie are served from a counter at the back. (You can also get lasagna if you need a break from British food.) Additional seating is available in the basement.

213 The Strand, WC2. ☎ 020/7427-0941. Tube: Temple (then a 5-min. walk north on Arundel Street and east on The Strand). Main courses: £5.75–£7.95 ($9–$12). AE, DC, V. Open: pub Mon–Fri 11 a.m.–11 p.m., Sat noon to 3 p.m.; food served Mon–Fri 11:30 a.m.–3 p.m., Sat noon to 2:30 p.m.

The George & Vulture
$$ The City   TRADITIONAL BRITISH

This historic City pub, dating from 1660, serves English lunches on its three floors. When you arrive, give your name and then head to the Jamaican pub across the passage for a drink; the staff will let you know when your table is ready. The pub offers daily specials and a regular menu that includes a mixed grill, a loin chop, and fried Dover sole filets. Potatoes and buttered cabbage are the standard vegetables, and the apple tart is always reliable. After you eat, you can explore the maze of pubs, shops, wine houses, and other old buildings nearby.

3 Castle Court, Cornhill, EC3. ☎ 020/7626-9710. Reservations accepted if you agree to arrive by 12:45 p.m. Tube: Bank (then a 5-minute walk east on Cornhill). Main courses: £6.65–£14.80 ($11–$24). AE, DC, MC, V. Open: Pub Mon–Sat 11 a.m.–11 p.m.; Sun noon to 10:30 p.m.; food served Mon–Fri noon to 2:30 p.m.

Gourmet Pizza Company
$ St. James's   PIZZA/PASTA

This large, bright eatery, frequented by workers in the area's shops and offices, provides an economical meal if you're in the West End — and a good choice if you need to please some pizza-loving kids. You can choose from 20 varieties of pizza — everything from a B.L.T. to one with Cajun chicken and prawns. About half the choices are vegetarian. The crusts are light and crispy and the toppings fresh and flavorful. If you don't want pizza, try the wild mushroom tortellini with chopped basil, tomato, and olive oil. Delicioso!

7–9 Swallow Walk (off Piccadilly), W1. ☎ 020/7734-5182. Tube: Piccadilly Circus (then a 5-minute walk west on Piccadilly and north on Swallow Street). Pizzas: £4.80–£8.45 ($7–$13). Pastas: £6.60–£8.45 ($10–$13). AE, DC, MC, V. Open: Mon–Sat noon to 3 p.m. and 5:00–10:30 p.m.

The Granary
$ Piccadilly Circus and Leicester Square   TRADITIONAL BRITISH

This country-style restaurant serves flavorful home-cooked dishes, listed daily on a chalkboard, including such favorites as lamb casserole with mint and lemon, pan-fried cod, or avocado stuffed with prawns, spinach, and cheese. Common vegetarian meals are meatless versions of *paella* (a Spanish rice dish), lasagne, and *korma* (curried vegetables with Greek yogurt). Having the same owners and many of the same staff for more than 25 years, this reliable restaurant also offers such traditional but tempting desserts as bread-and-butter pudding and Brown Betty (both served hot). Large portions guarantee that you'll be well filled. Kids enjoy the casual atmosphere and simple foods.

39 Albemarle St., W1. ☎ *020/7493-2978. Tube: Green Park (then a 5-minute walk east on Piccadilly to Albermarle) or Piccadilly Circus (then a 5-minute walk west on Piccadilly). Main courses: £7.90–£10.80 ($12–$16). MC, V. Open: Mon–Fri 11:30 a.m.– 7:30 p.m., Sat 11:30 a.m.–4:00 p.m.*

Hard Rock Café
$$ Mayfair   NORTH AMERICAN

This restaurant is one of a worldwide chain of rock-and-roll/American-roadside-diner-themed restaurants. Teens enjoy the rock memorabilia and loud music as well as the great burgers and shakes. Tasty vegetarian dishes are available, too. The portions are generous, and main dishes include salad and fries or baked potato. Consider the homemade apple pie if you have room for dessert. Be prepared to stand in line in the evenings.

150 Old Park Lane, W1. ☎ *020/7629-0382. Tube: Hyde Park Corner (take the Park Lane exit; Old Park Lane is just to the east of Park Lane). Main courses: £8.50–£15 ($13–$22). AE, MC, V. Open: Sun–Thurs 11:30 a.m.–12:30 a.m., Fri–Sat 11:30 a.m.–1 a.m.*

The Ivy
$$ Soho   BRITISH/FRENCH

Are you looking for a hip place to dine after enjoying the theater? The Ivy, with its 1930s look, tiny bar, glamour-scene crowd, and later-than-usual hours, fits the bill. The cooking features skillful preparations of fresh ingredients, with such popular dishes as white asparagus with sea kale and truffle butter and seared scallops with spinach, sorrel, and bacon. You can also enjoy Mediterranean fish soup, a great mixed grill, and traditional English desserts such as sticky toffee and caramelized bread-and-butter pudding.

1–5 West St., WC2. ☎ *020/7836-4751. Reservations required. Tube: Leicester Square (then a 5-minute walk north on Charing Cross Road; West Street is at the southeastern end of Cambridge Circus). Main courses: £8.75–£21.75 ($13–$33). Fixed-price menu: Sat–Sun lunch £15.50 ($23). AE, DC, MC, V. Open: Daily noon to 3 p.m. and 5:30 p.m. to midnight.*

Joe Allen

$$ Covent Garden   NORTH AMERICAN

Joe Allen is a low-profile place on a back street in Covent Garden. Its crowded dining room with checkered tablecloths is the sort of place where actors like to come after a performance to scarf down chili con carne or gnaw on barbecued ribs. The dependable food includes American classics with some international twists, and the set menu is a real value: After a starter (maybe *smoked haddock vichyssoise,* a cold soup with fish), you can choose main courses such as pan-fried parmesan-crusted lemon sole, Cajun chicken breast, and grilled spicy Italian sausages. If you're a tad homesick, try a burger, a brownie, and a Coke for consolation. Come before the show for the best prices, come after for potential star-gazing.

13 Exeter St., WC2. ☎ 020/7836-0651. Reservations recommended. Tube: Covent Garden (then a 5-minute walk south past the Market to Burleigh Street on the southeast corner of the Piazza and west on Exeter Street). Main courses: £8.50–£14.50 ($13–$22). Fixed-price menus: lunch Mon–Fri £12.50–£14.50 ($19–$22); pretheater dinner £13–£15 ($20–$22); Sun brunch £14.50–£16.50 ($22–$25). AE, MC, V. Open: Mon–Fri noon to 12:45 a.m., Sat 11:30 a.m.–12:45 a.m., Sun 11:30 a.m.–11:30 p.m.

Ken Lo's Memories of China

$$$$ Westminster and Victoria   CHINESE

Founded by the late Ken Lo, author of more than 30 cookbooks and once the host of a TV cooking show, this restaurant is one of the better (and certainly one of the more expensive) pan-Chinese restaurants in London. The interior decor is appealingly minimalist, and the service is impeccable. Spanning broadly divergent regions of China, the ambitious menu features Cantonese quick-fried beef in oyster sauce, lobster with handmade noodles, pomegranate prawn balls, and "bang-bang chicken" (a Szechuan dish), among many others.

67–69 Ebury Street (near Victoria Station), SW1. ☎ 020/7730-7734. Reservations recommended. Tube: Victoria Station (then a 10-minute walk west on Belgrave Street and south on Ebury Street). Main courses: £10–£30 ($15–$45). Fixed-price menus: 3-course lunch £19.50–£22 ($29–$33); dinner £27.50 ($41) for 3 courses, £30 ($45) for 5 courses; after-theater 3-course dinner £24.50 ($37). AE, DC, MC, V. Open: Daily noon to 2:30 p.m., 7:00–11:15 p.m.

Langan's Bistro

$$ Marylebone   BRITISH/FRENCH

The menu for this bistro is English with an underplayed (some may say underdeveloped) French influence. Behind a brightly colored storefront, the dining room is covered with clusters of Japanese parasols, rococo mirrors, paintings, and old photographs. Depending on the season, the fixed-price menu may start with a chicken-and-leek terrine or a pepper-and-brie tartlet and move on to brochette of lamb, grilled trout fillets, braised rabbit with mustard sauce, or baked cod. The dessert extravaganza known as "Mrs. Langan's chocolate pudding" is a must for chocoholics.

26 Devonshire St., W1. ☎ *020/7935-4531. Reservations recommended 3 days in advance. Tube: Regent's Park (then a 5-minute walk south on Portland Pl. and west on Devonshire Street). Fixed-price menus: lunch or dinner £17.50 ($26) for 2 courses, £19.50 ($29) for 3 courses. AE, DC, MC, V. Open: Mon–Fri 12:30–2:30 p.m. and 6:30–11:30 p.m., Saturday 6:30–11:00 p.m.*

L'Odeon

$$$$ Piccadilly Circus and Leicester Square   FRENCH/ INTERNATIONAL

L'Odeon had everyone talking when it opened. The interest had to do with its size and sophisticated interior as well as its food. Located in Nash Terrace, the huge second-floor dining room has arched windows overlooking the bustle of Regent Street and Piccadilly Circus. The service is efficient, although rather impersonal, but the food is always fresh and beautifully presented. For starters, try the layered foie gras and Serrano ham terrine or mussel saffron mousse. Main courses may include poached salmon with orange zest, roast chicken with parmesan, calf's liver with braised cabbage, or braised lamb.

65 Regent St. (entrance in Air Street), W1. ☎ *020/7287-1400. Reservations recommended. Tube: Piccadilly Circus (Air Street is the first turning on the south side of Regent Street). Main courses: £12.50–£20 ($19–$30). Fixed-price menus: lunch and pretheater £12.50–£13.50 ($19–$21). AE, DC, MC, V. Open: Mon–Sat noon to 2:30 p.m. and 5:30–11:00 p.m.*

Le Pont de la Tour

$$$$ South Bank   INTERNATIONAL

If you want a splendid view of the Thames and Tower Bridge, visit this upscale wine-and-dine emporium set within a mid-19th-century warehouse. Amid the brash hubbub of **Bar and Grill,** you can order a terrine of ham and foie gras or a half-lobster with roast peppers, olives, and fennel, among other fine dishes. The menu in the larger and more formal **Restaurant** offers such elegant foods as peppered duck with figs and port wine; lobster tortellini with ginger, coriander, and Asian greens; and an excellent Dover sole, which you can order grilled or *meunière* (rolled in flour and fried). Sir Terence Conran is the force behind these posh establishments.

36D Shad Thames, Butler's Wharf, SE1. ☎ *020/7403-8403. Reservations not accepted in the Bar and Grill, but required in the Restaurant. Tube: London Bridge (then a 10-minute walk east on Tooley Street and north on Lafon Street to Shad Thames). Main courses: Bar and Grill £9–£18 ($14–$27); Restaurant £16–£27 ($24–$40). Fixed-price menu: both venues, 3-course lunch Mon–Fri £28.50 ($47). AE, DC, MC, V. Open: Restaurant Mon–Fri noon to 3 p.m.; Mon–Sat 6–11 p.m., Sun noon to 3 p.m. and 6–11 p.m.; Bar and Grill daily 11:30 a.m.–11:00 p.m.*

Maggie Jones
$$ Kensington   TRADITIONAL BRITISH

At this trilevel restaurant with pine tables, the menu is all British, includ-
ing such traditional favorites as grilled leg of lamb chop with rosemary,
grilled trout with almonds, and Maggie's famous fish pie. For dessert, try
the *treacle* (molasses) tart. Everything tastes good and is reliably cooked,
but don't expect anything exceptional. By the way, the place is named
after Princess Margaret, who used to eat here.

6 Old Court Place (off Kensington Church Street), W8. ☎ 020/7937-6462. Reser-
vations required. Tube: High Street Kensington (then a 5-minute walk east on
Kensington High Street, north on Kensington Church Street, and east on Old Court
Pl.). Main courses: £5–£20 ($8–$30). AE, DC, MC, V. Open: Daily 12:30–2:30 p.m. and
6:30–11:00 p.m. (to 10:30 p.m. on Sunday).

Mona Lisa
$ Chelsea   ITALIAN/INTERNATIONAL

Make Mona Lisa your destination for lunch or dinner after walking the
length of King's Road, one of London's great shopping streets (from
Sloane Square the walk takes about 40 minutes, or you can hop on a bus).
A popular cafe by day, the place becomes a restaurant at night, although
they serve many of the same dishes for lunch and dinner. Everything is
homemade and fresh, and the ambience is informal and fun. The menu
includes many fish dishes, including seabass and Dover sole. Pasta da
Vinci, a house specialty, is pasta cooked in a paper bag with a sauce of
squid, mussels, and prawns. Salad lovers can try the Mona Lisa salad
with mozzarella, tomatoes, crispy bacon, avocado, and basil.

417 King's Road (near Millman's Street, just south of Beauford Street), SW10.
☎ 020/7376-5447. Tube: Sloane Square (then bus no. 11, 22, or 211; or a 40-minute
walk south on King's Road). Main courses: £3.95–£15.95 ($6–$24). MC, V. Open:
Mon–Sat 7 a.m.–11 p.m., Sun 9:00 a.m.–5:30 p.m.

The Museum Tavern
$ Bloomsbury   TRADITIONAL BRITISH

Across from the British Museum's front entrance, this ornate Victorian
pub is a convenient spot for a hearty lunch after perusing the Parthenon
sculptures. This place is self-service: You order food at the counter and
drinks at the bar and bring them to your table. Most of the main courses
are traditional pub staples: meat pies (chicken and ham; steak and
kidney; cottage), bangers and mash, fish-and-chips, lamb-and-rosemary
hot pot, quiche, salads, and lasagna. This place is a pub, remember, so
expect some cigarette smoke.

49 Great Russell St., WC1. ☎ 020/7242-8987. Tube: Russell Square (then a 5-minute
walk south on Montgomery Street, along the west side of Russell Square, to Great
Russell Street). Main courses: £5.45–£6.95 ($8–$11). AE, MC, V. Open: Mon–Sat

11 a.m.–11 p.m., Sun 11:00 a.m.–10:30 p.m. (food served daily to half an hour before closing).

Noor Jahan

$$ South Kensington   INDIAN

Noor Jahan is a neighborhood favorite in South Ken. The restaurant is small and unpretentious. The reliably good food includes moist and flavorful marinated chicken and lamb dishes cooked tandoori style in a clay oven. If you want to try one of their tasty specialties, consider chicken tikka, a staple of northern India, or the biriani dishes — where chicken, lamb, or prawns are mixed with basmati rice, fried in *ghee* (thick, clarified butter), and served with a mixed vegetable curry. If you're unfamiliar with Indian food, the waiters will gladly explain the dishes.

2A Bina Gardens (off Old Brompton Road). ☎ *020/7373-6522. Reservations recommended. Tube: Gloucester Road (then a 5-minute walk south on Gloucester Road, west on Brompton Road, north on Bina Gardens). Main courses: £7–£15.50 ($11–$23). Fixed-price menu: £18.50 ($28). AE, DC, MC, V. Open: Daily noon to 2:45 p.m. and 6:00–11:45 p.m.*

North Sea Fish Restaurant

$$ Bloomsbury   SEAFOOD

When they go to London, many people want to experience *real* fish-and-chips — not the generic frozen stuff that often passes for this traditional dish. Definitely try this unassuming chippie where the fish is *always* fresh. This place, with its sepia prints and red velvet seats, is pleasant, comfortable, and popular with adults and kids. You may want to start with grilled fresh sardines or a fish cake before digging into a main course of cod or haddock. The fish is most often served battered and deep-fried, but you can also order it grilled. The chips are almost as good as the fish.

7–8 Leigh St.(off Cartwright Gardens), WC1. ☎ *020/7387-5892. Reservations recommended. Tube: Russell Square (then a 10-minute walk north Marchmont Place and east on Leigh Street). Main courses: £6.95–£15.95 ($11–$24). AE, DC, MC, V. Open: Mon–Sat noon to 2:30 p.m. and 5:30–10:30 p.m.*

The Oratory

$$ South Kensington   MODERN BRITISH

Named for the nearby Brompton Oratory, a famous late-19th-century Catholic church, and close to the Victoria & Albert Museum and Harrods shopping, this funky bistro serves some of the best and least expensive food in posh South Ken. The high-ceilinged room is decorated in what I call Modern Rococo, with enormous glass chandeliers, patterned walls and ceiling, and wooden tables with wrought-iron chairs. Note the daily specials on the chalkboard, especially any pasta dishes. The homemade fish cakes, stir-fried prawns with noodles, and breast of chicken stuffed with Parma ham and fontina cheese are all noteworthy. For dessert, the sticky toffee pudding with ice cream is a melt-in-the-mouth delight.

232 Brompton Rd., SW3. ☎ 020/7584-3493. Tube: South Kensington (then a 5-minute walk north on Brompton Road). Main courses: £7–£13.50 ($11–$20). Fixed-price menu: lunch specials £3.50–£6.95 ($5–$10). MC, V. Open: Daily noon to 11 p.m.

Oxo Tower Brasserie
$$$ South Bank   FRENCH

This stylish brasserie sits atop the landmark Oxo Tower on the South Bank. Although the brasserie is less elegant than the adjacent Oxo Tower Restaurant, its food is marvelous and costs about half of what you pay to dine on tablecloths. The superlative river-and-city views are just as sublime, so book well in advance and insist on a window table. Order such tasty dishes as the tender and tart roast *poussin* (that's French for rabbit) with *rocket* (that's English for arugula), French beans, and a lemon and green olive butter; or the equally fine seared salmon with a spring onion mash and mustard sauce.

Oxo Tower Wharf, Barge House St., SE1. ☎ 020/7803-3888. Reservations essential at least 1 or 2 weeks in advance. Tube: Waterloo (the easiest foot route is to head north to the South Bank Centre and then follow the Thames pathway east to the Oxo Tower, about a 10-minute walk). Main courses: £13–£19.50 ($20–$29). Fixed-price menu: 3-course lunch £22 ($33). AE, DC, MC, V. Open: Daily noon to 3 p.m. and 5:30–11 p.m.

Pizzeria Condotti
$ Mayfair   PIZZA/PASTA

You can take your family to this lovely haven, with its fresh flowers and art-covered walls. The light, crisp pizzas arrive bubbling hot. Choices range from a simple margherita with mozzarella and tomato to the King Edward with potato, four cheeses, and tomato or the "American hot" with mozzarella, pepperoni, sausages, and hot peppers. Plenty of fresh salads and pastas are available, as well as a reasonably priced wine list. End your meal with a scoop of creamy tartufo ice cream made with chocolate liqueur.

4 Mill St. (just off Regent Street), W1. ☎ 020/7499-1308. Tube: Oxford Circus (then a 5-minute walk south on Regent Street, west on Conduit Street and north on Mill Street). Pizzas: £6.95–£8.50 ($11–$13). Pastas: £7.95 ($12). AE, DC, MC, V. Open: Mon–Sat 11:30 a.m. to midnight, Sun noon to 9 p.m.

Poons in the City
$$$ The City   CHINESE

Poons is famous for Cantonese specialties such as *lap yuk soom* (similar to tacos, with finely chopped wind-dried bacon) and *braised honeycomb* (a Chinese version of Yorkshire pudding and gravy). Pan-fried dumplings and deep-fried scallops make excellent starters. Other dishes feature crispy duck, prawns with cashews, and barbecued pork. The restaurant is on the ground floor of an office block less than a 5-minute walk from the Tower of London. At the end of the L-shaped restaurant is a simpler and less expensive 80-seat express cafe serving stir-fries and snacks.

2 Minster Pavement, Minster Court, Mincing Lane, EC3. ☎ 020/7626-0126. Reservations recommended for lunch. Tube: Monument (then a 5-minute walk east on Eastcheap and Great Tower Street and north on Mincing Lane). Main courses: £5–£9 ($8–$15). Fixed-price menus: lunch and dinner £22.50–£32 ($34–$48); express cafe lunch £5.50–£16.50 ($8–$25) per person (minimum of 2). AE, DC, MC, V. Open: Mon–Fri noon to 10:30 p.m.

Porter's English Restaurant

$$ Covent Garden   TRADITIONAL BRITISH

This comfortably informal restaurant specializes in English pies, including Old English fish pie; lamb and apricot; and ham, leek, and cheese. Forgo appetizers because the main courses, accompanied by vegetables and side dishes, are generous. If pie isn't your thing, try the bangers and mash, grilled sirloin, lamb steak, or pork chops. The puddings, including bread-and-butter pudding and steamed syrup sponge, are served hot or cold, with whipped cream or custard. The casual atmosphere makes this a good spot for families.

17 Henrietta St., WC2. ☎ 020/7836-6466. Reservations recommended. Tube: Covent Garden (then a 5-minute walk south on James Street; Henrietta Street is at the southwest corner behind Covent Garden Market). Main courses: £8.95–£22 ($14–$33). Fixed-price menu: £17.75 ($27). AE, DC, MC, V. Open: Mon–Sat noon to 11:30 p.m, Sun noon to 10:30 p.m.

Quaglino's

$$$$ St. James's   MODERN EUROPEAN

This power-charged megaeatery is *the* place for food and fun, with a huge sunken dining room that reminds you of an ocean liner's. The shellfish are always excellent, but other menu items are unreliable, as is the service. The menu changes often; choices may include goat cheese and caramelized onion tart, gnocchi with tomato-and-herb sauce, crab tartlet with saffron, or roasted cod and ox cheek with charcoal-grilled vegetables. Be sure to try the wonderfully delectable puddings, such as the vanilla *mascarpone* (a rich, white cream cheese) tart or *pannacotta* (thick cooked cream) with fresh figs.

16 Bury St., SW1. ☎ 020/7930-6767. Fax: 020/7839-2866. Reservations required at least 1 or 2 weeks in advance. Tube: Green Park (then a 10-minute walk northeast on Piccadilly, southeast on St. James's Street, and east on King Street to Bury Street). Main courses: £10.50–£18.50 ($16–$28). Fixed-price menu: (Mon–Thurs at lunch and pretheater dinner 5:30–6:30pm) £12.50–£15 ($19–$23). AE, DC, MC, V. Open: Daily noon to 3 p.m., Mon–Thurs 5:30–11:30 p.m., Fri–Sat 5:30 p.m.–12:30 a.m., Sun 5:30–10:30 p.m.

R.S. Hispaniola
$$$ The Strand   BRITISH/FRENCH

This former passenger boat is permanently moored in the Thames and provides good food and spectacular views of the river traffic. The menu changes often, with a variety of sturdy and generally well-prepared dishes, such as flambéed Mediterranean prawns with garlic, poached halibut on a bed of creamed spinach, rack of lamb flavored with rosemary and shallots, and a number of vegetarian dishes. The place can be fun and romantic — live music is played most nights — if a bit touristy.

River Thames, Victoria Embankment, Charing Cross, WC2. ☎ *020/7839-3011. Reservations recommended. Tube: Embankment (the restaurant a few steps from the station). Main courses: £9.95–£16.95 ($15–$25); £15 ($22) minimum per person. AE, DC, MC, V. Open: Mon–Fri noon to 2:30 p.m. and 6:30–11:00 p.m.; Sat 6:00– 11:30 p.m. Closed Dec 24–Jan 4.*

Rules
$$$ Covent Garden   TRADITIONAL BRITISH

If you want to eat classic British cuisine in a memorable (nay, venerable) setting, put on something reasonably dressy and head for Maiden Lane. Founded in 1798, Rules is London's oldest restaurant, numbering two centuries worth of prints, cartoons, and paintings among its decor. If you're game for game, go for it because that's what Rules is famous for. Ptarmigan, widgeon, partridge, and snipe — game birds shot at the restaurant's hunting seat — are roasted to order September through February. In recent years, they've added fish and a few vegetarian dishes, such as the wild mushroom lasagna in basil cream sauce.

35 Maiden Lane, WC2. ☎ *020/7836-5314. Reservations essential. Tube: Covent Garden (then a 5-minute walk south on James Street to Southampton Street behind Covent Garden Market and west on Maiden Lane). Main courses: £16.95–£22.50 ($25–$34). Fixed-price menu: Pretheater Mon–Fri 3–5 p.m. £19.95 ($30). AE, DC, MC, V. Open: Daily noon to midnight.*

San Lorenzo
$$$ Knightsbridge   ITALIAN

This fashionable restaurant was once a favorite of Princess Diana. Italian cuisine from all the regions of Italy, with a special nod toward Tuscany and the Piedmont, is the specialty. Seasonal fish, game, and vegetables appear in such dishes as risotto with fresh asparagus, partridge in white-wine sauce, and *tagliate di bue* (filet steak with arugula and balsamic vinegar). The fettuccine, gnocchi, and penne are all homemade. The food is reliably good, but some diners complain that too much attitude accompanies it.

22 Beauchamp Place, SW3. ☎ *020/7584-1074. Reservations required. Tube: Knightsbridge (then a 5-minute walk southwest on Brompton Road and south on Beauchamp Place). Main courses: £14.50–£20 ($22–$30). No credit cards. Open: Mon–Sat 12:30–3:00 p.m. and 7:30–11:30 p.m.*

Savoy Grill
$$$$ **The Strand** **TRADITIONAL BRITISH**

Like the hotel that houses it, the Savoy Grill caters to the rich, the powerful, the prestigious, and anyone else who can dress up and put together enough to afford the price of a meal. Service is impeccable, and the dining room is spacious but low key, with yew-paneled walls that give the space a warm, woody blush. If you like old-fashioned meat dishes, choose the daily special from the trolley: beef Wellington, roast sirloin, saddle of lamb, or pot-roasted guinea hen with horseradish crust. Otherwise, the menu changes twice a year and is based on seasonal specialties, such as oysters and partridge in September.

In The Savoy Hotel, Strand, WC2. ☎ 020-7420-2066. Reservations required. Tube: Charing Cross (then a 5-minute walk east along The Strand). Main courses: £13.50–£38 ($21–$57). AE, DC, MC, V. Open: Mon–Fri 12:30–2:30 p.m.; Mon–Sat 6:00–11:15 p.m. Closed August.

Shepherd's
$$$ **Westminster and Victoria** **TRADITIONAL BRITISH**

This popular restaurant sits between Tate Britain and Parliament. Regulars include a loyal crowd of barristers and MPs (a bell rings in the dining room to let them know it's time to go back to the House of Commons for a vote). Amid a nook-and-cranny setting of leather banquettes, sober 19th-century accessories, and English portraits and landscapes, you can dine on rib of Scottish beef with Yorkshire pudding, cream of watercress, hot salmon and potato salad with dill dressing, filet of lemon sole, or roast leg of lamb with mint sauce. You choose everything from a fixed-price menu but are given an impressive number of options.

Marsham Court, Marsham Street (at the corner of Page Street), SW1. ☎ 020/ 7834-9552. Reservations recommended. Tube: Westminster (then a 10-minute walk south on St. Margaret Place and Millbank and west on Westminster Street to Page and Marsham streets; or Pimlico, then north on Bessboro Street, John Islip Street, and Marsham Street). Fixed-price menus: £24 ($36) for 2 courses, £27 ($40) for 3 courses. AE, DC, MC, V. Open: Mon–Fri 12:30–2:45 p.m. and 6:30–11:00 p.m.

Simpson's-in-the-Strand
$$$ **The Strand** **TRADITIONAL/MODERN BRITISH**

Open since 1828, Simpson's offers an array of the best roasts in London — sirloin of beef, saddle of mutton with red-currant jelly, and Aylesbury duckling — served by a veritable army of formal waiters. (Remember to tip the tailcoated carver.) For a pudding, try the treacle roll and custard or Stilton with vintage port. You'll find all this downstairs, where the atmosphere is formal and dressy. They've now opened a more relaxed, brighter, lighter dining area on the second floor that's actually (gasp) nouvelle. You can also come here for a great real English breakfast.

100 The Strand (next to the Savoy Hotel), WC2. ☎ 020/7836-9112. Reservations required. Tube: Charing Cross (then a 5-minute walk east along The Strand). Main courses: Downstairs, £10.50–£22.95 ($16–$34); upstairs, £10.95–£19.50 ($16–$29). Fixed-price menus: Upstairs and downstairs, 2-course lunch and pretheater dinner £15.50 ($23); breakfast £15.50 ($23). AE, DC, MC, V. Open: Mon–Fri 7:15–10:15 a.m., 12:15–2:30 p.m. and 5:00–10:45 p.m.; Sat–Sun noon to 2:30 p.m. and 5–9 p.m.

The Stockpot
$ Piccadilly Circus and Leicester Square   BRITISH/CONTINENTAL

Now here's a dining bargain! This simple bilevel restaurant in the heart of the West End doesn't offer refined cooking, but the food is filling and the price is right — making it a good spot for families. You can find such fare as minestrone soup, spaghetti bolognese (the eternal favorite), braised lamb, and apple crumble on the fixed-price daily menu. (During peak dining hours, you may have to share the table with other guests.)

38 Panton St. (off Haymarket, opposite the Comedy Theatre), SW1. ☎ 020/7839-5142. Reservations accepted for dinner. Tube: Piccadilly Circus (then a 5-minute walk south on Haymarket and east on Panton Street). Main courses: £2.60–£6.50 ($4–$10). Fixed-price menus: 2-course lunch £3.70 ($6); 3-course dinner £6.40 ($10). No credit cards. Open: Mon–Sat 7 a.m.–11 p.m., Sun 7 a.m.–10 p.m.

Vong
$$$ Knightsbridge   THAI

This artily minimalist restaurant is a chic hangout for food groupies who can't get enough of chef/owner Jean-Georges Vongerichten's food. The cooking is subtle, innovative, and (usually) inspired. (Try the "black plate" sampler of six starters for a taste tour.) You can dine on perfectly roasted halibut or sublime lobster-and-daikon roll with rosemary-and-ginger sauce. Other temptations include the crab spring roll with vinegary tamarind dipping sauce and sautéed foie gras with ginger and mango, which literally melts in your mouth. The exotic desserts may include a salad of banana and passion fruit with white-pepper ice cream. You may get a same-day table if you dine early; the place starts filling up after 8 p.m.

In the Berkeley Hotel, Wilton Place, SW1. ☎ 020/7235-1010. Reservations required 7 days in advance. Tube: Knightsbridge (then a 3-minute walk east on Knightsbridge and south on Wilton Pl.). Main courses: £14.50–£20.95 ($22–$31). Fixed-price menus: Tasting £50 ($75); lunch £21 ($32); pre- and post-theater dinner £21 ($32). AE, DC, MC, V. Open: Mon–Sat noon to 2:30 p.m. and 6:00–11:30 p.m., Sun 6:00–10:30 p.m.

Wagamama Noodle Bar
$ Soho   JAPANESE

Try this trendsetting noodle bar modeled after the ramen shops of Japan if you're exploring Soho and want a delicious, nutritious meal uncontaminated by cigarette smoke. You enter along a stark, glowing hall with a busy open kitchen and descend to a large open room with communal tables. The specialties are ramen, Chinese-style thread noodles served in soups with various toppings, and the fat white noodles called *udon*. You can also order various rice dishes, vegetarian dishes, dumplings, vegetable and chicken skewers, and tempura. Your order is sent via radio signal to the kitchen and arrives the moment it's ready, which means that not everyone in a group is served at the same time. You may have to stand in line to get in, but it's worth the wait. Teens especially love the loud, hip, casual atmosphere.

10A Lexington St., W1. ☎ 020/7292-0990. Reservations not accepted. Tube: Piccadilly Circus (then a 5-minute walk north on Shaftesbury Avenue and Windmill Street, which becomes Lexington Street). Main courses: £4.85–7.50 ($7–$11). MC, V. Open: Mon–Thurs noon to 11 p.m., Fri–Sat noon to midnight, Sun 12:30–10:00 p.m.

Ye Olde Cheshire Cheese
$$ The City   TRADITIONAL BRITISH

Opened in 1667 and a one-time haunt of Samuel Johnson, Charles Dickens, and Fleet Street newspaper scandalmongers, Ye Olde Cheshire Cheese is London's most famous chophouse. The place contains six bars and two dining rooms and is perennially popular with families and tourists looking for some Olde London atmosphere. The house specialties include "ye famous pudding" (steak, kidney, mushrooms, and game), Scottish roast beef with Yorkshire pudding and horseradish sauce, and Dover sole. If those choices repulse the kids, they can choose sandwiches and salads.

Wine Office Court, 145 Fleet St., EC4. ☎ 020/7353-6170. Tube: Blackfriars (then a 10-minute walk north on New Bridge Street and west on Fleet Street). Main courses: £7–£15 ($11–$22). AE, DC, MC, V. Open: Mon–Sat noon to 11 p.m.; Sun noon to 3:30 p.m.; drinks and bar snacks daily 11:30 a.m.–11:00 p.m.

Zafferano
$$$$ Knightsbridge   ITALIAN

At Zafferano you find the best Italian food in London, served in a quietly elegant, attitude-free restaurant. You may not find a table, though, unless you reserve in advance. The semolina pastas are perfectly cooked and come with various additions, such as sausage and fennel seeds, pheasant parcels with rosemary, sweet chili garlic and crab, or meat and black truffle. The main courses, such as roast rabbit with Parma ham and polenta, charcoal-grilled chicken, and tuna with rocket and tomato salad, are deliciously simple and tender. For dessert, try the sublime tart with lemon and mascarpone.

15 Lowndes St., SW1. ☎ 020/7235-5800. Reservations required. Tube: Knightsbridge (then a 5-minute walk south on Lowndes Street, 2 streets east of Sloane Street). Fixed-price menus: 2-course lunch £18.50 ($28), 3-course lunch £21.50 ($32); 2-course dinner £29.50 ($44), 3-course dinner £35.50 ($53). AE, MC, V. Open: Daily noon to 2:30 p.m. and 7–11 p.m.

Index of Restaurants by Neighborhood

Bayswater

40% at Veronica's (Traditional/
Modern British, $$)

Bloomsbury

The Museum Tavern (Traditional
British, $)
North Sea Fish Restaurant
(Seafood, $$)

Chelsea

Aubergine (French, $$$$)
Bluebird (Modern European, $$$$)
Chelsea Kitchen (International, $)
Mona Lisa (Italian, $)

The City

Café Spice Namaste (Indian, $$)
Dickens Inn by the Tower
(Traditional/Modern British, $)
Fox & Anchor (Traditional British, $)
The George & Vulture (Traditional
British, $$)
Poons in the City (Chinese, $$$)
Ye Olde Cheshire Cheese (Traditional
British, $$)

Covent Garden

Food for Thought (Vegetarian, $)
Joe Allen (North American, $$)
Porter's English Restaurant
(Traditional British, $$)
Rules (Traditional British, $$$)

Holborn

The George (Traditional British, $$)

Kensington

Clarke's (Modern European, $$$)
Devonshire Arms (Traditional
British, $)
Maggie Jones (Traditional British, $$)

Knightsbridge

The Oratory (Modern British, $$)
San Lorenzo (Italian, $$$)
Vong (French/Thai, $$$)
Zafferano (Italian, $$$)

Marylebone

Café Suze (Pacific Rim/
International, $$)
Langan's Bistro (British/French, $$)

Mayfair

Hard Rock Café (North American, $$)
Pizzeria Condotti (Pizza/Pasta, $)

**Piccadilly Circus and
Leicester Square**

Asia de Cuba (Cuban/Asian, $$$)
The Granary (Traditional British, $)
L'Odeon (French, $$$$)
The Stockpot (British/Continental, $)

Soho

Chiang Mai (Thai, $$)
Crank's (Vegetarian, $)
Ed's Easy Diner (North American, $)
The Gay Hussar (Hungarian, $$$$)
The Ivy (British/French, $$)
Wagamama Noodle Bar (Japanese, $)

South Bank

Founders Arms (Modern British, $)
Le Pont de la Tour (International, $$$$)
Oxo Tower Brasserie (French, $$$)

South Kensington

Brasserie St. Quentin (French, $$)
Noor Jahan (Indian, $$)

St. James's

Fortnum & Mason (Traditional
British, $$)

Gourmet Pizza Company (Pizza/ Pasta, $)

Quaglino's (Modern European, $$$$)

The Strand

The George (Traditional British, $)

R.S. *Hispaniola* (British/French, $$$)

Savoy Grill (Traditional British, $$$$)

Simpson's-in-the-Strand (Traditional/ Modern British, $$$)

Westminster and Victoria

Ebury Wine Bar (British/International, $$)

Ken Lo's Memories of China (Chinese, $$$$)

Shepherd's (Traditional British, $$$)

Index of Restaurants by Cuisine

British/Continental

The Stockpot (Piccadilly Circus and Leicester Square, $)

British/French

The Ivy (Soho, $$)

Langan's Bistro (Marylebone, $$)

Shepherd's (Westminster and Victoria, $$$)

R.S. *Hispaniola* (The Strand, $$$)

British (Modern)

Dickens Inn by the Tower (The City, $)

40% at Veronica's (Bayswater, $$)

Founders Arms (South Bank, $)

The Oratory (Knightsbridge, $$)

Simpson's-in-the-Strand (The Strand, $$$)

British (Traditional)

Clarke's (Notting Hill, $$$)

Devonshire Arms (Kensington, $)

Dickens Inn by the Tower (The City, $)

Fortnum & Mason (St. James's, $$)

40% at Veronica's (Bayswater, $$)

Fox & Anchor (The City, $)

The George (The Strand, $)

The George & Vulture (The City, $$)

The Granary (Piccadilly Circus and Leicester Square, $)

Maggie Jones (Kensington, $$)

The Museum Tavern (Bloomsbury, $)

Porter's English Restaurant (Covent Garden, $$)

Rules (Covent Garden, $$$)

Savoy Grill (The Strand, $$$$)

Simpson's-in-the-Strand (The Strand, $$$)

Ye Olde Cheshire Cheese (The City, $$)

Chinese

Ken Lo's Memories of China (Westminster and Victoria, $$$$)

Poons in the City (The City, $$$)

Cuban/Asian

Asia de Cuba (Piccadilly Circus and Leicester Square, $$$)

French

Aubergine (Chelsea, $$$$)

Brasserie St. Quentin (South Kensington, $$)

L'Odeon (Piccadilly Circus and Leicester Square, $$$$)

Oxo Tower Brasserie (South Bank, $$$)

French/Thai

Vong (Knightsbridge, $$$)

Hungarian

The Gay Hussar (Soho, $$$$)

Indian

Café Spice Namaste (The City, $$)

Noor Jahan (South Kensington, $$)

International

Chelsea Kitchen (Chelsea, $)
Ebury Wine Bar (Westminster and
   Victoria, $$)
Le Pont de la Tour (South Bank, $$$$)

Italian

Mona Lisa (Chelsea, $)
San Lorenzo (Knightsbridge, $$$)
Zafferano (Knightsbridge, $$$)

Japanese

Wagamama Noodle Bar (Soho, $)

Modern European

Bluebird (Chelsea, $$$$)
Quaglino's (St. James's, $$$$)

North American

Ed's Easy Diner (Soho, $)
Hard Rock Café (Mayfair, $$)
Joe Allen (Covent Garden, $$)

Pacific Rim/International

Café Suze (Marylebone, $$)

Pizza/Pasta

Gourmet Pizza Company
   (St. James's, $)
Pizzeria Condotti (Mayfair, $)

Seafood

North Sea Fish Restaurant
   (Bloomsbury, $$)

Thai

Chiang Mai (Soho, $$)

Vegetarian

Crank's (Soho, $)
Food for Thought (Covent Garden, $)

Index of Restaurants by Price

$

Chelsea Kitchen (International,
   Chelsea)
Crank's (Vegetarian, Soho)
Devonshire Arms (Traditional British,
   Kensington)
Dickens Inn by the Tower
   (Traditional/Modern British,
   The City)
Ed's Easy Diner (North American,
   Soho)
Food for Thought (Vegetarian,
   Covent Garden)
Founders Arms (Modern British,
   South Bank)
Fox & Anchor (Traditional British,
   The City)
The George (Traditional British,
   The Strand)
Gourmet Pizza Company (Pizza/Pasta,
   St. James's)

The Granary (Traditional British,
   Piccadilly Circus and Leicester
   Square)
Mona Lisa (Italian, Chelsea)
The Museum Tavern (Traditional
   British, Bloomsbury)
Pizzeria Condotti (Pizza/Pasta,
   Mayfair)
The Stockpot (British/Continental,
   Piccadilly Circus and Leicester
   Square)
Wagamama Noodle Bar (Japanese,
   Soho)

$$

Brasserie St. Quentin (French, South
   Kensington)
Café Spice Namaste (Indian, The City)
Café Suze (Pacific Rim/International,
   Marylebone)
Chiang Mai (Thai, Soho)

Ebury Wine Bar (International, Westminster and Victoria)

Fortnum & Mason (Traditional British, St. James's)

40% at Veronica's (Traditional/Modern British, Bayswater)

The George & Vulture (Traditional British, The City)

Hard Rock Café (North American, Mayfair)

The Ivy (British/French, Soho)

Joe Allen (North American, Coven Garden)

Langan's Bistro (British/French, Marylebone)

Maggie Jones (Traditional British, Kensington)

Noor Jahan (Indian, South Kensington)

North Sea Fish Restaurant (Seafood, Bloomsbury)

The Oratory (Modern British, Knightsbridge)

Porter's English Restaurant (Traditional British, Covent Garden)

Ye Olde Cheshire Cheese (Traditional British, The City)

$$$

Asia de Cuba (Cuban/Asian, Piccadilly Circus and Leicester Square)

Clarke's (Traditional British, Kensington)

Oxo Tower Brasserie (French, South Bank)

Poons in the City (Chinese, The City)

R.S. *Hispaniola* (British/French, The Strand)

Rules (Traditional British, Covent Garden)

San Lorenzo (Italian, Knightsbridge)

Shepherd's (Shepherd's, Westminster and Victoria)

Simpson's-in-the-Strand (Traditional/Modern British, The Strand)

Vong (French/Thai, Knightsbridge)

Zafferano (Italian, Knightsbridge)

$$$$

Aubergine (French, Chelsea)

Bluebird (Modern European, Chelsea)

The Gay Hussar (Hungarian, Soho)

Ken Lo's Memories of China (Chinese, Westminster and Victoria)

Le Pont de la Tour (International, South Bank)

L'Odeon (French, Piccadilly Circus and Leicester Square)

Quaglino's (Modern European, St. James's)

Savoy Grill (Traditional British, The Strand)

Chapter 15

On the Lighter Side: Snacks and Meals on the Go

● ●

In This Chapter

▶ Grabbing a quick bite at sandwich shops, department stores, pasta parlors, and "chippies"

▶ Finding the best places for a spot of tea

▶ Treating yourself to ice cream

▶ Dining alfresco

● ●

*L*ondoners have a much less casual attitude toward food than Americans have. You won't see adults in London eating pretzels on the street or having a bite while traveling the Tube. And you don't find street vendors peddling hot dogs and other foods from carts (although you may see a fast-food van or two near major attractions).

Even the most frenetic Londoner likes to eat a proper, civilized "sit down" meal. So what's a too-rushed tourist to do?

Well, you can take in the all-American fast-food restaurants sprouting up all over Central London, including **Burger King, KFC, Pizza Hut,** and **McDonald's.** They're familiar, and your kids may clamor for them. But you're in London, after all; to help you enjoy snacks and light meals the London way, this chapter offers some interesting alternatives.

See the maps in Chapter 14 to find the locations of the eateries described in this chapter.

Cut off the Crust: Sandwich Bars

Sandwiches are an English invention (supposedly of the earl of Sandwich), and sandwich bars are a faster and cheaper alternative to sit-down restaurants and pubs. Most open early for breakfast and close in the afternoon. You can usually eat at a counter or in booths, or you can take your sandwich and go to the nearest park for an alfresco lunch. The bars sell coffee, tea, and nonalcoholic beverages.

Americans are sometimes confused by the way the English style their sandwiches. In general, the Brits use the word *mayonnaise* the way Americans use *salad*. *Tuna mayonnaise* or *egg mayonnaise* simply means "tuna salad" or "egg salad." The word *salad* is used in Britain to denote that lettuce and tomato have been added to a sandwich, as in "chicken with salad." At a sandwich bar, make sure that the sandwiches are *freshly cut* — meaning that they haven't been sitting around in the display case for hours.

The following sandwich bars are worth a bite:

✔ If you've dropped a bundle at Harrods and suddenly want to be frugal, just across the street is **Arco Bars of Knightsbridge** (46 Hans Crescent, SW1; ☎ **020/7584-6454**; Tube: Knightsbridge); a smaller location is just around the corner from the Knightsbridge Tube station (16 Brompton Arcade; ☎ **020/7584-3136**). Both are open Monday through Friday 7 a.m. to 6 p.m. and Saturday 8 a.m. to 6 p.m.

✔ Near Victoria Station, **Capri Sandwich Bar** (16 Belgrave Rd., NW1; ☎ **020/7834-1989**; Tube: Victoria) serves an imaginative variety of sandwiches. The bar is open daily 7:30 a.m. to 3:30 p.m.

✔ If you're in the vicinity of Euston Station, try the unpretentious but cheerful **Giovanni's Sandwich Bar** (152 North Gower St., at Euston Road; ☎ **020/7383-0531**; Tube: Euston), open daily 6:30 a.m. to 4:00 p.m.

In addition, the **Pret à Manger** chain, found throughout Central London, offers reliably fresh, inventive sandwiches and fast counter service. The best one is at 77–78 St. Martin's Lane, WC2 (☎ **020/7379-5335**; Tube: Leicester Square). It's open Monday through Thursday 7:30 a.m. to 9:00 p.m., Friday 7:30 a.m. to 11:00 p.m., Saturday 9 a.m. to 11 p.m., and Sunday 9 a.m. to 9 p.m.

Eat Hearty: Fish-and-Chips Joints

The English call a fish-and-chips place a *chippie*. At some chippies the food is wonderful; at others it's hideous. At the good places (the only ones I recommend), the fish (usually cod, haddock, or plaice) is fresh, the batter crisp, and the fries (chips) hand-cut. You can get tartar sauce, but the British also like to splash their fish-and-chips with malt vinegar.

The following restaurants all have sit-down and *takeaway* (what the Brits call American "takeout") service and welcome families with kids.

✔ **North Sea Fish Restaurant** (7–8 Leigh St., WC1; ☎ 020/7387-5892; Tube: Russell Square) is a restaurant (see Chapter 14), but it also offers takeaway service Monday through Saturday noon to 2:30 p.m. and 5:30 to 11:30 p.m. If the weather is good, take your meal over to Russell Square in the heart of Bloomsbury.

✔ **Rock & Sole Plaice** (47 Endell St., WC2; ☎ 020/7836-3785; Tube: Covent Garden) offers all-day takeaway service as well as a place to sit down and eat amid the bustle of the Covent Garden Piazza (tables are available on the lower level). Because of its location, this chippie is the most expensive of the lot, so prepare to pay at least £8 ($13) for a meal. It's open Monday through Saturday 11:30 a.m. to 11:30 p.m. and Sunday 11:30 a.m. to 10:00 p.m.

✔ **Fryer's Delight** (19 Theobald's Rd., WC1; ☎ 020/7405-4114; Tube: Chancery Lane or Holborn) is across from the Holborn Police Station. A plate of cod and chips is £4.25 ($7) if you eat in or £3.80 ($6) for takeaway; takeaway is available the same hours that the restaurant is open, Monday through Saturday noon to 11 p.m.

✔ **Golden Hind** (73 Marylebone Lane, W1; ☎ 020/7486-3644; Tube: Baker Street or Bond Street) is a few blocks south of Madame Tussaud's. This place is another bargain chippie where an average meal costs £5 ($8); hours are Monday through Saturday noon to 3 p.m. and 6 to 10 p.m.

✔ **Sea-Shell** (49–51 Lisson Grove, NW1; ☎ 020/7723-8703; Tube: Marylebone) is within easy walking distance west of Madame Tussaud's and is considered one of the best chippies in London. It's open Monday through Friday noon to 2 p.m. and 5:15 to 10:30 p.m., Saturday noon to 10:30 p.m., and Sunday noon to 2:30 p.m.

✔ **Seafresh Fish Restaurant** (80–81 Wilton Rd., SW1; (☎ 020/7828-0747; Tube: Victoria), offers a good cod fillet and great chips for about £8 ($13). It's open Monday through Saturday noon to 10:30 p.m.

✔ **Costas Fish Restaurant** (18 Hillgate St., W8; ☎ 020/7727-4310; Tube: Notting Hill Gate) is open Tuesday through Saturday noon to 2:30 p.m. and 5:30 to 10:30 p.m.

✔ **Geales** (2 Farmer St., W8; ☎ 020/7727-7969; Tube: Notting Hill Gate) is open Tuesday through Saturday noon to 3 p.m. and 6 to 11 p.m.

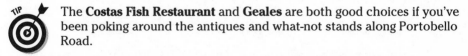

The **Costas Fish Restaurant** and **Geales** are both good choices if you've been poking around the antiques and what-not stands along Portobello Road.

Chomp Where You Shop: Department Store Restaurants

London is a great city for shopping, and you may not want to tear yourself away from the stores in order to get a bite to eat. The answer is to grab a bite at a department store restaurant. These eateries are convenient, but they aren't cheap. Here are a few of the most noteworthy:

✔ **Fortnum & Mason** (181 Piccadilly, W1; ☎ 020/7734-8040; Tube: Piccadilly) has three restaurants to choose from, the **Fountain** being the least expensive (see Chapter 14). Restaurant hours for the the Fountain are Monday through Saturday, 9 a.m. to 8 p.m.

✔ **Harrods** (87–135 Brompton Rd., SW1; ☎ 020/7730-1234; Tube: Knightsbridge), in addition to its ice-cream parlor and awe-inspiring Food Hall, offers its **Famous Deli Counter,** where you can perch on stools (no reservations) and pay too much for what's called "traditional Jewish food" but often isn't. It's open Monday through Saturday 10 a.m. to 6 p.m.

✔ **Harvey Nichols** (109–125 Knightsbridge, SW7; ☎ 020/7235-5250; Tube: Knightsbridge) is another Knightsbridge emporium with a restaurant, the **Fifth Floor at Harvey Nichols.** It's open Monday through Friday noon to 3 p.m. and for dinner 5:30 to 10:00 p.m., but eating there is pretty expensive. A better bet is the cafe, also on the fifth floor, where you can get a cup of tea and a salad or light meal; it's open Monday through Saturday 10 a.m. to 11 p.m. and Sunday 10 a.m. to 6 p.m. Like Harrods, Harvey Nichols has a fabulous food emporium where you can buy now and eat later.

Stop for a Spot of Tea: Simple and Lavish Teas

The stereotype is true in this case: Brits do drink tea. In fact, they drink 171 million cups per day (give or take a cup). Tea may be served fast-food style in paper cups, home-style in mugs, or more elegantly in bone china.

Casual tea rooms and pâtisseries

In the following comfortable neighborhood tearooms and pâtisseries, you can get a good cup of tea along with a scone or other pastry or a plate of tea sandwiches for about £3 to £10 ($5–$17):

✔ **Beverly Hills Bakery** (3 Egerton Terrace, SW3; ☎ 020/7584-4401; Tube: Knightsbridge) is noted for its muffins and serves light lunches from noon on. It's open Monday through Saturday 7:30 a.m. to 6:00 p.m. and Sunday 8:00 a.m. to 5:30 p.m.

✔ **Muffinski's** (5 King St., WC2; ☎ 020/7379-1525; Tube: Leicester Square) offers a great lowfat, homemade, vegetarian muffin. It's open Monday through Friday 8 a.m. to 7 p.m., Saturday 9 a.m. to 7 p.m., and Sunday 10 a.m. to 6 p.m.

✔ **Pâtisserie Cappucetto** (8 Moor St., W1; ☎ 020/7437-9472; Tube: Leicester Square) serves breakfast, sandwiches, soups, and superb desserts daily 7:30 a.m. to 11:30 p.m.

✔ **Pâtisserie Deux Amis** (63 Judd St., WC1; ☎ 020/7383-7029; Tube: Russell Square) is a good choice for a quick bite. It's open Monday through Friday 9:00 a.m. to 5:30 p.m. and Saturday and Sunday 9:00 a.m. to 1:30 p.m.

✔ **Pâtisserie Valerie** (44 Old Compton St., W1; ☎ 020/7437-3466; Tube: Leicester Square or Tottenham Court Road) has been around since 1926 and serves a mouthwatering array of pastries, but expect to stand in line night or day. It's open Monday through Friday 8 a.m. to 8 p.m., Saturday 8 a.m. to 7 p.m., and Sunday 9:30 a.m. to 6:00 p.m.

Pâtisserie Valerie has two branches in Marylebone (one at 105 Marylebone High St., W1; ☎ 020/7935-6240; Tube: Bond Street or Baker Street, and the other near Regent's Park at 66 Portland Place, W1; ☎ 020/7631-0467; Tube: Regent's Park). Both are open Monday through Friday 7:30 a.m. to 7:00 p.m., Saturday 8 a.m. to 7 p.m. and Sunday 9 a.m. to 6 p.m.

✔ **Richoux** has three old-fashioned tearooms situated in choice London locations. They serve food all day long, and they're kind to your budget: **Richoux-Knightsbridge,** (215 Brompton Rd., SW3; ☎ 020/7823-9971; Tube: Knightsbridge); **Richoux-Mayfair,** (41a South Audley St., W1; ☎ 020/7629-5228; Tube: Bond Street or Green Park); **Richoux-Piccadilly,** (172 Piccadilly, W1; ☎ 020/7493-2204; Tube: Piccadilly Circus).

Elegant spots for afternoon and high tea

A traditional afternoon English tea, which has cakes, sandwiches, and scones with clotted cream and jam, and which is "taken" in a high-toned hotel or restaurant, can be an afternoon affair or a nice alternative to lunch or dinner.

So what exactly, you ask, is the difference between afternoon tea and high tea?

✔ **Afternoon tea** is tea with cakes and/or sandwiches, served between 3 and 5 p.m.

✔ **High tea,** served from about 5 to 6 p.m., is a more elaborate affair: High tea includes a light supper with a hot dish, followed by dessert and tea.

These rather lavish affairs are expensive. You're paying for the location, the food, and the service. But at any one of the following places, you can get a very proper traditional tea without busting the bank or breaking a tooth:

✔ The **Palm Court Lounge,** in the Park Lane Hotel (Piccadilly, W1; ☎ 020/7499-6321; Tube: Hyde Park Corner or Green Park), requires that you make reservations. Teatime is daily 3:30 to 6:30 p.m., and afternoon tea runs £16 ($26).

✔ **Ritz Palm Court,** in the Ritz Hotel (Piccadilly, W1; ☎ 020/7493-8181; Tube: Green Park), requires reservations at least eight weeks in advance. Men must wear jackets and ties. Teatime is daily 2 to 6 p.m., and afternoon tea is £27 ($45).

✔ **Fortnum & Mason** (181 Piccadilly, W1; ☎ 020/7734-8040; Tube: Piccadilly Circus) offers two venues for tea. **St. James's** serves tea Monday through Saturday 3 to 5:30 p.m. at a cost of £16.50 ($27); the **Fountain** serves tea Monday through Saturday 3 to 6 p.m. for £12.95 ($21).

✔ **Palm Court at the Waldorf Meridien Hotel** (Aldwych, WC2; ☎ 020/7836-2400; Tube: Covent Garden) serves afternoon tea Monday through Friday 3 to 5:30 p.m., and holds tea dances (live music) on Saturdays 2:30 to 5:30 p.m. and Sundays 4:00 to 6:30 p.m. You must make reservations. If you want to attend the tea dance, men must wear jackets and ties. Afternoon tea runs £18 to £21 ($30–$35), and the tea dance £25 to £28 ($41–$46).

✔ **Georgian Restaurant,** on the fourth floor of Harrods (87–135 Brompton Rd., SW1; ☎ 020/7225-6800; Tube: Knightsbridge), serves high tea Monday through Saturday 3:45 to 5:30 p.m. (last order). It runs £18 ($30) per person.

✔ **Lanesborough** hotel (Hyde Park Corner, SW1; ☎ 020/7259-5599; Tube: Hyde Park Corner) requires reservations for high tea daily 3:30 to 5:30 p.m. (last order). The cost runs £20.50 ($34); the price goes up to £26.50 ($44) if you add strawberries and champagne.

Slurp Up Spaghetti: Pasta Parlors

If you're backpacking around London on a budget or you just want to save some dough, visit a pasta parlor for a plate of spaghetti or cannelloni. These places are open for lunch and dinner, and you can get a fixed-price meal that includes two or three courses for about £10 ($17).

Spaghetti House has several locations in Central London (the last two in the following list operate under different names):

- 20 Sicilian Ave., WC1; ☎ **020/7405-5215;** Tube: Holborn

- 30 St. Martin's Lane, WC2; ☎ **020/7836-1626;** Tube: Leicester Square

- 15 Goodge St., W1; ☎ **020/7636-6582;** Tube: Goodge Street

- **Vecchia Milano,** 74 Welbeck St., W1; ☎ **020/7935-2371;** Tube: Bond Street

- **Zia Teresa,** 6 Hans Rd., SW3; ☎ **020/7589-7634;** Tube Knightsbridge

All the preceding locations welcome children; they have high chairs and reduced-price kids' portions.

Another big pasta chain, **Cafe Uno,** with more than 20 branches, also provides these items for kids. The most popular branch is at 5 Argyll St., W1 (☎ **020/7437-2503;** Tube: Oxford Circus).

Nip in for a Treat: Ice Cream Stores

Nearly everybody likes ice cream, and **Häagen-Dazs** has several well-placed branches in tourist-heavy sections of London:

- 14 Leicester Sq.; ☎ **020/7287-9577;** Tube: Leicester Square

- Unit 6, Covent Garden Piazza; ☎ **020/7240-0436;** Tube: Covent Garden

- 83 Gloucester Rd., SW7; ☎ **020/7373-9988;** Tube: Gloucester Road

The preceding are nonsmoking places that welcome kids, provide high chairs, and offer children's portions. They're open daily 10 a.m. to 11 p.m. (sometimes to midnight in summer).

More upscale (and overpriced) is **Harrods Ice-Cream Parlour & Crêperie** (87 Brompton Rd., SW1; ☎ **020/7225-6628;** Tube: Knightsbridge), on the fourth floor of Harrods department store. It's open Monday, Tuesday, and Saturday 10:00 a.m. to 5:30 p.m. and Wednesday through Friday 10:00 a.m. to 6:30 p.m.

Farther west in Bayswater, you find **Winton's Soda Fountain** on the second floor of Whiteley's Shopping Centre (151 Queensway, W2; ☎ **020/7229-8489;** Tube: Bayswater or Queensway). It's open Monday through Thursday and Sunday 11 a.m. to 10 p.m. and Friday and Saturday 11 a.m. to 11 p.m.

Regent Milk Bar (362 Edgware Rd., W9; ☎ 020/7723-8669; Tube: Edgware Road) is a classic 1950s milk bar offering about a dozen flavors of ice cream. You can also get sandwiches and snacks. Popular with families, it's open daily 7:30 a.m. to 5:30 p.m.

Take Advantage of a Nice Day: Alfresco Dining

London may not be the perfect city for picnics. Rain can quickly put a damper on a picnic hamper, and nothing is quite as unappetizing as a wet sandwich. But on days when the weather cooperates, you may enjoy packing up some sandwiches and heading to a green spot to eat.

Delis and sandwich shops or expensive **Fortnum & Mason** or **Harrods,** whose Food Halls are legendary (see Chapter 19), can provide all the necessary picnic provisions, if you're in the West End. In neighborhoods outside of the West End (South Kensington or Marylebone, for example), you can go into any supermarket and generally find packaged sandwiches, crisps (potato chips), fresh fruit, and drinks.

In the West End, the **Embankment Gardens** is a pretty picnic spot, looking out on the Thames. This flower-filled strip of green is next to the Embankment Tube station, below The Savoy Hotel. You have to sit on benches instead of the grass and the traffic noise along the Embankment can be annoying, but it's still a nice place to know about.

Kensington Gardens (see Chapter 16) offers vast green lawns, frolicsome fountains, Kensington Palace, and the famous statue of Peter Pan. This spot is a favorite with children of all ages. The Princess Diana Memorial Playground in the garden's northwestern corner makes a wonderful play area. The park is close to all the great museums in South Ken. Adjacent **Hyde Park** is another lovely picnic site, particularly along the shores of Serpentine Lake. You can buy sandwiches and snacks at the Dell Restaurant (see Chapter 16) at the east end of the lake. In summer, bandstand concerts are given in the park.

The *royal parks* — **Green Park** and **St. James's Park** — are more sedate. You can choose to picnic on a lovely knoll and gaze upon Buckingham Palace.

Looking for an urban space good for people watching and with great views across the river? Picnic on the **South Bank** of the Thames, along the riverside promenade close to Royal Festival Hall and the National Theatre. Beside the busy Thames are trees and flowers — but no lawns for stretching out.

Part V
Exploring London

The 5th Wave   By Rich Tennant

In this part...

After you arrive at your hotel, unpack, and maybe grab a bite to eat, you can finally begin the real fun. Consult your list of must-sees, examine a street map and an Underground map, and prepare for your first taste of all that London offers.

If you're traveling with children, have limited time, or are a bit nervous about exploring on your own, turn to Chapter 18 for a list of guided tours. On the other hand, if you're raring to see the top sights on your own, you can find them — along with directions, open hours, and admission prices — in Chapter 16. Browse through Chapter 17's rundown of additional intriguing museums and sights (not the most popular, but definitely worth considering) to see your many options.

Check out Chapter 19 for some great tips on how to make the most of your shopping in London, as well as for specific stores to visit. In Chapter 20, you find some suggested London itineraries that include sightseeing strategies to help you enjoy the city on a *realistic* schedule. Finally, in Chapter 21, I wave you off at the train station and send you on your way to some fascinating places you can explore on a day trip. I think you'll love each and every one of them.

Chapter 16

London's Top Sights

*H*ere's the big question: What do you want to see and enjoy while you're in London? The possibilities are endless: fabulous museums, important historic sites, beautiful parks and gardens, and grand churches. Advance planning will ease your stress and save time when you reach this great city. In this chapter, I give you the information you need to make your itinerary fit your interests, time, and energy level.

To help you find your way around London, I recommend that you supplement my directions in this chapter with a *London A to Z* map. If you do get turned around, ask someone who's likely to know the area, such as a shop owner. Londoners are usually polite and helpful.

Because London is a city with 150 museums, 600 art galleries, and countless places of historic interest, you need to plan considerably for sightseeing. To help you pull together your itinerary, see the end of this chapter where I index the best attractions by neighborhood and type.

I arranged the sights in this chapter alphabetically. For locations, see the "London's Top Sights" map in this chapter. For kid-pleasing attractions, look for the Kid Friendly icon.

If you're a disabled visitor on wheels, you can still visit every sight that I mention in this chapter. Churches and museums provide wheelchair access, but you should call first because you may need to use a special entrance. The paths in the royal parks are generally flat and paved.

The sights in this chapter make up my roster of the most important, but they represent only the tip of the iceberg. Chapter 17 offers plenty more locations to choose from. To help in your planning, use the "Going 'My' Way" worksheet at the end of this guide. For useful information about planning workable itineraries based on the length of your trip, turn to Chapter 20.

London's Top Sights

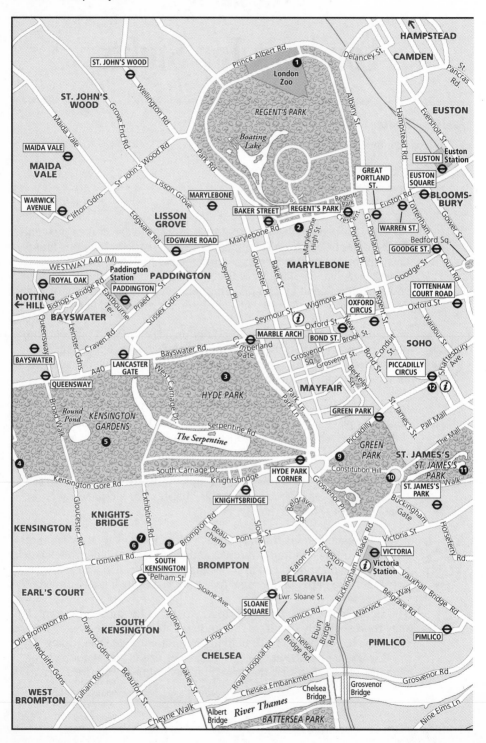

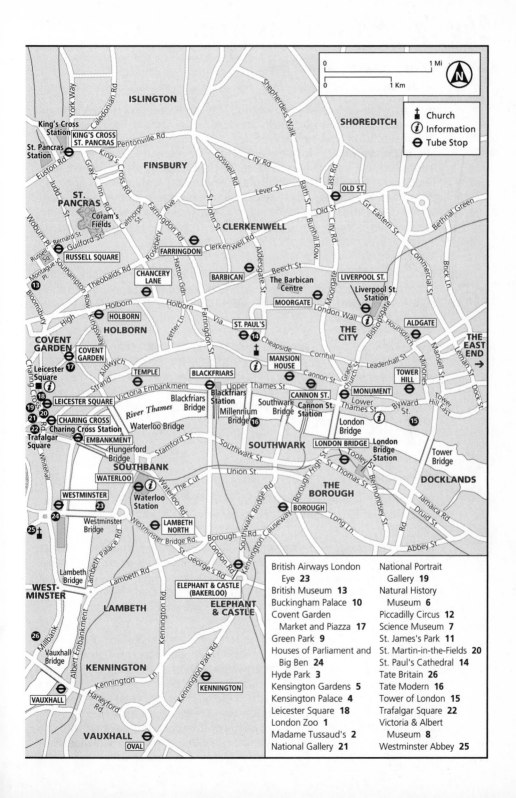

0 | 1 Mi
0 | 1 Km

N

✝ Church
ⓘ Information
⊖ Tube Stop

ISLINGTON

SHOREDITCH

King's Cross Station
KING'S CROSS ST. PANCRAS
St. Pancras Station
Pentonville Rd.

FINSBURY

City Rd.

OLD ST.

ST. PANCRAS

Coram's Fields

CLERKENWELL

Clerkenwell Rd.

RUSSELL SQUARE

FARRINGDON

CHANCERY LANE

BARBICAN

The Barbican Centre

LIVERPOOL ST.

Liverpool St. Station

ALDGATE

13

HOLBORN

HOLBORN

ST. PAUL'S

MOORGATE

London Wall

THE CITY

THE EAST END →

COVENT GARDEN

COVENT GARDEN

14

MANSION HOUSE

Leicester Square

TEMPLE

BLACKFRIARS

17

LEICESTER SQUARE

Blackfriars Station

CANNON ST.

TOWER HILL

MONUMENT

18

CHARING CROSS

River Thames

Blackfriars Bridge

Millennium Bridge

16

Southwark Bridge

Cannon St. Station

15

19
20
21
22

Charing Cross Station

Waterloo Bridge

London Bridge

Tower Bridge

Trafalgar Square

EMBANKMENT

Hungerford Bridge

SOUTHWARK

LONDON BRIDGE

London Bridge Station

DOCKLANDS

SOUTHBANK

WATERLOO

Waterloo Station

THE BOROUGH

WESTMINSTER

23

LAMBETH NORTH

BOROUGH

24

Westminster Bridge

25

WEST-MINSTER

Lambeth Bridge

ELEPHANT & CASTLE (BAKERLOO)

ELEPHANT & CASTLE

LAMBETH

26

Vauxhall Bridge

KENNINGTON

KENNINGTON

VAUXHALL

VAUXHALL

OVAL

British Airways London Eye **23**
British Museum **13**
Buckingham Palace **10**
Covent Garden Market and Piazza **17**
Green Park **9**
Houses of Parliament and Big Ben **24**
Hyde Park **3**
Kensington Gardens **5**
Kensington Palace **4**
Leicester Square **18**
London Zoo **1**
Madame Tussaud's **2**
National Gallery **21**
National Portrait Gallery **19**
Natural History Museum **6**
Piccadilly Circus **12**
Science Museum **7**
St. James's Park **11**
St. Martin-in-the-Fields **20**
St. Paul's Cathedral **14**
Tate Britain **26**
Tate Modern **16**
Tower of London **15**
Trafalgar Square **22**
Victoria & Albert Museum **8**
Westminster Abbey **25**

The Top Attractions from A to Z

British Airways London Eye
South Bank

As a piece of fast-track engineering, the 400-foot-high London Eye millennium observation wheel is impressive. Having ridden on it, I know that the observation pod feels safe. Each glass-sided elliptical module holds about 25 passengers, with enough space so you can move about freely. Although most people stand the entire time, you can sit on the available bench if you prefer. Lasting about 30 minutes (equivalent to one rotation), the ride (or *flight* as they call it) is remarkably smooth — even on windy days riders don't feel any nerve-twittering shakes. Providing that the weather is good, the wheel provides unrivaled views of London. It's scheduled to remain in operation until at least 2003.

For the London Eye, I recommend that you reserve your place (with a specific entry time) before you arrive; if you're ticketless, you can line up for a ticket at the office right behind the wheel, but you may have to wait an hour or two.

Bridge Road, SE1 (beside Westminster Bridge). ☎ *0870/500-0600 (advance credit-card booking; 50p [$1] booking fee added). Tube: Westminster (then a 5-minute walk south across Westminster Bridge; or Waterloo, then a 3-minute walk west along the riverside promenade). Admission: £7.95 ($13) adults, £6.45 ($11) seniors, £5.45 ($9) children under 16. Open: April–Oct daily 9 a.m.–10 p.m.; Nov–March daily 10 a.m.–6 p.m.*

British Museum
Bloomsbury

The British Museum ranks as the most visited attraction in London, with a splendid, wide-ranging collection of treasures from around the world.

Wandering through the museum's 94 galleries (see the map, "British Museum"), you can't help but be struck by humanity's enduring creative spirit. Permanent displays of antiquities from Egypt, Western Asia, Greece, and Rome are on view, as well as prehistoric and Romano-British, Medieval, Renaissance, Modern, and Oriental collections.

The most famous of the countless treasures are the superb **Parthenon Sculptures** (known in less politically correct times as the Elgin Marbles, brought to England in the 1801 by the seventh Lord Elgin) that once adorned the Parthenon in Athens (and which Greece desperately wants returned); the **Rosetta Stone** (which enabled archaeologists to decipher Egyptian hieroglyphics); the **Sutton Hoo Treasure,** an Anglo-Saxon burial ship, believed to be the tomb of a 7th-century East Anglian king; and **Lindow Man,** a well-preserved ancient corpse found in a bog. The museum's

British Museum

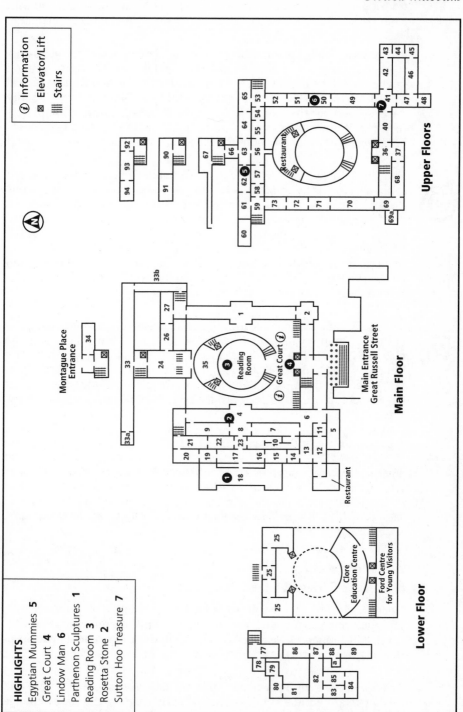

HIGHLIGHTS
Egyptian Mummies **5**
Great Court **4**
Lindow Man **6**
Parthenon Sculptures **1**
Reading Room **3**
Rosetta Stone **2**
Sutton Hoo Treasure **7**

ⓘ Information
⊠ Elevator/Lift
▥ Stairs

Upper Floors

Main Floor

Montague Place Entrance

Reading Room

Great Court

Main Entrance
Great Russell Street

Restaurant

Lower Floor

Clore Education Centre

Ford Centre for Young Visitors

ethnography collections are filled with marvelous curiosities: everything from a pair of polar-bear slacks worn by Eskimos to a Hawaiian god with a Mohawk haircut, found by Captain Cook and shipped back to London.

In November 2000, the museum's **Great Court** reopened with a glass-and-steel roof designed by Lord Norman Foster. Inaccessible to the general public for 150 years, the Great Court is now the museum's new central axis. In the center you find a circular building completed in 1857 that once served as the museum's famous **Reading Room.** Completely restored, it now houses computer terminals where visitors can access images and information about the museum's vast collections.

I suggest you give yourself at least three unhurried hours here. You can avoid big crowds by going on a weekday morning. If you get hungry along the way, the museum has a cafe and a restaurant in the Great Court and another cafe next to Room 12. You may want to pick up a *Visit Guide* to help you chart your way. It costs £2.50 ($3.75) and is available at the information desks in the Great Court. To enhance your enjoyment and understanding of the Parthenon Sculptures, pick up one of the sound guides available right outside Room 18 on the first floor, where the sculptures are exhibited; payment is by contribution.

If you have only limited time for the British Museum, consider taking one of the 90-minute highlight tours offered daily at 11 a.m. and 3 p.m; the cost is £7 ($11). The 60-minute focus tour, offered daily at 1 p.m. and Thursday and Friday at 5:30 and 7 p.m., covers some of the most important objects in the museum's collections; the cost is £5 ($8). You can get tickets and information for both tours at the information desk in the Great Court.

Great Russell St., WC1, between Bloomsbury Street and Montgomery Street ☎ *020/7636-1555. Tube: Russell Square (then a 5-minute walk south on Montgomery Street, along the west side of Russell Square, to the museum entrance on Great Russell Street). Admission: free. Most of the museum has wheelchair access via elevators; call for entrance information. Open: Mon 9 a.m.–5 p.m., Tues–Wed 9 a.m.–8 p.m., Thurs–Sat 9 a.m.–9 p.m., Sun 9 a.m.–8 p.m.; closed Jan 1, Good Friday, Dec 24–26.*

Buckingham Palace
St. James's Park and Green Park

Since 1837, when Victoria ascended the throne, all the majesty, scandal, intrigue, triumph, tragedy, power, wealth, and tradition associated with the British monarchy has been hidden behind the monumental facade of Buckingham Palace, the reigning monarch's London residence.

An impressive early-18th-century pile, the palace was rebuilt in 1825 and further modified in 1913. Late July or early August (the dates change

The power of the written word

The incredible literary collection that was once housed in the British Museum Reading Room (including its rare copy of the *Magna Carta,* the charter of liberties that was a forerunner to modern constitutions) has been moved to a remarkable new space in North London. For details, see the entry for the **British Library Exhibition Galleries** in Chapter 17.

yearly) to September, when the royal family isn't in residence, you can buy a ticket to get a glimpse of the impressive staterooms used by Elizabeth II and the other royals. You don't get a guided palace tour; you can wander at your own speed through 18 rooms, most of them baroque, filled with some of the world's finest artworks. In these rooms the Queen receives guests on official occasions. You leave via the gardens where the Queen holds her famous garden parties each summer. Budget about two hours for your visit.

On Monday through Thursday throughout the year, you can visit the **Royal Mews,** one of the finest working stables in existence, where the magnificent Gold State Coach, used in every coronation since 1831, and other royal conveyances are housed (and horses stabled). The **Queen's Gallery,** which features changing exhibits of works from the Royal Collection, has been closed for refurbishment but will reopen in time for the Queen's Golden Jubilee in June 2002.

You can charge tickets for Buckingham Palace tours by calling the Visitor Office at ☎ 020/7321-2233. Green Park also houses a ticket office, open daily July 29 to October 1; the office opens at 9 a.m. and closes at 4 p.m. or when the last ticket has been sold. Keep in mind that every visitor gets a specific time for entry into the palace, which is why phoning ahead for tickets is smart. You save yourself the time and bother of queuing for tickets outside the palace and then having to return hours later to get in. All phone-charged tickets are £12.50 ($19); at the ticket booth special rates are available for seniors, kids under 17, and families.

Buckingham Palace Road, SW1. Palace Visitor Office and Royal Mews ☎ 020/ 7839-1377 (9:30 a.m.–5:30 p.m.) or 020/7799-2331 (24-hour recorded info). Tube: St. James's Park (then a 10-minute walk north on Queen Anne's Gate and west on Birdcage Walk to Buckingham Gate); or Green Park (walk directly south through the park). Admission: Palace, £11 ($16) adults, £9 ($14) seniors, £5.50 ($8) children under 17, £27.50 ($41) families (2 adults/2 children under 17). Royal Mews, £4.30 ($6) adults, £3.30 ($4.45) seniors, £2.10 ($3.15) children, £10.70 ($16) families. Open: Palace, July 29–Oct 1 (these dates may vary by a day or two) daily 9:30 a.m.–4:15 p.m. Royal Mews, year-round Mon–Thurs noon to 4 p.m.; closed Dec 25–26. Visitors with disabilities must prebook for palace visits; Royal Mews is wheelchair accessible.

Changing of the Guard at Buckingham Palace
St. James's Park

Free of charge, you can stand outside Buckingham Palace and watch the Changing of the Guard. The Foot Guards of the Household Division of the Army, the Queen's personal guard, carry out the ritual. The Old Guard forms in the palace forecourt before going off duty and handing everything over to the New Guard, which leaves Wellington Barracks at precisely 11:27 a.m. and marches to the palace via Birdcage Walk, usually accompanied by a band. The Guard consists of three officers and 40 men, but this number decreases when the Queen is away. The entire ceremony takes around 40 minutes. If you can't find a spot at the front of the railings of Buckingham Palace, you can see pretty well from the Victoria Memorial in front of the palace.

The pageantry of the Changing of the Guard is no longer a daily occurrence. The event takes place at 11:30 a.m. daily April 1 to early June but only on alternate days at other times of the year. To avoid disappointment, make sure to call ahead or check the Web site listed in the next paragraph.

Buckingham Palace Road, SW1. ☎ *020/7799-2331 (24-hour recorded info). Internet:* www.LondonTown.com/changingguards.phtml. *Tube: St. James's Park (then a ten-minute walk north on Queen Anne's Gate and west on Birdcage Walk to Buckingham Gate); or Green Park (walk directly south through the park). Admission: Free.*

Royal scandals

Things came to a head for the scandal-ridden House of Windsor after Princess Diana's death in 1997, when national polls showed that the British public viewed the monarchy as aloof, out of touch, and a waste of taxpayers' money. The Queen was so shocked at the findings (so out of touch) that she hired a Washington-style spin doctor to boost the family's sagging ratings. The results have been mixed, and royal scandals continue. In April 2001, Sophie Rhys-Jones (who's trying unsuccessfully to pass herself off as Diana II), wife of Prince Edward, was caught in a royally embarrassing blackmail scheme by a newspaper reporter posing as a rich sheik and potential client of her public relations firm. Lambasted by the press for the way she used her royal connections for personal gain, she was forced by the Queen to give up her lucrative job. By the way, did you know the Windsors are really the Saxe-Coburg-Gothas? They changed their German name at the onset of World War I. And they have their own official Royal Web site, www.royal.gov.uk, although you won't find any scandals on it.

More changing of the Guard

If you miss the Changing of the Guard or the event doesn't take place on the day of your visit, you can still get an eyeful of London pageantry by attending the **Mounted Guard Changing Ceremony** at the Horse Guards Building in Whitehall. The ceremony takes place daily Monday through Saturday at 11 a.m. and Sunday at 10 a.m. No ticket is required, but arrive early for a good view. To get there, take the tube to Charing Cross and walk south from Trafalgar Square along Whitehall (about a 5-minute walk); the Horse Guards Building will be on your right.

Covent Garden Market and Piazza
Covent Garden

In 1970, the old market — the noisy, bustling public market where vendors hawked everything under the sun — moved out of Covent Garden and the area became the site of one of London's earliest and most successful urban recycling efforts. The market buildings now house dozens of enticing shops and eating and drinking places. The wrought-iron stalls in the former Flower Market are loaded with vendors. The piazza in front may be the most popular public gathering place outside of Trafalgar Square; the space is always "heaving," as the Brits say. Covent Garden is also the home of the **Royal Opera House** (see Chapter 23) and two excellent museums: the **Transport Museum** and the **Theatre Museum** (see Chapter 17 for descriptions of both).

Tube: Covent Garden (when you come out of the tube stop you're in Covent Garden; the Market and piazza is a 1-minute walk south in a pedestrian-only zone).

Houses of Parliament and Big Ben
Westminster

Big Ben is synonymous with the city of London. The **Houses of Parliament,** situated along the Thames, house the landmark clock tower containing **Big Ben.** Designed by Sir Charles Barry and A.W.N. Pugin, the impressive Victorian buildings were completed in 1857. Covering approximately 8 acres, they occupy the site of an 11th-century palace of Edward the Confessor.

At one end (Old Palace Yard) you find the **Jewel House,** built in 1366 and once the treasury house of Edward III, who reigned from 1327 to 1377. The best view is from Westminster Bridge, but if you prefer, you can sit in the **Stranger's Gallery** to hear Parliament debate.

Previously, overseas visitors had to go through an elaborate procedure weeks in advance of their trip in order to tour the Houses of Parliament. Now, however, 75-minute guided tours are available Monday through Saturday for an eight-week period every summer (generally from the second week in August until the end of September). The tours cost £5.25 ($8), and booking your ticket in advance is recommended. The London ticket office in Westminster Hall (at the Houses of Parliament) opens in mid-July. You can reserve by phone at ☎ 020/7344-9966 or order tickets online at www.ticketmaster.co.uk. For the rest of the year, the procedure for getting a tour is much more difficult. If you're interested, you can find details on the Web at www.parliament.uk.

Bridge Street and Parliament Square, SW1. ☎ *020/7219-3000; 020/7219-4272 for the House's schedule and topics of debate. Tube: Westminster (you can see the clock tower with Big Ben directly across Bridge Street when you exit the tube). Admission: free. For tickets, join the line at St. Stephen's entrance. Open: Stranger's Gallery, Mon–Wed 2:30–10:30 p.m., Thurs 11:30 a.m.–7:30 p.m., most Fridays 9:30 a.m.– 3:00 p.m. Parliament isn't in session late July to mid-Oct or on weekends.*

Hyde Park
Westminster

With adjoining Kensington Gardens, Hyde Park offers 630 acres of lushly landscaped lawns, magnificent flower beds, avenues of trees, and a 41-acre lake known as the **Serpentine,** where you can row and sail model boats. **Rotten Row,** the park's famous 300-year-old riding track, was the country's first public road to be lit at night. At the northeastern tip, near Marble Arch, is **Speakers' Corner,** a famous Sunday-morning venting spot for anyone who wants to climb up on a soapbox. Hyde Park, once the private hunting domain of the royals, including Henry VIII, is now open to everyone and is one of the largest urban free parks in the world.

Free band concerts are held in the park's bandshell on Sundays and Bank Holidays May to August, and the Dell Restaurant (☎ 020/7706-0464) at the east end of the Serpentine offers cafeteria-style food and drinks Monday through Friday 10 a.m. to 4 p.m. in winter (to 5 p.m. on weekends) and 10 a.m. to 6 p.m. in summer (to 7 p.m. on weekends). The park is a pleasant place for an hour's stroll, but staying longer is tempting.

Bounded by Knightsbridge to the south, Bayswater Road to the north, and Park Lane to the east. ☎ *020/7298-2100. Tube: Marble Arch or Lancaster Gate on the north side (the park is directly across Bayswater Road) or Hyde Park Corner in the southeast corner of the park. Open: Daily dawn to midnight.*

Kensington Gardens
Kensington

Kensington Gardens adjoins Hyde Park west of the lake known as the Serpentine. Children especially love the famous bronze statue of **Peter Pan,** located north of the Serpentine Bridge. Commissioned in 1912 by

Big Ben tolls for thee

Big Ben is not the name of the clock tower or its clock. It's the name of the largest bell that you hear booming in that famous hourly chime. Some believe that the bell was named after Sir Benjamin Hall, the commissioner of works when the bell was hung in 1859. Others maintain that Big Ben was named for a champion prizefighter of the time, Ben Gaunt.

The 5-ton clock mechanism housed in the 316-foot tower kept ticking until 1976, when it succumbed to "metal fatigue" and had to be repaired. At night, new energy-efficient lighting now gives the illuminated clock faces a greenish tinge. The light at the very top is lit when Parliament is in session.

Trivia buffs will be interested to know that the minute hand on each of the tower's four clocks is as large as a double-decker bus.

Peter Pan's creator, J. M. Barrie, the statue marks the spot where Peter Pan in the book *Peter Pan in Kensington Gardens* entered the gardens to get to his home on Serpentine island.

The park is also home to the **Albert Memorial,** an ornate neo-Gothic memorial honoring Queen Victoria's husband, Prince Albert; the lovely **Italian Gardens;** and the free **Serpentine Gallery** (☎ **020/7298-1515**), which is gaining a reputation for showing cutting-edge art and is open daily (except December 24 to 27 and January 1) 10 a.m. to 6 p.m. The **Princess Diana Memorial Playground** is in the northwestern corner of the park. If the weather is fine, give yourself enough time for a leisurely stroll — at least a couple of hours.

Bounded by Kensington Palace Gardens and Palace Green on the west, Bayswater Road on the north, Kensington Road and Kensington Gore on the south. ☎ *020/ 7298-2100. Tube: High Street Kensington (then a 10-minute walk east on Kensington High Street) or Queensway (which is directly across from the northwest corner of the park). Open: Daily dawn to midnight.*

Kensington Palace
Kensington Gardens

Kensington Palace was used as a royal residence until 1760. Victoria was born in this palace, and here in 1837, she was informed she was the new Queen of England (and could move to the grander Buckingham Palace). One wing of Kensington Palace was Princess Diana's London home after her divorce from Prince Charles.

The palace is home to Princess Margaret and the duke and duchess of Kent, so portions of it are closed off to visitors. But you can see the **State**

Apartments and the **Royal Ceremonial Dress Collection's** "Dressing for Royalty" exhibit, which takes visitors through the process of being presented at court, from the first visit to the tailor/dressmaker to the final bow or curtsy. Dresses worn by Queen Victoria, Queen Elizabeth II, and Princess Diana are on display. The freshly restored **King's Apartment** features a magnificent collection of Old Masters. Give yourself about 1½ hours to view the palace.

For a pleasant and not-too-expensive tea or snack after visiting Kensington Palace, stop in at **The Orangery** (☎ **020/7376-0239**) in the gardens adjacent to the palace. The restaurant is open daily noon to 6 p.m. Lunches cost about £7 ($10); from 3 p.m. you can get a good tea for £6.95 to £12.95 ($10 to $19).

The Broad Walk, Kensington Gardens, W8. ☎ 020/7937-7079. Tube: Queensway on the north side (then a 10-minute walk south through the park) or High Street Kensington on the southwest side (then a 10-minute walk through the park). Open: Daily 10 a.m.–5 p.m. Admission: £8.80 ($13) adults, £6.90 ($10) seniors/children 5 and older. Wheelchair accessible, despite some stairs; however, call first.

Leicester Square
Soho

Leicester (pronounced *Les*-ter) Square is a crowded place with a big-city buzz. Mimes, singers, and street entertainers of all kinds vie for attention. Once a dueling ground, the square is now a pedestrian zone and the heart of West End entertainment. A half-price ticket booth (no phone) for theater, opera, and dance is at the south end of the square (see Chapter 23). In the square's center, surrounded by movie theaters and restaurants, is **Leicester Square Gardens,** with four corner gates named for William Hogarth, Sir Joshua Reynolds, John Hunter, and Sir Isaac Newton, all of whom once lived or worked in the area. You also find statues of William Shakespeare and Charlie Chaplin, a bow to theater and cinema. You probably won't want to linger long, but just walking through the square can be fun. If you're traveling with kids, this area is one place with a restroom (coin-operated).

Tube: Leicester Square (take the Leicester Square exit and you're in the pedestrian-only zone that leads to the square).

London Zoo
Regent's Park, Marylebone

The 36-acre London Zoo is Britain's largest, with about 8,000 animals in various species-specific houses. The best attractions are the **Insect House** (bird-eating spiders), the **Reptile House** (huge monitor lizards and a 15-foot python), the **Sobell Pavilion for Apes and Monkeys,** and the **Lion Terraces.** In the **Moonlight World,** special lighting effects simulate night for the nocturnal creatures, so you can see them in action. The newest exhibit, Web of Life, in the **Millennium Conservatory,** brings together special animal displays with interactive activities to show the interconnectedness and diversity of different life forms. The **Children's Zoo,** with interactive exhibits placed at low height, is designed for 4- to 8-year-olds. Many families budget almost an entire day for the zoo; I recommend that you give it at least three hours.

In 2001, a number of measures were established to protect London Zoo's animals against foot-and-mouth disease. All visitors must walk across disinfected matting upon entering. Visitors are also being asked whether they have been on a farm with animals or in contact with farm animals in the last seven days. If so, the zoo asks these visitors to postpone their visit to the Zoo until the foot-and-mouth outbreak is over. The Children's Zoo is closed to London Zoo's visitors as an extra precaution. For up-to-date information, you can check out the zoo's Web site at www.londonzoo.co.uk.

A fun way to arrive at the London Zoo is by water. The **London Waterbus Co.** (☎ 020/7482-2550) operates single and return trips in snug converted canalboats along the Regent's Canal from Warwick Crescent in Little Venice to Camden Lock Market. Take the tube to Warwick Avenue and walk south across Regent's Canal, and then you can see the moorings. Trips from both locks depart daily 10 a.m. to 5 p.m. The round-trip fare is £4 ($7).

At the north end of Regent's Park, NW1. ☎ *020/7722-3333; Internet:* www.londonzoo.co.uk. *Tube: Regent's Park (then bus C2 north on Albany Street to Delaney Street, 10-minute or a half-hour walk north through the park) or Camden Town (then a 12-minute walk south on Parkway, following the signs). Admission: £10 ($15) adults, £8.50 ($13) seniors/students/disabled, £7 ($12) children 3–14, £30 ($45) families (2 adults/2 children). Open: March–Oct daily 10:00 a.m.–5:30 p.m.; Nov–Feb daily 10 a.m.–4 p.m.;closed Dec 25.*

Madame Tussaud's
Marylebone

Madame Tussaud's wax museum is a world-famous tourist attraction and a fun spot for older kids. The question is: Do you want to pay the admission and devote the time to see the collection of lifelike figures? (Once in, you need at least 1½ hours to see everything.) The original moldings of members of the French court, to whom Madame Tussaud had direct access (literally, because she made molds of their heads after they were guillotined during the French Revolution), are undeniably fascinating. And animatronic gadgetry makes the **Spirit of London** theme ride fun. But the **Chamber of Horrors** is definitely for the ghoulish (parents with younger kids may want to think twice about wandering here). This exhibit allows you to see one of Jack the Ripper's victims lying in a pool of (wax?) blood and likenesses of mass murderers, such as Gary Gilmore and Charles Manson. You can see better stars next door, at the **London Planetarium** (see Chapter 17). The new **Superstars** exhibit features Hollywood faves like Nicolas Cage and Samuel L. Jackson.

When the Prince and Princess of Wales separated, their mannequins at Madame Tussaud's were moved slightly apart. When they divorced, Diana was moved to the end of the royal line, but after her death she was brought down from the royal enclosure so that people can get closer to her (or it, I should say).

Go early to beat the crowds; better still, reserve tickets one day in advance, then go straight to the head of the line. You can order tickets by phone or online (see the next paragraph for contact information).

Marylebone Road, NW1. ☎ 020/7935-6861; Internet: www.madame-tussauds.com. *Tube: Baker Street (then a 2-minute walk east on Marylebone Road). Admission: £11.95 ($18) adults, £9.45 ($13) seniors, £8.45 ($12) children under 16; children under 4 not admitted. Combination tickets (including the planetarium): £14.45 ($21) adults, £11.25 ($17) seniors, £9.95 ($15) children under 16. Open: June–Aug 9:00 a.m.–5:30 p.m. daily; Sept–May 10:00 a.m.–5:30 p.m. Mon–Fri, Sat–Sun 9:20 a.m.–5:30 p.m. Wheelchair accessible via elevators, but call first because only three chair-users are allowed in at a time.*

National Gallery
Trafalgar Square, St. James's

If you're passionate about great art, then you'll think that the National Gallery is paradise. This museum houses one of the world's most comprehensive collections of British and European paintings. All the major schools from the 13th to the 20th century are represented, but the Italians get the lion's share of wall space, with works by artists such as Leonardo da Vinci, Botticelli, and Raphael. The French Impressionist and post-Impressionist works by Monet, Manet, Seurat, Cézanne, Degas, and van Gogh are splendid. And because you're on English soil, check out at least a few of Turner's stunning seascapes, Constable's landscapes, and Reynolds' society portraits. And you won't want to miss the Rembrandts. Budget at least two hours to enjoy the gallery. The second floor has a good restaurant for lunch, tea, or snacks.

Use the free computer information center to make the most of your time at the gallery. The center allows you to design a tour based on your preferences (a maximum of 10 paintings from the 2,200 entries) and prints out a customized tour map. You can also rent a portable audio tour guide for £3 ($4.50). Every painting has a reference number. Punch in the appropriate number to hear information about any work that interests you.

Trafalgar Square, WC2. ☎ 020/7747-2885. Tube: Charing Cross (then a 2-minute walk north across Trafalgar Square). Admission: Free, but special exhibits may require paying a fee, usually around £5 ($8). Open: Mon–Tues and Thurs –Sun 10 a.m.–6 p.m., Wed 10 a.m.–9 p.m.; closed Jan 1, Good Friday, Dec 24–26. The entire museum is wheelchair accessible.

Picture-perfect Queen Mum

The Royal Family portrait commissioned by the National Portrait Gallery to celebrate the Queen Mother's 100th birthday (in 2000) is the newest royal addition to go on display in the National Portrait Gallery. Artist John Wonnacott painted the canvas that portrays Queen Elizabeth, Prince Phillip, Prince Charles, and Princes William and Harry in conversation with the Queen Mother in the White Drawing Room in Buckingham Palace. Interestingly, Prince William — Charles' firstborn and thus the second in line to the throne — dominates the picture.

National Portrait Gallery
Trafalgar Square

What do these people all have in common: Sir Walter Raleigh, Shakespeare (wearing a gold earring), Queen Elizabeth I, the Brontë sisters, Winston Churchill, Oscar Wilde, Noël Coward, Mick Jagger, and Princess Di? You can find lifelike portraits of them, as well as nearly every other famous English face, at the National Portrait Gallery. The portraits are arranged in chronological order. The earliest portraits are in the **Tudor Gallery;** portraits from the 1960s to the 1980s are displayed in the **Balcony Gallery.** The rooftop cafe provides great West End views. Plan on spending at least two hours, but getting sidetracked here is easy, so you may want more time.

St. Martin's Place (off Trafalgar Square behind the National Gallery), WC2. ☎ 020/ 7306-0055. Tube: Leiceister Square (then a 2-minute walk south on Charing Cross Road). Admission: Free; audio tour £3 ($5). Open: Mon 11 a.m.–6 p.m., Tues–Sat 10 a.m.–6 p.m., Sun noon to 6 p.m. All but the landing galleries are wheelchair accessible; call first for entry instructions.

Natural History Museum
South Kensington

Filled with magnificent specimens and exciting displays relating to natural history, this museum houses the national collections of living and fossil plants, animals, and minerals. The most popular attraction in this enormous Victorian-era museum is the huge **Dinosaurs** exhibit, with 14 complete skeletons and a trio of full-size, robotic Deinonychus lunching on a freshly killed Tenontosaurus. Bug-filled **Creepy Crawlies** is another popular kid pleaser. The sparkling gems and crystals in the **Mineral Gallery** literally dazzle, and in the **Meteorite Pavilion** you can see fragments of rock that crashed into the earth from the farthest reaches of the galaxy. The museum offers enough to keep you occupied for at least two hours.

Cromwell Road, SW7. ☎ *020/7942-5000. Tube: South Kensington (the tube station is on the corner of Cromwell Road and Exhibition Road, at the corner of the museum). Admission: Free. Open: Mon–Sat 10:00 a.m.–5:50 p.m., Sun 11:00 a.m.– 5:50 p.m. Nearly all the galleries are flat or ramped for wheelchair users; call for instructions on entering the building.*

Piccadilly Circus
The West End

Nearly everyone who visits London wants to see Piccadilly Circus, which lies at the beginning of the West End. Piccadilly Circus, along with neighboring Leicester Square, is London's equivalent to New York's Times Square. Around the landmark statue of Eros, jostling crowds pack the pavements and an international group of teens heads for the **Pepsi Trocadero,** the area's mega-entertainment center (see Chapter 17). Regent Street at the west side of the circus and Piccadilly at the south end are major shopping streets (see Chapter 19). Piccadilly, traditionally the western road out of town, was named for the "picadil," a ruffled collar created by a 17th-century tailor named Robert Baker.

Tube: Piccadilly Circus.

Science Museum
South Kensington

The Science Museum is a popular tourist attraction that covers the history and development of science, medicine, and technology. The state-of-the-art interactive displays tickle the brains of 7- to 12-year-olds, and the **Garden Galleries** provide construction areas, sound-and-light shows, and games for younger kids. The fascinating displays include the Apollo 10 space module, an 1813 steam locomotive, Fox Talbot's first camera, and Edison's original phonograph. The **Wellcome Wing,** which opened in summer 2000, is devoted to contemporary science and has an **IMAX 3-D film theater.** Give yourself at least two hours, more if you're going to see the film.

Exhibition Road, London SW7. ☎ *020/7942-4454. Tube: South Kensington (a sign-posted exit in the Underground station goes directly to the museum). Admission: Museum free; call for cost of IMAX tickets. To book IMAX tickets in advance call* ☎ *0870/870-4868. Open: Daily 10 a.m.–6 p.m.; closed Dec 24–26. All galleries are wheelchair accessible.*

St. James's Park and Green Park
Westminster

Henry VIII acquired these two adjoining royal parks in the early 16th century. St James's Park, the prettier of the two, was landscaped in 1827 by John Nash in a picturesque English style with an ornamental lake and promenades. **The Mall,** the processional route between Buckingham

Green with envy

Green Park is called Green Park because it's the only royal park without any flower beds. Why? A popular story has it that one day, as Charles II was walking through the park with his entourage, he announced that he was going to pick a flower and give it to the most beautiful lady present. This lady happened to be a milkmaid and not Queen Catherine, his wife. The queen was livid and ordered that all flowers be removed from the park (a horticultural version of "Off with their heads!").

Palace and Whitehall and Horse Guards Parade, is the route used for major ceremonial occasions. Prince Charles and his sons live at **St. James's Palace,** and the Queen Mum resides at **Clarence House** next door. The residences — closed to visitors — are between The Mall and **Pall Mall** (pronounced *Pell Mell*), a broad avenue running from Trafalgar Square to St. James's Palace.

Bounded by Piccadilly to the north, Regent Street to the east, Birdcage Walk and Buckingham Palace Road to the south, and Grosvenor Place to the west. ☎ *020/ 7930-1793. Tube: Green Park (the tube station is right at the northeast corner of Green Park) or St. James's Park (then a 5-minute walk north on Queen Anne's Gate to Birdcage Walk, the southern perimeter of St. James's Park). Open: Daily dawn–dusk.*

St. Paul's Cathedral
The City of London

After the Great Fire of 1666 destroyed the city's old cathedral, the great architect Christopher Wren was called upon to design St. Paul's, a huge and harmonious Renaissance-leaning-toward-baroque building (see "St. Paul's Cathedral" map in this chapter). During World War II, Nazi bombing raids wiped out the surrounding area but spared the cathedral, so Wren's masterpiece, capped by the most-famous dome in London, rises majestically above a crowded sea of undistinguished office buildings. Grinling Gibbons carved the exceptionally beautiful choir stalls, which are the only impressive artworks inside.

Christopher Wren is buried in the **crypt,** and his epitaph, on the floor below the dome, reads LECTOR, SI MONUMENTUM REQUIRIS, CIRCUMSPICE ("Reader, if you seek his monument, look around you"). His companions in the crypt include Britain's famed national heroes: the Duke of Wellington, who defeated Napoleon at Waterloo, and Admiral Lord Nelson, who took down the French at Trafalgar during the same war. But many people want to see St. Paul's simply because Lady Diana Spencer wed Prince Charles here in what was billed as "the fairy-tale wedding of the century."

St. Paul's Cathedral

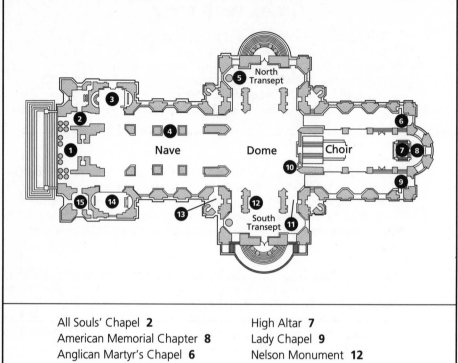

All Souls' Chapel **2**	High Altar **7**
American Memorial Chapter **8**	Lady Chapel **9**
Anglican Martyr's Chapel **6**	Nelson Monument **12**
Chapel of St. Michael	Pulpit **10**
& St. George **14**	St. Dunstan's Chapel **3**
Dean's Staircase **15**	Staircase to Library,
Entrance to Crypt	Whispering Gallery & Dome **13**
(Wren's grave) **11**	Wellington Monument **4**
Font **5**	West Doorway **1**

You can climb up to the **Whispering Gallery** for a bit of acoustical fun or gasp your way up to the very top for a breathtaking view of London. You can see the entire cathedral in an hour or less.

St. Paul's is now linked to the Tate Modern on the South Bank by the pedestrian-only **Millennium Bridge,** designed by Lord Norman Foster.

St. Paul's Churchyard, Ludgate Hill, EC4. ☎ *020/7246-8348. Tube: St. Paul's (then a 5-minute walk west on Ludgate to cathedral entrance on St. Paul's Churchyard). Admission: £5 ($8) adults, £4 ($6) seniors/students, £2.50 ($3.75) children. Tours: Guided tours daily 11:00 a.m., 11:30 a.m., 1:30 p.m., 2:00 p.m.; £2.50 ($3.75) adults, £2 ($3)* *seniors, £1 ($1.50) children under 10. Audio tours (available 8:30 a.m.–3:00 p.m.) £3.50 ($4.75) adults, £2.50 ($3.75) seniors/students. Open: Mon–Sat 8:30 a.m.–4:00 p.m.; galleries Mon–Sat 9:30 a.m.–4:00 p.m.; no sightseeing on Sunday (services only). The cathedral is wheelchair accessible by service entrance near the South Transept; ring the bell for assistance.*

Tate Britain
Pimlico

The Tate Gallery took this name to distinguish it from its new counterpart, Tate Modern, which opened in May 2000. Tate Britain retains the older (pre-20th century) collections of exclusively British art. Among the masterpieces on display are dreamy works by the British pre-Raphaelites, the celestial visions of William Blake, bawdy satirical works by William Hogarth, genteel portraits by Sir Joshua Reynolds, pastoral landscapes by John Constable, and the shimmering seascapes of J.M.W. Turner. Plan on spending at least two hours here. The gallery has a restaurant and a cafe on the lower level.

Millbank, Pimlico SW1. ☎ 020/7887-8000. Tube: Pimlico (then a 10-minute walk south on Vauxhall Bridge Road to the river and north on Millbank to the museum entrance). Bus: For a more scenic route, take bus 77A, which runs south along The Strand and Whitehall to the museum entrance on Millbank. Admission: Free; varying admission fees for special exhibits (for advance ticket sales call ☎ 020/ 7420-0055); audio tours £3 ($4.50). Open: daily 10:00 a.m.–5:50 p.m. Most of the galleries are wheelchair accessible, but call first for details on entry.

Tate Modern
South Bank

The former Bankside Power Station is the setting for the fabulous Tate Modern, which opened in May 2000. Considered one of the three or four top modern art museums in the world, it houses the Tate's collection of international 20th-century art, displaying major works by some of the most influential artists of this century: Pablo Picasso, Henri Matisse, Salvador Dalí, Marcel Duchamp, Henry Moore, and Frances Bacon among them. A gallery for the 21st-century collection exhibits contemporary art. Fans of contemporary art and architecture shouldn't miss this new star on the London art scene. Plan on spending at least two hours. The museum is now linked to St. Paul's Cathedral by the pedestrian-only **Millennium Bridge,** designed by Lord Norman Foster.

25 Sumner Street, SE1. ☎ 020/7887-8000. Tube: Southwark (then a 10-minute walk north along Blackfriars Road and east along the riverside promenade) or Blackfriars (then a10-minute walk south across Blackfriars Bridge). Admission: Free; varying admission fees for special exhibits. Open: Sun–Thurs 10 a.m.–6 p.m.; Fri–Sat 10 a.m.–10 p.m.; closed Dec 24 – 26, Jan 1.

That's the way the bridge bounces

Lord Norman Foster's $28-million **Millennium Bridge** linking Tate Modern to St. Paul's got off to a very wobbly start on its opening day, June 10, 2000. This much-publicized, highly visible, high-tech pedestrian span had one slight problem: It swayed and bounced so much that people couldn't walk on it. Seems that the "untraditional" suspension system of aluminum and stainless steel wasn't doing in real life what it had done on paper. The bridge had to be closed immediately to determine whether major repairs were needed. Bitter Londoners immediately compared the bridge fiasco to another major millennial dud: the Dome, which didn't open on time and had dismal attendance. When Foster's bridge reopened, the same problem occurred, and it was closed for a second time. In Fall 2001, however, the bridge was deemed safe and opened to the public.

Tower of London

The City of London

The Tower of London offers enough to keep you captivated for a good three to four hours, but *make sure* that you save time for the **Crown Jewels,** which include the largest diamond in the world (the 530-carat Star of Africa) and other breathtaking gems set into royal robes, swords, sceptres, and crowns.

The Tower of London (see the map, "Tower of London" in this chapter) is the city's best-known and oldest historic site. In 1066, William the Conqueror built that tower, which served as his fortress and later as a prison, holding famous captives such as Sir Walter Raleigh and Princess Elizabeth I. Anne Boleyn and Catherine Howard (two of the eight wives of Henry VIII), the 9-day queen Lady Jane Grey, and Sir Thomas More were among those unlucky individuals who got their heads chopped off on **Tower Green.** According to Shakespeare, the two little princes (the sons of Edward IV) were murdered in the **Bloody Tower** by henchmen of Richard III — but the story is controversial among modern historians.

You can attend the nightly **Ceremony of the Keys,** the ceremonial locking-up of the Tower by the Yeoman Warders. For free tickets, write to the Ceremony of the Keys, Waterloo Block, Tower of London, London EC3N 4AB, and request a specific date but also list alternate dates. At least six weeks' notice is required. You must send a self-addressed stamped envelope (British stamps only) or two International Reply Coupons with all requests. If you have a ticket, a Yeoman Warder will admit you at 9:35 p.m.

Tower of London

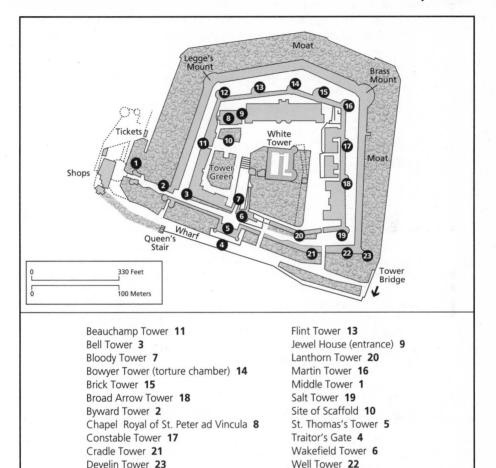

Beauchamp Tower **11**	Flint Tower **13**
Bell Tower **3**	Jewel House (entrance) **9**
Bloody Tower **7**	Lanthorn Tower **20**
Bowyer Tower (torture chamber) **14**	Martin Tower **16**
Brick Tower **15**	Middle Tower **1**
Broad Arrow Tower **18**	Salt Tower **19**
Byward Tower **2**	Site of Scaffold **10**
Chapel Royal of St. Peter ad Vincula **8**	St. Thomas's Tower **5**
Constable Tower **17**	Traitor's Gate **4**
Cradle Tower **21**	Wakefield Tower **6**
Develin Tower **23**	Well Tower **22**
Devereux Tower **12**	

 Huge black ravens hop around the grounds of the Tower of London. An old legend says that the British Commonwealth will end when the ravens leave the tower. Their wings have been clipped as a precaution.

 In the bad old days, important prisoners often arrived at the tower by boat. You can, too. **Catamaran Cruisers** (☎ **020/7987-1185**) provides daily ferry service between Embankment Pier (Tube: Embankment) and Tower Pier. A one-way ticket is £5.70 ($9) adults and £3.80 ($6) children under 16. See Chapter 18 for more options.

Tower Hill, EC3. ☎ 020/7709-0765. Tube: Tower Hill (then a 5-minute walk west and south on Tower Hill). Bus: You can take the eastbound bus 25 from Marble Arch, Oxford Circus, or St. Paul's; it stops at Tower Hill, north of the entrance. Admission:

£11.30 ($16) adults, £8.50 ($13) seniors/students, £7.50 ($11) children 5–15, £34 ($51) families (2 adults, 3 children). Tours: Free 1-hour guided tours of the entire compound are given by the Yeoman Warders (also known as "Beefeaters") every half hour, starting at 9:30 a.m. (Sun 10:00 a.m.) from the Middle Tower near the main entrance. The last guided walk starts about 3:30 p.m. in summer or 2:30 p.m. in winter; weather permitting. Open: March–Oct Mon–Sat 9 a.m.–5 p.m., Sun 10 a.m.–4 p.m.; Nov–Feb Tues–Sat 9 a.m.–4 p.m., Sun 10 a.m.–4 p.m.; closed Jan 1 and Dec 24–26. Wheelchair access onto the grounds is available, but many of the historic buildings can't accommodate wheelchairs.

Trafalgar Square

St. James's

Trafalgar Square is a roaringly busy traffic interchange surrounded by historic buildings, such as St. Martin-in-the-Fields church and the National Gallery. Besides being a major tourist attraction, Trafalgar Square is the site of many large gatherings, such as political demonstrations and holiday celebrations. The square honors military hero Horatio, Viscount Nelson (1758–1805), who lost his life at the Battle of Trafalgar. **Nelson's Column,** with fountains and four bronze lions at its base, rises 145 feet above the square. At the top, a 14-foot-high statue of Nelson (5 feet 4 inches tall in real life) looks commandingly toward **Admiralty Arch,** passed through by state and royal processions between Buckingham Palace and St. Paul's Cathedral. You don't need more than a few minutes to take in the square (the National Gallery across the street and the National Portrait Gallery behind it will take up more of your time).

The neoclassical church on the northeast corner of Trafalgar Square was the precursor for dozens of similar-looking churches throughout colonial New England. Designed by James Gibbs, a disciple of Christopher Wren, **St. Martin-in-the-Fields (☎ 020/7930-0089)** was completed in 1726; the 185-foot spire was added about 100 years later. The **Academy of St. Martin-in-the-Fields,** a famous music ensemble, frequently performs here. Lunchtime concerts are held on Monday, Tuesday, and Friday at 1 p.m., and evening concerts are held Thursday through Saturday at 7:30 p.m. Concert tickets are £6 to £15 ($10 to $24). For reservations by credit card, call **☎ 020/7839-8362.** The church is open Monday through Saturday 10 a.m. to 6 p.m. and Sunday noon to 6 p.m.; admission is free.

Café-in-the-Crypt (☎ 020/7839-4342), one of the West End's most pleasant restaurants, is in the crypt of St. Martin-in-the-Fields and serves up helpings of traditional English home cooking daily 10 a.m. to 8 p.m. The busy crypt also contains the **London Brass Rubbing Centre (☎ 020/7437-6023),** which provides paper, metallic waxes, and instructions on how to rub your own replica of historic brasses. Prices range from £3 to £15 ($4.50 to $23.00). This activity is a great diversion for kids 10 and up. The center is open Monday through Saturday 10 a.m. to 6 p.m. and Sunday noon to 6 p.m.

Bounded on the north by Trafalgar, on the west by Cockspur Street, and on the east by Whitehall. Tube: Charing Cross (the Underground station has an exit to the square).

Victoria & Albert Museum
South Kensington

The Victoria & Albert (known as the V&A) is the national museum of art and design. In the 145 galleries, filled with fine and decorative arts from around the world, you find superbly decorated period rooms, a fashion collection spanning 400 years of European designs, Raphael's designs for tapestries in the Sistine Chapel, the Silver Galleries, and the largest assemblages of Renaissance sculpture outside Italy and of Indian art outside India. The Canon Photography Gallery shows work by celebrated photographers. In November 2001, the museum opened its spectacular new British Galleries. Allow at least two hours just to cover the basics.

Cromwell Road, SW7. ☎ 020/7942-2000. Tube: South Kensington (the museum is across from the Underground station). Admission: Free. Open: Thurs–Tues 10 a.m.– 5:45 p.m., Weds 10 a.m.–10 p.m.; closed Dec 24–26. The museum is wheelchair accessible (only about 5% of the exhibits include steps).

Westminster Abbey
Westminster

The Gothic and grand Westminster Abbey is one of London's most important historic sites. (See map, "Westminster Abbey.") The present abbey dates mostly from the 13th and 14th centuries, but a church has been on this site for more than a thousand years. Since 1066, when William the Conqueror became the first English monarch to be crowned here, every successive British sovereign except for two (Edward V and Edward VIII) has sat on the **Coronation Chair** to receive the crown and scepter. In the **Royal Chapels,** you can see the **chapel of Henry VII,** with its delicate fan vaulting, and the **tomb of Queen Elizabeth I,** who was buried in the same vault as her Catholic half-sister, Mary I, and not far from her rival Mary Queen of Scots. In **Poets' Corner,** some of England's greatest writers (including Chaucer, Dickens, and Thomas Hardy) are interred or memorialized. Other points of interest include the College Garden, cloisters, chapter house, and the Undercroft Museum, which contains the Pyx Chamber with its display of church plate, the silver owned by the church. In September 1997, the abbey served as the site of Princess Diana's funeral. The abbey is within walking distance of the Houses of Parliament.

Broad Sanctuary, SW1. ☎ 020/7222-7110. Tube: Westminster (then a three-minute walk west following Parliament Square to Broad Sanctuary). Bus: The 77A going south along The Strand, Whitehall, and Millbank stops near the Houses of Parliament, near the Abbey. Admission: Abbey and Royal Chapels, £5 ($7) adults, £3 ($4.50) seniors/students, £2 ($3) children 11–16, £10 ($15) families (2 adults, 2 children).

Westminster Abbey

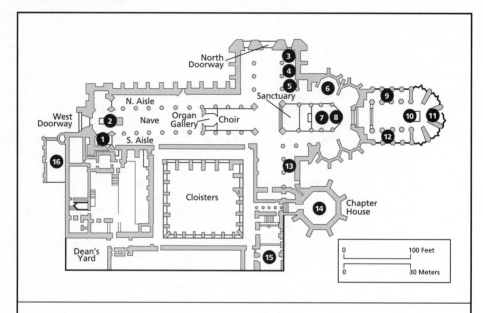

Bookshop **16**

Chapel of St. John the Baptist **6**

Chapel of St. John the Evangelist **5**

Chapter House **14**

Henry V's Chantry **8**

Poets' Corner **13**

Royal Air Force Chapel **11**

St. Andrew's Chapel **3**

St. Edward's Chapel
(Coronation Chair) **7**

St. George's Chapel **1**

St. Michael's Chapel **4**

Tomb of Mary I &
Elizabeth I **9**

Tomb of Henry VII **10**

Tomb of Mary,
Queen of Scots **12**

Tomb of the Unknown Warrior/
Memorial to Churchill **2**

Undercroft Museum and
Pyx Chamber **15**

Chapter House, Pyx Chamber, and Museum, free with Super Tour (see following information on guided tours) or £2.50 ($3.75) adults, £1.30 ($2) children. Guided tours: Led by an Abbey Verger £8 ($12); Super Tours £3 ($4.50) (tours led by an Abbey Verger are longer and more comprehensive than the Super Tours); call for times; tickets for tours at Enquiry Desk in the Abbey; audio tours £2 ($3). Open: Cathedral, Mon–Fri 9:00 a.m.–4:45 p.m. (last admission 3:45 p.m.), Sat 9:00 a.m.–2:45 p.m.; no sightseeing on Sunday (services only). Cloisters, daily 10 a.m.–6 p.m. Chapter house, Pyx Chamber, and Undercroft Museum, daily 10 a.m.–4 p.m. College Garden, April–Sept 10 a.m.– 6 p.m., Oct–March 10 a.m.–4 p.m. Ramped wheelchair access is available via the Cloisters; ring the bell for assistance.

LONDON TATTLER

Oscar Wilde's window

In 1995, 100 years after Oscar Wilde's release from Reading Gaol (where he was imprisoned after his trial for "gross indecency"), the Church of England finally recognized his immortal genius with a memorial window at Westminster Abbey. But because his name is nowhere to be seen in the abbey, the blue window with its abstract design is the kind of dubious honor that would no doubt provoke a witty quip from the great playwright. Maybe something like, "Clear glass wasn't good enough for me; it had to be stained."

Index of Top Attractions by Neighborhood

Bloomsbury
British Museum
City of London
St. Paul's Cathedral
Tower of London

Covent Garden
Covent Garden Market and Piazza

Kensington and South Kensington
Kensington Gardens
Kensington Palace
Natural History Museum
Science Museum
Victoria & Albert Museum

Marylebone
London Zoo
Madame Tussaud's

Piccadilly Circus and Leicester Square
Piccadilly Circus
Leicester Square

Pimlico
Tate Britain

South Bank
British Airways London Eye
Tate Modern

St. James's
Buckingham Palace
National Gallery
National Portrait Gallery
St. James's Park and Green Park

Trafalgar Square
Westminster
Houses of Parliament and Big Ben
Hyde Park
Westminster Abbey

Index of Attractions by Type

Churches

St. Paul's Cathedral
Westminster Abbey

Museums

British Museum
Madame Tussaud's
National Gallery
National Portrait Gallery
Natural History Museum
Science Museum
Tate Britain
Tate Modern
Victoria & Albert Museum

Palaces and other historic buildings

Buckingham Palace
Houses of Parliament and Big Ben

Kensington Palace
Tower of London

Parks, gardens, and the zoo

Hyde Park
Kensington Gardens
London Zoo
St. James's Park and Green Park

Squares

Covent Garden Market and Piazza
Leicester Square
Piccadilly Circus
Trafalgar Square

Viewpoints

British Airways London Eye

Chapter 17

More Cool Things to See and Do

*I*f you think you've "done" London because you've marveled at Westminster Abbey, seen where the Queen lives, wandered through St. Paul's Cathedral, toured the Tower of London, and feasted your eyes on the masterpieces in the British Museum and the National Gallery, think again. London is a teeming treasure trove of possibilities large and small: glorious gardens, magnificent mansions, singular museums, ancient corners, historic churches, and many themed attractions that fill you in on the history and flavor of majestic London Town. This chapter highlights only a few of the many activities that you can find to tickle your fancy and make the most of your visit. (See the map "More London Sights.")

I also cover four major attractions just outside Central London and easily accessible by Tube or train — **Hampstead Heath, Hampton Court Palace, Kew Gardens,** and **Windsor Castle.** You can spend the better part of a day visiting any one of these sights — all trips well worth your time — before returning to Central London in time for a play or concert in the evening.

More London Sights

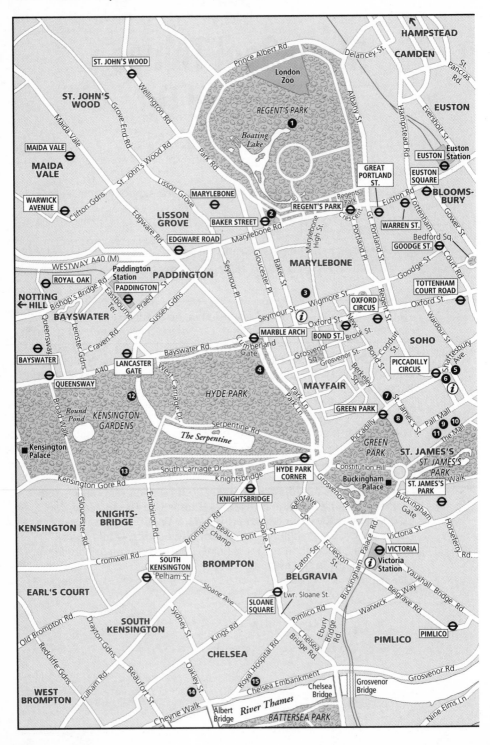

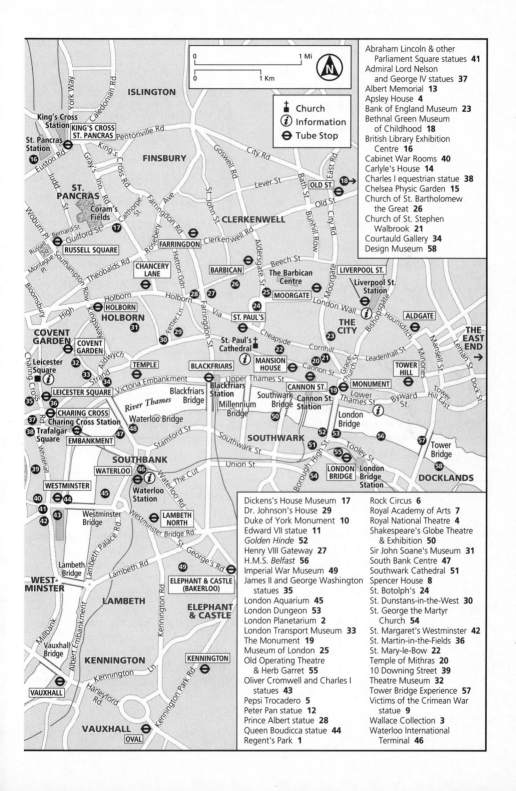

Abraham Lincoln & other
  Parliament Square statues **41**
Admiral Lord Nelson
  and George IV statues **37**
Albert Memorial **13**
Apsley House **4**
Bank of England Museum **23**
Bethnal Green Museum
  of Childhood **18**
British Library Exhibition
  Centre **16**
Cabinet War Rooms **40**
Carlyle's House **14**
Charles I equestrian statue **38**
Chelsea Physic Garden **15**
Church of St. Bartholomew
  the Great **26**
Church of St. Stephen
  Walbrook **21**
Courtauld Gallery **34**
Design Museum **58**

Dickens's House Museum **17**
Dr. Johnson's House **29**
Duke of York Monument **10**
Edward VII statue **11**
Golden Hinde **52**
Henry VIII Gateway **27**
H.M.S. *Belfast* **56**
Imperial War Museum **49**
James II and George Washington
  statues **35**
London Aquarium **45**
London Dungeon **53**
London Planetarium **2**
London Transport Museum **33**
The Monument **19**
Museum of London **25**
Old Operating Theatre
  & Herb Garret **55**
Oliver Cromwell and Charles I
  statues **43**
Pepsi Trocadero **5**
Peter Pan statue **12**
Prince Albert statue **28**
Queen Boudicca statue **44**
Regent's Park **1**

Rock Circus **6**
Royal Academy of Arts **7**
Royal National Theatre **4**
Shakespeare's Globe Theatre
  & Exhibition **50**
Sir John Soane's Museum **31**
South Bank Centre **47**
Southwark Cathedral **51**
Spencer House **8**
St. Botolph's **24**
St. Dunstans-in-the-West **30**
St. George the Martyr
  Church **54**
St. Margaret's Westminster **42**
St. Martin-in-the-Fields **36**
St. Mary-le-Bow **22**
Temple of Mithras **20**
10 Downing Street **39**
Theatre Museum **32**
Tower Bridge Experience **57**
Victims of the Crimean War
  statue **9**
Wallace Collection **3**
Waterloo International
  Terminal **46**

The following sights are fully or partially wheelchair accessible; visitors with disabilities should call the attraction to find out about special entrances, ramps, and elevator locations:

- Bank of England Museum
- Bethnal Green Museum of Childhood
- Bramah Tea & Coffee Museum
- British Library Exhibition Galleries
- Chelsea Physic Garden
- Courtauld Gallery
- Design Museum
- Hampton Court
- Imperial War Museum
- London Aquarium

- London Dungeon
- London Planetarium
- London Transport Museum
- Museum of London
- Regent's Park
- Rock Circus
- Royal Academy of Art
- Royal Botanic Gardens (Kew Gardens)
- Theatre Museum
- Tower Bridge Experience
- Wallace Collection

Sights for History Buffs

You can't escape history in London. The past is woven into the very fabric of the city, and it's why many visitors want to come here. The "history" contained in the sights in this section is as old as Rome, as new as the current Prime Minister, and as dramatic as the events of World War II.

Cabinet War Rooms

Westminster

You can almost hear the air-raid sirens here. In this 21-room underground bunker, Prime Minister Winston Churchill and his War Cabinet planned out the military campaigns of World War II. The site has been meticulously preserved, right down to the nightshirt and cigar waiting by Churchill's bed. Give yourself an hour to explore the site.

Clive Steps, King Charles Street, SW1. ☎ *020/7930-6961. Tube: Westminster (then a 10-minute walk west, staying on the north side of the street, to Parliament Street, turn right to reach King Charles Street). Admission: £4.80 ($8) adults, £3.50 ($5) seniors/students, children under 16 free; a free self-guided audio tour comes with your ticket. Open: April–Sept 9:30 a.m.–6:00 p.m., Oct–March 10 a.m.–6 p.m. (last admission 5:15 p.m.).*

Imperial War Museum

Lambeth

The former insane asylum known as Bedlam is now devoted to the insanity of war. You can see a wide range of weapons and equipment, including a Battle of Britain Spitfire, a German one-man submarine, a Mark V tank, and a rifle once carried by Lawrence of Arabia. Other exhibits include coded messages, forged documents, espionage equipment from World War I to the present, and multimedia presentations about the Blitz and trench warfare. The Holocaust Gallery documents one of history's darkest episodes through film, photos, and artifacts, many shown for the first time. Enough history is on display to keep you occupied for a couple of hours.

Lambeth Road, SE1. ☎ 020/7416-5320. Tube: Lambeth North (then a 10-minute walk south on Kennington, south of Westminster Bridge Road, and east on Lambeth Road). Admission: £6.50 ($10) adults, £5.50 ($8) students, seniors and children under 16 free; admittance for everyone free after 4:30 p.m. Open: Daily 10 a.m.–6 p.m.

Museum of London

City of London

The Museum of London may be the most comprehensive city museum anywhere in the world. Located in the original square-mile Londinium of the Romans and overlooking the city's Roman and medieval walls, the museum includes archaeological finds; paintings and prints; social, industrial, and historical artifacts; and costumes, maps, and models to recount the city's history from prehistoric times to today. Give yourself at least an hour to skim through the collections; although, spending more time than that is easy.

150 London Wall (in the Barbican district near St. Paul's Cathedral), EC2. ☎ 020/7600-3699. Tube: St. Paul's (then a 10-minute walk north on St. Martin Le Grand and Aldersgate). Open: Mon–Sat 10:00 a.m.–5:50 p.m., Sun noon to 5:50 p.m. Admission: £5 ($8) adults, £3 ($4.50) children/students/seniors; £12 ($18) families (2 adults/3 children); admission free after 4:30 p.m. Closed Dec 24–26 and Jan 1.

10 Downing Street

St. James's

The prime minister's residence is a place on many visitors' "must see" lists, so I'm sorry to tell you that there's nothing to see except a heavily guarded gate. By peering through the gate you can get a glimpse, on the right side, of No. 10, the official residence of the British PM since 1732. The Chancellor of the Exchequer resides next door at No. 11, and No. 12 serves as the office of the chief government whip, responsible for maintaining discipline and cooperation in the vociferous House of Commons.

Prime time Prime Minister

Of course, London gossip swirls around 10 Downing Street just as it does around Buckingham Palace. In 1999, Cherie Blair, wife of poll-sensitive Prime Minister Tony Blair, announced that she was pregnant with the couple's fourth child. Mrs. Blair, a high-powered lawyer specializing in employment law, made it known (when she was seven months pregnant) that she thought her husband should take advantage of the paternity leave policy his Labour government has incorporated into law. (Since 1999, new fathers in Britain have the right to take up to 13 unpaid weeks off work during the first 5 years of their children's lives.) Mr. Blair, a seasoned spin-meister, was uncharacteristically tongue-tied by his wife's suggestion. Whether to take unpaid leave was obviously not a question of financial hardship. Cherie Blair, QC (Queen's Counsel), the first prime minister's wife to hold a full-time job, reputedly earns three times the $175,000 annual salary of her prime minister husband. In the end, Prime Minister Blair took a week off when his wife gave birth to a son, Leo. Gossip swirled again in July 2000, when the Blair's 16-year-old son, Euan, was arrested in Leicester Square for drunkenness. And again in 2001, when Cherie Blair outpolled the Queen as "Britain's most powerful woman."

These three small brick terrace houses, built on a cul-de-sac in 1680, stand in sharp contrast to the enormous 19th-century offices lining Whitehall, the government quarter around Downing Street.

10 Downing St., SW1. Tube: Westminster (then a 5-minute walk north on Parliament Street and Whitehall).

Attractions for Art Lovers

In addition to the great art museums described in Chapter 16, London is home to many smaller and less-visited galleries. The works in the Courtauld Gallery and the Wallace Collection are first-rate, and the Royal Academy serves as a grand venue for special shows.

Courtauld Gallery

The Strand

If you like paintings by the Impressionists, visit the Courtauld Gallery, which boasts one of the greatest collections outside Paris. Masterpieces by all the great names — Degas, Renoir, Cézanne, Manet, Monet, and Gauguin — are all on view in this suprisingly little-known museum. Give yourself at least an hour, preferably two.

Somerset House, The Strand, WC2. ☎ *020/7873-2526. Tube: Temple (then a 5-minute. walk north on Arundel Street and west on The Strand). Admission: £4 ($6)* *adults, £2 ($3) students, free for children under 18. Open: Mon–Sat 10 a.m.–6 p.m., Sun noon to 6 p.m.*

Royal Academy of Arts

St. James's

Housed in 18th-century Burlington House, the site of Britain's first art school, the Royal Academy presents major exhibits throughout the year and mounts a renowned (and usually jam-packed) Summer Exhibition of juried works from around the United Kingdom. Give yourself about an hour.

Burlington House, Piccadilly, W1. ☎ 020/7300-8000. Tube: Piccadilly Circus (then a 5-minute walk down Piccadilly; the Academy is on the north side of the street just before the Burlington Arcade). Admission: Varies according to exhibit but usually £7 ($11) adults, £4.50 ($7) seniors, £2.50 ($3.75) children 11–18, £1 ($1.50) children under 11. Open: Sat–Thurs 10 a.m.–6 p.m. (last admission 5:30 p.m.), Fri 10:00 a.m.–8:30 p.m.

Wallace Collection

Marylebone

The palatial town house of the late Lady Wallace is the setting for a spectacular collection of art and armaments. You can enjoy outstanding French works by the likes of Watteau and Fragonard, as well as masterpieces from the Dutch (Frans Hals and Rembrandt), English, Spanish, and Italian schools. Decorative art and ornaments from 18th-century France and European and Asian armaments are also on display. Give yourself at least an hour.

Hertford House, Manchester Square, W1. ☎ 020/7935-0687. Tube: Baker Street (then a 10-minute walk south on Baker Street to the museum entrance on the north side of Manchester Square). Admission: Free. Open: Mon–Sat 10 a.m.–5 p.m., Sun noon to 5 p.m.

Literary Landmarks

Writers have been drawn to London for centuries and have left their literary imprints all over this vast metropolis. Listed in this section are some of the unique places associated with writers who lived in London, as well as one of the world's great storehouses of literary treasures.

British Library Exhibition Centre

Marylebone

Opened in 1998, this literary offshoot of the British Museum (see Chapter 16) houses some of the world's most famous books, maps, manuscripts, and documents, including a copy of the Magna Carta, the illustrated

Lindisfarne Gospel from Ireland, *The Diamond Sutra* (the world's earliest-dated printed book), Shakespeare's first folio, and handwritten manuscripts by authors such as Jane Austen and Thomas Hardy. Multimedia exhibits trace the story of book production. Give this sight at least an hour; allow more time if you love literature or literary history.

Euston Road, NW1. ☎ *020/7412-7332. Tube: King's Cross/St. Pancras (then a 5-minute walk west on Euston; the museum entrance is just beyond Midland Road). Admission: Free. Open: Mon and Wed–Fri 9:30 a.m.–6:00 p.m., Tues 9:30 a.m.– 8:00 p.m., Sat 9:30 a.m.–5:00 p.m., Sun 11 a.m.–5 p.m.*

Carlyle's House

Chelsea

Thomas Carlyle (author of *The French Revolution*) and his wife, Jane (a wit and noted letter writer), lived in this pretty 1708 Queen Anne terrace house from 1834 to 1881. Furnished as it was during their residence, the house is an accurate representation of middle-class Victorian domestic life. Carlyle's "soundproof" study in the skylit attic is filled with memorabilia — his books, a letter from Benjamin Disraeli, personal effects, a writing chair, and even his death mask. You can browse through in about a half-hour.

24 Cheyne Row, SW3. ☎ *020/7352-7087. Tube: Sloane Square (then a 20-minute walk south on Lower Sloane Street and Hospital Road to Cheyne Walk and north on Cheyne Row; or from Sloane Square take bus 11, 19, or 22). Admission: £3.50 ($5) adults, £1.90 ($2.85) children. Open: April–Oct Wed–Sun 11 a.m.–4:30 p.m.*

Dickens's House Museum

Bloomsbury

Charles Dickens lived in many places, but he and his family called this Bloomsbury house home from 1837 to 1839. Here the great author penned *The Pickwick Papers, Oliver Twist,* and *Nicholas Nickleby,* the poignant and famous portrayals of Victorian England. The museum contains the world's most comprehensive Dickens library, portraits, illustrations, and rooms furnished exactly as they were in Dickens's time. You can see everything in a half-hour, but allow more time if you're a Dickens' fanatic.

48 Doughty St., WC1. ☎ *020/7405-2127. Tube: Russell Square (then a 10-minute walk up Guilford Street and turn right on Doughty Street; the museum is on the east side of the street). Admission: £3.50 ($5) adults, £2.50 ($3.75) seniors, £1.50 ($2.25) for children. Open: Mon–Fri 9:45 a.m.–5:00 p.m., Sat 10 a.m.–5 p.m.*

Dr. Johnson's House

Holborn

Hidden away in a tiny square north of Fleet Street is the Queen Anne house where Dr. Samuel Johnson, best known as the lexicographer who compiled one of the first dictionaries of the English language, lived (quite humbly) from 1748 to 1759. A copy of the original dictionary is on display, along with Johnson memorabilia. The restored 17th-century house is close to Ye Olde Cheshire Cheese pub (see Chapter 14), a favorite haunt of the good doctor, who was celebrated as a storyteller of the first order. You can see everything on view here in about a half-hour.

17 Gough Sq., EC4. ☎ *020/7353-3745. Tube: Temple (then a 10-minute walk north on Arundel Street to Fleet Street and east on Fleet Street to Dunstan's Court; Gough Square is to one side of Dunstan's Court). Admission: £3 ($4.50) adults, £2 ($3) seniors/students. Open: May–Sept Mon–Sat 11:00 a.m.–5:30 p.m., Oct–April Mon–Sat 11 a.m.–5 p.m.*

Intriguing Museums of All Shapes, Sorts, and Sizes

London's museums are surprisingly varied in their scope and substance. In addition to all the great art museums described in Chapter 16 and earlier in this chapter (see "Attractions for Art Lovers"), the city has museums dedicated to theater, architecture, design, medicine, and money.

Bank of England Museum

City of London

Devoted capitalists enjoy the Bank of England Museum, housed in the enormous Bank of England building. The museum chronicles changes in the banking industry since the Bank of England's beginnings in 1694, when funds were needed to finance the war against France's Louis XIV. On display are documents from famous customers (including George Washington), gold bullion, bank notes (forged and real), and coins. Interactive video displays present information about today's high-tech world of finance and a reconstructed 18th-century Banking Hall. You can see it all in less than an hour.

Bartholomew Lane, EC2. ☎ *020/7601-5545. Tube: Bank (then a 5-minute walk east on Threadneedle Street, turn left on Bartholomew's Lane for the museum entrance). Admission: Free. Open: Mon–Fri 10 a.m.–5 p.m.*

Old Operating Theatre & Herb Garret

Southwark

The Old Operating Theatre is not for the faint of heart. The roof garret of the church of St. Thomas, once attached to St. Thomas's Hospital, contains Britain's oldest operating theater (from 1822), where students could witness surgical procedures on poor (literally and figuratively) patients. You'll shudder over the collection of mid-19th-century "state-of-the-art" medical instruments, including amputation saws. The theater was in use long before the advent of anesthesia in 1846. Prior to that time, if a patient had a limb amputated, only a blindfold and a bottle of liquor were provided (and you thought your HMO was bad). The herb garret was used for the storage and curing of medicinal herbs.

9A St. Thomas St., SE1. ☎ 020/7955-4791. Tube: London Bridge (then a 5-minute walk east on St. Thomas Street). Admission: £3.50 ($5) adults, £2.25 ($3.50) seniors, £1.60 ($2.40) children. Open: Daily 10:30 a.m.–5 p.m.; closed Dec 20–Jan 5.

Design Museum

South Bank

This museum houses the kind of collection that makes visitors say, "I remember those." If you're a design enthusiast — or want to see how commercial design affects our everyday lives — be sure to check out this place. Classical, kitsch, modern, surreal, and innovative — from Corbusier chairs to the Coke bottle — are all chronicled here. Plus the river views are great. Plan to spend at least an hour.

Butlers Wharf, Shad Thames, SE1. ☎ 020/7403-6933. Tube: Tower Hill (then a 10-minute walk across Tower Bridge to Butler's Wharf east of the bridge on the South Bank; or London Bridge, then a 10-minute walk east along The Queen's Walk beside the Thames). Admission: £5.50 ($8) adults, £4 ($6) seniors/children, £15 ($22) families (2 adults/2 children). Open: Mon–Fri 11:30 a.m.–6 p.m., Sat–Sun 10:30 a.m.–6 p.m.

Sir John Soane's Museum

Holborn

The house of Sir John Soane (1753–1837), architect of the Bank of England, is an eccentric cache of ancient sculpture, artifacts, and art mixed in with odd architectural perspectives, fool-the-eye mirrors, flying arches, and domes. This captivating Holborn attraction is rarely crowded, which makes spending an hour even more of a treat. The oldest piece in the house is the 3,300-year-old sarcophagus of Pharaoh Seti I. Top prize in the picture gallery goes to William Hogarth's satirical and sometimes bawdy series from *The Rake's Progress.*

13 Lincoln's Inn Fields, WC2. ☎ 020/7405-2107. Tube: Holborn (then a 5-minute walk south on Kingsway to Lincoln's Inn Fields; the museum entrance is on the north side of the street). Admission: Free. Guided tours: Sat at 2:30 p.m., £3($4.50). Open: Tues–Sat 10 a.m.–5 p.m., first Tues of every month 6–9 p.m.

Theatre Museum

Covent Garden

The National Collections of the Performing Arts are housed at this branch of the Victoria & Albert Museum (see Chapter 16). Spend an hour or so checking out the collections related to British theater, ballet, opera, music-hall pantomime, puppets, circus, and rock and pop music (both past and present). Kids enjoy the daily stage make-up demonstrations. The costume workshops use costumes from the Royal Shakespeare Company and the Royal National Theatre.

Russell Street, WC2. ☎ *020/7945-4700. Tube: Covent Garden (then a 3-minute walk south to Russell Street on the east side of Covent Garden Piazza). Admission: £4.50 ($7) adults, £2.50 ($3.75) seniors/students, free for children under 16. Open: Tues–Sun 10 a.m.–6 p.m. (last admission 5:30 p.m.)*

Activities for Teens

If you have teens in tow, you may wonder where to take them so that they won't feel as though their interests are being completely ignored. The choices in this section — all places where teens hang out — provide a few screams, a wonderland of games, and some really loud music.

London Dungeon

South Bank

Don't bring young children unless you want to pay for therapy, but teens seem to love the grisly re-creations of medieval torture and executions presented at this house of horrors. You find a scream (literally) around every corner. Amid the tolling bells, dripping water, and caged rats, you can face Jack the Ripper or witness a simulated burning at the stake. If you're hungry after all the murder and mayhem, you're in luck: A Pizza Hut is on the premises.

28–34 Tooley St., SE1. ☎ *020/7403-7221. Tube: London Bridge (the exhibit is across from the station). Admission: £9.95 ($15) adults, £8.50 ($13) students, £6.50 ($10) seniors/children under 15. Children 14 and under must be accompanied by an adult. Not recommended for young children. Open: April–Sept daily 10:00 a.m.–6:30 p.m. (last admission 5:30 p.m.); Oct–March daily 10:00 a.m.–5:30 p.m. (last admission 4:30 p.m.).*

Pepsi Trocadero

Piccadilly Circus

This "total entertainment complex" is right on Piccadilly Circus. The lead attraction is **Segaworld,** which offers various rides, including Max Drop, the world's first indoor freefall ride (don't eat for at least an hour before), and 400 ear-splitting, eye-popping video games and simulators. The Rock Circus (see the next listing), an offshoot of Madame Tussaud's, is another big draw. Theme restaurants include the ersatz **Rainforest Café** (which doesn't pretend its proceeds go to support the rain forests), and the 1950s-style **Ed's Easy Diner.** Plan to spend some time, because the Pepsi Trocadero is designed and packaged in such a way that after you're in, finding your way out again seems to take forever.

Piccadilly Circus. ☎ *0891/881-100. Tube: Piccadilly Circus (then a 2-minute walk to the northeast side). Admission: Segaworld is free, but games and rides cost 20p–£3 (30¢–$4.50). Open: Sun–Thurs 10 a.m. to midnight, Fri–Sat 10 a.m.–1 a.m.*

Rock Circus

Piccadilly Circus

This popular outpost of Madame Tussaud's wax musuem (see Chapter 16) presents the history of rock and pop music. The audio-animatronic performers move and sing golden oldies and more recent chart toppers. You and your kids can enjoy plenty of memorabilia and a sensory overload of videos and personal stereo sound. (Of course, hearing the songs they grew up with called "oldies" is always disconcerting for adults.)

Pepsi Trocadero, Piccadilly Circus, W1. ☎ *020/7734-7203. Tube: Piccadilly Circus (it's on the north side). Admission: £8.25 ($12) adults, £6.95 ($11) seniors/students, £5.95 ($9) children under 16. Open: Mon–Tues 11:00 a.m.–5:30 p.m., Wed–Sun 10:00 a.m.–5:30 p.m.*

Places That Please Kids

The little(r) ones probably won't have much interest in London's art museums and historic buildings. But the city offers all kinds of diversions for pre-teens, including a museum crammed with antique toys and attractions related to the sea, the stars, and the subway (Tube).

Bethnal Green Museum of Childhood

Bethnal Green

A branch of the Victoria & Albert Museum (see Chapter 16), this museum specializes in toys from the past and present. You can find a staggering collection of dolls, many with elaborate period costumes, and fully furnished dollhouses ranging from simple cottages to miniature mansions. Optical toys, marionettes, puppets, tin soldiers, war toys, toy trains and aircraft, and a display of clothing and furniture relating to the social history of childhood make this museum an enchanting place to invest a couple of hours.

Cambridge Heath Road, E2. ☎ *020/8980-2415. Tube: Bethnal Green (then a 5-minute walk north on Cambridge Heath Road to the museum entrance on the east side of the street). Admission: Free. Open: Mon–Thurs and Sat–Sun 10 a.m.–5:50 p.m.*

London Aquarium

South Bank

London's subterranean aquarium, located right beside the British Airways London Eye (see Chapter 16), may be a bit disappointing if you've been to any of the great aquariums in the United States. Neverthe-less, children enjoy observing its more than 350 species of fish and aquatic invertebrates, including sharks, graceful stingrays, man-eating piranha, and sea scorpions. Exhibits, a couple with floor-to-ceiling tanks, re-create marine habitats from around the world. Plan on spending at least an hour — more if you can't pull the kids away.

Bridge Road (beside Westminster Bridge), SE1. ☎ 020/7967-8000. Tube: Waterloo (then a 5-minute walk west along the river). Admission: £8 ($12) adults, £6.50 ($10) seniors, £5 ($8) children, £22 ($33) families (2 adults/2 children). Open: Daily 10 a.m.– 6 p.m. (last admission 5 p.m.).

London Planetarium

Marylebone

In the planetarium's show, you get to accompany a spaceship of travel-ers forced to desert their planet and travel through the solar system, vis-iting its major landmarks and witnessing spectacular cosmic activity. Partnered with Madame Tussaud's wax museum (see Chapter 16), this planetarium takes you on a journey to very different stars from the ones cast in wax next door. The planetarium offers many kid-friendly hands-on exhibits (including one that lets you see what shape or weight you'd be on other planets). You can also hear Stephen Hawking talk about myste-rious black holes. Give this sight at least a couple of hours.

Marylebone Road, NW1. ☎ 020/7935-6861. Tube: Baker Street (then a 1-minute walk east on Marylebone Road). Admission: £7 ($10) adults, £5.60 ($8) seniors, £4.85 ($7) children under 16. Children under 5 not admitted. Combination ticket: for Planetarium and Madame Tussaud's, £14.45 ($22) adults, £11.30 ($17) seniors, £10 ($15) children. Open: Daily 9:00 a.m.–5:30 p.m. Half-hour shows begin at 10 a.m. or 10:30 a.m. depending on season.

London Transport Museum

Covent Garden

Housed in a splendid Victorian building (once the Flower Market at Covent Garden), this museum chronicles the development of the city's famous Underground and double-decker red bus system. A fabulous col-lection of historic vehicles, including an 1829 omnibus, a horse-drawn bus, and London's first trolley bus, are on display. Several KidZones offer interactive exhibits that enable younger visitors to operate the controls of a Tube train, get their tickets punched, and play with touch-screen technology. After two hours, you may have to drag them away.

The Piazza, WC2. ☎ 020/7379-6344. Tube: Covent Garden (then a 2-minute walk west to the Piazza; the museum is in the southeast corner). Admission: £5.50 ($8) adults, £2.95 ($4.50) seniors/children, £13.95 ($21) families (2 adults/2 children). Open: Sat–Thurs 10 a.m.–6 p.m., Fri 11 a.m.–6 p.m. (last admission at 5:15 p.m.).

To See or Not to See: Shakespeare Sights

If you don't have time to visit Stratford-upon-Avon (see Chapter 21), where the great poet and dramatist William Shakespeare was born and died, you can visit two Shakespeare-associated sights on London's South Bank.

Shakespeare's Globe Theatre & Exhibition

South Bank

At this full-size replica of Shakespeare's Globe Theatre, just east of its original site, you can take guided tours through the theater and its workshops. You can find out about the days of Shakespeare and Elizabethan theater: what audiences were like, the rivalry among the theaters, the cruel bear-baiting shows, and the notorious Southwark Stews (a nearby area where prostitutes plied their trade). Watching a Shakespeare play from one of the benches in this roofless "wooden O" is a memorable experience, though the hard benches can be rough on the backside. See Chapter 22 for details on obtaining tickets for one of the performances presented May through September.

If you plan to see a Shakespeare play at the Globe, you can have a snack, tea, or a full meal in the theater itself. No reservations are required at **The Globe Café**; it's open daily May through September 10 a.m. to 11 p.m. and October through April 10 a.m. to 6 p.m. Make reservations ahead for lunch or dinner at **The Globe Restaurant ☎ 020/7928-9444**), open daily noon to 2:30 p.m. and 6 to 11 p.m.

New Globe Walk (just west of Southwark Bridge), SE1. ☎ *020/7902-1500. Tube: Mansion House (then a 10-minute walk across Southwark Bridge; the theater is visible on the west side along the river). Tours: £7.50 ($11) adults, £6 ($9) seniors/students, £5 ($8) children, £23 ($34) family. Open: Oct–April daily 10 a.m.–5 p.m., May–Sept (performance season) daily 9 a.m.–noon.*

Southwark Cathedral

South Bank

Chaucer and Shakespeare both worshiped at Southwark Cathedral. London's second-oldest church after Westminster Abbey, Southwark (pronounced *Suthick*) Cathedral is in what was London's first theater district (as well as a church-sanctioned center of prostitution). Although the cathedral was partially rebuilt in 1890, a great deal of history is associated with this 15th-century church. In under 30 minutes, you can see the entire site, including the Shakespeare memorial window and a 13th-century wooden effigy of a knight. Lunchtime concerts are regularly given on Monday and Tuesday; call for exact times and schedules.

Montague Close (just west of London Bridge) SE1. ☎ 020/7367-6700. Tube: London Bridge (then a 5-minute walk across London Bridge Road to Cathedral Street). Admission: Free, but a £2 ($3) donation is suggested. Open: Daily 8 a.m.–6 p.m.

Ships Ahoy! Nautical London

The River Thames, London's watery artery to the English Channel, is full of all kinds of watercraft. In Chapter 18, I tell you about touring the Thames by boat. This section details two intriguing ships that you can visit.

H.M.S. Belfast

South Bank

The *Belfast,* a huge Royal Navy cruiser built in 1938 and used in World War II, is now moored in the Thames near London Bridge opposite the Tower of London. Tours of this floating 10,500-ton museum allow visitors to see all seven decks. On-ship exhibits are devoted to the history of the ship and the Royal Navy. You and your kids can witness a re-created surface battle. Plan to spend about 90 minutes.

Morgan's Lane, Tooley Street (between Tower Bridge and London Bridge), SE1. ☎ 020/7940-6300. Tube: London Bridge (then a 10-minute walk north across Tooley Street and north on Hays Lane toward the entrance on the river). Admission: £5.40 ($8) adults, £4 ($6) seniors/students, children under 16 free. Open: Nov–March daily 10 a.m.–5 p.m.; April–Oct daily 10 a.m.–6 p.m. (last admission 45 minutes before closing).

Golden Hinde

South Bank

A full-scale reconstruction of Sir Francis Drake's 16th-century flagship, complete with a crew dressed in Tudor costumes, the *Golden Hinde* was built in Devon but launched in San Francisco in 1973 to commemorate Drake's claiming of California for Queen Elizabeth I. Like the original, this ship circumnavigated the globe, sailing more than 140,000 miles before becoming a permanent floating museum in 1996. A self-guided tour of the fully rigged ship, once the home to 20 officers and gentlemen and between 40 to 60 crew members, takes about a half-hour.

St. Mary Overie Dock, Cathedral Street (west of London Bridge), SE1. ☎ 08700/118-700. Tube: London Bridge (then a 5-minute walk west on Bedale and Cathedral streets). Admission: £2.50 ($3.75) adults, £2.10 ($3.15) seniors, £1.75 ($2.60) children, £6.50 ($10) families (2 adults/2 children). Open: Mon–Fri 10:00 a.m.–5:30 p.m., some weekends (call first).

Architectural Highlights and Stately Homes

Stepping into one of London's great mansions, you can see what life lived on a grand scale was really like. The capital is also full of intriguing monuments, including one called, simply, The Monument, and famous bridges, such as Tower Bridge, which you can visit high above the Thames.

Apsley House

St. James's

Once known as Number One London because it was the first house past the toll-gate into London, this magnificent neoclassical mansion designed by Robert Adam and built between 1771 and 1778 was the London residence of the first duke of Wellington. The last great London town house, Apsley contains original collections that are mostly intact. After his phenomenal military career, which included defeating Napoléon at Waterloo in 1815, the duke was one of the most popular men in England. Apsley House, with its sumptuous interiors and treasure trove of paintings, china, swords, and military honors, reflects the first duke's position as the most powerful commander in Europe. A free, audio guide explains it all on a self-guided tour that lasts about an hour. The family is still in residence, although you never see them.

Hyde Park Corner, W1. ☎ 020/7499-5676. Tube: Hyde Park Corner (Exit 3 brings you up next to the house). Admission: £4.50 ($7) adults, £3 ($4.50) seniors, children under 18 free. Open: Tues–Sun 11 a.m.–5 p.m.

The Monument

City of London

This 202-foot-high Doric column was designed by Sir Christopher Wren and commemorates the Great Fire of 1662, which allegedly began in nearby Pudding Lane and swept through London. The Monument is the tallest isolated stone column in the world — you'll know just how tall if you climb the 311 steps to the viewing platform at the top.

Monument Street (just north of London Bridge), EC3. ☎ 020/7626-2717. Tube: Monument (you get out right across the street). Admission: £1.50 ($2.25) adults, 50p (75¢) children. Open: Daily 10:00 a.m.–5:40 p.m.

Spencer House

St. James's

The late Princess Diana is probably the most famous member of the Spencer family, but she never lived in her family's ancestral London home, built for the first Earl Spencer in 1766. The house, one of London's most beautiful private palaces, hasn't been a private residence since 1927. Brilliantly restored and opened as a museum in 1990, its rooms are filled with period furniture and art loans from Queen Elizabeth, the Tate Britain, and the Victoria & Albert Museum. Guided tours (the only way to see the place) take about an hour.

27 St. James's Place, SW1. ☎ *020/7499-8620. Tube: Green Park (then a 5-minute walk south on Queen's Walk to St. James's Place on your left). Admission: £3.50 ($5) adults. Children under 10 not admitted. Open: Sun 10:30 a.m.–4:45 p.m. Closed Jan and Aug.*

Tower Bridge Experience

Southwark

The "experience" lets you get inside one of the world's most famous bridges to find out why, how, and when it was built. Harry, a Victorian bridge worker brought to life by animatronics, tells you the story of this famous drawbridge with its pinnacled towers and how the mechanism for raising the bridge for ship traffic actually works. You also meet the architect's ghost and visit a miniature music hall. The experience takes about 90 minutes. The spectacular views up and down the Thames from the bridge's glass-enclosed walkways double the value of this attraction.

North Pier, Tower Bridge, SE1. ☎ *020/7378-1928. Tube: Tower Hill (then a 10-minute walk south to the north pier of Tower Bridge). Admission: £6.25 ($9) adults, £4.25 ($6) seniors/students/children 5–15. Open: April–Oct daily 10:00 a.m.–6:30 p.m.; Nov–March daily 9:30 a.m.–6:00 p.m. (last admission 75 minutes before closing).*

For fans of Princess Di

If you're a true Princess Diana fan, note that she's buried on a picturesque island on the Oval Lake at **Althorp**, the Spencer family estate in Northamptonshire. The grounds are open for a limited time each year in July and August, but you can view the island from across the lake only.

Admission is £11 ($17) adults, £9 ($13) seniors, £5 ($8) children, and £27 ($40) families (2 adults, 2 children). The charge includes admission to the Diana Museum set up by her brother, Earl Spencer. The museum contains an exhibit celebrating Diana's childhood, her royal wedding (including her famous wedding gown), and her charitable works. I advise that you book your tickets in advance by calling ☎ 0870/167-9000. You can also buy day-of tickets (first-come, first-served) from the Northampton Visitor Centre by phone (☎ 01604/238-977) or online (www. tickets.com). For the most up-to-date information visit the Web site at www. althorp-house.co.uk.

Parks and Gardens

Part of London's charm comes from its giant green parks, small neighborhood squares, and special gardens. You never have to feel oppressed by too much brick and concrete in this city. If the mood strikes, you may want to visit one of the lovely spots described in this section.

Chelsea Physic Garden

Chelsea

Hidden behind high brick walls, the Chelsea Physic Garden is the second-oldest surviving botanical garden in England and one of London's most beautiful places. The garden, containing more than 7,000 exotic herbs, shrubs, trees, and flowers, plus England's earliest rock garden, was founded in 1673 by the Worshipful Society of Apothecaries to develop medicinal and commercial plant species. Cotton seeds from this garden launched an industry in the new colony of Georgia. The garden is small enough (3½ acres) to wander through in an hour, but budget some more time if you love plants.

Swan Walk, 66 Royal Hospital Rd., SW3. ☎ *020/7352-5646. Tube: Sloane Square (then a 15-minute walk south on Lower Sloane Street and west to the end of Royal Hospital Road). Bus: Southbound bus 11, 19, or 22 from Sloane Square Admission: £4 ($5) adults, £2 ($3) students/children 5–15. Open: April–Oct Wed 2–5 p.m., Sun 2–6 p.m.; daily 2–5 p.m. during the Chelsea Flower Show in May.*

Regent's Park

Marylebone

Regent's Park spans 400 acres of green, mostly open parkland fringed by imposing Regency terraces. The park is the home of the **London Zoo** (see Chapter 16). People come here to play soccer, cricket, tennis, and softball; boat in the lake; visit **Queen Mary's Rose Garden** (which includes an outdoor theater — see Chapter 22); and let their kids have fun in the many playgrounds. The sight offers summer lunch and evening bandstand concerts as well as puppet shows and other children's activities on weekdays throughout August. The northernmost section of the park rises to the summit of **Primrose Hill,** which provides fine views of Westminster and the City. The restrooms by Chester Gate, on the east side of the park, offer facilities for persons with disabilities.

Just north of Marylebone Road and surrounded by the Outer Circle road. ☎ *020/7 486-7905. Advance booking for Open Air Theatre (operating late May to early Sept)* ☎ *020/7486 7905. Tube: Regent's Park or Baker Street (then a 5-minute walk north to the south end of the park). Open: Daily 5 a.m. to dusk.*

Royal Botanic Gardens, Kew

Located 9 miles southwest of Central London, the **Royal Botanic Gardens** at Kew — more familiarly known as Kew Gardens — are a gift to garden lovers. A trip to Kew takes the better part of a day to allow for travel time and garden strolling, but the enjoyment that you receive is well worth the time investment. On display in the 300-acre gardens is a marvelous array of specimens first planted in the 17th and 18th centuries. Orchids and palms are nurtured in the Victorian glass pavilion hothouse. The site contains a lake, aquatic gardens, a Chinese pagoda, and even a royal palace. **Kew Palace,** the smallest and most lovely of the former royal compounds, is where King George III went insane. **Queen Charlotte's Cottage** served as the mad king's summer retreat.

Tired of the Tube? Why not take a boat to Kew Gardens? April to late September, vessels operated by the **Westminster Passenger Service Association** (☎ 020/7930-4721) leave from Westminster Pier daily 10:15 a.m., 11:15 a.m., noon, and 2 p.m. Round-trip fares for the 90-minute journey are about £10 ($15) adults, £8 ($12) seniors, and £5 ($8) children. The last boat from Kew usually departs around 5.30 p.m. (depending on the tide).

Kew. ☎ 020/8332-5000. Tube: Kew Gardens (then a 10-minute walk west on Broomfield Street to Victoria Gate entrance on Kew Road). Admission: £6.50 ($10) adults, £4.50 ($7) seniors, children 5–16 free. Tours: March–Nov free 1-hour tours daily at 11 a.m. and 2 p.m. Open: Gardens, daily 9:30 a.m. to dusk; glass pavilion closes 1 hour before gardens; Kew Palace, April–Oct Sat–Sun 11:00 a.m.–5:30 p.m. Closed Dec 25 and Jan 1.

A Quaint Village just a Tube Ride Away

The London that you see today was once a series of separate villages. The nearby village of Hampstead, with its adjacent heathland, still retains its rural charm and makes for an excellent excursion.

Hampstead and Hampstead Heath

Although only 15 minutes by Tube from Central London, **Hampstead** maintains its old-world charm. (See the map "Hampstead.") It's filled with Regency and Georgian houses (many set in lovely gardens) favored by artists and writers from Keats to John Le Carré. **Flask Walk,** the village's pedestrian mall, provides an eclectic assemblage of historic pubs, shops, and chic boutiques. The village itself has lots of old alleys, steps, courts, and groves just begging to be explored.

Hampstead

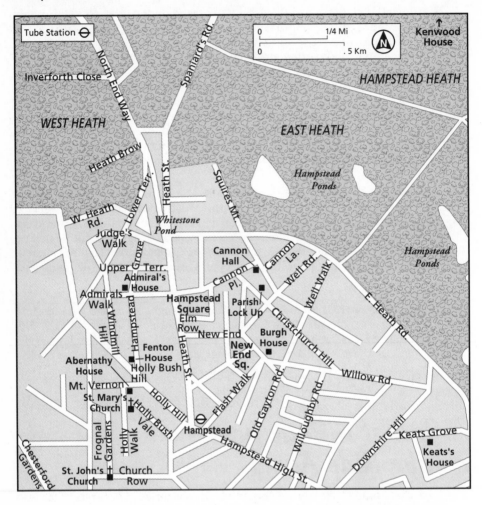

Adjacent **Hampstead Heath** is 800 acres of high parkland offering an opportunity for picnicking, swimming, and fishing. On a clear day you can see St. Paul's Cathedral and even the hills of Kent. An excursion here takes up at least a half day or more.

Tube: Hampstead (the Tube stop is a minute from Flask Walk) or Hampstead Heath (Parliament Hill, right behind the Tube stop, leads up into to the park itself).

Kenwood House

This lovely neoclassical villa sits on the shore of Kenwood Lake in the northern section of Hampstead Heath. The villa was remodeled in the 1760s by Robert Adam. Inside, you find a small but impressive collection of paintings (with works by Rembrandt, Vermeer, Gainsborough, Turner, and Reynolds) and jewelry. You can get something to eat in the cafeteria in the former coach house. For a remarkable summer outdoor concert experience, visit the Kenwood Lakeside concert (see Chapter 23 for information).

Hampstead Lane (Hampstead), NW3. ☎ *020/8348-1286. Tube: Archway (then bus 210 west along Highgate and Hampstead Lane). Admission: Free. Open: April–Oct daily 10 a.m.–6 p.m.; Nov–March daily 10 a.m.–4 p.m.*

Royal Castles and Palaces

Everyone wants to see Buckingham Palace, the Queen's London residence. But another royal residence, accessible year-round, awaits in nearby Windsor. Just as memorable is Hampton Court, another great royal compound from the time of Henry VIII.

Hampton Court Palace

In 1514, Cardinal Wolsey began building the splendid Tudor Hampton Court in East Moseley, Surrey, 13 miles west of London on the north side of the Thames. Henry VIII nabbed Hampton Court for himself and made it a royal residence, which it remained until 1760. The **Anne Boleyn Gate,** with its 16th-century astronomical clock, and the **Great Hall,** with its hammer-beam ceiling, are remnants from Hampton Court's Tudor days. Later, the palace was much altered by Sir Christopher Wren for William and Mary. Wren also designed the famous **Maze,** where visitors can wander in dizzy confusion. Inside the enormous palace are various state apartments and private rooms, including the **King's Dressing Room,** the Tudor kitchens, wooden carvings by Grinling Gibbons, Italian paintings, and guides dressed in period costumes. The manicured Thames-side gardens are lovely. You find a cafe and restaurant on the grounds. You need a full day for this excursion.

Hampton Court, East Moseley, Surrey. ☎ *020/8781-9500. Train: Frequent trains from Waterloo Station make the half-hour trip to Hampton Court Station; the round-trip fare costs about £4.50 ($7). Admission: £10.50 ($17) adult, £8 ($12) seniors/students, £7 ($11) children. Open: Mid-March–mid-Oct Tues–Sun 9:30 a.m.–6:00 p.m., Mon 10:15 a.m.–6:00 p.m.; mid-Oct–mid-March Tues–Sun 9:30 a.m.–4:30 p.m., Mon 10:15 a.m.–4:30 p.m. Closed Dec 24–26, Jan 1.*

Windsor Castle

Windsor is one of the queen's official residences. The castle, with its imposing skyline of towers and battlements rising from the center of the 4,800-acre Great Park, is located in Windsor, Berkshire, 20 miles from the center of London. The castle has been used as a royal residence since its construction by William the Conqueror approximately 900 years ago. The **State Apartments** that are open to visitors range from the intimate chambers of Charles II to the enormous Waterloo Chamber, built to commemorate the

Ghost palace

So many people, from staff to visitors, have reported encounters with Catherine Howard's ghost in the "haunted gallery" at Hampton Court that psychologists from the University of Hertfordshire conducted an investigation to see if they could find a scientific explanation for the phenomenon — the results were inconclusive. Catherine, the fifth wife of King Henry VIII, was locked up in Hampton Court prior to her beheading for adultery in 1542. One day she supposedly escaped and in desperation ran along the 40-foot gallery to pound on the king's door and beg for mercy. Sightings in this gallery of a running, screaming apparition have been reported for centuries.

victory over Napoléon in 1815. All are furnished with important works of art from the Royal Collection. **Queen Mary's Dollhouse,** designed by Sir Edwin Lutyens as a present for Queen Mary in 1921, is a marvelous palace in miniature. **St. George's Chapel,** a Gothic masterpiece of the 14th century, is the burial place of ten monarchs and the home of the Order of the Garter.

April through June, the **Changing of the Guard** takes place at 11 p.m. Monday through Saturday (on alternate days the rest of the year). From the ramparts of Windsor you can look down on the playing fields of **Eton College,** where aristocrats have been sending their boys for generations. All the royals attend the famous school in the charming town of **Eton** across the Thames Bridge. Give yourself a full day for this excursion.

Windsor. ☎ *01753/869-861. Train: Trains leave every half-hour from Waterloo Station for the 50-minute trip (the stop is Windsor & Eton); the round-trip fare is about £6 ($9). Admission: £11 ($17) adults, £9 ($13) seniors/students, £5.50 ($8) children 17 and under, £27.50 ($41) families (2 adults, 2 children). Open: Nov–Feb daily 9:45 a.m.–4:00 p.m. (last admission 3 p.m.); March–Oct daily 9:45 a.m.–5:30 p.m. (last admission 4 p.m.). Closed March 28, June 16, Dec 25–26, Jan 1.*

Greenwich: The Center of Time and Space

Time is of the essence in Greenwich, a town and borough of Greater London, about 4 miles east of The City. The world's clocks are set according to Greenwich Mean Time, and visitors from around the globe flock here to stand on the **Prime Meridian,** the line from which the world's longitude is measured. Greenwich offers enough to keep you fully occupied for a full day, and it makes a great outing for kids.

The easiest and most interesting route to get to Greenwich is by Dock-lands Light Rail from Tower Hill Gateway, which takes you past Canary Wharf and all the new Docklands development. The one-way fare is £1.50 ($2.25). Take the train to Island Gardens, the last stop, and then walk through the foot tunnel beneath the Thames to Greenwich. You come out next to the *Cutty Sark.* **Catamaran Cruisers (☎ 020/7987-1185)** runs a year-round fleet of boats from Embankment Pier to Greenwich Pier. A round-trip ticket is £7.50 ($11) adults, £5.65 ($8) seniors, and £4.10 ($6) children.

All the attractions in Greenwich are clearly signposted, and you can reach them on foot. The Greenwich Tourist Information Centre (46 Greenwich Church St.; ☎ **020/8858-6376**) is open daily 10 a.m. to 5 p.m. The center offers 1½ to 2-hour walking tours (at 12:15 and 2:15 p.m.) of the town's major sights for £4 ($6). Reservations aren't necessary, but you may want to call first to make certain that the schedule hasn't changed. If you take the walking tour, you get 20% off admission to the **National Maritime Museum** and **Old Royal Observatory.**

If you're looking for a nice spot for lunch, try the **Green Village Restaurant** (11–13 Greenwich Church St.; ☎ **020/8858-2348**). The restaurant serves several kinds of fresh fish (try the fish pie if it's available), American-style burgers, salads, and omelets. It's open daily 11 a.m. to midnight.

The Greenwich Passport saves you money if you're planning to visit the major attractions. The passport provides admission to the *Cutty Sark,* the National Maritime Museum, and the Royal Observatory (see the following entries). The cost is £12 ($18) adults and £9.60 ($14) seniors and students. You can obtain the Passport at the Tourist Infor-mation Centre or at any of the three attractions it covers.

Cutty Sark

The majestic *Cutty Sark,* berthed on the River Thames, is the last of the tea-clipper sailing ships. It was launched in 1869 and first used for the lucrative China Sea tea trade. Later, the ship carried wool from Australia and after that (up until the end of World War II) served as a training ship. Today, the hold contains a rich collection of nautical instruments and paraphernalia. You can visit the ship on a self-guided tour and see every-thing in under an hour. Kids seem to enjoy the experience of being aboard the old ship as much as adults.

King William Walk. ☎ 020/8858-3445. Admission: £3.50 ($5) adults, £2.50 ($3.75) children, £8.50 ($13) families (2 adults, 2 children). Open: Daily 10 a.m.–5 p.m.

National Maritime Museum

The paintings of ships are boring, but the National Maritime Museum also displays sailing crafts and models and an extensive exhibit on Lord

Nelson, which includes hundreds of his personal artifacts (including the coat he was wearing when he was shot at the Battle of Trafalgar). You can sail through in about a half-hour.

In Greenwich Park. ☎ *020/8312-6608. Admission: £7.50 ($11) adults, £6 ($9) seniors/ students, free for children 16 and under. Open: Daily 10 a.m.–5 p.m. (June–Sept 9 until 6 p.m.)*

Royal Observatory Greenwich

After leaving Queen's House (see the next entry), you can huff your way up the hill in the park to explore the center of time and space, the **Prime Meridian** (longitude 0 degrees). Of particular interest inside the observatory is the collection of original 18th-century chronometers (marked H1, H2, H3, and H4), beautiful instruments that were developed to help mariners chart longitude by time instead of by the stars. The Prime Meridian line and the various astronomical gadgets in the observatory appeal to the imaginations of older kids.

In Greenwich Park. ☎ *020/8312-6608. Admission: £6 ($9) adults, £4.80 ($7) seniors/ students, free to children under 16. Open: Daily 10 a.m.–5 p.m. (June–Sept 9 until 6 p.m.).*

Queen's House

Adjacent to the National Maritime Museum is the splendidly restored Queen's House, designed by Inigo Jones in 1616 and later used as a model for the White House. The museum was the first classical building in England. The house was commissioned by Anne of Denmark, the wife of James I, and completed in 1635 (with later modifications). You can visit the royal apartments on a self-guided tour that takes about a half-hour. Special exhibits are also held here.

In Greenwich Park. ☎ *020/8312-6608. Admission: £7.50 ($11) adults, £6 ($9) seniors/ students, £3.75 ($6) children. Open: Daily 10 a.m.–5 p.m.*

Royal Naval College

Near the *Cutty Sark,* the Royal Naval College occupies the site of Greenwich Palace, which stood here from 1422 to 1620 and was the birthplace of Henry VIII, Mary I, and Elizabeth I. Badly damaged by Cromwell's troops during the English Civil War, the palace was later torn down, and in 1696 a naval hospital for retired seamen was erected in its place. The Thames-side buildings, designed by Sir Christopher Wren, became the Naval College in 1873 and are today a UNESCO-designated World Heritage Site. The only rooms open to visitors are the chapel and the imposing **Great Hall** with its dazzling painted ceiling. The body of Lord Nelson lay in state here in 1805.

King William Walk. ☎ *020/8858-2154. Admission: Free. Open: Daily 2:30–4:45 p.m.*

Chapter 18

Seeing London by Guided Tour

● ●

In This Chapter
▶ Taking the bus
▶ Cruising the river
▶ Touring London on foot

● ●

*L*ondon, a vast metropolis with centuries of history, offers something for everyone. Whether you love history, gardens, the arts, or royalty, you can find sights and events of interest. But how do you know where to begin discovering London? Ideally, you can examine the lists of sights in Chapters 16 and 17 and make some wise choices based on your preferences. Then you can use public transportation to visit your selections and spend as much time as you have available for each site. However, some people may find a general city overview to be helpful. And some travelers have only a couple of days to cover the most popular sights, such as Buckingham Palace and Westminster Abbey. Some visitors to London may not be able to comfortably use the Underground subway system or walk long distances. In these cases, a guided tour may be just the ticket.

This chapter provides information on all kinds of tours; you can travel on a motor coach, a boat, or your own shoe leather.

The Lay of the Land: Getting Oriented by Bus

The general sightseeing companies offer variations of two basic half-day orientation tours by bus:

> ✔ An excursion that covers sights in the West End, including a visit to Westminster Abbey and a chance to see the Changing of the Guard at Buckingham Palace (however, see the following paragraph).

> ✔ An excursion that heads east into The City, with stops at St. Paul's Cathedral and the Tower of London.

Many folks take tours that include Buckingham Palace because they think a tour is the easiest way to see the Changing of the Guard. Keep in mind that the Changing of the Guard is no longer a daily occurrence; it takes place every *other* day August 1 through March 31 (see Chapter 16 for details). If the event is not scheduled to occur the day you take your tour, you'll probably visit the Household Cavalry in Whitehall instead. This alternative sight is less impressive but still noteworthy.

The following sections describe the main sightseeing tours that travel by bus (also see Evan Evans in the section "River Views: Cruising Down the Thames" later in this chapter for another bus-tour option):

✔ **Golden Tours** (office at 4 Fountain Square, 123–151 Buckingham Palace Rd.; ☎ **800/456-6303** in the United States or 020/7233-7030; Internet: www.goldentours.co.uk; Tube: Victoria) offers many guided excursions. Their comfortable buses have restrooms, and the certified guides have certifiable senses of humor. The daily *Historic & Modern London* tour is a full-day outing that includes the West End, Westminster Abbey, the Changing of the Guard, the City of London, St. Paul's Cathedral, the Tower of London, and a cruise from the Tower down to Charing Cross Pier; the fee includes a pub lunch, a tea aboard ship, and all admission prices, so this tour is a good value.

The cost is £53 ($79) for adults and £46 ($69) for kids under 16. Tours depart from the office on Buckingham Palace Road and from other points in Central London. Courtesy pick-up service is available from several hotels. You can book your tickets in person, by phone, or online, or you can ask your hotel concierge to do it for you.

✔ **Original London Sightseeing Tours** (box office at Baker Street Station Forecourt, corner of Baker Street and Marylebone Road; ☎ **020/8877-1722;** Internet: www.theoriginaltour.com; Tube: Baker Street) allows you to pick and choose what you see and how much time you spend at each location. This company maintains a fleet of double-decker buses (many of them open on top), and offers hop-on/hop-off service at more than 90 boarding points around the city. The *Original London Sightseeing Tour* provides live commentary. The tour, not including time for your stops, lasts 90 minutes and covers every major sight in Central London and the South Bank. A multilingual version of the tour is also available. In addition, the company operates **City Connectors,** which are buses without commentary, that shuttle from one sight to the next and include stops at shopping areas. One ticket, valid for 24 hours, lets you take all tours and ride City Connectors.

The company offers a timesaving **Fast Track ticket service** for many London attractions. On the bus, for no additional charge, you can buy tickets for the Tower of London, museums, and other places that are on your itinerary. When you arrive, you don't have to stand in line for tickets.

You can get tickets online or at the box office. After you have your ticket, you can begin the tour at any one of 90 different pick-up spots throughout the city (look for "Original London Tour" on London bus stop signs). Tours depart every 15 minutes daily 9 a.m. to 6 p.m. (in summer, every 5 minutes until 9 p.m.). A ticket good for 24 hours on all tour routes costs £14 ($21) for adults and £7.50 ($11) for children under 16.

✔ **Visitors Sightseeing Tours** (☎ 020/7636-7175; Internet: www. visitorsightseeing.co.uk) offers the *Big Bus Tour,* which passes every major sight and offers live commentary and hop-on/hop-off service on open-top buses. The company also provides more individualized tours, including day tours to places outside of London (such as Stonehenge). London tours, available daily, are conducted on luxury buses with certified guides; tour prices vary according to the itinerary. You can see the complete selection of tours by visiting their Web site, and you can then get tickets by phone for the tour of your choice. Tours leave from the Departure Lounge, Royal National Hotel, Bedford Way (Tube: Russell Square).

On Monday, Wednesday, Friday, and Sunday at 6:50 p.m., Visitors Sightseeing Tours offers a macabre tour called *Ghosts, Ghouls & Ancient Taverns* that explores sights associated with Jack the Ripper and the medieval plague and stops in at a couple of pubs along the way. The cost is £17 ($26) adults, £15 ($22) seniors; the tour isn't recommended for children under 14.

River Views: Cruising Down the Thames

For many people, a boat trip down the Thames is one of the grand highlights of a trip to London. Children especially enjoy these trips on the water. Sightseeing boats regularly ply the river between Westminster and the Tower of London; some continue downstream to Greenwich (site of the Prime Meridian, *Cutty Sark,* and Old Royal Observatory) and upstream to Kew Gardens and Hampton Court (see Chapter 17 for details on these two sights and Greenwich). As you float past, you can view many of London's great monuments: the Houses of Parliament, Westminster Abbey, St. Paul's Cathedral, and the Tower Bridge. The main departure points along the Thames are at Westminster Pier (Tube: Westminster), Waterloo Pier (Tube: Waterloo), Embankment Pier (Tube: Embankment), Tower Pier (Tube: Tower Hill), and Greenwich Pier (Tube: Greenwich). For recorded information on these tours, call the general London transportation line at ☎ 0839/123-432.

You may enjoy the river tours that the following companies provide (see also **Golden Tours** in the preceding section, "The Lay of the Land: Getting Oriented by Bus"):

✔ **Evan Evans** (☎ 020/7950-1777; Internet: www.evanevans.co.uk) offers three river cruises in addition to daily coach tours of London. A daily lunch cruise aboard the *Silver Bonito* costs £17.50 ($28) per person. Another daily offering starts with a guided boat tour of the Thames, disembarks for a tour of the Tower of London, and continues by bus to The City and St. Paul's; the price is £30.50 ($46) for adults and £28.50 ($43) for children ages 3 to 16. A daily full-day tour takes in Westminster Abbey, continues to Buckingham Palace for the Changing of the Guard, includes a lunch cruise on the Thames, and returns by bus to St. Paul's and the Tower of London. The price is £53.50 ($80) for adults and £48.50 ($73) for children.

✔ **Catamaran Cruisers** (☎ 020/7987-1185; Internet: www.catamaran cruisers.co.uk) runs a year-round fleet of boats on the Thames. A ticket from Embankment Pier to Greenwich costs £8.50 ($13) for adults (slightly higher in July and August), £7.65 ($11) for seniors, and £5 ($7) for children. From April to October, the company offers a nightly (6:30, 7:30, and 10:30 p.m.) 50-minute circular cruise from Embankment Pier that passes most of London's major floodlit monuments (the same cruise is available during the day as well). All the boats provide live commentary and have a fully licensed bar. The cost is £6.70 ($10) for adults and £4.70 ($7) for children. If you want a half-hour trip on the river from Embankment Pier to the Tower of London or the other way around, Catamaran Cruisers is the place to try. A one-way ticket in either direction is £5.70 ($9) for adults and £3.50 ($5) for children.

✔ **Westminster Passenger Services** (☎ 020/7930-4721) operates boats year-round from Westminster Pier, across from the Houses of Parliament, to Kew Gardens and Hampton Court. The round-trip fare between Westminster and Kew is £11 ($16) adults, £5 ($7) child; from Westminster to Hampton Court the round-trip fare is £14 ($21) adults, £7 ($10) children.

Splendid Scenery, Fine Food: Dining on the River

If you just want a romantic river dining experience, **Bateaux London** (☎ 020/7925-2215) offers a nightly dinner cruise that leaves Embankment Pier (Tube: Embankment) at 7:15 p.m. and returns at 10:45 p.m. The cruise, which includes a four-course dinner with live music and after-dinner dancing, costs £58 ($87) per person Sunday to Wednesday, £60 ($90) per person Thursday to Saturday.

A one-hour lunch cruise with a three-course set menu and live commentary is offered Monday through Saturday at £21 ($31) per person; the cruise departs from Embankment Pier at 12:15 p.m. A two-hour, three-course Sunday lunch jazz cruise departs from Embankment Pier at 12:15 p.m. and costs £35 ($52) per person.

Advance reservations are required for all Bateaux London cruises, and a "smart casual" dress code (no sweat pants or running shoes) is in effect.

Walk This Way: Taking a Walking Tour

Nothing beats walking as a means of getting acquainted with a city. And walking tours give you the additional benefit of a knowledgeable guide providing reliable information. This form of exploration is great for people with special interests (such as architecture, history, or literature). And older children usually enjoy walking tours as well. The weekly events listed in *Time Out* magazine, available at every newsstand in London, include dozens of intriguing walks; a walk goes on every day.

If you want to follow detailed strolls on your own, check out the 11 tours offered in *Frommer's Memorable Walks in London* (published by Hungry Minds, Inc.). The following companies offer enjoyable guided walking tours:

- **London Walks** (☎ 020/7624-3978; Internet: www.london.walks.com) is the oldest walking tour company in London. It offers a terrific array of tours, including *Jack the Ripper's London, Christopher Wren's London, Oscar Wilde's London,* and *The Beatles' Magical Mystery Tour.* Different walks are available for every day of the week, rain or shine; they last about two hours and end near an Underground station. You don't need to reserve in advance. A London Walk costs £5 ($8) for adults and £4 ($6) for students with ID; kids are free if accompanied by a parent. Call or check the Web site for departure points and schedules.

- **Stepping Out** (☎ 020/8881-2933; Internet: www.walklon.ndirect.co.uk) offers guided walking tours of several London neighborhoods, including Southwark on the South Bank. One off-beat theme walk called *Brothels, Bishops and the Bard* explores the Clink (the oldest prison in London), Shakespeare's memorial window in Southwark Cathedral, and the site of the original Globe Theatre. The cost is £5 ($8) for adults and £4 ($6) for seniors/students. Call or check the Web site for departure points and schedules.

Chapter 19

Shopping in Paradise: London's Stores and Markets

● ●

In This Chapter

▶ Getting your VAT refund

▶ Using sound judgment at the duty-free airport shops

▶ Taking your purchases through Customs

▶ Visiting the big department stores

▶ Shopping Knightsbridge and the West End

● ●

L ondon is one of the world's great shopping meccas. If shopping is on your agenda, you can find any item that you're looking for. But you won't find many bargains, except during the department stores' big sales in January and July (see the sidebar "Saving on the London sales," later in this chapter).

Surveying the Shopping Scene

You get the best values on goods that are manufactured in England. Items from The Body Shop, Filofax, or Dr. Martens cost less than they do in the United States. Other potentially good values include woolens and cashmeres, English brands of bone china, English toiletries, antiques, used silver, old maps and engravings, and rare books. You can also do well with French products; the prices are almost as good as Paris offers.

You may be surprised — and perhaps disappointed — at the number of big U.S. chains that have opened stores in London. But in addition to the familiar chains and megastores, London is still the home of hundreds of small, unique specialty shops and boutiques to delight the eye and empty the wallet.

Normal shopping hours are Monday through Saturday 10:00 a.m. to 5:30 p.m., with a late closing (7 or 8 p.m.) on Wednesday or Thursday. The law allows stores to be open for six hours on Sunday, usually 11 a.m. to 5 p.m.

Table 19-1 lists conversions for U.S. and U.K. sizes.

Table 19-1		The Right Fit: Size Conversions	
U.S.	*U.K.*	*U.S.*	*U.K.*
Women's Clothes		*Women's Shoes*	
8	10	4½	3
10	12	5½	4
12	14	6½	5
Women's Clothes		*Women's Shoes*	
14	16	7½	6
16	18	8½	7
18	20	9½	8
Men's Clothes/Shirts		*Men's Shoes*	
Sizes are the same		7	6
		8	7
		9	8
		10	9
		11	10
		12	11

Getting the VAT Tax Back

The *VAT* (value-added tax) in London and throughout the United Kingdom is 17.5%. You have to pay this tax on every retail item. Anyone who isn't a resident of the European Union can get a VAT refund, but every store requires a minimum purchase to qualify. The exact amount varies from store to store, although the minimum expenditure is £50 ($75). Not every store honors this minimum: It's £100 ($150) at Harrods, for example. But qualifying for a tax refund is far easier in Britain than in almost any other country in the European Union.

VAT isn't charged on goods shipped out of the country, no matter how much you spend. You can avoid VAT and the hassle of lugging large packages back with you by having London stores ship your purchases for you; many are happy to do so. However, shipping charges can *double* the cost of your purchase, and you may also have to pay U.S.

duties when the goods arrive. Instead of this costly strategy, consider paying for excess baggage (rates vary with the airlines).

To get a VAT refund, you must get a VAT refund form from the retailer, and the retailer must complete the form at the time of purchase. Don't leave the store without a completed refund form. Don't let any merchant tell you that you can get refund forms at the airport.

You can get back about 15% of the 17.5% VAT that you pay on your purchases. (You can't get back the entire amount.) To obtain your refund, follow these steps:

1. **Ask the store whether it does VAT refunds and how much the minimum purchase is.**

2. **If you've spent the minimum amount, ask for the VAT refund paperwork. The retailer must fill out a portion.**

3. **Fill out your portion of the form (name, address).**

4. **Present the form — along with the goods — at the VAT Refunds counter in the airport.**

You're required to show the goods at your time of departure, so don't pack them in your checked luggage; put them in your carry-on instead.

After the paperwork is stamped, you have two choices:

✔ You can mail in the papers and receive your refund in a British check (no!) or a credit-card refund (yes!).

✔ You can go directly to the Cash VAT Refund desk at the airport and get your refund in cash.

The bad news: If you accept cash other than British pounds sterling, you lose money on the conversion rate. Many stores charge a flat fee for processing your refund, so £3 to £5 ($4.50–$8) may be automatically deducted from the total refund. Even so, you may still be saving a bundle.

If you're traveling from London to other countries in the European Union, don't apply for your VAT refund at the London airport. Apply for all your VAT refunds at one time at your final destination, prior to departure from the European Union.

Choosing Wisely at Duty-Free Shops

Many visitors to London and other cities take advantage of the duty-free shopping at the airports. The *duty* they avoid paying in these shops is the local tax on the items (like state sales tax in the United

States), not any import duty that may be assessed by the U.S. Customs office. Duty-free shopping is big business at airports. Heathrow Airport's Terminal 4 resembles a shopping mall, and the other terminals also offer a good bit of shopping and not much crossover between brands.

Before you decide to spend your preboarding time shopping, consider this fact: Not every item in a duty-free area is a bargain. Airport prices for souvenirs and candy bars, for example, are higher than elsewhere in London. Duty-free prices on luxury goods are usually fair but not bargain basement. Liquor and cigarettes, on the other hand, are often much less expensive than in the United States. If you do find yourself shopping in the airport stores, watch for special promotions and coupons that can save you some pounds at the time of purchase.

Don't postpone your shopping until you get to the airport. And if you do intend to shop the duty-free stores, familiarize yourself with London prices beforehand, so you know what is a good value and what isn't. And understand that buying items at a duty-free shop before flying home does *not* exempt them from counting toward your U.S. Customs limits (monetary or otherwise).

Getting Your Goodies Through Customs

The Customs authority doesn't impose limits on how much loot **U.S. citizens** can bring home from a trip abroad, but it does put limits on how much they can bring back for free. You may bring home $400 worth of goods duty-free, providing you've been out of the country at least 48 hours and haven't used the exemption in the past 30 days. Here's some additional information about the limit and Customs law:

✔ The law includes not more than 1 liter of an alcoholic beverage (you must be over 21).

✔ The law includes not more than 200 cigarettes and 100 cigars.

✔ Antiques more than 100 years old and works of art are exempt from the $400 limit, as is anything you mail home from abroad.

✔ You may mail up to $200 worth of goods to yourself (marked "For Personal Use") and up to $100 worth to others (marked "Unsolicited Gift") once each day, as long as the package doesn't include alcohol or tobacco products.

✔ You must pay an import duty on anything over these limits, a flat rate of 10% duty on the next $1,000 worth of purchases.

✔ You must show proof of ownership for any expensive items, such as cameras or laptop computers, that you take with you to the United Kingdom. If you don't have proof (such as sales receipts or insurance forms), you can register the items before your trip using Custom Form 4457, available through the U.S. Customs Service (see the next paragraph).

Be sure to have your receipts with you. For more specific guidance, write to the **U.S. Customs Service** (P.O. Box 7407, Washington, D.C. 20044 ☎ **202/927-6724**), requesting the free pamphlet *Know Before You Go.* Or check out the details on the Customs Department Web site at www.customs.ustreas.gov.

Returning **Canadian citizens** are allowed a C$300 exemption and can bring back, free of duty, 200 cigarettes, 2.2 pounds of tobacco, 40 imperial ounces (1.2 quart) of liquor, and 50 cigars. You should declare all valuables that you're taking with you to the United Kingdom, such as expensive cameras, on the Y-38 Form before departure from Canada. For a clear summary of Canadian rules, write for the booklet *I Declare,* issued by Revenue Canada (2265 St. Laurent Blvd., Ottawa K1G 4KE; ☎ **800/461-9999** or 613-993-0534).

The duty-free allowance for returning **Australian citizens** is A$400 (A$200 for those under 18). Citizens can bring home, free of duty, 250 cigarettes or 250 grams of loose tobacco, and 1.125 liters of alcohol. Australian citizens who'll be returning home with valuable goods they already own (for example, foreign-made cameras) should file form B263 before leaving. For more information, contact Australian Customs Services (GPO Box 8, Sydney NSW 2001; ☎ **02/9213-2000**).

The duty-free allowance for **New Zealand citizens** is NZ$700. Citizens over 17 can bring in 200 cigarettes, or 50 cigars, or 250 grams of tobacco, or a mix of all three if the combined weight doesn't exceed 250 grams; plus 4.5 liters of beer and wine, or 1.125 liters of liquor. To avoid paying duty on goods you already own (cameras and the like), fill out a certificate of export before you leave, listing the valuables you are taking out of the country. For more information, contact New Zealand Customs (50 Anzac Ave., P.O. Box 29, Auckland; ☎ **09/359-6655**).

Checking Out the Big Names

London is full of department stores. Some, like world-famous Harrods, may be familiar to you. Others, like Harvey Nichols, may be pleasant surprises. All these established department stores have their own style and personality.

Saving on the London sales

Traditionally, London stores hold sales in January and July. In recent times, the July sales have begun in June or earlier. The January sale is the main event, and it generally starts after the first week (when round-trip airfares are low).

The January sale at Harrods is the most world famous, but nearly every other store has a big sale at the same time. Discounts usually range from 25% to 50% at the major stores, such as Harrods and Selfridges. At Harrods, you'll find the best buys on the store's logo souvenirs, English china, and English designer brands such as Jaeger.

Fenwick of Bond Street

Mayfair

Fenwick of Bond Street is a high-style women's fashion store. Fenwick (pronounced "*Fen*-ick") was founded in 1891 and offers an impressive collection of designer women's wear, ranging from moderately priced ready-to-wear items to more expensive designer fashions. Fenwick also sells an array of lingerie in all price ranges.

63 New Bond St., W1. ☎ *020/7629-9161. Tube: Bond Street. Open: Mon–Tue and Thurs–Sat 10:00 a.m.–6:30 p.m. and Wed 10 a.m.–8 p.m.*

Fortnum & Mason

St. James's

Fortnum & Mason, down the street from the Ritz hotel, holds two *royal warrants* (a royal warrant is a form of official patronage the store can use in its advertising) and is the Queen's London grocer (but don't expect to see Her Majesty in the store). Amid a setting of deep-red carpets and crystal chandeliers, you can find everything from pâté de foie gras to Campbell's soup. The grocery department carries the finest foods from around the world, and on the other floors you find bone china, crystal, leather, antiques, and stationery departments. Dining choices include the **Patio, St. James's,** and **The Fountain** (see Chapter 14).

181 Piccadilly, W1. ☎ *020/7734-8040. Tube: Piccadilly Circus. Open: Mon–Sat 10:00 a.m.–6:30 p.m.*

Harrods

Knightsbridge

Harrods may be the most famous department store in the world. Carrying one of the coveted green plastic Harrods bags that you get with your purchase can provide you with a sense of accomplishment. The store's 300 departments offer merchandise that's breathtaking in its range, variety, and quality. Best of all are the Food Halls, stocked with a huge variety of foods and several cafes.

87–135 Brompton Rd., SW1. ☎ 020/7730-1234. Tube: Knightsbridge. Open: Mon–Sat 10 a.m.–7 p.m.

Harvey Nichols

Knightsbridge

Harvey Nichols, the late Princess Diana's favorite store, has its own gourmet food hall and fancy restaurant, the **Fifth Floor,** and is crammed with designer home furnishings, gifts, and fashions. Women's clothing is the largest segment of its business, a familiar fact to those fans of the British TV series *Absolutely Fabulous.* Harvey Nicks, as it's called, doesn't compete with Harrods because it features a much more upmarket, fashionable image.

109–125 Knightsbridge, SW1. ☎ 020/7235-5000. Tube: Knightsbridge. Open: Mon, Tues, and Sat 10 a.m.–7 p.m., Wed–Fri 10 a.m.–8 p.m., and Sun noon to 6 p.m.

Liberty

St. James's

Liberty provides six floors of fashion, china, home furnishings, upholstery fabrics, scarves, ties, luggage, and gifts. The store is best known for its Liberty Prints — fine quality fabrics, typically in floral patterns. These distinctive fabrics are highly sought after by interior decorators because they add an unmistakable touch of England to any room decor.

214–220 Regent St., W1. ☎ 020/7734-1234. Tube: Oxford Circus. Open: Mon–Wed 10:00 a.m.–6:30 p.m, Thurs 10 a.m.–8 p.m., Fri–Sat 10 a.m –7 p.m., Sun noon to 6 p.m.

Harrods loses royal warrant

The London gossip columns were ablaze early in 2000 when Prince Philip withdrew his royal warrant (a sign of official royal patronage) from Harrods, claiming that the royal household just didn't use the store as much as it used to. Harrods just happens to be owned by Mohamed Al Fayed, father of Dodi Al Fayed, who was killed with Princess Diana in that famous car crash. The elder Mr. Al Fayed, an Egyptian who's been denied U.K. citizenship, has made some startling allegations against the House of Windsor, claiming that the deaths of Diana and his son were not accidental. Could that be the real reason that Harrods is now warrantless?

Finding a drugstore

The English refer to a drugstore as a chemist's shop. All over London, you can find **Boots the Chemist** stores. In terms of size and convenience, the best one is just across from Harrods (at 72 Brompton Rd., SW3; ☎ 020/7589-6557; Tube: Knightsbridge). In addition to medicine, Boots sells film, pantyhose (called *tights*), sandwiches, and all of life's little necessities. The store is open Monday through Friday 8:30 a.m. to 7:00 p.m. and Saturday 9 a.m. to 7 p.m. One of the most centrally located chemists is **Bliss the Chemist** (5 Marble Arch, W1; ☎ 020/7723-6116; Tube: Marble Arch) open daily 9 a.m. to midnight. **Zafash Pharmacy** (233–235 Old Brompton Rd., SW5; ☎ 020/7373-2798; Tube: Earl's Court) is London's only 24-hour pharmacy.

Marks & Spencer

Mayfair

Marks & Spencer is a private-label department store that offers basics of all kinds. The merchandise at both locations is high quality, if a bit conservative.

458 Oxford St., W1 (☎ 020/7935-7954; Tube: Marble Arch) and 173 Oxford St., W1 (☎ 020/7437-7722; Tube: Oxford Circus). Open: Mon–Fri 9 a.m.–8 p.m., Sat 9:00 a.m.–7:30 p.m., and Sun noon to 6 p.m.

Selfridges

Mayfair

Selfridges is one of the largest department stores in Europe. The store has been redone to attract upscale customers, but the vast size of the store provides room for less expensive mass-marketed lines as well. More than 500 divisions sell everything from artificial flowers to groceries. The Miss Selfridge boutique, on one side of the store near the cosmetics department, features teen fashions, hotshot clothes, accessories, makeup, and moderately priced cutting-edge fashions. While on this side of the store, you can visit the cafe.

400 Oxford St., W1. ☎ 020/7629-1234. Tube: Bond Street or Marble Arch. Open: Mon–Wed 10 a.m.–7 p.m., Thurs and Fri 10 a.m.–8 p.m., Sat 9:30 a.m.–7:00 pm., and Sun 11:30 a.m.–6:00 p.m.

Taking It to the Street (Markets)

Markets make for fun shopping because you never know what you may find. The places listed in this section are for adventurous shoppers who like to browse and dawdle.

Portobello Road

Kensington Church Street dead-ends at the Notting Hill Gate Tube station, which is the jumping-off point for **Portobello Market** (No phone; Tube: Notting Hill Gate), the famous London street market along Portobello Road. Portobello (market and road) is a magnet for collectors of virtually anything from precious junk to precious antiques. The market is mainly open Saturday 6 a.m. to 5 p.m. You may find that perfect Regency commode you've always been looking for. But mixed in with the good things is a lot of overpriced junk, so you have to wade through to find anything worthwhile. Now that everything's been discovered and designated *collectible,* the prices are often too high.

The Portobello Market on a busy Saturday is prime pickpocketing territory. Keep an eye or a hand on your wallet or purse.

If you want to check out the shops along Portobello Road, I advise that you visit during the week. Approximately 90 antiques and art shops are open here during the week when the street market is closed. Weekdays are a better time for serious collectors to shop, because they get more attention from dealers and aren't distracted by the throngs of shoppers.

Covent Garden

The **Covent Garden Market** (☎ 020/7836-9136; Tube: Covent Garden) includes retail stores and two different markets (the kind with stalls) open daily 9 a.m. to 5 p.m. Traders sell all kinds of goods at the busy **Apple Market.** Much of the merchandise is what the English call *collectible nostalgia,* which includes glassware and ceramics, leather goods, toys, clothes, hats, and jewelry. Antiques dealers predominate on Mondays. The backside of Covent Garden is the home of **Jubilee Market** (☎ 020/7836-2139), a bit more downscale market where you can find cheap clothes and books. Some of London's best shopping is available at the restored hall on The Piazza and at specialty shops in the area (see "The West End: More famous shopping streets and stores," later in this chapter).

Chelsea and Antiquarius

In a rambling old building, the **Chelsea Antiques Market** (253 King's Rd., SW3; ☎ 020/7352-5686; Tube: Sloane Square) offers endless bric-a-brac browsing possibilities. This market is definitely a good place to search out old or rare books. You're likely to run across Staffordshire dogs, shaving mugs, Edwardian buckles and clasps, ivory-handled razors, old velours, lace gowns, wooden tea caddies; and that's just the beginning. The market is closed on Sunday.

Another good market is **Antiquarius** (131–141 King's Rd., SW3; ☎ 020/7351-5353; Tube: Sloane Square), where more than 120 dealers offer specialized merchandise — usually of the small, domestic variety, such as antique and period jewelry, porcelain, silver, first-edition books, boxes, clocks, prints, and paintings. The shops and booths are generally open Monday through Saturday from 10 a.m. to 6 p.m.

Shopping in Knightsbridge and the West End

London's two major shopping areas are Knightsbridge and the West End. You can find some of London's most famous and most impressive stores along several key streets in these two neighborhoods. You also find all the department stores listed in "Checking Out the Big Names," earlier in this chapter.

Knightsbridge: Home of Harrods

The home of department stores Harrods and Harvey Nichols, Knightsbridge is the second-most famous of London's retail districts (see the map "Knightsbridge and Chelsea Shopping").

Brompton Road (home to Harrods) runs southwest from the Knightsbridge Tube stop. Beauchamp Place (pronounced *Beech*-um), one of the streets running south from Brompton Road, is only one block long, but it's full of the kinds of trendy, upscale shops where young British aristocrats buy their clothing for "the season." In the 1980s, the future Princess Diana and other young blue bloods and yuppies were dubbed "the Sloane Rangers" because this area near Sloane Square was their favorite shopping grounds (and Range Rovers were their favorite cars). Cheval Place, running parallel to Brompton Road to the north, is lined with designer resale shops. Sloane Street, where you can find plenty of fashion boutiques, runs south from the Knightsbridge Tube stop to Sloane Square and the beginning of Chelsea.

The **Map House of London** (54 Beauchamp Place, SW3; ☎ 020/ 7589-4325; Tube: Knightsbridge) is an ideal place to find a sophisticated souvenir, maybe an antique map, an engraving, or an old print of London; a century-old original engraving can cost as little as £15 ($22).

Chelsea: The young and the antique

Chelsea is famous for King's Road (Tube: Sloane Square). This road is the area's main street and, along with Carnaby Street, is branded in Londoner's minds (those over 40, that is) as the street of the Swinging Sixties. About one-third of King's Road is devoted to antiques markets and *multistores* (large or small groups of indoor stands, stalls, and booths within one enclosure); another third houses design trade

Shopping in Knightsbridge and Chelsea

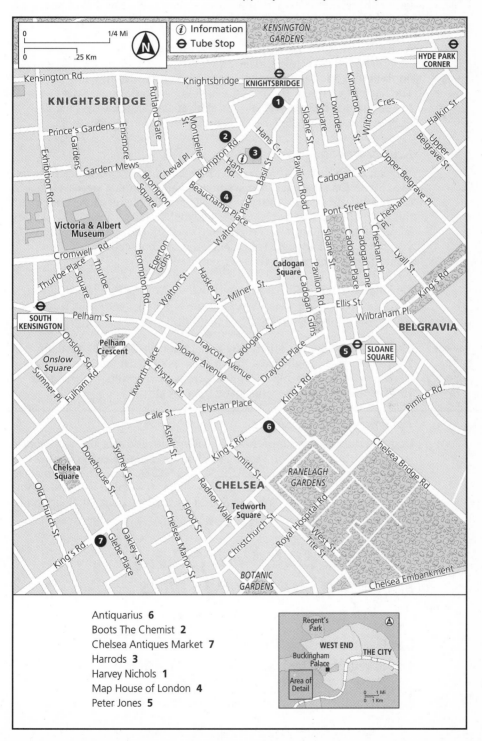

Antiquarius **6**
Boots The Chemist **2**
Chelsea Antiques Market **7**
Harrods **3**
Harvey Nichols **1**
Map House of London **4**
Peter Jones **5**

showrooms and stores of household wares, and the remaining third is faithful to the area's teenybopper roots. King's Road begins on the west side of the Sloane Square Tube stop.

A Chelsea emporium founded in 1877, **Peter Jones** (Sloane Square, SW1; ☎ 020/7730-3434; Tube: Sloane Square) is known for household goods, household fabrics and trims, china, glass, soft furnishings, and linens. The linen department is one of the best in London. You may also want to check out the **Chelsea Antiques Market** and **Antiquarius** (see the section "Taking It to the Street (Markets)" earlier in this chapter).

Kensington: Street chic

You can reach Kensington, west of Knightsbridge, by taking the Tube to High Street Kensington, the area's preeminent shopping street. Many of this neighborhood's retail shops cater to street chic teens. Although this strip offers a few staples of basic British fashion, most of the stores feature items that stretch and are very, very short or very, very long; very, very tight; and very, very black. And, of course, they sell the clunky shoes that go with these ensembles.

Kensington Church Street, running north to Notting Hill, is one of the city's main shopping avenues for antiques, selling everything from antique furniture to Impressionist paintings.

The **Children's Book Centre** (237 Kensington High St., W8; ☎ 020/7937-7497; Tube: High Street Kensington) is the best place in London to go for children's books. Fiction is arranged according to age, up to 16. The center also sells videos and toys for kids.

Holborn: Heigh-ho, Silver!

Don't let the slightly out-of-the-way Holborn location, or the facade's lack of charm, put you off visiting the **London Silver Vaults** (Chancery House, 53–63 Chancery Lane, WC2; ☎ 020/7242-3248; Tube: Chancery Lane). Downstairs are the real vaults — 40 in all — filled with a staggering collection of old and new silver and silverplate, plus a collection of jewelry.

The West End: More famous shopping streets and stores

The key shopping areas in the West End are

- ✔ **Oxford Street** for affordable shopping
- ✔ **Regent Street** for fancier shops and more upscale department stores and specialty dealers
- ✔ **Piccadilly** for older established department stores

✔ **Jermyn Street** for traditional English luxury goods

✔ **Bond Street** for chic upscale fashion boutiques

✔ **Covent Garden** for all-purpose shopping, often with a hipper edge

✔ **St. Martin's Court** (between Charing Cross Road and St. Martin's Lane) for prints, posters, and books

Around Piccadilly Circus: A bit of everything

Piccadilly Circus is considered to be the center of London. For the best shopping in this area, head south from the Piccadilly Tube stop along Piccadilly (the street) or northwest along Regent Street. The following are some of the most renowned stores around Piccadilly Circus:

✔ **Burberry** (18–22 Haymarket, SW1; ☎ 020/7930-3343; Tube: Piccadilly Circus) sells those famous raincoats, plus top-quality men's shirts, sportswear, knitwear, and accessories.

✔ **Hatchards** (187 Piccadilly, W1; ☎ 020/7439-9921; Tube: Piccadilly Circus) was established in 1797 and is London's most historic and atmospheric bookstore.

✔ **Tower Records** (1 Piccadilly Circus, W1; ☎ 020/7439-2500; Tube: Piccadilly Circus) is one of the largest tape and CD stores in Europe. This store is practically a tourist attraction in its own right.

Jermyn Street: Traditional luxury

Two-block-long Jermyn Street lies a block south of Piccadilly between St. James's Street and Duke Street. Many of the posh men's haberdashers and toiletry shops along this street have been doing business for centuries and cater to the royals. They include the following:

✔ **Farlows** (5 Pall Mall, SW1; ☎ 020/7839-2423; Tube: Piccadilly Circus) is famous for fishing and shooting equipment and classic country clothing.

✔ **Floris** (89 Jermyn St., SW1; ☎ 020/7930-2885; Tube: Piccadilly Circus) is a small mahogany-clad store that's been selling its own line of soaps and perfumes since 1851.

✔ **Hilditch & Key** (73 Jermyn St., SW1; ☎ 020/7930-5336; Tube: Piccadilly Circus) has been selling perhaps the finest men's shirts in the world for more than a century. These quality goods are 100% cotton, cut by hand, and sport buttons fashioned from real shell.

✔ **Taylor of Old Bond Street** (74 Jermyn St., SW1; ☎ 020/7930-5544; Tube: Piccadilly Circus) was established in 1954 and is devoted to the shaving and personal hygiene needs of men. The store offers the world's finest collection of shaving brushes, razors, and combs, plus soaps and hair lotions.

Shopping in the West End

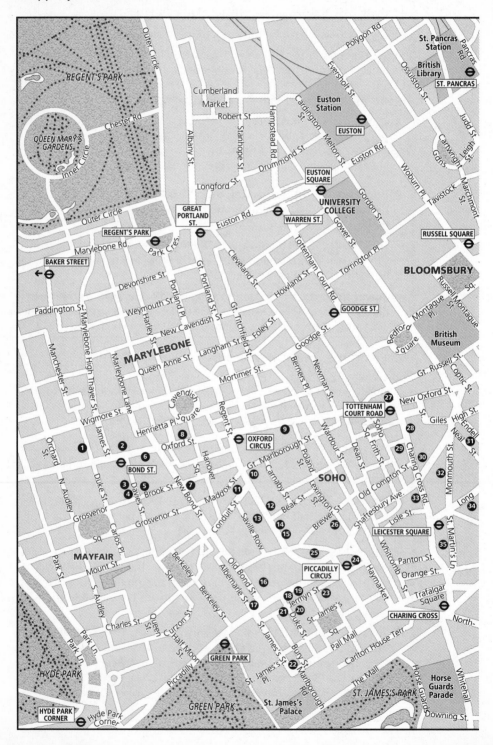

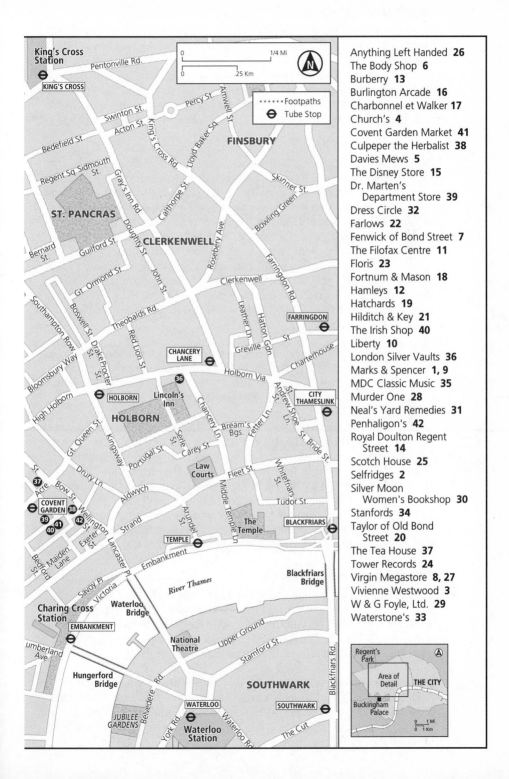

Anything Left Handed **26**
The Body Shop **6**
Burberry **13**
Burlington Arcade **16**
Charbonnel et Walker **17**
Church's **4**
Covent Garden Market **41**
Culpeper the Herbalist **38**
Davies Mews **5**
The Disney Store **15**
Dr. Marten's
    Department Store **39**
Dress Circle **32**
Farlows **22**
Fenwick of Bond Street **7**
The Filofax Centre **11**
Floris **23**
Fortnum & Mason **18**
Hamleys **12**
Hatchards **19**
Hilditch & Key **21**
The Irish Shop **40**
Liberty **10**
London Silver Vaults **36**
Marks & Spencer **1, 9**
MDC Classic Music **35**
Murder One **28**
Neal's Yard Remedies **31**
Penhaligon's **42**
Royal Doulton Regent
    Street **14**
Scotch House **25**
Selfridges **2**
Silver Moon
    Women's Bookshop **30**
Stanfords **34**
Taylor of Old Bond
    Street **20**
The Tea House **37**
Tower Records **24**
Virgin Megastore **8, 27**
Vivienne Westwood **3**
W & G Foyle, Ltd. **29**
Waterstone's **33**

Regent Street: Upscale specialties

Regent Street begins in a grand sweeping curve on the west side of Piccadilly Circus and heads north to intersect with Oxford Street. This majestic thoroughfare is lined with upscale department stores and specialty boutiques. The **Burlington Arcade** is a must-see if you're in this area. This famous glass-roofed Regency passage, running from Piccadilly to Burlington Gardens, is lit by wrought-iron lamps and decorated with clusters of ferns and flowers. The arcade is lined with intriguing shops and boutiques.

Savile Row, synonymous with hand-tailored men's suits, lies a block west of Regent Street. Its once-countercultural counterpart — in the early Beatles' years — is **Carnaby Street,** now a sad tourist attraction trying to trade in on a vanished past; Carnaby Street is a block east of Regent Street. **Royal Doulton Regent Street** (154 Regent St., W1; ☎ 020-7734-3184; Tube: Piccadilly Circus or Oxford Circus) carries English bone china, including Royal Doulton, Minton, and Royal Crown Derby. (The January and July sales are excellent.) **Scotch House** (84–86 Regent St., W1; ☎ 020-7734-0203; Piccadilly Circus) is known globally for its selection of cashmere and wool knitwear for men, women, and children; the store also sells tartan garments and accessories, as well as Scottish tweed classics.

If you're left-handed, you're in luck at **Anything Left Handed** (57 Brewer St., off Regent Street, W1; ☎ 020/7437-3910; Tube: Piccadilly Circus). This unique store sells practical items — everything from scissors to corkscrews — for the southpaws in the world.

Do I need to tell you what you can find at **The Disney Store,** 140 Regent St., W1 (☎ 020/7287-6558; Tube: Piccadilly Circus), which you see as you walk farther north toward Oxford Street? If you're looking for non-Disney toys, you couldn't do any better than **Hamleys** (188–196 Regent St., W1; ☎ 020/7494-2000; Tube: Piccadilly Circus). The finest toy shop in the world, Hamleys stocks more than 35,000 toys and games on seven floors of fun and magic. You can get everything from cuddly stuffed animals and dolls to radio-controlled cars, train sets, model kits, board games, outdoor toys, and computer games.

Oxford Street: Affordable big names

Instead of beginning your shopping adventure on Regent Street, you may want to visit Oxford Street first, getting out at the Oxford Circus, Bond Street, or Tottenham Court Road Tube stop. Oxford Street is more affordable than Regent Street — not as stylish, but offering a good variety and quantity of merchandise.

If you are a chronic organizer who can't live without your Filofax, head immediately for **The Filofax Centre** (21 Conduit St., W1; ☎ 020/7499-0457; Tube: Oxford Circus). At this store on Conduit Street, which leads west from Regency Street, you can find the entire range of inserts and books at prices that are about half of what they are in the States. **The**

Body Shop stores are based in the U.K but are now all over the States; however, prices at the London branches are much lower. You can stock up on their politically and environmentally correct beauty, bath, and aromatherapy products at their location at 375 Oxford St., W1 (☎ 020/7409-7868; Tube: Bond Street). You find other branches in every shopping zone in London.

The **Virgin Megastore** has two Oxford Street locations. The larger is at 14–16 Oxford St., W1 (☎ 020/7631-1234; Tube: Tottenham Court Road). The other is at 527 Oxford St., W1 (☎ 020/7491-8582; Tube: Oxford Circus). Thousands of current CDs in every genre are sold, and you can hear the release on headphones at listening stations before making a purchase.

Bond Street: Designer chic

Bond Street, running parallel to Regent Street on the west and connecting Piccadilly with Oxford Street, is home to all the hot international designers and is London's answer to New York's Fifth Avenue. Bond Street is divided into New (northern section) and Old (southern portion). Very expensive fashion boutiques line Bond Street and the adjacent streets. **Davies Street,** running south from outside the Bond Street Tube station, is just one of the area's choicer streets; **Davies Mews** is an upscale shopping zone noted for its antiques dealers. You can access the area from the north by the Bond Street Tube stop and from the south by Green Park.

Vivienne Westwood (6 Davies St., W1; ☎ 020/7629-3757; Tube: Bond Street) is one of the hottest British designers for women. This flagship store carries a full range of jackets, skirts, trousers, blouses, dresses, and evening dresses. **Church's** (133 New Bond St., W1; ☎ 020/7493-1474; Tube: Bond Street) sells classy shoes easily recognized by the fashion elite. Chocolate connoisseurs should visit **Charbonnel et Walker** (1 The Royal Arcade, 28 Old Bond St., W1; ☎ 020/7491-0939; Tube: Green Park), famous for its hot chocolate (buy it by the tin) and strawberries-and-cream chocolates.

Around Leicester Square: Music and memorabilia

Leicester Square itself boasts only giant movie palaces and touristy restaurants (and a reduced-price ticket booth). But the streets around Leicester Square are filled with shops selling rare books, prints, and posters, some relating to the performing arts.

The Leicester Square shops include:

- ✔ **Dress Circle** (57–59 Monmouth St., WC2; ☎ 020/7240-2227; Tube: Leicester Square) specializes in show-business memorabilia for all West End and Broadway shows.

- ✔ **MDC Classic Music** (31–32 St. Martin's Lane, WC2; ☎ 020/7240-0270; Tube: Leicester Square), sitting right next to the English

National Opera, specializes in opera recordings; you receive expert knowledge and personal service.

✔ **Stanfords** (12–14 Long Acre, WC2; ☎ 020/7836-1321; Tube: Leicester Square) was established in 1852, and is the world's largest map shop (many of its maps, which include worldwide touring and survey maps, are unavailable elsewhere). Stanfords is also London's best travel bookstore.

Charing Cross Road: A book lover's delight

Charing Cross Road is a book lover's paradise because of its vast number of bookstores, selling both new and old volumes. Many of these places sell maps and guides, too, including the tourist's necessity, *London A to Z*. Some of the most fascinating bookstores include the following:

✔ **Murder One** (71–73 Charing Cross Rd., WC2; ☎ 020/7734-3483; Tube: Leicester Square) specializes in crime, romance, science fiction, and horror books. Crime and science-fiction magazines, some obscure, are also available.

✔ **Silver Moon Women's Bookshop** (64–68 Charing Cross Rd.; ☎ 020/7836-7906; Tube: Tottenham Court Road) stocks thousands of titles by and about women, including a large selection of lesbian-related books. Plus the shop offers videos and jewelry.

✔ **Waterstone's** (121 Charing Cross Rd.; ☎ 020/7434-4291; Tube: Tottenham Court Road) is a U.K. chain with branches all over London. You can find the latest releases and well-stocked sections of books currently in print.

✔ **W & G Foyle, Ltd.** (113–119 Charing Cross Rd., WC2; ☎ 020/7440-3225; Tube: Tottenham Court Road) claims to be the world's largest bookstore, with an impressive array of hardcovers and paperbacks, as well as travel maps, records, videotapes, and sheet music.

Covent Garden: Something for everyone

Try to save some of your shopping energy for Covent Garden, home of what may be the most famous "market" in all of England: the **Covent Garden Market** (see "Taking It to the Street (Markets)," earlier in this chapter).

Excellent English soaps, toiletries, and aromatherapy goods, as well as herbal goods, are available throughout the market and surrounding streets, including at the following shops:

✔ **Culpeper the Herbalist** (8 The Market, Covent Garden, WC2; ☎ 020/7379-6698; Tube: Covent Garden) sells food, bath, and aromatherapy products as well as dream pillows, candles, sachets, and that popular favorite: the battery-operated aromatherapy fan.

> ✔ **Neal's Yard Remedies** (15 Neal's Yard, off Shorts Garden, WC2; ☎ 020/7379-7222; Tube: Covent Garden) is noted the world over for its all-natural, herbal-based bath, beauty, and aromatherapy products in cobalt-blue bottles.
>
> ✔ **Penhaligon's** (41 Wellington St., WC2; ☎ 020/7836-2150; Tube: Covent Garden) is an exclusive-line Victorian perfumery dedicated to good grooming. Choose from a large selection of perfumes, after-shaves, soaps, candles, and bath oils for women and men.

Also in Covent Garden you can find **Dr. Martens Department Store** (1–4 King St., WC2; ☎ 020/7497-1460; Tube: Covent Garden), the flagship for internationally famous "Doc Marts" shoes. Prices are far better here than they are in the States.

Farther along, at 14 King St., is **The Irish Shop** (☎ 020/7379-3625; Tube: Covent Garden), which sells a wide variety of articles shipped directly from Ireland, including colorful knitwear, traditional Irish linens, hand-knitted Aran fisherman's sweaters, and Celtic jewelry.

And you can finish off at **The Tea House** (15A Neal St., WC2; ☎ 020/ 7240-7539; Tube: Covent Garden), which sells everything associated with tea, tea drinking, and teatime.

Index of Stores by Merchandise

Antiques
Antiquarius (Chelsea)
Chelsea Antiques Market (Chelsea)
Map House of London (Knightsbridge)

Bath and hygiene products
The Body Shop (Mayfair)
Culpeper the Herbalist (Covent Garden)
Floris (St. James's)
Neal's Yard Remedies (Covent Garden)
Penhaligon's (Covent Garden)
Taylor of Old Bond Street (St. James's)

Books and maps
Children's Book Centre (Kensington)
Hatchards (St. James's)
Murder One (Soho)
Silver Moon Women's Bookshop (Soho)
Stanfords (Covent Garden)
W & G Foyle, Ltd. (Soho)
Waterstone's (Soho)

Candy
Charbonnel et Walker (Mayfair)

Clothing
Burberry (St. James's)
Hilditch & Key (St. James's)
Scotch House (St. James's)
Vivienne Westwood (Mayfair)

Drug stores (chemists)
Bliss the Chemist (Bayswater)
Boots the Chemist (Knightsbridge)
Zafash Pharmacy (South Kensington)

Department stores
Fenwick of Bond Street (Mayfair)
Fortnum & Mason (St. James's)
Harrods (Knightsbridge)
Harvey Nichols (Knightsbridge)
Liberty (Mayfair)
Marks & Spencer (Mayfair)
Selfridges (Mayfair)

Housewares and china

Peter Jones (Chelsea)
Royal Doulton Regent Street
    (St. James's)

Markets

Antiquarius (Chelsea)
Chelsea Antiques Market (Chelsea)
Covent Garden Market (Covent
    Garden)
Portobello Market (Notting Hill)

Miscellaneous

Anything Left Handed (Soho)
Dress Circle (Soho)
The Filofax Centre (Covent Garden)
The Irish Shop (Covent Garden)
The Tea House (Covent Garden)

Music

MDC Classic Music (Covent Garden)
Tower Records (St. James's)
Virgin Megastore (Soho and Mayfair)

Shoes

Dr. Martens Department Store
    (Covent Garden)

Silver

London Silver Vaults (Holborn)

Sporting goods

Farlows (St. James's)

Toys

The Disney Store (St. James's)
Hamleys (St. James's)

Chapter 20

Four Great London Itineraries

*E*very London visitor must face one problem: how to see as much as possible in a limited amount of time. You're lucky if you have an entire week or even more. But what if you have only three or five days at your disposal? What if you're bringing the family along? These questions are what this chapter is all about. If you budget your time wisely and choose your sights carefully, you can make the most of a limited schedule or a trip with the kids.

Start with two basic premises. The first is that you won't have as much time as you'd like, so you need to be selective because you simply can't see everything. The second is that you want to see the highlights of London without turning your trip into a test run for the London Marathon; to avoid racing around requires some advance planning because London is a huge place.

This chapter offers four easy-to-do suggested daily itineraries. They're intended for first-timers but include places that returning visitors (such as myself) always want to see again. The first itinerary covers the big sights. The next two are a little more adventurous. The itinerary for families visits the top spots and then heads to family-friendly destinations just outside the city. Each of these itineraries is a mix of sights and experiences. I don't believe in sending you to three museums in one day; the result is sensory overload, and you would end up not seeing anything.

The itineraries are commonsense, limited-time suggestions only, however. You may want to spend your days doing something else entirely. Maybe you'd really rather spend an entire day in the British Museum, instead of a couple of hours. Maybe shopping in Chelsea and cafe hopping in Soho is more appealing to you than watching the

Changing of the Guard at Buckingham Palace. Go for it! London can be enjoyed in countless ways that have nothing to do with traditional sightseeing.

For complete descriptions of the sights, plus exact street addresses, opening hours, and admission prices, see Chapters 16 and 17.

London in Three Days

Three days doesn't seem like a very long time. But in that short period, you can hit most of the key sights in London and enjoy a memorable trip.

Start your trip on **Day one** with a visit to majestic **Westminster Abbey,** visiting the Royal Tombs and Poets' Corner. Afterward, because they're right next door, stroll around the **Houses of Parliament.** Unless you queue up to hear a debate, or take one of the guided tours available from the August through September (see Chapter 16 for details), you won't be able to get inside, but you can enjoy a great riverside view from Westminster Bridge. On the opposite side of the Thames is the **British Airways London Eye,** a new 450-foot-high observation wheel. Reserve in advance for the trip up and over London, otherwise you may spend at least a half-hour in line for a ticket and another hour before your scheduled "flight." You're not far from **Tate Britain,** so if you're in the mood to look at great English art, head over to Pimlico. Renting a self-guided audio tour will add to your enjoyment. Later in the afternoon, explore **Piccadilly Circus,** the teeming epicenter of London's West End. You find great shopping on Regent Street, Piccadilly, and Jermyn Street (see Chapter 19 for shopping). If you haven't already reserved a seat for a **West End show,** you may want to stop by the half-price ticket booth in **Leicester Square** to see what's available (see Chapter 22 for info on theaters). Have dinner in Soho before the show (See Chapter 14 for restaurants).

Greet **Day two** with a walk through **Green Park.** You're on your way to **Buckingham Palace** to witness the pageantry of the **Changing of the Guard** (check beforehand to make certain that it's taking place that day). For details on touring the State Rooms of Buckingham Palace during August and September, see Chapter 16. Reserve tickets in advance, so you know your specific entry time; otherwise, you may have to wait in line for an hour or more to get in. If you're not touring the palace itself, visit the **Royal Mews.** From Buckingham Palace you can stroll down The Mall, through **St. James's Park,** passing **Clarence House,** home of the Queen Mother, and **St. James's Palace,** London home of Prince Charles and his two sons.

Trafalgar Square, London's grandest and certainly most famous plaza, is your next stop. You can have lunch or tea at the **National Gallery's**

restaurant or at **Café-in-the-Crypt** in St. Martin-in-the-Fields church on the east side of the square. Spend your afternoon viewing the treasures of the **National Gallery.** Renting one of the self-guided audio tours will help you to hone in on the most important paintings in the collection. After dinner in the Covent Garden area or on the Thames (see Chapter 18 for cruises), head to one of the bars, pubs, or clubs I describe in Chapter 24.

On **Day three,** arrive as early as you can at the **Tower of London** and immediately hook up with one of the one-hour guided tours led by the Beefeaters. Later, you can explore the precincts on your own, making certain you allot enough time to see the **Crown Jewels.** From the Tower, head over to nearby **St. Paul's Cathedral,** which you can see in about a half-hour.

The **British Museum,** your next stop, has enough to keep you occupied for several days; if you want to see only the highlights, allow yourself a minimum of two hours. Finish off your afternoon in Knightsbridge at **Harrods** (see Chapter 19), the most famous department store in London, and perhaps the world. Knightsbridge and adjacent South Kensington offer innumerable dining options (see Chapter 14).

London in Five Days

This section assumes that you've already followed the suggested itineraries (see the preceding section) for your first three days.

Day four begins at the **National Portrait Gallery,** where you can find the likeness of just about every famous British person you've ever heard of. Renting one of the self-guided audio tours is a good idea. From the portrait gallery you can easily walk to **Covent Garden Market** (see Chapter 19). Scores of interesting shops are in and around the market, and Covent Garden Piazza, a lively hub filled with restaurants, makes a perfect spot for lunch. Spend your afternoon strolling in **Kensington Gardens** and visiting **Kensington Palace,** once the London home of Princess Diana. Then go for a traditional English dinner at **Rules,** London's oldest restaurant, or **Simpson's-in-the-Strand** (see Chapter 14). Are you up for a play or a concert tonight? Then check your theater options in Chapter 22.

Day five begins with a morning at the museum of your choice. Choosing among the three major South Kensington museums — the **Natural History Museum,** the **Science Museum,** and the **Victoria & Albert Museum** — is entirely a matter of taste. If you like modern art, the newly opened **Tate Modern** on the South Bank is the place to spend your morning. (See Chapter 16 for a description of all the museums.) In the afternoon, expand your horizon with a short trip outside the city. Chapter 17 offers descriptions of the **Royal Botanic Gardens** at Kew,

Hampton Court, Windsor Palace, Hampstead Heath, and **Greenwich.**
None of these places is terribly far away; the trips to reach them take
anywhere from 20 minutes to an hour. You can be back in time for dinner.

London in Seven Days

How time flies! By now, if you've followed the suggested itineraries for
the last five days (see the preceding two sections), you've seen most of
the major sights in London.

On **Day six,** you're ready for a day trip. Riding in one of Britain's
sleek new trains is terrific fun. The only problem is that you have to
decide where you want to go. In Chapter 21, I give you the lowdown
on six places, each remarkable in its own way. Do you want to see
Shakespeare's birthplace in **Stratford-upon-Avon** or the famous prehistoric stone circle called **Stonehenge?** Do you want to spend a day
by the seaside in **Brighton** or strolling around ancient **Canterbury** with
its mighty cathedral? Or perhaps head to **Bath** to discover its splendid
Georgian crescents. You can reach most of these places in 90 minutes
or less.

Day seven is your last day in London, and you'll want it to be special.
In the morning, visit **Madame Tussaud's** wax museum or one of the
museums you haven't yet seen. Afterward, stroll through **Hyde Park** and
stop at **Apsley House,** the London home of the first duke of Wellington.
This house gives you a glimpse of what life was like inside one of
London's great private palaces. If it's Sunday, you may instead want to
visit **Spencer House,** the family home of the late Princess Diana. You can
also do some last-minute shopping, if you prefer. Check out London's
various shopping neighborhoods in Chapter 19, and then make your
way to the major shopping arteries: Knightsbridge, Oxford Street,
Bond Street, King's Road in Chelsea, or Regent Street. A traditional
afternoon tea at one of London's great hotels (see Chapter 15) makes
a delightful end to the afternoon. After that? You've booked theater
tickets, haven't you?

London with Kids

So you want to spend five days in London and bring along your kids?
No problem. I have a few suggestions to keep you *and* your kids excited
and entertained. For tips on traveling with kids, see Chapter 4.

Don't schedule too much on **Day one.** Exercise helps ward off jet lag.
After sitting in a plane for several hours the best option may be to take
smaller children to one of London's great parks, so they can run and let
off steam. Depending on where your hotel is located, your destination
may be **Hyde Park, Kensington Gardens, Green Park, St. James's Park,**

or **Regent's Park.** If you're traveling with teens, you may want to introduce them to the city by taking a stroll through London's four royal
parks, following the **Princess Diana Commemorative Walk.**

You can begin more focused sightseeing on **Day two.** Consider a guided
bus tour that helps orient everyone and gives you at least a glimpse of
all the major sights (see Chapter 18). Several outfits provide tours on
double-decker buses — always a treat for kids. After the tour, make
the **British Airways London Eye** your first stop. Reserve your
ticket beforehand to avoid waiting in a long line. Afterward, cross
Westminster Bridge and stroll over to view the **Houses of Parliament**
and **Big Ben** (hopefully the clock strikes the hour while you're in the
vicinity). And because it's close at hand, use this opportunity to visit
Westminster Abbey. Younger children may not get much out of the
place, but you will. Later in the afternoon, take a ferry ride down the
Thames to the **Tower of London;** you can catch the ferry at the piers
near the Houses of Parliament. After you're inside, hook up with one of
the Beefeater tours. If you're with a child ages 10 to 17, you may want
to have dinner at the **Hard Rock Café** in Mayfair (see Chapter 14).

Begin **Day three** at the **Natural History Museum** in South Kensington,
where the dinosaur exhibit captures the imaginations of both the
young and the old(er). If your child's a budding Einstein, the **Science
Museum** with its many hands-on, interactive exhibits may be a better
choice. Afterward, if you have small children in tow, stroll over to
Kensington Gardens for a look at the famous statue of Peter Pan.
The new **Princess Diana Memorial Playground** in the northwest
corner of Kensington Gardens enchants little ones. You can have lunch
in **The Orangery** of adjacent Kensington Palace, or make your way to
Café-in-the-Crypt in St. Martin-in-the-Fields church in Trafalgar Square;
you find a brass-rubbing center in the church, too. If you're with a
teen, you may want to spend the morning or afternoon in **Madame
Tussaud's wax museum;** some of the gorier exhibits are unsuitable for
young children. In the evening, older kids and teens may also enjoy one
of the West End's razzmatazz musicals. If a dinner and a play for just
the two of you sounds good, you can get a baby sitter for the little ones
(see the Appendix for a reputable service).

Make **Day four** a day trip to **Brighton** on the Sussex coast (see Chapter
21). The quick trip takes less than an hour. After you arrive, you can
visit the **Royal Pavilion** and take the kids over to **Palace Pier,** a spot
filled with games and souvenir stands. If the weather's warm, you can
rent a deck chair and sit on the beach. Brighton is a fun place just to
stroll around, with plenty to keep you and the family entertained.

On **Day five,** head out to **Hampton Court Palace,** another quick train
ride of less than an hour (see Chapter 17). Hampton Court offers much
to explore, so give yourself at least four hours. Small children may not
get much out of the visit, but they will probably be intrigued by the
staff wearing period costumes. You can eat on the premises. Save the

best part for last: The famous Maze in the gardens brings out the kid in everyone. Finally, return to London for a good night's rest before flying out the next morning.

More Tips for Organizing Your Time

If you organize your days efficiently and with commonsense, you can make the most of your visit to London. Disorganized travelers waste a lot of time, show up at the museum on the day it's closed, and end up in the nether regions of Tooting Bec because they hopped the wrong Underground line. Don't assume that every museum or site is open every day, all day. Take a moment to look at the details that I provide for each attraction in Chapters 16 and 17. And carry a copy of *London A to Z*.

An average top sight takes about two hours to visit, after you're actually inside. Some (Buckingham Palace and the Royal Mews) take more; others (Westminster Abbey and St. Paul's) take less. But other variables enter in: whether or not you're taking a guided tour (usually about an hour to 90 minutes, no matter where), if you have kids in tow, or if lines move slowly due to the crowds of visitors. Predicting how much time you'll spend at a major attraction, such as the British Museum and the National Gallery, is difficult. But as a general rule, you can "do" about three or four sights in a day if you're pushing yourself, fewer if you're not.

Many of London's major sights are concentrated in specific areas, so walking is the best way to see several sights in a short period of time. To cover larger areas, I recommend that you take the fast and convenient Underground.

Try to hit the very top sights on your list early in the day, preferably when they open, or late in the afternoon. Visit the places that are really important to you when you're feeling fresh and when they're less crowded. I mean, in particular, Buckingham Palace (when it's open to the public during August and September), the Tower of London, Westminster Abbey, and Madame Tussaud's. Westminster Abbey, to cite just one example, can receive upward of 15,000 visitors per day!

Unless you have adrenaline to spare, try to unwind a little before you begin your round of after-dark diversions. You may need some down time between the end of your sightseeing day and the beginning of your evening activities. I suggest that you head back to your hotel to take a shower or bath, to curl up with a novel or the evening paper for an hour, or maybe to catch a quick snooze to recharge your batteries.

Chapter 21

Exploring beyond London: Five Great Day Trips

. . . .

In This Chapter

▶ Taking the best day trips from London

▶ Getting there and back

▶ Deciding what to see and do after you arrive

. . . .

*I*n comparison to the United States, England is a small country. You can visit countless places on a one-day side trip from London.

In Chapter 17, I describe the easiest side trips from London: **Kew Gardens, Hampton Court Palace, Windsor Palace,** and **Greenwich.** In this chapter, I venture out to some of England's most popular, impressive, and famous places: Bath, Brighton, Canterbury, Stratford-upon-Avon, and Stonehenge. By train, all these sites are less than two hours from London (see the map "Side Trips from London").

By Train or by Car: Weighing the Options

Because of England's small size and easy-access train and road networks, this country is a joy to explore.

From London you can reach Bath, Brighton, and Canterbury, in 90 minutes or less by train and in about two hours by car. The train trip to Stratford-upon-Avon or to Salisbury (the closest large town to Stonehenge) is about two hours; it's about three hours by car. If you get an early start you can explore any one of these places, have lunch, and still be back in London in time for dinner.

The following sections help you decide whether train travel or automotion is for you.

Side Trips from London

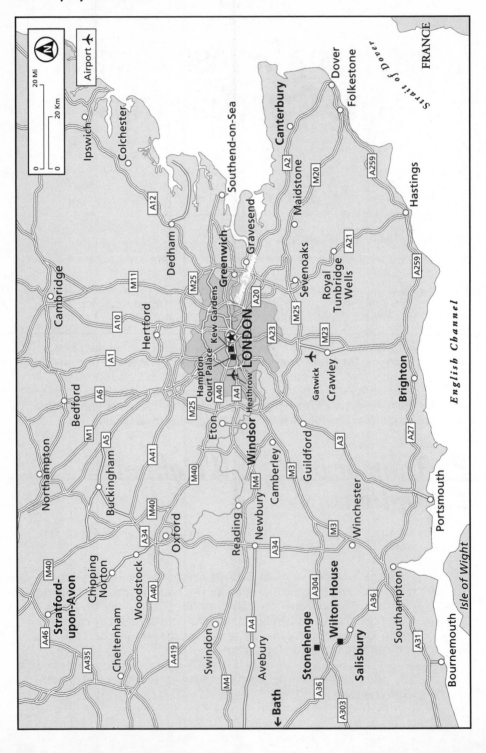

Taking the train

If you plan to travel around England by train, get a pass from **BritRail Travel International,** 500 Broadway, New York, NY 10036 (☎ **866/ BRITRAIL** or 877/677-1066 in the U.S; Internet: www.britrail.net), before you arrive. The BritRail Southeast Pass gets you to three of the towns in this chapter (but not to Bath or Stratford-upon-Avon). Trains offer first- and standard-class seating — first-class cars are less crowded and seats are roomier and more comfy. Because the train trips to destinations in this chapter aren't very long, standard-class may be fine for most travelers. The cost for first-class travel for any three days in an eight-day period is $106 adults and $31 children (5 to 15 years); standard-class is $73 adults and $21 children. You can also obtain four-day and seven-day Southeast Passes. See Chapter 3 for more information on BritRail.

Taking a car: Driving on the left, passing on the right

I always suggest that people travel by train instead of driving. Much of your car trip will be on motorways without much scenery, so what's the point? But some people want to drive, no matter what. If you're one of those people, this section is for you.

Before you even consider renting a car, ask yourself whether you're comfortable driving with a steering wheel on the right-hand side of the vehicle while shifting with your left hand (you can get an automatic, but it costs considerably more). Remember, you must drive on the left and pass on the right.

Although the car-rental market in Britain is highly competitive, renting a car here costs more than in the United States — unless, that is, you can find a special promotional offer from an airline or a car-rental agency. Most U.K. car-rental agencies accept U.S. driver's licenses. In most cases you must be 23 years old (21 in some instances), no older than 70, and have had your U.S. license for more than a year.

You can often get a discount on car-rental rates if you reserve 48 hours in advance through the toll-free reservations offices. Weekly rentals are almost always less expensive than daily rates. And the rate, of course, depends on the size of the vehicle.

When you make your reservation, ask whether the quoted price includes the 17.5% VAT and unlimited mileage. Then find out whether *personal accident insurance* (PAI), *collision-damage waiver* (CDW), and any other insurance options are included. If they aren't a part of the deal, which is usually the case, be sure to ask how much they cost. When you drive in any foreign country (or anywhere, for that matter), arrange for as much coverage as possible.

Some credit card companies offer the collision-damage waiver and other types of insurance for free if you use that card to pay for the rental. If you're planning to rent a car, check with your credit-card company to see what's covered, or you may end up paying for coverage you already have.

Bath: Hot Mineral Springs and Cool Georgian Magnificence

Bath, 115 miles west of London, is a beautiful spa town on the Avon River (see "Bath" map). Since the days of the ancient Celts — and later the Romans — Bath has been famous for its hot mineral springs. In 1702, Queen Anne frequented the soothing, sulfurous waters and transformed Bath into a spa for the elite. Aristocrats, socialites, social climbers, and flamboyant dandies such as Beau Nash have added to the spa's fashionable and fascinating history. The great author Jane Austen used Bath as an upwardly genteel setting for her class-conscious plots.

Today, the spa is a grand legacy from the Georgian era, boasting beautiful curving *crescents* (a row of houses built in a long curving line) and classically inspired buildings of honey-colored stone. Must-sees are the **Roman Baths Museum** and adjoining **Pump Room** (where visitors can continue the long tradition of sipping water while listening to music), the adjacent **Abbey,** and the **Assembly Rooms** (once used for balls and gaming).

Getting there

Trains for Bath leave from London's Paddington Station every half-hour; the trip takes about 90 minutes. The off-peak (after 9 a.m.) round-trip fare is about £30 (higher on Fridays). By car, take the M4 to Junction 18, and then drive a few miles south on A46.

Finding information and taking a tour

Bath's Tourist Information Centre (☎ **01225/477-761;** Internet: www.visitbath.co.uk), located in the center of town on the square in front of Bath Abbey, provides free, guided walks. The tours leave from outside the **Pump Room** Monday through Friday at 10:30 a.m. and 2 p.m., Saturday at 10:30 a.m., and Sunday at 10:30 a.m. and 2 p.m. Additional walks are offered at 7 p.m. nightly from May through October. From May through September, the information center is open Monday through Saturday 9:30 a.m. to 6:00 p.m. and Sunday 10 a.m. to 4 p.m. The rest of the year, the center is open Monday through Saturday 9:30 a.m. to 5:00 p.m. and Sunday 10 a.m. to 4 p.m.

Bath

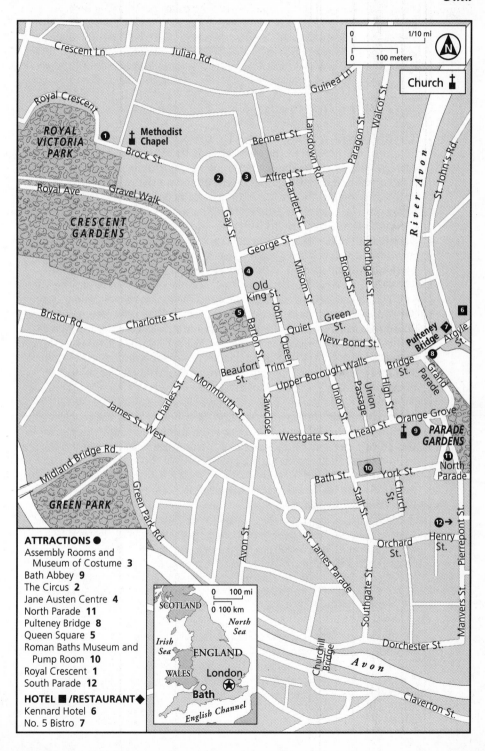

ATTRACTIONS ●
Assembly Rooms and
  Museum of Costume **3**
Bath Abbey **9**
The Circus **2**
Jane Austen Centre **4**
North Parade **11**
Pulteney Bridge **8**
Queen Square **5**
Roman Baths Museum and
  Pump Room **10**
Royal Crescent **1**
South Parade **12**
HOTEL ■ /RESTAURANT◆
Kennard Hotel **6**
No. 5 Bistro **7**

The **Bath Pass** offers admission to every attraction in Bath (more than 30 in all, including the Roman Baths Museum) and special discounts at shops and restaurants. A one-day Bath Pass costs £19 ($28) adults, £12 ($18) children 5 to 16; a two-day pass is £29 ($43) adults, £22 ($33) children; and a three-day pass costs £39 ($58) adults, £25 ($37) children. You can buy the Bath Pass at the Tourist Information Centre.

Seeing the sights

The Romans — who arrived in A.D. 75 — built the huge complex at the center of the **Roman Baths Museum** (☎ 01225/477-785), beside Bath Abbey. When visitors enter, they receive a portable self-guided audio tour keyed to everything on display, including the original Roman baths and heating system; the audio tour is fun, informative, and very well done. Admission is £6.90 ($12). The museum is open daily October through March 9:30 a.m. to 5:00 p.m., April through September 9 a.m. to 6 p.m., and August 9 a.m. to 9 p.m.

Overlooking the Roman baths is the late-18th-century **Pump Room** (☎ 01225/477-7785), where the fashionable assembled to sip the vile-tasting but reputedly health-promoting water. You're welcome to taste it for yourself, if you dare. Admission is free. In the Pump Room, you can enjoy *elevenses* (morning tea), lunch, or afternoon tea to a background of live music. Main courses cost £9 to £10 ($14–$15), a fixed-price lunch menu is £12 to £13 ($18–$20), and afternoon tea is £6 to £8 ($9–$12). The Pump Room is open Monday through Saturday 9:30 a.m. to 4:40 p.m. and Sunday 10:30 a.m. to 4:30 p.m.

Step inside **Bath Abbey** (☎ 01225/422-462) and view the graceful fan vaulting, the great East Window, and the ironically simple memorial to Beau Nash, the most flamboyant of the dandies who frequented Bath in its heyday. Admission is by donation. April through October, the abbey is open Monday through Saturday 9 a.m. to 6 p.m. (to 4:30 p.m. November through March); year-round, it's open Sunday 1:00 to 2:30 p.m. and 4:30 to 5:30 p.m.

Another classic building worth visiting is the **Assembly Rooms** (Bennett Street; ☎ 01225/477-789), the site of all the grand balls and social climbing in 18th-century Bath. Admission is free unless you want to visit the excellent **Museum of Costume** that's part of the complex. Admission is £4.20 ($6) adults, £3.75 ($6) seniors/students, and £3 ($4.50) children 6 to 18. Both are open daily 10 a.m. to 5 p.m.

Bath's newest attraction, the **Jane Austen Centre** (40 Gay St.; ☎ 01225/443-000) is located in a Georgian town house on an elegant street where Austen once lived. Exhibits and a video convey a sense of what life in Bath was like during the Regency period. Admission is £4 ($6). The center is open Monday through Saturday 10 a.m. to 5 p.m. and Sunday 10:30 a.m. to 5:30 p.m.

Bath is a wonderful walking town, filled with beautiful squares and sweeping residential crescents. Stroll along the **North Parade** and the **South Parade, Queen Square,** and **The Circus** and be sure to have a look at the **Royal Crescent,** a magnificent curving row of 30 town houses designed in 1767 by John Wood the Younger. Regarded as the epitome of England's *Palladian style* (a classical style incorporating elements from ancient Greek and Roman buildings), the Royal Crescent is now designated a World Heritage site. **No. 1 Royal Crescent (☎ 01225/428-126)** is a gorgeously restored 18th-century house with period furnishings. Admission is £4 ($6) adults, £3 ($4.50) seniors/students/children. Mid-February through October, the house is open Tuesday through Sunday 10:30 a.m. to 5:00 p.m. (to 4:00 p.m. in November).

Pulteney Bridge, built in 1770, spans the River Avon a few blocks south of the Assembly Rooms. The bridge is one of the few in Europe lined with shops and restaurants.

Staying in style

If you want to spend the night in Bath, try the **Kennard Hotel** (11 Henrietta St., Bath BA2 6LL; ☎ **01225/310-472;** Fax: 01225/460-054; Internet: www.kennard.co.uk). On the east side of Pulteney Bridge, within walking distance of everything in Bath, this elegant hotel with 13 guest rooms occupies a beautifully restored 1794 Georgian town house. The rates are £88 to £110 ($132–$165) double, breakfast included. American Express, MasterCard, and Visa are accepted.

Dining out

A popular French eatery in Bath's city center is **No. 5 Bistro** (5 Argyle St., ☎ **01225/444-499**). The chef at this pleasant, smoke-free restaurant produces mouth-watering dishes that may include choices such as Provençal fish soup, chargrilled loin of lamb, or vegetarian offerings such as roast stuffed peppers or vegetable gratin. Main courses are £13 to £14 ($19–$21). The bistro is open Mondays 6:30 to 10:30 p.m., and Tuesday through Saturday noon to 2:30 p.m. and 6:30 to 10:30 p.m. American Express, MasterCard, and Visa are accepted.

Brighton: Fun beside the Seaside

On the Sussex coast, a mere 50 miles south of London, Brighton is England's most famous, and probably most popular, seaside town (see "Brighton" map). Brighton was a small fishing village until the Prince Regent, who would become George IV, became enamored of the place and had the incredible Royal Pavilion built. Where royalty moves, fashion follows, and Brighton eventually became one of Europe's most fashionable towns. The lovely Georgian terraces that you see every-where date from this period. Later in the 19th century, when breathing sea air was prescribed as a cure-all for everything from depression to tuberculosis, the Victorians descended in hordes. Today, Brighton is a commuter suburb of London and a popular place for conventions and romantic weekend getaways. Gays and lesbians are very much a part of the local and visitor scene.

Brighton is a compact town, and the easiest way to get around is on foot. Forget about that frantic need for sightseeing and relax. Relaxation is what Brighton is all about. This place is for leisurely strolling, either in the town or along the seaside promenades. The town is small enough so you won't get lost and large enough to offer some good cultural diversions.

Brighton

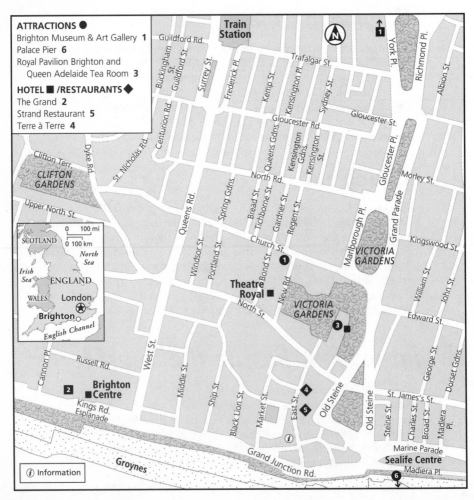

ATTRACTIONS ●
Brighton Museum & Art Gallery **1**
Palace Pier **6**
Royal Pavilion Brighton and
   Queen Adelaide Tea Room **3**
HOTEL ■ /RESTAURANTS ◆
The Grand **2**
Strand Restaurant **5**
Terre à Terre **4**

Getting there

Connex South Central has more than 40 trains a day from London's Victoria Station. The trip takes about an hour. If you travel off-peak (after 9 a.m.), a round-trip ticket costs about £14 ($21). If you're driving, the M23 from central London leads to Brighton. The drive should take about an hour, but if roads are clogged it may take twice that time.

Finding information

Brighton's **Tourist Information Centre** (10 Bartholomew Sq.; ☎ 01273/292-599) is opposite the town hall, about a 10-minute walk south from the train station. The center is a good place to pick up info on current events and a Gay Information Sheet listing gay guesthouses, pubs, and clubs. If you fall in love with Brighton and decide to stay overnight, you can reserve a room at the information center. The center is open Monday through Friday 9 a.m. to 5 p.m., Saturday 10 a.m. to 5 p.m., and Sunday 10 a.m. to 4 p.m. (summer only).

Seeing the sights

Brighton's one must-see attraction is the **Royal Pavilion** (☎ 01273/290-900), set in a small landscaped park bounded by North Street, Church Street, Olde Steine, and New Road. The pavilion is one of the most extraordinary palaces in Europe. John Nash redesigned the original farmhouse and villa on this site for George IV (when the king was still Prince Regent), who lived here with his mistress, Lady Conyngham, until 1827.

The exterior, as crazily wonderful as anything King Ludwig of Bavaria dreamed up, is an Indian fantasy of turrets and minarets. The interior, decorated in a Chinese style, is sumptuous and fantastically extravagant. The king's brother, William IV, and Queen Victoria later used the pavilion. Admission is £4.50 ($7) adults. The pavilion is open daily October through May 10 a.m. to 5 p.m. and June through September 10 a.m. to 6 p.m.

 Before you leave the pavilion, consider having lunch or a *cream tea* (tea and scones served with clotted cream and strawberry preserves) in the superbly restored **Queen Adelaide Tea Room** (☎ 01723/292-736), open daily 10:30 a.m. to 4:30 p.m. (to 5 p.m. in summer). Queen Adelaide, who used this suite in 1830, didn't appreciate the epicurean tastes of her husband, George IV. Dismissing his renowned French chefs, she reverted back to British cuisine so dreary that Lord Dudley complained "you now get cold pâté and hot champagne." The lunch selections and cream teas range from £4 to £6 ($6–$9).

Close to the Royal Pavilion, on Church Street, you find the small **Brighton Museum & Art Gallery** (☎ 01273/290-900), with some interesting collections of Art Nouveau and Art Deco furniture, glass, and ceramics, plus a Fashion Gallery. It's a good place to wile away an hour. Admission is free, and it's open Monday and Tuesday and Thursday through Saturday 10 a.m. to 5 p.m. and Sunday 2 to 5 p.m.

The town's famous amusement area, **Palace Pier,** jutting out into the sea just south of the Royal Pavilion, was built in the late 19th century. Today the pier is rather tacky but worth visiting nonetheless. At night, all lit up with twinkling lights, this place is almost irresistible. Spend half an hour, but don't expect to find much more than junk food and arcade games.

Brighton and neighboring Hove stretch out along the English Channel. The entire **seafront** is a pebbly public beach used for swimming and sunning. Promenades for strolling are all along the seafront. If you're into sunbathing *au naturel,* Brighton has the only nude beach in England, about a mile west of Brighton Pier. You'll recognize it when you get there.

Staying in style

The grandest place to stay is **The Grand** (King's Road, Brighton, Sussex BN1 2FW; ☎ **01273/321-188;** Fax: 01273/202-694; Internet: www. grandbrighton.co.uk). Built in 1864 right on the seafront, this huge, dazzlingly white resort hotel is five-star luxury throughout. The 200 guest rooms are spacious and predictably gorgeous, done mostly in blues and yellows, with big tile baths. The most expensive have sea-facing balconies and floor-to-ceiling double-glazed windows. The special weekend and "Leisure" rates can cut the rack rate almost in half. Rack rates are £230 to £250 ($345–$375) double, with an English breakfast included. American Express, Diners Club, MasterCard, and Visa are accepted.

Dining out

One of the hippest (and friendliest) places for dining is the bow-fronted **Strand Restaurant** (6 East St.; ☎ **01273/747-096**), which serves Modern British cuisine. The ever-changing fixed-price menu, including two or three courses for a set price, is an extremely good value. Herby home-made vegetable soup, pâté, or mussels cooked with fresh cream, wine, and garlic may be followed by chicken breast with leeks and blue cheese sauce, artichoke-and-pesto lasagna, or lamb chops with gravy and a dessert. Main courses are £8 to £15 ($12–$23). The restaurant is open daily 12:30 to 10:00 p.m. (to 10:30 p.m. on weekends). American Express, Diners Club, MasterCard, and Visa are accepted.

For a new outlook on vegetarian food, try **Terre à Terre** (71 East St.; ☎ **01273/729-051**). Considered the best vegetarian restaurant in England, perhaps in all Europe, this place elevates meatless cuisine to an art form. The food is impeccably fresh and beautifully presented. You can eat your way through the menu with the Terre à Tapas, a superb selection of all their best dishes, big enough for two. Main courses are £10 to £12 ($15–$18). The restaurant is open Tuesday through Saturday noon to 10:30 p.m., Sunday 10:00 a.m. to 10:30 p.m. (brunch 10 a.m. to 1 p.m.), and Monday 6:00 to 10:30 p.m. Reservations are recommended. Diners Club, MasterCard, and Visa are accepted.

Canterbury: Tales from the Great Cathedral

Magnificent **Canterbury Cathedral** is one of the glories of England. Spinning the yarns found in *The Canterbury Tales,* Chaucer's pilgrims made their way here. For nearly 400 years, the devout, in search of miracles, salvation, and a bit of adventure, trekked to the cathedral's shrine of Thomas à Becket, archbishop of Canterbury, who was murdered in 1170 by henchmen of Henry II. (The pilgrims didn't stop coming until Henry VIII had the shrine destroyed in 1538.) Modern pilgrims, today called "day-trippers," continue to pour into the Kentish city of Canterbury on the river Stour, 62 miles east of London. They come to see the cathedral, of course, but also to visit the host of small museums and to enjoy the picturesque town surrounding it. (See the map "Canterbury.")

Getting there

Canterbury has two train stations, Canterbury East and Canterbury West, and you can easily walk to the city center from either one. From London's Victoria Station trains run about every half-hour to Canterbury East. Hourly trains from London's Charing Cross stop at Canterbury West. The journey takes 1½ hours and costs about £15 ($22) for a day return. For schedules and information, call ☎ **0345/484-950.** To drive from London, take the A2 and then the M2; Canterbury is signposted all the way. The city center is closed to cars, but you find several parking areas close to the cathedral.

Finding information and taking a tour

At the **Visitors Information Centre** (34 St. Margaret's St.; ☎ **01227/766-567;** Internet: www.canterbury.co.uk), near St. Margaret's Church, you can buy tickets for daily guided-tour walks of the city and cathedral. The walks leave from here at 11:30 a.m. (July 8 through September 18) and 2 p.m. (April 11 through October 27). The cost is £3.50 ($5) adults, £3 ($4.50) seniors/students/children under 14, and £8.50 ($13) families (2 adults/2 children). Easter through September, the center is open Monday through Saturday 9:30 a.m. to 5:30 p.m. and Sunday 10 a.m. to 4 p.m.; the rest of the year, the center is open Monday through Saturday from 9:30 a.m. to 5:00 p.m.; the Sunday opening remains in effect until December only.

Canterbury

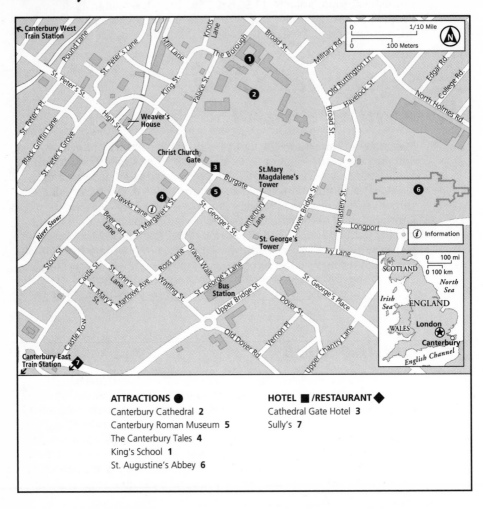

ATTRACTIONS ●

Canterbury Cathedral **2**
Canterbury Roman Museum **5**
The Canterbury Tales **4**
King's School **1**
St. Augustine's Abbey **6**

HOTEL ■ **/RESTAURANT** ◆

Cathedral Gate Hotel **3**
Sully's **7**

Canterbury Historic River Tours, Weavers House, 1 St. Peter's St.
(☎ 07790/534-744), offers half-hour boat trips on the Stour River with
a commentary on the history of the buildings you pass. April through
September, river conditions permitting, boats depart each half-hour
from 10 a.m. to 5 p.m. Monday through Saturday, and Sunday from
11 a.m. to 4 p.m. Tickets are £4.50 ($7) adults and £3.50 ($5) children.
Umbrellas are available in case of rain. The boats leave from behind
the 15th-century Weavers House (access via the Weavers restaurant
garden).

Seeing the sights

Make your first stop the imposing **Canterbury Cathedral** (11 The Precincts; ☎ 01227-762-862), a magnificent structure that was the first major expression of the Gothic style in England. The crypt dates from about 1100, and the cathedral itself (rebuilt after a fire) from the 13th century, with a bell tower added in the 15th century.

Although Henry VIII destroyed Becket's shrine, its site is still marked in the Trinity Chapel, near the high altar. Noteworthy features of the cathedral include a number of panels of rare stained glass and the medieval royal tombs of Henry IV and Edward the Black Prince. Admission is £3.50 ($5) adults and £1.50 ($2.25) children/students/seniors. Guided tours (based on demand) cost £3 ($5) adults, £2.50 ($3.75) students/seniors, and £1.50 ($2.25) children. The cathedral is open Monday through Friday 9 a.m. to 5 p.m. (to 4:30 p.m. November through March), Saturday 9:00 a.m. to 2:30 p.m., Sunday 12:30 to 2:30 p.m. and 4:30 to 5:30 p.m.; closed to sightseeing during services.

As you stroll the cathedral grounds, you may encounter flocks of well-behaved boys and girls wearing blazers and ties: They attend **King's School,** the oldest public school in England, housed in several fine medieval buildings north of the cathedral.

Off High Street, near the cathedral, is the entertaining exhibition known as **The Canterbury Tales** (23 St. Margaret's St.; ☎ 01227/454-888), where the pilgrimages of Chaucerian England are recreated in tableaux. On audio headsets you can hear five of Chaucer's *Canterbury Tales* and the story of the murder of St. Thomas à Becket. Give yourself 45 minutes to an hour to see/hear the entire show. Admission is £5.90 ($9) adults, £4.90 ($7) seniors/students/children 5 to 16. The attraction is open daily February 19 through June and September through October 10 a.m. to 5 p.m.; July through August 9:30 a.m. to 5:30 p.m.; November through February 18 10:00 a.m. to 4:30 p.m.

Two millennia ago, the conquering Romans were living in Canterbury, which they called Cantuaria. Their daily lives are chronicled in the small but fascinating **Canterbury Roman Museum** (☎ 01227/785-575), in the excavated Roman levels of the city between the cathedral and High Street on Butchery Lane. Admission is £2.20 ($3.30) adults, £1.45 ($2.25) seniors/students, and £1.10 ($1.65) children. The museum is open Monday through Saturday 10 a.m. to 5 p.m. (Sunday 1:30 to 5:00 p.m. from June through October).

Although the cathedral gets the lion's share of attention in Canterbury, another Christian site predates it by about 600 years. Set in a spacious park, about a 10-minute walk east from the center of town, you find the atmospheric ruins of **St. Augustine's Abbey** (Longport; ☎ 01227/673-345), founded in 598 and one of the oldest Anglo-Saxon monastic sites in the country. This World Heritage site offers interactive audio tours. Admission is £2.60 ($4) adults and £2.50 ($3.75) seniors/students. The site is open daily April through September 10 a.m. to 6 p.m., October 10 a.m. to 5 p.m., and November through March 10 a.m. to 4 p.m.; closed December 24 to 26 and January 1.

Trek another five minutes east from St. Augustine's Abbey to visit the oldest parish church in England. **St. Martin's Church** (North Holmes Road; ☎ **01227/459-482**), founded by Queen Bertha (the French wife of Saxon King Ethelbert), was already in existence when Augustine arrived from Rome to convert the natives in 597. Admission is free, and the church is open daily 9 a.m. to 5 p.m.

Staying in style

If you're planning an overnight in Canterbury and want, like the pilgrims of yore, to stay near the cathedral, you can't get any closer than the **Cathedral Gate Hotel** (36 Burgate, Canterbury, Kent CT1 2HA; ☎ **01227/464-381**; Fax: 01227/462-800; E-mail: cgate@cgate.demon.co.uk). Dating from 1438, the 27-room hotel adjoins Christchurch Gate and overlooks the Buttermarket. The guest rooms are comfortable and modestly furnished, with sloping floors, massive oak beams, and winding corridors — what else would you expect from a hotel built more than 500 years ago? Rates are £81 ($121) double, continental breakfast included. American Express, Diners Club, MasterCard, and Visa are accepted.

Dining out

One of the best restaurants in Canterbury is **Sully's,** in the County Hotel (High Street; ☎ **01227/766-266**). You can choose from a selection of traditional English dishes or try one of the more imaginatively conceived platters or seasonal specialties. Reservations are recommended. A fixed-price lunch is £17 ($26); a fixed-price dinner goes for £23 to £28 ($35–$42). American Express, Diners Club, MasterCard, and Visa are accepted. The restaurant is open daily 12:30 to 2:20 p.m. and 7 to 10 p.m.

Stratford-upon-Avon: In the Footsteps of the Bard

Stratford-upon-Avon is a shrine to the world's greatest playwright, William Shakespeare, who was born, lived much of his life, and is buried in this market town on the Avon River, 91 miles northwest of London. In summer, crowds of international tourists overrun Stratford, which aggressively hustles its Shakespeare connection. (See map, "Stratford-upon-Avon.")

Stratford-upon-Avon

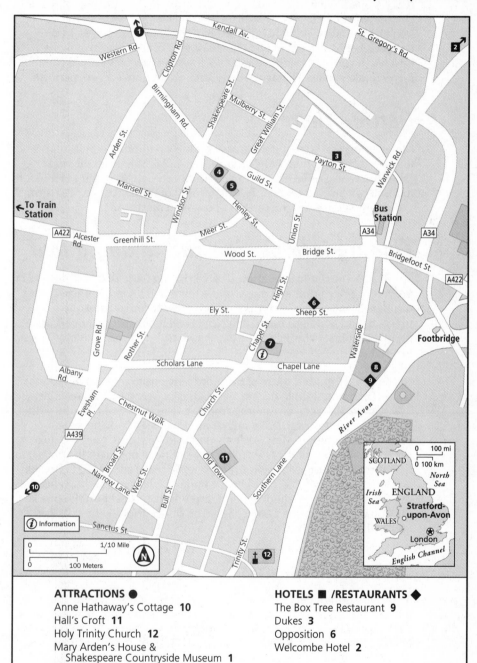

ATTRACTIONS ●
Anne Hathaway's Cottage **10**
Hall's Croft **11**
Holy Trinity Church **12**
Mary Arden's House &
    Shakespeare Countryside Museum **1**
New Place/Nash's House **7**
Royal Shakespeare Theatre **8**
Shakespeare Centre **5**
Shakespeare's Birthplace **4**

HOTELS ■ /RESTAURANTS ◆
The Box Tree Restaurant **9**
Dukes **3**
Opposition **6**
Welcombe Hotel **2**

Stratford boasts many Elizabethan and Jacobean buildings, but it's not really a quaint village anymore. If you're arriving by train, your first glimpse will be of a vast litter-strewn parking lot across from the station. Don't let this sight put you off. The charms of Stratford haven't been completely lost — you find lots of charming corners as you explore. Besides the literary pilgrimage sights, the top draw in Stratford is the **Royal Shakespeare Theatre,** where Britain's foremost actors perform.

Getting there

Direct trains leave frequently from London's Paddington Station; the journey takes two hours and costs about £22 ($33) for an off-peak (after 9:30 a.m.) or weekend round-trip ticket. Call ☎ **0345/484-950** for information and schedules. To drive from London, take the M40 toward Oxford and continue to Stratford-upon-Avon on the A34.

Finding information and taking a tour

Stratford's **Tourist Information Centre** (Bridgefoot; ☎ **01789/293-127**) provides information and maps of the town and its major sites. Easter through October, the center is open Monday through Saturday 9 a.m. to 6 p.m. and Sunday 11 a.m. to 5 p.m.; November through February, it's open Monday through Saturday 9 a.m. to 5 p.m., and Sunday 11 a.m. to 4 p.m.

Guide Friday guided tours of Stratford leave from outside the tourist office. Open-top double-decker buses depart every 15 minutes daily 9:30 a.m. to 5:30 p.m. in summer. You can take the one-hour ride without stops or get off and on at any or all the town's five Shakespeare properties, including Mary Arden's House in Wilmcote (see the next section). The tour ticket is valid all day but does not include admission into any of the houses. The tours cost £8.50 ($12) adults, £7 ($10) seniors/students, £2.50 ($3.75) children under 12, and £19.50 ($28) families (2 adults and up to 4 children). You can buy your ticket on the bus, at the Tourist Information Centre, or at the Guide Friday office, 14 Rother St. (☎ **01789/294466**).

Seeing the sights

A combination ticket that you can buy at your first stop gets you into the five sites administered by the Shakespeare Birthplace Trust: **Shakespeare's Birthplace, Anne Hathaway's Cottage, New Place/ Nash's House, Mary Arden's House,** and **Hall's Croft.** The ticket costs £12 ($18) adults, £11 ($17) seniors/students, £6 ($9) children, and £29 ($43) families (2 adults, 3 children).

A logical place to begin your tour is **Shakespeare's Birthplace,** (Henley Street; ☎ **01789/204016**) where the Bard, son of a glover and wool merchant, first saw the light of day on April 23, 1564. You enter through the modern **Shakespeare Centre,** where you can spend a few minutes browsing the exhibits that illustrate his life and times. The house, filled with Shakespeare memorabilia, is actually two 16th-century half-timbered houses joined together. His father's shop was on one side, and the family residence was on the other. After visiting the bedroom where wee Willie was (probably) born, the Elizabethan kitchen, and other rooms, you can walk through the garden. Admission is £6 ($9) adults, £5.50 ($8) senior citizens/students, £2.50 ($3.75) children, £15 ($22) families (2 adults, 3 children). The Birthplace is open daily March 20 to October 19 9 a.m. to 5 p.m. (Sunday from 9:30 a.m.); October 20 to March 19 9:30 a.m. to 4 p.m. (Sunday from 10 a.m.). It's closed December 24 to 26.

To visit **Anne Hathaway's Cottage** (Cottage Lane, Shottery [about a mile south of Stratford]; ☎ 01789/292-100), take a bus from Bridge Street or, better still, walk there along the well-marked country path from Evesham Place. Anne Hathaway, who came from a family of yeomen farmers, lived in this lovely thatched cottage before she married 18-year-old Shakespeare (a May-December marriage in reverse, although Anne was only 25). Many original 16th-century furnishings, including the *courting settle* (a type of bench that courting couples often sat on), are preserved inside the house, which was occupied by Anne's ancestors until 1892. Before leaving be sure to stroll through the beautiful garden and orchard. Admission is £4.50 ($7) adults, £2 ($3) children, and £11 ($16) families (2 adults, 3 children). The cottage is open daily from March 20 to October 19 9:30 a.m. to 5 p.m. and off-season 9:30 a.m. to 4 p.m. (from 10 a.m. on Sunday). The cottage is closed January 1, Good Friday, and December 24 to 26.

Shakespeare retired in 1610 to **New Place** (Chapel Street; ☎ 01789/204-016). By that time, he was a relatively prosperous man whose plays had been seen by Queen Elizabeth. New Place was a Stratford house that he'd purchased a few years earlier and where he was to die in 1616. The house was later torn down and, today, only the gardens remain. To reach the site from his birthplace, walk east on Henley Street and south on High Street, which becomes Chapel Street. Visitors enter through **Nash's House,** which belonged to Thomas Nash, husband of Shakespeare's granddaughter. The house contains 16th-century period rooms and an exhibit illustrating the history of Stratford. Adjoining the house is a knot garden landscaped in an Elizabethan style. Admission is £3.50 ($5) adults, £1.80 ($2.50) children, and £8.50 ($13) families (2 adults, 3 children). Opening hours are the same as Shakespeare's Birthplace (except Good Friday and January 1, when New Place opens at 1:30 p.m.).

Shakespeare's daughter, Susanna, probably lived with her husband, Dr. John Hall, in **Hall's Croft** (Old Town; ☎ 01789/292-107), a magnificent Tudor house with a walled garden. From New Place, continue south on Chapel and Church Streets and turn east on Old Town to reach Hall's

Croft. The house is furnished in the style of a middle-class 17th-century home. On view are exhibits illustrating the theory and practice of medicine in Dr. Hall's time. Opening times and admissions are the same as for Nash's House (see the preceding paragraph).

Shakespeare died on his birthday, at age 52, and was buried in **Holy Trinity Church** (Old Town; ☎ **01789/266-316**), a beautiful parish church beside the Avon River. His wife Anne, his daughter Susanna, and Susanna's husband, John Hall, lie beside him in front of the altar. A bust of the immortal bard looks down upon the gravesite. I find it a bit odd that the inscription on the tomb of the man who wrote some of the world's most enduring lines is little more than trivial verse, ending with "and curst be he who moves my bones." Obviously William Shakespeare didn't want to leave Stratford — ever. Admission to the church is free, but a small donation is requested to see Shakespeare's tomb. March through October, you can visit the church from Monday through Saturday 8:30 a.m. to 6 p.m. (to 4 p.m. the rest of the year); year-round, the church is open Sunday 2 to 5 p.m.

About 3½ miles north of Stratford on the A34 (Birmingham) road is **Mary Arden's House & Shakespeare Countryside Museum** (Wilmcote; ☎ **01789-204-016**), the last of the five Shakespeare shrines. For more than 200 years, Palmers Farm, a Tudor farmstead with an old stone dovecote and outbuildings, was identified as the girlhood home of Mary Arden, Shakespeare's mother. Recent evidence revealed, however, that Mary Arden actually lived in the house next door, at Glebe Farm. In 2000, the house at Glebe Farm was officially redesignated as the Mary Arden House. Dating from 1514, the house contains country furniture and domestic utensils; in the barns, stable, cowshed, and farmyard you find an extensive collection of farming implements illustrating life and work in the local countryside from Shakespeare's time to the present. Admission is £5 ($7) adults, £2.50 ($3.75) children, and £13.50 ($20) families (2 adults, 3 children). Opening times are the same as for all the other Shakespeare sites.

Experiencing Hamlet or Twelfth Night As You Like It

The **Royal Shakespeare Theatre** (Waterside, Stratford-upon-Avon CV37 6BB; ☎ **01789/295-623**) is the home of the **Royal Shakespeare Company,** which typically stages five Shakespeare plays during a season running from November through September. You can reserve seats through a North American or a British travel or ticket agent, or online at Ticketmaster (www.ticketmaster.co.uk) or First Call (www.first-call.co.uk). A few tickets are always held for sale on the day of a performance; but if you wait until you arrive in Stratford, you may not be able to get a good seat. The box office is open Monday through Saturday 9 a.m. to 8 p.m. but closes at 6 p.m. on days when no performances are on the schedule. Ticket prices are £6 to £46 ($10–$74).

Staying in style

During the long theater season, reserve in advance if you're planning to sleep, perchance to dream, in Stratford. However, the **Tourist Information Centre** (Bridgefoot; ☎ **01789/293-127**) can help you find accommodations.

If you want to stay in the lap of luxury, try the **Welcombe Hotel** (Warwick Road, Stratford-upon-Avon, Warwickshire CV37 ONR; ☎ **01789/295-252;** Fax: 01789/414-666; Internet: www.welcombe. co.uk). Located 1½ miles northeast of the town center, this top-of-the-line, full-service hotel is in one of the country's great Jacobean houses. The largest of the 68 guest rooms are big enough for tennis matches; in the smaller rooms you'd have to content yourself with table tennis. You can enjoy an 18-hole golf course and 157 acres of grounds. Rates begin at £175 ($254) for a double, English breakfast included. Diners Club, MasterCard, and Visa are accepted.

Dukes (Payton Street, Stratford-upon-Avon, Warwickshire CV37 6UA; ☎ **01789/269-300;** Fax: 01789/414-700; Internet: www.astanet.com/ get/ dukeshtl) is a charming choice for the budget-conscious. The hotel was formed from two Georgian town houses and is located in Stratford's center, near Shakespeare's birthplace. The nicely restored public areas and 22 guest rooms are attractive. Many amenities usually found in more expensive hotels are available. The hotel's restaurant serves good English and continental cuisine. No children under 12 are accepted. Rooms go for £65 to £100 ($97–$150) double, English breakfast included. American Express, MasterCard, and Visa are accepted.

Dining out

The river Avon with its gliding white swans is right outside the windows of **The Box Tree Restaurant** (Waterside; ☎ **01789/293-226**) in the Royal Shakespeare Theatre. The menu offers French, Italian, and English cuisine, and you can dine by candlelight after a performance. Reservations are required (a special phone for reservations is available in the theater lobby). The matinee lunch costs £16 ($24). Three-course fixed-price dinners cost £26 to £27 ($39–$41) on Friday and Saturday. American Express, MasterCard, and Visa are accepted. The restaurant is open noon to 2:30 p.m. on matinee days and Monday through Saturday 5:45 p.m. to midnight.

Opposition (13 Sheep St.; ☎ **01789/269-980**), housed in a 16th-century building in the heart of Stratford, offers a historic setting and moderate prices. Lunch and dinner choices are a mix of traditional and Modern British cuisine. Reservations are recommended. Main courses are £6.75 to £15.50 ($10–$23). The restaurant accepts MasterCard and Visa and is open daily noon to 2 p.m. and 5 to 11 p.m.

Salisbury and Stonehenge: Gothic Splendor and Prehistoric Mysteries

The tall slender spire of Salisbury Cathedral rises up from the plains of Wiltshire like a finger pointing toward the heavens. Salisbury, or New Sarum as it was once called, lies in the valley of the Avon River, 90 miles southwest of London. Filled with Tudor inns and tearooms and dominated by its beautiful cathedral, this old market town is often overlooked by visitors eager to see Stonehenge, about 9 miles away. (See the map "Salisbury.")

Salisbury

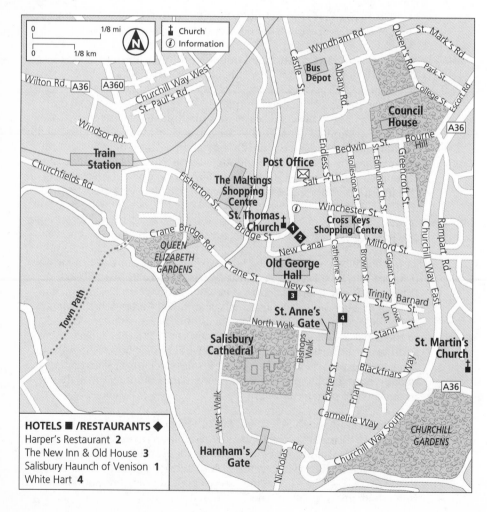

| 0 | 1/8 mi |
| 0 | 1/8 km |

N

✝ Church
ⓘ Information

Wyndham Rd.
Queen's Rd.
St. Mark's Rd.
Castle St.
Albany Rd.
Park St.
College St.
Escort Rd.
Wilton Rd. **A36**   **A360**
Churchill Way West
St. Paul's Rd.
Bus Depot
Council House   **A36**
Windsor Rd.
Bedwin St.
Endless St.
St. Edmunds Ch. St.
Greencroft St.
Bourne Hill
Train Station
Post Office ✉
Salt Ln.
Rollestone St.
Churchfields Rd.
Fisherton St.
The Maltings Shopping Centre
ⓘ
Winchester St.
St. Thomas Church ■ ❶ ❷
Cross Keys Shopping Centre
Greencroft St.
Rampart Rd.
Crane Bridge Rd.
Bridge St.
New Canal
Catherine St.
Brown St.
Milford St.
Gigant St.
Churchill Way East
QUEEN ELIZABETH GARDENS
Old George Hall
Crane St.
New St. ❸
Ivy St.
Trinity St.
Barnard St.
Lowe's Ln.
Town Path
St. Anne's Gate
North Walk
❹
Stann St.
Salisbury Cathedral
Bishops Walk
St. Martin's Church ✝
Exeter St.
Friary Ln.
Blackfriars Way
A36
West Walk
CHURCHILL GARDENS
HOTELS ■ /RESTAURANTS ◆
Harper's Restaurant **2**
The New Inn & Old House **3**
Salisbury Haunch of Venison **1**
White Hart **4**
Harnham's Gate
Nicholas Rd.
Carmelite Way
Churchill Way South

Getting there

From London's Waterloo Station hourly Network Express trains run to Salisbury; the journey takes about 1½ hours and costs about £22 ($33) for an off-peak (after 9:30 a.m.) round-trip ticket. For information and schedules, call ☎ **0345/484-950.** If you're driving from London, head west on the M3 to the end of the run, continuing the rest of the way on the A30.

Finding information

Salisbury's **Tourist Information Centre** is on Fish Row (☎ **01722/334-956**). October through April, the center is open Monday through Saturday 9:30 a.m. to 5:00 p.m.; June through September, it's open Monday through Saturday 9:30 a.m. to 6:00 p.m. and Sundays 10:30 a.m. to 4:30 p.m.

Seeing the sights

Visitors eager to see Stonehenge often overlook the lovely old market town of Salisbury, but I suggest that you try to spend a bit of time wandering through Salisbury Cathedral.

Salisbury

Despite an ill-conceived renovation in the 18th century, the **Salisbury Cathedral's** (The Close; ☎ **01722/323-279**) 13th-century structure remains the best example in England of Early English and Perpendicular Gothic style. The 404-foot spire is the tallest in the country. The beautiful 13th-century octagonal **chapter house** possesses one of the four surviving original texts of the *Magna Carta.* Adding to the serene beauty of the cathedral are the cloisters and an exceptionally large **close,** comprising about 75 buildings. The suggested donation for admission is £3.50 ($5) for the cathedral and 50p (75¢) for the chapter house. May through August, the cathedral is open daily 8:30 a.m. to 8:30 p.m. (to 6:30 p.m. September through April).

In the town of Wilton, 3 miles west of Salisbury on the A30, is **Wilton House** (☎ **01722/746-720**), one of England's great country estates. The home of the earls of Pembroke, the house is noted for its 17th-century staterooms by the celebrated architect Inigo Jones. Shakespeare's troupe is believed to have entertained here. Several centuries later in this house, General Eisenhower and his advisers made preparations for the D-Day landings at Normandy. Beautifully maintained furnishings and paintings by Van Dyck, Rubens, Brueghel, and Reynolds fill the house. You can visit a reconstructed Tudor kitchen and Victorian laundry, plus the "Wareham Bears," a collection of some 200 miniature dressed teddy bears. The 21-acre grounds include rose and water gardens, riverside and woodland walks, and a huge adventure playground for children. Admission is £7.25 ($11) adults and £4.50 ($7) children 5 to 15. Easter through September, the house and grounds are open daily 11 a.m. to 6 p.m. (last admission 5 p.m.); in October it's open daily from 10:30 a.m. to 5:30 p.m. (last admission 4:30 p.m.). If you're without a car, you can take the bus that stops on New Canal, a 10-minute walk north of Salisbury train station; check with the tourist office for schedules.

Stonehenge

About 9 miles north of Salisbury, at the junction of the A303 and the A344/A360, you find one of the world's most renowned prehistoric sites and one of England's most popular attractions, the prehistoric stone circle known as **Stonehenge (☎ 01980/624-715)**. If you're not driving, hop on one of the Wilts & Dorset buses that depart from the Salisbury train station daily between 11 a.m. and 2 p.m.; the trip takes about 40 minutes, and the round-trip fare is about £5 ($8). The crowds can be overwhelming as the day wears on, so arrive as early as possible.

Stonehenge is a stone circle of megalithic pillars and lintels built on the flat Salisbury Plain. Experts believe that the site is from 3,500 to 5,000 years old. Many visitors to Stonehenge are disappointed to find that Stonehenge isn't as enormous as they envisioned, and is now surrounded by a fence that keeps sightseers 50 feet from the stones. Keep in mind, however, that many of the stones, which weigh several tons, were mined and moved from distant quarries in a time before forklifts, trucks, and dynamite.

Stonehenge was probably a shrine and/or ceremonial gathering place of some kind. The old belief that Stonehenge was built by the Druids has been discredited (it's probably older than the Celtic Druids). A popular theory is that the site was an astronomical observatory because it's aligned to the summer solstice and can accurately predict eclipses based on the placement of the stones. But in an age when experts think they know everything, Stonehenge still keeps its tantalizing mysteries to itself. Admission is £4.20 ($6) adults, £3.20 ($5) students/seniors, and £2.20 ($3.30) children. The site is open daily from March 16 through May and September through October 15, 9:30 a.m. to 6:00 p.m.; June through August, 9 a.m. to 7 p.m.; and October 16 to March 15, 9:30 a.m. to 4:00 p.m.

Staying in style

A Salisbury landmark since Georgian times, the **White Hart** (1 St. John St., Salisbury, Wiltshire SP1 2SD; ☎ **01722/327-476;** Fax: 01722/412-761; Internet: www.heritagehotels.com) was totally renovated in 1995. The hotel offers accommodations in the older section of the building or in a new motel-like section in the rear. A good restaurant is on site. Rates are £115 to £140 ($160–$210) double. The hotel accepts American Express, MasterCard, and Visa.

If you're looking for an inexpensive but atmospheric (and smoke-free) B&B, try **The New Inn & Old House** (39–47 New St., Salisbury, Wiltshire SP1 2PH; ☎ **01722/327-679**). This 15th-century building, with a walled garden backing up to the Cathedral Close Wall, offers seven well-appointed oak-beamed guest rooms. The Inn restaurant serves reasonably priced meals. Rates are £50 to £70 ($75–$105) double, continental breakfast included. American Express, MasterCard, and Visa are accepted.

Dining out

Looking for simple, healthy, homemade food? Go to **Harper's Restaurant** (7–9 Ox Row, Market Square; ☎ **01722/333-118**). You can order from two menus, one featuring cost-conscious bistro-style platters and the other a longer menu with all-vegetarian pasta dishes. Reservations are recommended. Main courses are £8.50 to £12.50 ($13–$19) and fixed-price meals £8 ($12) at lunch and £13 ($20) at dinner. American Express, MasterCard, and Visa are accepted. The restaurant is open Monday through Saturday noon to 2 p.m. and 6:30 to 9:30 p.m. and Sunday 6:00 to 9:30 p.m. (October through May, the place is closed on Sunday).

The **Salisbury Haunch of Venison** (1 Minster St.; ☎ **01722/322-024**) is a creaky-timbered 1320 chophouse and pub that serves English roasts and grills. The house specialty is roast haunch of venison with *bubble and squeak* (mashed potatoes and cabbage). Main courses are £9 to £13 ($14–$20), with pub platters at £4 to £6 ($6–$9). American Express, MasterCard, and Visa are accepted. The restaurant is open daily noon to 2:30 p.m. and Monday through Saturday 7:00 to 9:30 p.m. The pub is open Monday through Saturday 11 a.m. to 11 p.m. and Sunday noon to 10:30 p.m. The pub is closed Christmas through Easter.

Part VI

Living It Up after the Sun Goes Down: London Nightlife

The 5th Wave   By Rich Tennant

The new soccer team from the UK, "The London Fog", has just scored the winning goal, and in celebration, the team members are ripping off their double breasted trench coats, and tossing them into the stands!

In this part...

*L*ondon, for some people, is synonymous with the performing arts. Year-round, on every evening of the week, you find someone performing something somewhere. Planning a night out here isn't the problem — choosing from among all the possibilities is where the difficulty lies.

Because theater is unquestionably the most popular of the city's cultural choices — for many visitors, a trip to London wouldn't be complete without seeing at least one play or musical — I begin this part by giving you the lowdown on the theater scene in Chapter 22. But if theater isn't your thing, you won't be lacking for other diversions. In Chapter 23, I highlight London's other performing arts: grand opera, symphonic concerts, modern and classical ballet, and countless musical recitals.

Nightlife in London is certainly not restricted to the "high arts," however. In Chapter 24, I introduce you to some of the many places where you can rub elbows with Londoners and perhaps have a pint or two — pubs, bars, clubs, discos, cabarets, and jazz spots.

Chapter 22

Experiencing the Grand Tradition: London's Theater Scene

· ·

In This Chapter

▶ Getting the inside scoop on London's theater scene

▶ Finding out what's on and where

▶ Getting tickets

▶ Enjoying pre- or post-theater dinner

· ·

*I*n the United States, people think of New York City as *the* theater capital. But from a global perspective, London may hold that title, based on the number of offerings and the quality of the performances. Of course, London didn't attain this stature overnight. The city has been building its theatrical reputation since the Elizabethan era, when Shakespeare, Marlowe, and others were staging their plays in a South Bank theater district.

Plays and musicals are staged all over the city in approximately 100 theaters, but the commercial hits are centered in the West End (the site of approximately 50 theaters). The **Barbican** and the **South Bank** area also provide major theater venues. Just like New York, London is the home of many *fringe* venues (the equivalent of Off- or Off-Off-Broadway theaters).

This chapter gives you the information you need in order to take advantage of London's long theater tradition.

Seeing the Big — and Not So Big — Shows

Before you begin to consider which plays or musicals to attend, you need some basic information. You should know that booking a seat before you leave is the best way to ensure that you get to enjoy the performance of your dreams, especially if you want to see one of the hot musicals or a big-name star in a limited-run show. Hit shows such as *The Lion King* can be sold out months in advance.

Do you know what you should wear for your evening at the theater? You certainly don't have to dress to the nines, but if you arrive in a sweat suit and running shoes you'll be pretty conspicuous. (No one would be rude enough to say anything, of course.) London theater audiences are, on the whole, pretty well dressed. I can't give you any hard and fast rules here, just use common sense and "try to look nice," as my mum used to say.

With these critical details in mind, you can begin to orient yourself to the London theater scene. The following sections provide the basics.

Visiting Theaterland

The West End theater district — also called Theaterland — is concentrated in the area around Piccadilly Circus, Leicester Square, and Covent Garden. But the theaters at the **Barbican** and **South Bank Centre** (see the next section) are theatrically considered West End venues as well.

I can't guarantee that you'll like whatever play you see in the West End. But you can expect that the production values and the performances will be of the highest quality. Major British stars with international screen reputations regularly perform in the West End, although you're just as likely to see a show starring someone you've never heard of but who's well known in England. You can also expect to find a few American plays and musicals because the crossover between London and New York is increasing. And here's some good news: Tickets are considerably cheaper here than in New York. In London, you rarely pay more than £35 ($52) for the best seats in the house.

London's theater offerings always include new plays, long-run favorites, and revivals of the classics, as well as Shakespeare. Some of the shows in the West End have been running for years and show no sign of winding down, for example Agatha Christie's *Mousetrap* and Andrew Lloyd Webber's *Phantom of the Opera*. In general, evening performances are Monday through Saturday and, depending on the show, matinees are on Wednesday or Thursday and Saturday. Some shows have added Sunday performances, too. Matinees are a couple of pounds cheaper than evening performances.

Plays in the West End have varying curtain times. Evening performances may begin at 7:30, 8, or 8:30 p.m., and matinees at 1:30, 2, or 2:30 p.m. Check your ticket to be certain because if you're late you won't be admitted until the second act or a suitable pause in the action. (If it's a one-act play, good luck.) Londoners take their theater very seriously (even the comedies), so don't be one of those obnoxious latecomers who whines that the Tube was late. If you come laden with packages, you can check them in the coatroom. Don't tip the usher who shows you to your seat. Talking and noisily unwrapping pieces of candy during the performance will be frowned on — especially if I'm in the audience.

In London, theaters don't hand out play programs free of charge to every patron. If you want a program, you must buy it. They usually cost £2 to £3 ($3–$4.50).

Finding a ticket bargain beyond the West End

I can't list all the theaters in Theaterland, but I need to highlight three standout venues. They're geographically outside London's West End, but they are still considered part of the West End theater community.

- ✔ The **Barbican Centre** (Silk Street, EC2; Tube: Barbican), a multi-arts center in The City, is the London home of the prestigious **Royal Shakespeare Company** (☎ 020/7638-8891), which performs in the 1,156-seat **Barbican Theatre.** Other plays are performed in **The Pit,** a 200-seat studio theater. Also in the complex you find bars, cafes, and restaurants. Ticket prices vary from show to show, but they generally are less than those for commercial hits in the West End; theatergoers under 25 and over 60 qualify for special reductions. The box office (☎ 0208/7638-8891) is open daily 9 a.m. to 8 p.m. Call ☎ 020/7382-7297 for 24-hour recorded info on all Barbican Centre events, or you can check out the performance calendar on the Web at www.rsc.org.uk.

- ✔ The **South Bank Arts Centre** (South Bank, SE1; Tube: Waterloo) is home to the **Royal National Theatre** (☎ 020/7452-3000), which performs in three theaters: the **Olivier** (1,160 seats), **Lyttelton** (890 seats), and **Cottesloe** (a smaller theater-in-the-round). The Royal National performs Shakespeare, but it is just as likely to offer a new David Hare work or a Tennessee Williams revival. Ticket prices are slightly lower than at the commercial theaters on the other side of the river, generally £10 to £29 ($15–$46) for evening performances and £9 to £25 ($15–$41) for matinees. Unsold seats are offered at even lower prices two hours before curtain. The facility also houses cafes, bars, and a good bookstore. The box office is open Monday through Saturday 10 a.m. to 8 p.m. For information on performances, call ☎ 020/7452-3400 (Monday through Saturday 10 a.m.–11 p.m.). You can find all performances and an online booking form at www.nationaltheatre.org.uk.

✔ **Shakespeare's Globe Theatre** (New Globe Walk, Bankside, SE1; ☎ 020/7401-9919; Tube: Cannon Street or London Bridge) is the newest addition to the South Bank theater scene. The Globe presents a June-through-September season of the Bard's plays in a reconstructed oak-and-thatch open-air Elizabethan theater (performances may be cancelled because of rain). The benches can be numbing, but the discomfort is worth the opportunity to see Shakespeare performed not far from the original theater and right beside the Thames. Check out www.shakespeares-globe.org for current performances.

Exploring the fringe

In many ways, fringe theater is London's real theatrical heartbeat. The *fringe,* London's equivalent of New York's Off- or Off-Off-Broadway, is now commonly called *Off West End.* (When my own play, *Beardsley,* was produced in London, it was on the fringe.) Groups performing on the fringe don't have the big bucks to mount lavish West End productions, but they often hope that their shows will be critical hits and move to the West End. With the overabundance of acting talent in London, the fringe is where you may see tomorrow's stars acting today and next season's hit in its original bare-bones form. The plays performed on the fringe are sometimes controversial or experimental, but for true theater lovers they can provide a stimulating alternative to the tradition and glamour of the West End. The performance spaces for fringe productions are usually smaller than for West End shows (sometimes tiny, sometimes above a pub), and the ticket prices are usually much lower (rarely more than £10/$15). Fringe theaters and spaces adapted to fringe productions are scattered far and wide, so consult a *London A to Z, Time Out,* or call the theaters directly for directions on how to find them.

Enjoying outdoor theater

What could be more fun than watching a good play performed under the stars? The **Regent's Park Open Air Theatre** (Regent's Park, NW1; ☎ 020/7486-2431; Tube: Baker Street) has a May-to-August season. This large venue offers theater seats but no roof, so rain may cancel the show. You find the theater on the north side of Queen Mary's Rose Garden. Ticket prices range from £8.50 to £23 ($13–$35); you can check out the program on the theater's Web site, www.open-air-theatre.org.uk. **Shakespeare's Globe** (see the previous section "Beyond the West End") is another venue that's open to the heavens.

Finding Out What's On

You know that you want to attend a play, but how do you find out what's playing where? You can find details for all London shows, concerts, and other performances in the daily London newspapers: the *Daily Telegraph,* the *Evening Standard,* the *Guardian,* the *Independent,* and the *Times.* Another good source is the free booklet *London Planner,* available at the British Travel Centre (1 Regent St.) or by mail from a British Tourist Authority travel office (see the Appendix for contact info). For the most comprehensive listings of London theatrical performances, plus thumbnail synopses of the plots and (usually scathing) critical opinion, buy a copy of the weekly magazine *Time Out,* available at London newsstands on Wednesdays for £1.95 ($3), or see its Web site at www.timeout.com. The Web is one of the best places to search in advance for information on plays and performances currently running in London. You may find the following sites useful:

- ✔ www.londontheatre.co.uk
- ✔ www.keithprowse.com
- ✔ www.albemarle-london.com
- ✔ www.timeout.com

Getting Tickets

If you have your heart set on seeing a major London theatrical performance, here's my best advice: Order your tickets in advance — before you leave home — to ensure that you have a seat (see Chapter 9 for ordering advance tickets).

Buying from a box office

But if you're in London and decide then that you want to see a show, you may still be able to get a seat. Even though an announcement has been made that a show is sold out, you can often buy a ticket from the theater's box office, which usually opens at 10 a.m. Ticket cancellations occur, and last-minute house seats go on sale the day of the performance or an hour before. Many London theaters offer standby seats, sold an hour before the performance to students and seniors with proper ID. If you want to save a few pounds, matinees are somewhat cheaper than evening performances.

If you don't have time to go to the box office and have a major credit card handy, call the theater directly. You can find the phone numbers in the papers and in *Time Out.* Many London theaters accept telephone credit-card bookings at regular prices (plus a minimal fee of about £1.50/$2.25). They'll hold your tickets at the box office, where you pick them up any time up to a half-hour before the curtain. By buying directly from the box office, you don't have to pay the commission fee (up to 30%) charged by ticket agencies.

Buying a ticket in "the stalls" doesn't mean that you'll be seated in the ladies' powder room. It means that you may have one of the best seats in the house. *Stalls* is the British term for first-floor orchestra. Most of the West End theaters are fairly old, which means that they may have *boxes* for sale as well. These box seats will be on the sides of the second or third tier.

Using ticket agencies

All over the West End, ticket agencies boldly advertise that they have tickets to the sold-out hit shows. Most of these places are legitimate, but their commission fees vary. If you choose to use the services of a ticket agency rather than booking directly with the box office (see the preceding section), I recommend that you call, stop in, or book online at one of the following trustworthy agencies:

- ✔ **Globaltickets/Edwards & Edwards** maintains a counter at the Britain Visitor Center (1 Regent St., SW1; ☎ **020/7734-4555** or 020/7734-4500; Internet: www.globaltickets.com; Tube: Piccadilly Circus). The counter is open Monday through Friday 10:15 a.m. to 6:15 p.m. and Saturday and Sunday 10 a.m. to 4 p.m. You pay a variable commission on top of the ticket price.

- ✔ The **Albemarle Booking Agency** (74 Mortimer St., London, W1; ☎ **020/7637 9041**; Internet: www.albemarle-london.com; Tube: Oxford Circus or Goodge Street) is another long-established agency, open Monday through Friday 10 a.m. to 6 p.m. and Saturday 10 a.m. to 5 p.m. Albemarle maintains dedicated theater desks at several of London's ritzier hotels, including the **Savoy,** the **Park Lane Hilton,** the **Dorchester,** and **Claridge's.** Its commission fee of 25% on top of the ticket price is what you can expect to pay for just about any theater booking made through a hotel concierge.

Two trustworthy agencies accept credit-card bookings 24 hours a day and charge a 25% commission:

- ✔ **First Call** (☎ **01293/453-744**; Internet: www.firstcalltickets.com)

- ✔ **TicketMaster** (☎ **0870/606-9999**; Internet: www.ticketmaster.co.uk)

You can pick up your tickets at the box office.

Before you buy any ticket from any agency, the agent must tell you the face value of the tickets (you can ask to see them). Before you sign the charge receipt, be sure to check the seat numbers, the face value of the tickets, and the agent's booking fee. If you're making a telephone booking, the agent must disclose the face value of the tickets, their locations, and whether you have a restricted view.

Beware of unlicensed ticket agencies that charge far more than the face value of the ticket plus a very hefty commission fee. A commission fee should *never* be more than 30% of the regular ticket price. Reputable ticket agencies belong to the Society of Ticket Agents and Retailers (STAR) and always advertise this fact.

 The **Society of London Theatres** (☎ **020/7836-0971**) operates a half-price ticket booth in the clock tower building by the gardens in Leicester Square (Tube: Leicester Square). The booth has no telephone info line, so you have to show up in person to see what's on sale that day. The booth is open Monday through Saturday noon to 6:30 p.m. and noon to 2 p.m. for matinees (which may be on Wednesday, Thursday, Saturday, or Sunday). Tickets are sold only on the day of performance. This transaction is a cash-only affair; no credit cards or traveler's checks are accepted. You pay exactly half the price plus a nominal fee (usually about £3/$4.50). The most popular shows usually won't be available, but you may luck out. Tickets for the English National Opera and other events are sometimes available as well. You may want to stop by in any case to pick up a free copy of *The Official London Theatre Guide,* which lists every show with addresses and phone numbers and includes a map of the West End theater district.

 You see ticket agencies around Leicester Square advertising half-price or reduced-price tickets. Keep in mind that the Society of London Theatres operates the only official half-price ticket booth. At these other places, you may be sold a reduced-price ticket for a seat that just happens to be in the last row of the balcony or a seat with a restricted view. And wave away those pesky scalpers who hang out in front of mega-hits. They may indeed be selling (for an astronomical price) a valid ticket. But some of these *touts,* as they're called, also forge tickets, which means that you'll be out of cash and out of a show. By law, any tout must disclose the face value of the ticket, so you know exactly what the mark-up is. The best advice: Don't deal with them.

Dining before or after the Performance

Will you eat dinner before or after your theatrical experience? By eating beforehand, you may feel too rushed to make the curtain. Eating late is more fun and relaxed, but hunger pangs may mar your theater enjoyment, and not every restaurant is open late.

Many of the restaurants that I review in Chapter 14 serve pretheater meals. These places are geared for the theater crowd, so they know your time is limited. Pretheater menus are usually served 5:30 to 7 p.m. Your choices are limited to a set menu, but you can be out by 7:30 p.m. or earlier. The prices are usually a good value.

The following restaurants (all listed in Chapter 14) are close to West End theaters and have pretheater menus:

- ✔ **The Ivy,** 1–5 West St., Soho, WC2; ☎ **020/7836-4751;** Tube: Leicester Square

- ✔ **Joe Allen,** 13 Exeter St., Covent Garden, WC2; ☎ **020/7836-0651;** Tube: Covent Garden

- ✔ **L'Odeon,** 65 Regent St. (entrance on Air Street), Piccadilly Circus, W1; ☎ **020/7287-1400;** Tube: Piccadilly Circus

- ✔ **Quaglino's,** 16 Bury St., St. James's, SW1; ☎ **020/7930-6767;** Tube: Green Park

- ✔ **Rules,** 35 Maiden Lane, Covent Garden, WC2; ☎ **020/7836-5314;** Tube: Covent Garden

- ✔ **Simpson's-in-the-Strand,** 100 The Strand (next to the Savoy Hotel), WC2; ☎ **020/7836-9112;** Tube: Charing Cross

Just be certain to book a table beforehand. If you're dining outside the West End, allot extra time to order, eat, pay the bill, get your coats, and then hop on the Tube or hail a taxi to make the curtain.

If you're not fussy about what you eat and just want to keep your stomach from growling during the performance, fast-food joints are plentiful in Leicester Square and Piccadilly Circus. And if you're going farther afield — to the **Barbican** or **South Bank Centre** — you can ward off impending hunger pangs with a light meal or a sandwich at one of the cafes or restaurants on the premises.

I'm not a big one for late dining, and in the West End the final curtain rarely comes down before 10:30 p.m. (at the opera the performance usually isn't over until 11 p.m.). If you're dining after the show, find out whether the restaurant of your choice is open (the late-night dining custom isn't as established in London as in New York). And if you're using the Tube, remember that most lines end service at 11:30 p.m. or midnight at the very latest. You may want to have dinner before the show and dessert and coffee afterward.

Chapter 23

Raising the Curtain: London's Performing Arts

. . . .

In This Chapter

▶ Going to symphony, chamber-music, and rock concerts

▶ Seeing opera and dance performances

▶ Finding out what's playing

▶ Getting tickets

. . . .

*L*ondon is a mecca of the performing arts. Whether you enjoy
symphony or rock concerts, operas or classical ballets, you can
feed your need for music or dance. Take your pick from the city's own
Royal Opera, Royal Ballet, English National Opera, or London Symphony
Orchestra. Or see one of the internationally renowned groups or
performers for which London is a tour stopover. This chapter gives you
the information that you need to plan your trip to include the performing
arts.

Finding Out What's Where

London newspapers have arts or culture sections in their Sunday
editions, and you can access many of them on the Web to check
performing-arts schedules. You find the most comprehensive listings
in the *Times* (www.Sunday-times.co.uk) and the *Telegraph* (www.
telegraph.co.uk). For a weeklong list of what's happening, check
Time Out, available at newsstands on Wednesdays and on the Web at
www.timeout.com.

Artsline (☎ **020-7388-2227;** Internet: www.artsline.org.uk) provides
advice on disabled accessibility to London arts and entertainment
events.

Purchasing Tickets

If you want to attend a musical event or a dance performance, I recommend that you go to the box office to buy tickets or call the venue and order tickets by phone. Buying direct saves you from paying a big commission fee. Generally, by using a credit card, you can order tickets from the box office — or online — before you leave home and pick them up in London.

The following agencies accept credit-card bookings 24 hours a day, all charging at least 25% commission:

- ✔ **Keith Prowse** (☎ **800/669-7469** in the U.S. or 0293/453-744; Internet: www.keithprowse.com)

- ✔ **Albemarle Booking Agency** (☎ **020/7637-9041**; Internet: www.albemarle-london.com)

- ✔ **TicketMaster** (☎ **0870/606-9999**; Internet: www.ticketmaster.co.uk)

- ✔ **Globaltickets** (☎ **020/7734-4555**; Internet: www.globaltickets.com)

Enjoying a Night at the Opera

London is home base to two major opera companies. The **Royal Opera** enjoys the most international prestige. It performs operas in the original languages and boasts the most famous international singers. Its home is the **Royal Opera House** (Covent Garden, WC2E; ☎ **020/7304-4000** info line; Tube: Covent Garden), which recently reopened after a years-long state-of-the-art refurbishment that added two smaller venues — the **Linbury Studio Theatre** and the **Glore Studio Theatre.** Ticket prices for grand opera run £8 to £150 ($12–$225). For a summary of the opera (and ballet) season, check the Web site www.royalopera.org. If you have your heart set on seeing an opera at the Royal Opera, book as far ahead as you possibly can — I'm talking weeks, not days. The season runs September through July.

The **English National Opera** (usually referred to as the ENO) beats the Royal Opera in popularity and inventiveness. It performs at the **London Coliseum** (St. Martin's Lane, WC2N; ☎ **020/7632-8300** for box office, open 24 hours Monday through Saturday for phone bookings, 10 a.m. to 6 p.m. in person; Tube: Leicester Square). The operas are all sung in English. Seats run £6 to £66 ($9–$99); unsold seats go on sale at reduced prices three hours before a performance; special prices are available for student and senior standby seats. The opera season runs September through July. You can see the ENO program and book online by going to its Web site at www.eno.org.

The following two venues also offer you the opportunity to see opera during your time in London:

- ✔ The **Holland Park Theatre** (Holland Park, W8; ☎ **020/7602-7856;** Tube: Holland Park), London's most charming stage, uses the ruins of a Jacobean mansion in Holland Park as a backdrop for a mid-June through August season of opera. Tickets run £15 to £25 ($23–$41). You can view the performance schedule and book tickets online at www.operahollandpark.com.

- ✔ For nearly 130 years the **D'Oyly Carte Opera Company** (☎ **020/ 7793-7100**) has been performing the comic operas of Gilbert & Sullivan. Venues change, and the schedule is irregular, so I advise that you check out the company's Web site at www.doylycarte.ork.uk for current information.

Enjoying Bach, Beethoven, and Brahms

London offers some of the world's finest classical and chamber music. This section describes your choices for enjoying classical music.

From the Barbican to the Royal Albert

The home base for the **London Symphony Orchestra** (Internet: www.lso.co.uk) is the **Barbican Hall** at the Barbican Centre (Silk Street, EC2Y; ☎ **020/7638-8891** for 24-hour recorded info; Tube: Barbican), the concert hall portion of a giant performing-arts complex in The City. You may also catch a performance by the **Royal Philharmonic Orchestra** (Internet: www.rpo.co.uk), which plays concerts here and at the Royal Albert Hall, another all-purpose venue for classical music.

The **Royal Albert Hall** (Kensington Gore, SW7; ☎ **020/7589-8212;** Tube: High Street Kensington) is an enormous circular domed concert hall that has been a landmark in South Kensington since 1871. The box office is open daily 9 a.m. to 9 p.m.; ticket prices vary by the event.

A summer tradition: Going to the Proms

From mid-July through mid-September, fans of classical and pops concerts attend the wildly popular concert series called the *Proms.* Featuring musicians from all over Europe, Proms concerts are held at the **Royal Albert Hall** (see the preceding section), where they began in 1895. For Proms concerts, all seats are removed from the orchestra and gallery level. Reserved seats are available, but devotees stand for a close look at the orchestras. Starting in July, you can book seats through the Royal Albert Hall box office at ☎ 020/7589-8212. To get one of the 1,000 standing room places (£3/$4.50), you have to queue up on the day of the performance. You can check out the Proms schedule on the Web at www.bbc.co.uk/proms.

The South Bank Centre

The **South Bank Centre** (South Bank, SE1; ☎ 020/7960-4242; Tube: Waterloo) presents approximately 1,200 classical music and dance concerts per year. Performances are held year-round in three separate auditoriums: The **Royal Festival Hall** presents symphonic works performed by a variety of orchestras (some British, some international). The **Queen Elizabeth Hall,** a smaller venue, offers chamber music concerts and dance programs. The **Purcell Room,** an intimate setting, is ideal for recitals. You can get tickets and information on all three venues at the box office (level 1, Belvedere Rd.; open 10 a.m. to 9 p.m.) or online at www.sbc.org.uk; prices vary for each event. For credit-card bookings, call ☎ 020/7960-4242.

Chamber music in Wigmore Hall

Wigmore Hall (36 Wigmore St., W1; ☎ 020/7935-2141; Tube: Bond Street) is a beautifully renovated, century-old concert hall used for chamber-music and solo concerts and recitals. You can find performance information on the Web at www.wigmore-hall.org.uk.

Chamber-music performances are also held in the **Purcell Room** at the **South Bank Centre** (see the preceding section). Prices vary for every concert.

Romantic concerts by candlelight

Evening candlelit concerts of baroque music are performed weekly (usually on Thursday, Friday, and Saturday night) at 7:30 p.m. in the lovely church of **St. Martin-in-the-Fields,** Trafalgar Square, W1 (☎ 020/7839-8362 for credit-card bookings; Tube: Charing Cross). Lunch-time concerts are usually held on Monday, Tuesday, and Friday at 1 p.m. Tickets run £6 to £15 ($9–$23).

Music under the stars

Kenwood House (Hampstead Lane, NW3; ☎ 020/7413-1443; Tube: East Finchley), a picturesque lakeside estate on Hampstead Heath, is the setting for **Kenwood Lakeside Concerts,** a series of outdoor concerts held at 7:30 p.m. on Saturdays in July and August. A free shuttle bus runs between the East Finchley Tube station and the concert bowl. From Central London, you need at least 20 minutes to get to the Tube stop, and another 15 minutes for the ride on the shuttle bus. Tickets cost £6 to £20 ($9–$30).

Finding the Dance Venues

The **Royal Ballet** performs at the **Royal Opera House** and the **English National Ballet,** and other visiting companies perform at the **London Coliseum** (see the section "Enjoying a Night at the Opera" for details).

Refurbished in 1998, **Sadler's Wells** (Rosebery Avenue, Islington EC1R; ☎ 020/7863-6000; Tube: Angel) is well known for its contemporary dance, theater, and music productions and as a venue for solo performers. Sadler's Wells also manages the **Peacock Theatre** (Portugal Street, WC2; ☎ 020/7863-8222; Tube: Covent Garden), a home for dance in the West End, and the **Lillian Baylis Theatre** (Arlington Way, EC1; ☎ 020/7713-6000; Tube: Farringdon), a smaller venue for dance and performance. Programs for all three theaters are listed on the Web at www.sadlers-wells.com.

The **Place Theatre** (17 Duke's Rd., WC1; ☎ 020/7387-0161; Internet: www.theplace.org.uk; Tube: Euston) is the main venue for contemporary dance in the United Kingdom. **Riverside Studios** (Crisp Road, W6; ☎ 020/8237-1111; Internet; www.riversidestudios.co.uk; Tube: Hammersmith) is an arts center that showcases theater, cinema, and dance.

Braving the Mega Concerts: They Will, They Will Rock You

When the rock and pop stars play London, they need a *huge* arena to hold their shrieking fans. The two biggest venues are **Wembley Stadium** (Empire Way, Wembley, Middlesex; ☎ 020/8902-8833; Tube: Wembley Park) and the **Earl's Court Exhibition Centre** (Warwick Road, SW5; ☎ 020/7385-1200; Tube: Earl's Court).

A much smaller (by that I mean less than 70,000 seats) rock-and-pop venue is the **Brixton Academy** (211 Stockwell Rd., SW9; ☎ 020/7771-3000; Tube: Brixton).

Another big-event hall is **Shepherd's Bush Empire** (Shepherd's Bush Green, W12; ☎ 020/7711-3000; Tube: Shepherd's Bush). And sometimes the old **Royal Albert Hall** (see the section "From the Barbican to the Royal Albert" earlier in this chapter) rocks, too.

Chapter 24

Enjoying a Pint: Pubs, Clubs, and Bars

Maybe your idea of a perfect evening is going to an elegant hotel bar for a cocktail, or sitting back in a historic pub and quaffing a pint of ale. In this chapter, I help you find a fun and fitting nightspot. And if you need music to make you happy, this chapter can point you in the direction of your kind of beat. For locations, see the "London Clubs, Pubs, and Bars" map.

Doing the Pub Crawl

A great way to experience real-life London is to do *a pub crawl,* that is, walk from pub to pub and sample the different brews. If you're accustomed to ordering a typical American beer with a rather conventional name, you may be bowled over by the colorful names and vast assortment of British beers on tap in a pub. You can find Courage Best, Old Speckled Hen, Wadworths 6X, Brakspears, Friary Meux, and Ind Coope Burton, to name just a few. Although you can get a hard drink at both bars and pubs, when you're in a pub you're better off confining yourself to beer because pubs don't often carry all the ingredients necessary for a mixed drink (the way U.S. bars do). See the sidebar "A beer primer: Are you bitter or stout?" to familiarize yourself with your beer choices. Of course, if you find just the right pub, you can order a pint, get comfortable, and spend the evening. You can even order a good meal; see Chapter 13 for more on pub grub.

London Clubs, Pubs, and Bars

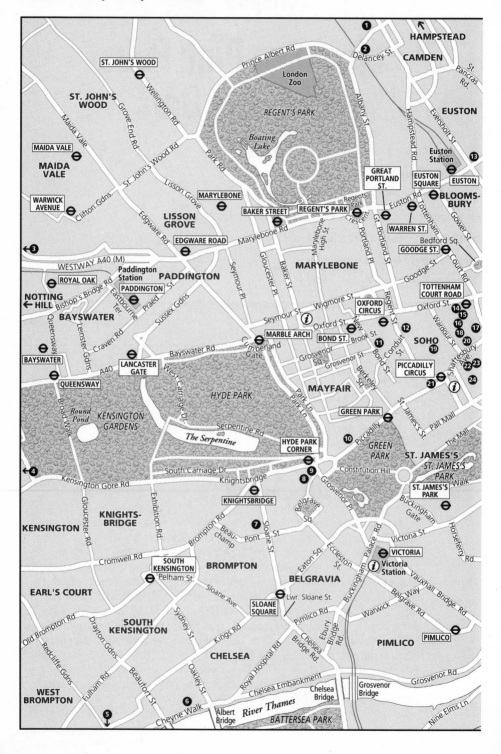

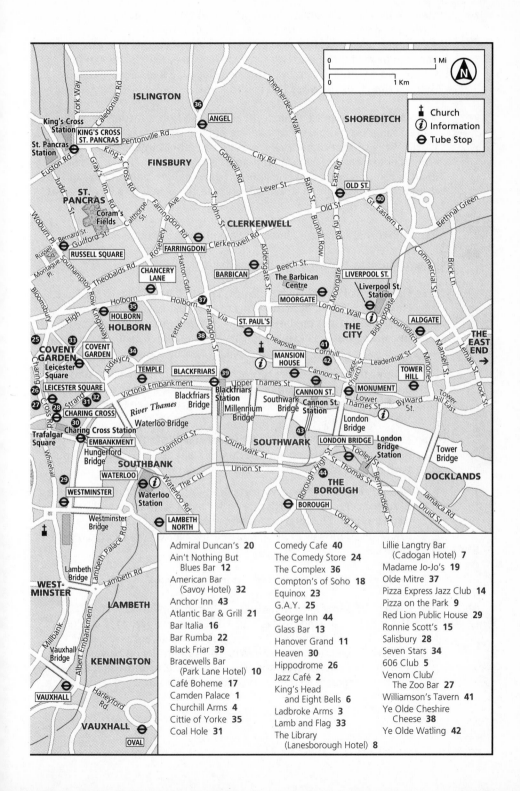

ISLINGTON

SHOREDITCH

King's Cross
Station

St. Pancras
Station

FINSBURY

ST. PANCRAS

Coram's
Fields

CLERKENWELL

RUSSELL SQUARE

CHANCERY LANE

BARBICAN

The Barbican Centre

LIVERPOOL ST.

Liverpool St. Station

HOLBORN

MOORGATE

ST. PAUL'S

ALDGATE

THE CITY

THE EAST END

COVENT GARDEN

Leicester Square

MANSION HOUSE

TEMPLE

BLACKFRIARS

TOWER HILL

LEICESTER SQUARE

CHARING CROSS

Blackfriars Station
Blackfriars Bridge
Millennium Bridge

Upper Thames St.

CANNON ST.

Southwark Cannon St. Station
Bridge

MONUMENT

Charing Cross Station

River Thames
Waterloo Bridge

London Bridge

Trafalgar Square

EMBANKMENT

Hungerford Bridge

SOUTHWARK

LONDON BRIDGE London Bridge Station

Tower Bridge

DOCKLANDS

SOUTHBANK

WATERLOO

WESTMINSTER

Waterloo Station

THE BOROUGH

BOROUGH

Westminster Bridge

LAMBETH NORTH

WEST-MINSTER

LAMBETH

Lambeth Bridge

Vauxhall Bridge

KENNINGTON

VAUXHALL

VAUXHALL

OVAL

Legend:
† Church
(i) Information
⊖ Tube Stop

0 — 1 Mi
0 — 1 Km
N

Admiral Duncan's **20**	Comedy Cafe **40**	Lillie Langtry Bar (Cadogan Hotel) **7**
Ain't Nothing But Blues Bar **12**	The Comedy Store **24**	Madame Jo-Jo's **19**
American Bar (Savoy Hotel) **32**	The Complex **36**	Olde Mitre **37**
Anchor Inn **43**	Compton's of Soho **18**	Pizza Express Jazz Club **14**
Atlantic Bar & Grill **21**	Equinox **23**	Pizza on the Park **9**
Bar Italia **16**	G.A.Y. **25**	Red Lion Public House **29**
Bar Rumba **22**	George Inn **44**	Ronnie Scott's **15**
Black Friar **39**	Glass Bar **13**	Salisbury **28**
Bracewells Bar (Park Lane Hotel) **10**	Hanover Grand **11**	Seven Stars **34**
Café Boheme **17**	Heaven **30**	606 Club **5**
Camden Palace **1**	Hippodrome **26**	Venom Club/ The Zoo Bar **27**
Churchill Arms **4**	Jazz Café **2**	Williamson's Tavern **41**
Cittie of Yorke **35**	King's Head and Eight Bells **6**	Ye Olde Cheshire Cheese **38**
Coal Hole **31**	Ladbroke Arms **3**	Ye Olde Watling **42**
	Lamb and Flag **33**	
	The Library (Lanesborough Hotel) **8**	

Most pubs adhere to strict hours governed by Parliament: Monday through Saturday 11 a.m. to 11 p.m. and Sunday noon to 10:30 p.m. Americans take note: Pubs don't ask for or expect a service charge, and you never tip the bartender; the best you can do is offer to buy him or her a drink. Ten minutes before closing a bell rings, signaling that it's time to order your last round.

A movement is afoot to abolish the strict pub hours throughout the United Kingdom. The laws restricting pub hours were passed during World War I so that munitions workers and others involved in the war effort couldn't spend too much time drinking at their "local." The change requires an Act of Parliament to deregulate pub hours, but the drinkers who want pubs to remain open til the wee hours have a great deal of public support.

Remember that pubs are almost always full of cigarette smoke.

When you're in The City, try these pubs:

- **Cittie of Yorke** (22 High Holborn, WC1; ☎ 020/7242-7670; Tube: Holborn or Chancery Lane) has the longest bar in Britain and looks like a great medieval hall — an appropriate appearance because a pub has existed at this location since 1430.

- **Seven Stars** (53 Carey St., WC2; ☎ 020/7242-8521; Tube: Holborn) is tiny and modest except for its collection of Toby mugs and law-related art. The pub is located at the back of the law courts, so lots of barristers drink here — it's a great place to pick up some British legal jargon.

- **Olde Mitre** (Ely Place, EC1; ☎ 020/7405-4751; Tube: Chancery Lane), named after an inn built on this site in 1547, is a small pub with an eccentric assortment of customers.

- **Black Friar** (174 Queen Victoria St., EC4; ☎ 020/7236-5650; Tube: Blackfriars) is an Edwardian wonder made of marble and bronze Art Nouveau. The interior features bas-reliefs of mad monks, a low-vaulted mosaic ceiling, and seating carved out of gold marble recesses.

When you're in West London, try the following pubs:

- **Churchill Arms** (119 Kensington Church St., W8; ☎ 020/7727-4242; Tube: Notting Hill Gate or High St. Kensington) is loaded with Churchill memorabilia. The pub hosts an entire week of celebration leading up to Sir Winston's birthday on November 30. Visitors are often welcomed like regulars here, and you'll find the overall ambience to be down-to-earth and homey.

> ✔ **Ladbroke Arms** (54 Ladbroke Rd., W11; ☎ **020/7727-6648;** Tube: Holland Park) strays a bit from a traditional pub environment with its jazz in the background and rotating art prints, but it makes for a pleasant stop and a good meal. This pub's changing menu may include such items as chicken breast stuffed with avocado and garlic steak in pink peppercorn sauce.

If you want to try a truly historic pub, check out my suggestions in Chapter 27.

A beer primer: Are you bitter or stout?

Most of the pubs in London and throughout the United Kingdom are tied to a particular brewery and sell only that brewery's beers (an outside sign displays the brewery name). Independent pubs can sell more brands than a tied pub. Either way, you still have to choose from what may seem like a bewildering variety of brews. The colorful names of individual brews don't provide much help — you can only wonder what Pigswill, Dogs Bollocks, Hobgoblin, Old Thumper, or Boondoggle taste like. The taste of any beer, whether on draught or in a bottle, is crafted by the brewery and depends on all sorts of factors: the water, the hops, the fermentation technique, and so on. You can get a few U.S. and international brands, but imports are more expensive than the homegrown products.

When you order beer in a pub, you need to specify the type, the brand, and the amount (pint or half-pint) that you want. Asking the bartender to recommend something based on your taste preferences is perfectly okay. Just remember that most English beer is served at room temperature. Here are some brief descriptions that may come in handy in a pub:

- ✔ **Bitter,** what most locals drink, is a clear, yellowish traditional beer with a strong flavor of hops.

- ✔ **Real ale,** a bitter that's still fermenting (alive) when it arrives from the brewery that's pumped and served immediately.

- ✔ **Ale** isn't as strong as bitter and has a slightly sweeter taste. You can order light or pale ale in a bottle; export ale is a stronger variety.

- ✔ **Lager,** when chilled, is probably closest to an American-style beer. Lager is available in bottles or on draught.

- ✔ **Shandy,** equal parts bitter and lemonade (sometimes limeade or ginger beer, a nonalcoholic, very gingery ginger ale), is for those individuals who like a sweet beverage that's only partially beery.

- ✔ **Stout** is a dark, rich, creamy version of ale. Guinness is the most popular brand. A black and tan is half lager and half stout.

Feeling the Beat: Music and Dancing

Whether you want to cool down to some cool jazz or boogie to a big beat, this section can help you find the right nightspot for you.

Jazzing up the night

Small, smoky jazz clubs are common in London. In Soho, **Ronnie Scott's** (47 Frith St., W1; ☎ 020/7439-0747; Tube: Tottenham Court Road) has been London's preeminent jazz club for years, with dependably high-caliber performances. Bring a full wallet, because you have to order food (meals or snacks) on top of the £15 to £20 ($22–$30) admission.

In Earl's Court, the **606 Club** (90 Lots Rd., SW10; ☎ 020/7352-5953; Tube: Earl's Court or Fulham Broadway) is a basement club where young British jazz musicians play. You don't have to pay a cover charge to get in, but you do have to order food. And to pay the musicians, the establishment adds to your bill an additional charge of £5 ($8) Sunday through Thursday and about $1 more on Friday and Saturday. You can find good food and diverse music (Afro-Latin jazz to rap) at the **Jazz Café** (5 Parkway, NW1; ☎ 020/7916-6060; Tube: Camden Town). Admission is £12 to £18 ($18–$27).

In Soho, try the **Pizza Express Jazz Club** (10 Dean St., W1; ☎ 020/7439-8722; Tube: Tottenham Court Road). Big names from the American jazz scene regularly perform in this intimate venue, and you can enjoy pizza, too. The club is open daily 7:45 p.m. to midnight, and the admission is £15 to £20 ($22–$30). In Knightsbridge, mainstream jazz is performed in the basement Jazz Room of **Pizza on the Park** (11 Knightsbridge, SW1; ☎ 020/7235-5273; Tube: Hyde Park Corner). The club is open daily from 7:30 p.m., with sets at 9:15 and 11:15 p.m.; admission is £16 to £18 ($24–$27). Neither club's cover charge includes food.

London's only authentic blues venue is the **Ain't Nothing But Blues Bar** (20 Kingly St., W1; ☎ 020/7287-0514; Tube: Oxford Circus). The club features local acts and touring American bands. Expect long lines on weekends. Hours are Monday through Thursday, 6 p.m. to 1 a.m.; Friday and Saturday, 6 p.m. to 3 a.m.; and Sunday 7:30 p.m. to midnight. Free every night except Friday and Saturday after 8:30 p.m.; cover charge varies from £3 to £5 ($5–$8).

Catching a cabaret or laughing at the comics

Both gays and straights enjoy the drag/cabaret shows at **Madame Jo-Jo's** (8–10 Brewer St., Soho, W1; ☎ 020/7734-2473; Tube: Leicester

Square). The shows produced in its plush theater/bar are a campy and fun tradition. The club is open daily 10 p.m. to 4 a.m., and tickets cost £5 to £10 ($8–$15).

The Comedy Store (1A Oxendon St., off Piccadilly Circus, SW1; ☎ 020/ 7344-0234; Tube: Piccadilly Circus) is London's best showcase for established and rising comic talent. Visitors must be 18 or older. Doors open at 6:30 p.m., and shows start at 8:00 p.m.; the cover charge is £12 ($18). Seats are not reserved, so arrive early to get a good spot. The **Comedy Cafe** (66 Rivington St., EC2; ☎ 020/7739-5706; Tube: Old Street) is another good place to sample stand-up London style. Doors open at 7:00 p.m., and shows start at 8:30 p.m.; the cover is £3 ($5) on Thursday, £10 ($15) on Friday, and £12 ($18) on Saturday.

Shaking your groove thang at the clubs

London is a large, multicultural city, and its music scene reflects its diversity. In the London clubs, you can listen to drum 'n' bass, indie, Asian underground (or tabla 'n' bass, as it's called), chemical beats (don't ask), breakbeats, techno, trance, psychedelic, and many others.

I must warn you: The London club scene is overwhelmingly a late-night youth scene. If you're a woman under 30 who can squeeze into a leather miniskirt and a sleeveless zip-up top, or a man under 30 who wears Doc Martens and an earring, you'll probably fit in. The action doesn't really get hot until about midnight.

Cover charges vary according to day of the week and what band is playing. For more options, check out the music and clubs listings in *Time Out* (Internet: www.timeout.com), a weekly entertainment magazine.

The Complex, in Islington (1–5 Parkfield St., N1; ☎ 020/7288-1986; Tube: Angel), frequently books live bands; the club has four floors with different dance vibes on each. Hours are Friday and Saturday 10 p.m. to 7 a.m.; admission is £10 to £12 ($15–$18).

The **Equinox** (Leicester Square, WC2; ☎ 020/7437-1446; Tube: Leicester Square) boasts London's largest dance floor and one of the largest lighting rigs in Europe. A diverse crowd dances to equally diverse music, including dance hall, pop, rock, and Latin. The hours are Monday through Saturday 9 p.m. to 3 a.m., and the cover is £7 to £12 ($11–$18).

The **Hippodrome** (at the corner of Cranbourn Street and Charing Cross Road, WC2; ☎ 020/7437-4311; Tube: Leicester Square) is a cavernous place with a great sound system and lights to match. This club was a favorite of Princess Diana during her early club-hopping days; now the place is tacky, touristy, and packed on weekends. The hours are Monday through Saturday 9 p.m. to 3 a.m., and the cover is £7 to £12 ($11–$18).

Venom Club/The Zoo Bar (13–17 Bear St., WC2; ☎ **020/7839-4188;** Tube: Leicester Square) features a trendy Euro-androgynous crowd and music so loud you have to use sign language. The club boasts the slickest, flashiest, most psychedelic decor in London, and even 35-year-olds come here. The hours are daily 9 p.m. to 3 a.m., and the cover is £3 to £5 ($5–$8) after 10 p.m.

Bar Rumba (36 Shaftesbury Ave., W1; ☎ **020/7287-2715;** Tube: Piccadilly Circus) is all over the map musically; every night this club features a different type of music, including jazz fusion, phat funk, hip hop, drum 'n' bass, soul, R&B, and swing. The minimum age for admittance is 21 on Saturday and Sunday and 18 on Monday through Friday. Hours are Monday through Thursday 10 p.m. to 3 a.m., Friday 10 p.m. to 4 a.m., Saturday 9 p.m. to 6 a.m., and Sunday 8 p.m. to 1 a.m. The cover is £3 to £12 ($5–$18).

The **Hanover Grand** (6 Hanover St., W1; ☎ **020/7499-7977;** Tube: Oxford Circus) is funky and down and dirty on Thursday, but otherwise cutting-edge and always crowded. Age and gender are not always easy to distinguish here. Hours are Monday through Saturday 10 p.m. to 4 a.m., and the cover £10 to £12 ($5–$18).

Housed in a former theater, the **Camden Palace** (1A Camden High St., NW1; ☎ **09062/100-200;** Tube: Camden Town) draws a young all-night crowd addicted to trendy downtown costumes. The music varies from night to night, so call in advance. The club is open Tuesday and Wednesday 9 p.m. to 2 a.m., Friday 10 p.m. to 6 a.m., and Saturday 10 p.m. to 8 a.m. The cover is £5 ($8) on Tuesday and Wednesday and £7 to £20 ($11–$30) on Friday and Saturday.

Unwinding in Elegance

Maybe you just want a quiet, romantic spot where you and your significant other can enjoy a cocktail and actually talk to one another for a change. Or perhaps you're looking for a sophisticated place to enjoy a pre- or post-theater drink. The following establishments are just the ticket. They're located in grand hotels and offer a bit of privacy from the crowds. Jackets and ties are required for gents at the American Bar; a "smart casual" dress code is in effect at the others, so leave your jeans and sneakers in the hotel room.

Where's the bartender who's known for his special concoctions, the Savoy Affair and the Prince of Wales, as well as what's reputedly the best martini in town? You can find him at the **American Bar** (in the Savoy Hotel, The Strand, WC2; ☎ **020/7836-4343;** Tube: Charing Cross Road or Embankment), one of London's most sophisticated gathering places

Bracewells Bar (in the Park Lane Hotel, Piccadilly, W1; ☎ 020/7499-6321; Tube: Green Park or Hyde Park) is chic and nostalgic, with a plush decor of Chinese lacquer, comfortable sofas, and soft lighting.

Looking for high ceilings, leather chesterfields, oil paintings, grand windows, and old-world charm? Visit **The Library** (in the Lanesborough Hotel, 1 Lanesborough Place, SW1; ☎ 020/7259-5599; Tube: Hyde Park Corner), one of London's poshest drinking retreats. Its collection of ancient cognacs is unparalleled in town.

At the **Lillie Langtry Bar** (in the Cadogan Hotel, Sloane Street, SW1; ☎ 020/7235-7141; Tube: Sloane Square or Knightsbridge), you can go back in time to the charm and elegance of the Edwardian era, when Lillie Langtry, an actress and a society beauty (and a mistress of Edward VII), lived here. Writer Oscar Wilde — often a guest in Lillie's home and in this hotel — is honored on the drinks menu by his favorite libation, the Hock and Seltzer (see Chapter 8 for a description of the hotel).

Seeking Spots for Night Owls

Except for the die-hards in the all-night discos, Londoners retire to bed fairly early. Restaurants and bars routinely close before midnight. But a few places in restless, nightclub-heavy Soho stay open late to accommodate night owls:

- ✔ **Bar Italia** (22 Frith St., W1; ☎ 020/7437-4520; Tube: Tottenham Court Road) is open 24 hours for coffee and serves a limited snack menu.

- ✔ **Atlantic Bar & Grill** (20 Glasshouse St., W1; ☎ 020/7734-4888; Tube: Piccadilly Circus) is open for drinks Monday through Saturday to 3 a.m. You may have wait in line for a place to sit.

- ✔ **Café Boheme** (13–17 Old Compton St., W1; ☎ 020/7734-0623; Tube: Tottenham Court Road or Leicester Square) offers a chance to get a drink until 3 a.m. Monday through Wednesday, until 11:30 p.m. Sunday, and 24 hours Thursday through Saturday.

Finding Gay Clubs and Discos

To be where it's happenin', stroll along Old Compton Street in Soho (Tube: Leicester Square). You may want to duck into **Admiral Duncan's** (54 Old Compton St., W1; ☎ 020/7437-5300) or the two-floor **Compton's of Soho** (53–55 Old Compton St., W1; ☎ 020/7479-7961). Both of these gay bar/pubs are Soho institutions, open Monday through Saturday noon to 11 p.m. and Sunday noon to 10:30 p.m.

The city's largest women-only bar is the bilevel **Glass Bar** (West Lodge, Euston Square Gardens, 190 Euston Rd., NW10; ☎ **020/7387-6184;** Tube: Euston). The bar has a "smart casual" dress code and is open Tuesday through Friday 5 p.m. until "late," Saturday 6 p.m. until "late," and Sunday 2 to 7 p.m.; you can't get in after 11:30 p.m. Monday through Saturday.

In terms of size, central location, and continued popularity, the best gay (and everyone else) disco in London is **Heaven** (Under the Arches, Craven Street, WC2; ☎ **020/7930-2020;** Tube: Charing Cross or Embankment). The place is open Monday and Wednesday 10:30 p.m. to 3:00 a.m., Friday 10:30 p.m. to 6:00 a.m., and Saturday 10:30 p.m. to 5:00 a.m. Admission varies from £3 to £10 ($5–$17).

G.A.Y. (London Astoria, 157 Charing Cross Rd., Soho, WC2; ☎ **0906/ 100-016;** Tube: Tottenham Court Road) is the biggest gay dance venue in Europe. Hours are Saturday 10:30 p.m. to 5:00 a.m., and admission is £10 ($17).

Check the gay listings in *Time Out* for nightclubs that have dedicated gay nights, as well as *Frommer's Gay & Lesbian Europe* (published by Hungry Minds, Inc.), which has extensive coverage of London's gay scene.

Part VII
The Part of Tens

The 5th Wave

By Rich Tennant

"Oh, Will— such passion, such pathos, such despair and redemption. I've never read a more moving grocery list."

In this part...

This part contains lots of "extra" fun. You can have a wonderful time in London without reading a word of this part, or you can use it to enhance your trip. If you've been to London once or twice already and are now ready to expand your explorations, these chapters can give you a few good ideas.

I unveil the stories behind ten famous London statues in Chapter 25. In Chapter 26, I describe ten historic London churches, and in Chapter 27, I tell you about ten extra-special London pubs.

Chapter 25

Striking a Pose: Ten Famous London Statues

. . . .

In This Chapter

▶ Enjoying the statues of royalty: The good, the bad, and the ugly

▶ Checking out London's other statues: From Abraham Lincoln to Queen Boudicca

. . . .

*U*nlike pigeons, people don't really pay too much attention to statues of public figures anymore, do they? People prefer creations found in museums, with the names of famous sculptors affixed to them. The whole idea of casting a bronze of an important public figure just doesn't fit with the modern world view. Who'd qualify for such an honor in this day and age?

In England, the only person today who may be considered deserving of such a monument is the late Princess Diana (at least in the general public's opinion). But the city is filled with bronze statues commemorating all sorts of individuals from the past. This chapter offers ten (or so) that may be of interest to you or that you may run into at some point during your London stay and think "Who *is* that?" (for the location of each, see the map "More London Sights" in Chapter 17).

Admiral Lord Nelson

In Trafalgar Square (Tube: Charing Cross), perched atop the 145-foot Nelson's Column, one of London's most famous monuments, is a statue of (you guessed it) **Admiral Lord Nelson.** Horatio Viscount Nelson was the victor over the French and Spanish fleet at the 1805 Battle of Trafalgar and is Britain's best-known naval hero. On the column he's 17 feet high (and had to be hoisted up in three sections), but in real life he was all of 5 feet, 4 inches tall. (Also in Trafalgar Square is an equestrian statue of **George IV,** who considered himself a gentleman but was nobody's idea of a hero.)

Charles 1

In 1633, French sculptor Hubert LeSueur completed the equestrian statue of **Charles I** that stands (or rather sits) at the north end of Whitehall, just south of Trafalgar Square (Tube: Charing Cross). For no discernable reason, royals seem to have elevated egos and think of themselves as larger than life. So Charlie, who came in at just 5 feet tall, had the sculptor tack another foot onto his frame. In real life, alas, the monarch lost whatever symbolic stature the extra foot gave him when Cromwell chopped off his head in 1649. However, history has many strange twists and turns: This statue was sold to a scrap dealer who was supposed to destroy it but instead shrewdly buried the piece in his garden. In 1660, when the monarchy was restored and Charles II ascended the throne, the scrap dealer was able to sell the new king the undamaged statue. The figure didn't go up in its present spot on Whitehall — with a pedestal by great architect Sir Christopher Wren — until 1765.

Duke of York and Edward VII

Just north of St. James's Park, at the midpoint of Carlton House Terrace (Tube: Charing Cross), you find the **Duke of York Monument.** So who was the duke of York (not Prince Andrew), and why did he warrant this massive 7-ton statue? Those are very good questions, and I'm completely unable to answer them. He was the second son of George III (who was on the throne when America gained its independence from Britain), and when he died he was massively in debt. Sir Richard Westmacott's 1834 sculpture, which rests on a column of pink granite, was funded by withholding a day's pay from every soldier in the Empire. I ask you, was that fair? Some wags have speculated that the duke's statue was placed high up so his creditors couldn't reach him.

The monument looms over Waterloo Place, an enclave of aristocratic elegance and one of London's greatest examples of urban planning. At the entrance of Waterloo Place you find a statue of **Edward VII,** chiseled by Sir Bertram Mackennal in 1921 to honor the king who gave his name to the Edwardian era. The son of Queen Victoria, "Eddie" had to wait until he was 60 before he could ascend the throne, and he died nine years later. But not all is royal in Waterloo Place: You also find a statue dedicated to the victims of the Crimean War.

Henry VIII

Wouldn't you say that Henry VIII is England's best-known king? You may have "seen" him in plays, movies (such as *Anne of the Thousand Days* and *A Man for All Seasons*), and that great Masterpiece Theatre TV series *The Six Wives of Henry VIII.* Henry VIII was a huge man, with huge appetites, and he wouldn't take no for an answer. (He didn't have to, he was king.) The much-married Merrie Monarch has never been considered anyone's idea of a role model, so maybe that explains why London has only one statue of him. You can see it atop the **Henry VIII Gateway** on West Smithfield (Tube: Barbican). In 1702 the stonemasons who built St. Paul's Cathedral built the gateway, which commemorates Henry's giving of St. Bartholomew Hospital to The City — a gift made possible by his dissolution of the monasteries.

James II and George Washington

Two notable statues flank the main entrance of the National Gallery, across from Trafalgar Square (Tube: Charing Cross). On the left is British sculptor Grinling Gibbons's fine statue of **James II,** from 1636, a year after James ascended the throne. Because he immediately levied new taxes and sought to restore Catholicism to England, this monarch never caught on in the public popularity polls. In fact, he was ousted from the throne and spent the rest of his life in exile in France. The **George Washington** statue on the right is a Jean Antoine Houdon replica of a statue in the capitol building in Richmond, Virginia. A gift from that state, the statue arrived in London with boxes of earth for the base, so the first American president would always be able to stand on American soil.

Oliver Cromwell

The small garden in front of the Houses of Parliament (Tube: Westminster) contains a statue of **Oliver Cromwell,** Lord Protector of England from 1653 to 1658. This fanatical Puritan led the Parliamentary armies during the Civil War that dethroned Charles I. Under Cromwell's "protectorate," at least 30,000 Irish men, women, and children were massacred, and vast tracts of Ireland handed over to the English. Small wonder that Irish members of Parliament were outraged when Cromwell's statue, by Hamo Thorneycroft, was unveiled in 1899. In fact, Parliament ultimately refused to pay for it, and Lord Rosebery, the prime minister, shelled out the money himself. Cromwell, a sword in one hand and a Bible in the other, appears to be averting his eyes from the bust of **Charles I** (the king he had beheaded — see "Charles I," earlier in this chapter), which you can see across the street above the doorway of the St. Margaret's Westminster church.

Peter Pan

Children love the famous statue of **Peter Pan,** north of the Serpentine Bridge in Kensington Gardens (Tube: High St. Kensington). Commissioned in 1912 by Peter Pan's creator, J. M. Barrie, the bronze sculpture by George Frampton marks the spot where Peter Pan touched down in the gardens. Of course, this kid could fly — he didn't have to take the Tube like the rest of us. Peter Pan was an adored fantasy hero long before he became a psychological "syndrome" for men who refuse to grow up. He was to children of earlier generations what Harry Potter is to the kids of today. Maybe, eventually, there'll be a Harry Potter statue in Paddington Station.

Prince Albert

Prince Albert of Saxe-Coburg-Gotha (a name the royals changed to Windsor at the onset of World War I) was the handsome German consort of Queen Victoria. When he died at age 42 in 1861, the grief-stricken queen donned the black widow's weeds she'd wear for the rest of her long life. London has two statues of Prince Albert. One is at the rejuvenated **Albert Memorial** in Kensington Gardens (see Chapter 16). The other stands in the center of Holborn Circus (Tube: Holborn) — that one has been dubbed "the politest statue in London" because the prince is seen raising his hat.

Queen Boudicca

Who, you may wonder, is the wild-haired superwoman in the horse-drawn chariot at the north end of Westminster Bridge (Tube: Westminster)? She's **Queen Boudicca** (or Boadicea), that's who, with her fearless warrior-daughters. "Bo" was a fierce Celtic queen who fought back the invading Romans and died in A.D. 60. Thomas Hornicraft created the sculpture in the 1850s; the figure was placed at its current site in 1902.

Winston Churchill and Abraham Lincoln

Parliament Square (Tube: Westminster) boasts more outdoor sculptures than any other place in London. Unless you're a student of British history, most of the bronze gentlemen (**Sir Robert Peel, Benjamin Disraeli, the 14th earl of Derby,** and **General Jan Smuts**) ranged around the square won't mean anything to you. But you may recognize two of them. **Sir Winston Churchill,** the prime minister during World War II (see entry for Cabinet War Rooms in Chapter 17) is at his most bulldoggish in Ivor Roberts-Jones's 1975 sculpture, standing in the square's northeast corner. A statue of **Abraham Lincoln** by Augustus Saint-Gaudens stands across the street on the west side of the square. The statue was a gift from the city of Chicago, which has the 1887 original in Lincoln Park.

Chapter 26

Making Amens: Ten Noteworthy London Churches

Westminster Abbey and **St. Paul's Cathedral** (see Chapter 16) are giant repositories of English history and get the lion's share of visitor attention in London. But the city boasts scores of smaller churches also worth visiting. The area known as the City of London is especially rich in neoclassical churches designed by Sir Christopher Wren (1632–1723) after the disastrous Great Fire of 1666. One of England's greatest architects, and certainly its most prolific, Wren designed St. Paul's.

This chapter explores ten London churches that you may want to check out on your ramblings around town (for their locations, see the map "More London Sights" in Chapter 17).

Church of St. Bartholomew the Great

On the east side of Smithfield Square, EC1 (Tube: Barbican), is a rare 16th-century gatehouse, and perched atop the gatehouse sits an even rarer late-16th-century timber-frame house predating the Great Fire. The gatehouse opens onto the grounds of the **Church of St. Bartholomew the Great,** a little-visited gem that just happens to be the oldest parish church in London. The church was part of an Augustinian priory founded in 1123. Over the centuries, the building has somewhat miraculously escaped major damage — despite being used at various times as stables and a printing office (where Benjamin Franklin worked in 1725). The 15th-century cloisters are to your right as you enter. Inside the church is a "weeping" 17th-century statue of Edward Cooke (the marble condenses moisture from the air), the tomb of Rahere, the priory's founder, and a lovely *oriel* (a projecting bay) window.

If you leave the churchyard by using the gate in the far right corner, you come out on **Cloth Fair,** a street with gabled houses from 1604. Like St. Bartholomew's, they're among the very few surviving buildings predating the disastrous Great Fire that leveled much of London in 1666.

Church of St. Stephen Walbrook

Walbrook, EC4 (Tube: Cannon Street), a lane in the heart of The City, was the site of a brook that was paved over in medieval times. Today, the lane houses the **Church of St. Stephen Walbrook,** one of Sir Christopher Wren's finest works. By the 18th century, the fame of this church had spread throughout Europe, and many still consider it the most beautiful church in London. Its splendid dome served as a model for the one at St. Paul's Cathedral. The altar beneath the dome was sculpted from *travertine* (a porous mineral) in 1956 by British sculptor Henry Moore, who had reservations about tackling the job because he was an agnostic. "Henry, I'm not asking you to take the service," said the rector who offered Moore the commission. "I understand that you're a bit of a chiseler; just do your job."

St. Botolph's

I think it's appropriate to include in this chapter a church dedicated to England's patron saint of travelers: **St. Botolph's** on Aldersgate Street, EC1 (Tube: Barbican), close to the **Museum of London** (see Chapter 17). The church interior has a fine barrel-vaulted roof. Actually, three City churches are dedicated to St. Botolph, and all are located beside now-vanished gates into the city. At one time, instead of being greeted by ATMs and currency-exchange windows, travelers could pause and give thanks to Botolph for their safe journey to London.

St. Dunstan's-in-the-West

The octagonal **St. Dunstan's-in-the-West,** on Fleet Street, EC4 (Tube: Temple), is a fine early example of Gothic Revival architecture. That was the style in fashion when an earlier church that survived the Great Fire of 1666 was replaced between 1829 and 1833. The large clock on the tower is something of a historical curiosity: The clock dates from 1671 and was installed by the congregation as an offering of thanks because the church hadn't burned down. Every 15 minutes, two giant clubs strike a bell that has been tolling for more than 330 years. People take clocks, watches, and timepieces for granted nowadays, but this clock was the first in London to have a double face and to have minutes marked on the dial.

St. George the Martyr Church

Also in Southwark, next to the remains of Marshalsea Prison on Borough High Street, SE1 (Tube: Borough), you find **St. George the Martyr Church.** The church is probably more famous for its literary associations than for any intrinsic beauty of the structure itself. This church is where Dickens's fictional heroine Little Dorrit is baptized and, at one point, is forced to spend the night when she's locked out of the Marshalsea debtors' prison; later she's married in this church. A stained-glass window in the east wall shows her at prayer.

St. Margaret's Westminster

St. Margaret's Westminster, the parish church of the House of Commons since 1614, is on St. Margaret Street, SW1 (Tube: Westminster) and often mistaken for Westminster Abbey next door. St. Margaret's is notable for its glorious above-the-altar East Window, whose stained glass was presented by Ferdinand and Isabella of Spain to commemorate the marriage of their daughter, Catharine of Aragon, to Arthur, the son of Henry VII. By the time the glass arrived, Arthur had died and Henry VIII, his younger brother, had wed Catherine, the first of his eight wives (he divorced her for Anne Boleyn). The weddings of poet John Milton (1656) and statesman (and future prime minister) Winston Churchill (1908) were held in this church.

St. Martin-in-the-Fields

St. Martin-in-the-Fields, on Trafalgar Square, WC2 (Tube: Charing Cross), was a stylistic prototype for hundreds of churches constructed in 18th-century New England. James Gibbs, who was influenced by the churches of Sir Christopher Wren, designed the church in 1726. Furniture designer Thomas Chippendale, painters Sir Joshua Reynolds and William Hogarth, and Nell Gwynn, mistress of Charles II, are buried within. For details about the concerts held here, see the description of St. Martin's under "Trafalgar Square" in Chapter 16.

St. Mary-le-Bow

Established in the 11th century, **St. Mary-le-Bow,** on Bow Lane, EC4 (Tube: Mansion House), is one of London's most venerable churches.

The structure that originally stood here was a casualty of the Great Fire of 1666; the steepled church that you see today is a work by Sir Christopher Wren, who modeled it after Rome's Church of the Basilica of Maxentius. According to tradition, a true *Cockney* (a native of the East End of London) is someone born within hearing distance of the bells of St. Mary-le-Bow. In the churchyard's garden is a statue of Captain John Smith, a one-time parishioner who left London to become one of the first settlers of Jamestown, Virginia (he's the one who was saved by Pocahontas).

Southwark Cathedral

Southwark Cathedral, on Montague Close, SE1 (Tube: London Bridge), is one of the oldest buildings in Southwark and also one of the most beautiful (see Chapters 17 and 25). A church has occupied this site for at least a thousand years; before that, a Roman villa was located here.

London's second-oldest church after **Westminster Abbey,** Southwark Cathedral, in the 12th century, was the first Gothic church to be erected in London. Today, you see the 15th-century cathedral (with Victorian restorations) that once served London's rowdy South Bank theater district. Chaucer and Shakespeare both worshiped here, and Shakespeare's brother Edmund was buried here in 1607.

Besides a memorial to the immortal Bard, the church contains a 13th-century wooden effigy of a knight, one of the oldest surviving wooden effigies in England. John Harvard, founder of Harvard University, was baptized in this church.

Temple of Mithras

Not far from **St. Stephen Walbrook,** at the entrance to Temple Court on Queen Victoria Street, EC4 (Tube: Mansion House), you find the remains of what's probably London's oldest church site. This church isn't a Christian church, however, but a third-century Roman temple, the **Temple of Mithras.** Unearthed during 1954 excavations and raised to its present level, the temple is shaped like a tiny Christian basilica with a central nave and two aisles. The temple was used by the Mithraic cult, which had its origins in Persia and was brought to London by Roman soldiers in the second century. At one time, when the Roman Empire still ruled the Western world, Mithraism was as popular as Christianity. Archaeologists speculate that the pagan temple was destroyed in the fourth century, when Christianity became the official religion of the Empire. Some of the sculptures that were found in the temple are displayed in the **Museum of London** (see Chapter 17).

Chapter 27

Enjoying a Pint of Ale and a Bit of History: Ten London Pubs

In This Chapter

▶ Enjoying some pub history

▶ Finding a pub with character

*P*ublic houses, better known as pubs, have been a way of life in London and throughout the United Kingdom for centuries. Chapter 13 offers information about London pubs (and Chapters 15 and 24 also mention some intriguing pubs). But I could write an entire guide just on the pubs of London because the city has hundreds of them. Not all these pubs are old, of course, and not all have the kind of character that accumulates over centuries of drinking, talking, smoking, and eating. But dozens upon dozens of these pubs date back anywhere from a century to more than 400 years.

This chapter offers descriptions of ten more pubs. Each of these places has some special story, history, or association attached to it (for their locations, see the map "London's Clubs, Pubs, and Bars" in Chapter 24). All are open regular pub hours of Monday through Saturday 11:00 a.m. to 11:30 p.m.; some are open Sunday noon to 10:30 p.m.

Anchor Inn

The **Anchor Inn** (Park Street, SE1; ☎ 020/7407-1577; Tube: Southwark) was frequented by 18th-century figures such as Samuel Johnson, who produced the first *Dictionary of the English Language;* playwright Oliver Goldsmith, whose most famous work is *She Stoops to Conquer;* and painter Sir Joshua Reynolds, first president of the Royal Academy. The Anchor Inn has a nice riverside terrace.

Coal Hole

Opened in the early 19th century, the **Coal Hole** (91 The Strand, WC2; ☎ 020/7836-7503; Tube: Covent Garden) got its name from the coal haulers who unloaded their cargo on the Thames nearby. One of Central London's larger pubs, the Coal Hole has many theatrical connections because of its West End location. Famous mid-19th-century Shakespearean actor Edmund Kean used to hire rowdies, get them drunk here, and then send them off to heckle his rivals in other theaters.

George Inn

One of the city's most historically important pubs is the **George Inn** (in George Inn Yard off Borough High Street, SE1; ☎ 020/7407-2056; Tube: Borough). It's the last remaining example in London of an old style–coaching inn, with balconies (called galleries) around the inner court. The George was doing business during the reign of Henry VIII, and some claim it actually dates back to Chaucer's era.

King's Head and Eight Bells

Chelsea's intimate, club-like **King's Head and Eight Bells** (50 Cheyne Walk, SW3; ☎ 020/7352-1820; Tube: Sloane Square) opened more than 400 years ago, around 1580. Back then, of course, the area was rural; Henry VIII's country house stood nearby. Later, celebrated artists and writers such as Dante Gabriel Rossetti, Thomas Carlyle (whose house is now a museum; see Chapter 17), Oscar Wilde, Laurence Olivier, and Vivien Leigh made their homes in Chelsea, one of the prettiest (and now one of the most expensive) parts of London. The neighborhood's still filled with literary and other luminaries, so keep your eyes open if you stop in here. You never know who may pop in.

Lamb and Flag

The **Lamb and Flag** (33 Rose St., WC2; ☎ 020/7497-9504; Tube: Leicester Square) was once known by the grisly name "Bucket of Blood" because prizefighters battered one another into a bloody pulp during matches held for betting customers. The pub, a rare survivor of the Great Fire of 1666, has a couple of literary associations to offset its unsavory past. In the 19th century, this place was one of Charles Dickens's favorite taverns. A couple of centuries earlier, poet John

Dryden was attacked and beaten just outside, probably because of a lampoon that he directed at the earl of Rochester. Every year on December 16, the pub commemorates the anniversary of the attack with a Dryden Night.

Red Lion Public House

Civil servants and members of Parliament frequent the **Red Lion Public House** (48 Parliament St., SW1; ☎ 020/7930-5826; Tube: Westminster). So many MPs stop in here that the pub rings a special bell before a vote is taken, allowing the lawmakers to get back in time. Charles Dickens stopped in once for a pint of beer — he was 11 years old at the time (life was different back then).

Salisbury

I'm partial to the **Salisbury** (90 St. Martin's Lane, WC2; ☎ 020/7836-5863; Tube: Leicester Square) because I used to hang out there. The pub sits right in the heart of the West End theater district, dates from 1852, and has a beautifully preserved art nouveau interior with marble fittings, cut-glass mirrors, and brass statuettes. Like the **Lamb and Flag** noted earlier, the Salisbury was once famous for bare-knuckle prizefights — but that was long before my time.

Williamson's Tavern

Williamson's Tavern (in Groveland Court, off Bow Lane, EC4 ☎ 020/7248-6280; Tube: St. Paul's) was the residence of the Lord Mayor of the City of London before the nearby Mansion House was built. The tavern stands behind a 17th-century gate presented to the Lord Mayor by William and Mary. The building later served as an inn. Inside you can have a drink and one of its famous steak sandwiches.

Ye Olde Cheshire Cheese

Ye Olde Cheshire Cheese (Wine Office Court, 145 Fleet St., EC4; ☎ 020/7353-6170; Tube: Blackfriars) was established in 1667, but a tavern stood on this site as early as 1590 (see Chapter 14). The earlier tavern burned down in the Great Fire of 1666 and was quickly rebuilt — in fact, Ye Old Cheshire Cheese was the first pub to reopen after the fire. Downstairs, you can see charred wooden beams bearing witness to the massive fire that destroyed a large portion of London. This pub was one of Charles Dickens's favorite hangouts, and he usually sat at a table to the right of the fireplace on the first floor.

Ye Olde Watling

Ye Olde Watling (29 Watling St., EC4; ☎ **020/7248-6252;** Tube: Mansion House) is a 17th-century pub that the great architect Sir Christopher Wren used as an office when St. Paul's Cathedral was being constructed. The pub was built from timber taken from dismantled sailing ships.

Appendix

Quick Concierge

●●

*H*ow do you use the telephones? Where can you find your embassy or consulate? The Quick Concierge offers quick answers to a variety of "where do I?" and "how do I?" questions. Some of this information is found in the text but repeated here for your convenience; some of it is new.

Fast Facts: London

Ambulance

For an ambulance, call ☎ **999**.

American Express

The main Amex office is at 6 Haymarket, SW1 (☎ 020/7930-4411; Tube: Piccadilly Circus). Full services are available Monday–Friday 9 a.m.–5:30 p.m. and Saturday 9 a.m.–4 p.m. At other times — Saturday 4 p.m.– 6 p.m. and Sunday 10 a.m.–5 p.m. — only the foreign-exchange bureau is open. Additional Amex offices are at 78 Brompton Rd., Knightsbridge SW3 (☎ 020/7584-3431; Tube: Knightsbridge); 84 Kensington High St., Kensington W8 (☎ 020/7795-8703; Tube: Kensington High St.); 51 Great Russell St., Bloomsbury WC1 (☎ 020/7404-8700; Tube: Russell Sq.); and 1 Savoy Court, The Strand WC2 (☎ 020/7240-1521; Tube: Charing Cross).

ATMs

ATMs, also called "*cashpoints*," are widely available at banks throughout Central London. The most popular networks are Cirrus (☎ 800/424-7787; Internet: www. mastercard.com/atm) and Plus (☎ 800/843-7587; Internet: www.visa. com/atms).

Baby-sitters

Pippa Pop-ins (430 Fulham Rd., SW6 1DU; ☎ 020/7385-2458; Fax: 020/7385-5706) is a fully licensed children's care facility.

Business Hours

Banks are usually open Monday–Friday 9:30 a.m.–3:30 p.m.

Business offices are open Monday–Friday 9 a.m.–5 p.m. London stores generally open at 9 a.m. and close at 6:30 p.m., staying open to 7 p.m. one night a week.

Pubs are allowed to stay open Monday–Saturday 11 a.m. to 11 p.m. and Sunday noon to 10:30 p.m. Some bars stay open past midnight.

Camera Repair

Sendean, 105–109 Oxford St., 1st floor, W1 (☎ 020/7439-8418), gives free estimates and does quick work. It's open weekdays 9:30 a.m.–5:30 p.m. (Fridays until 6 p.m.) and accepts MasterCard and Visa.

Country Code and City Code

The country code for England is 44. London's telephone area code is 020. If you're calling a London number from outside the city, use 020 followed by the eight-digit number. If you're calling within London, leave off the 020 and dial only the eight-digit number.

Credit Cards

American Express, Diners Club, MasterCard, and Visa are widely accepted in London and throughout the United Kingdom. If your card gets lost or stolen in London, call the following U.K. numbers: Visa ☎ 01604/230-230 (☎ 800/645-6556 in the U.S. for Citicorp Visa); American Express ☎ 01273/696-933 (☎ 800/221-7282 in the U.S.); MasterCard ☎ 01702/362-988 (☎ 800/307-7309 in the U.S.); Diners Club ☎ 0800/460-800 (☎ 800/525-7376 in the U.S.).

Currency

Britain's unit of currency is the pound sterling (£). Every pound is divided into 100 pence (p). Coins come in denominations of 1p, 2p, 5p, 10p, 20p, 50p, £1, and £2. Notes are available in £5, £10, £20, and £50 denominations.

Currency Exchange

In London you can easily exchange cash or traveler's checks by using a currency-exchange service called a bureau de change. You find them at the major London airports, at any branch of a major bank, at all major rail and Underground stations in Central London, at post offices, and at American Express or Thomas Cook offices.

Every major bank in Central London has a foreign currency window where you can exchange traveler's checks or cash. The major banks with the most branches include Barclays Bank (☎ 020/7441-3200), Midland Bank (☎ 020/7599-3232), and NatWest (☎ 020/7395-5500).

Doctors and Dentists

In an emergency, contact Doctor's Call at ☎ 07000/372-255. Some hotels also have physicians on call. Medical Express, 117A Harley St., W1 (☎ 020/7499-1991; Tube: Oxford Circus), is a private clinic with walk-in medical service (no appointment necessary) Monday–Friday 9 a.m.–6 p.m. and Saturday 9:30 a.m.–2:30 p.m. For dental emergencies, call Eastman Dental Hospital, 56 Gray's Inn Rd., WC1 (☎ 020/7915-1000; Tube: King's Cross).

Electricity

British current is 240 volts, AC cycle, roughly twice the voltage of North American current, which is 115–120 volts, AC cycle. You won't be able to plug the flat pins of your appliance's plugs into the holes of British wall outlets without suitable converters or adapters (available from an electrical supply shop). Be forewarned that you'll destroy the inner workings of your appliance (and possibly start a fire) if you plug an American appliance directly into a European electrical outlet without a transformer.

Embassies and High Commissions

London is the capital of the United Kingdom and therefore the home of all the embassies, consulates, and high commissions. United States: 24 Grosvenor Sq., W1 (☎ 020/7499-9000; Tube: Bond St.). Canada: MacDonald House, 38 Grosvenor Sq., W1 (☎ 020/7258-6600; Tube: Bond St.). Ireland: 17 Grosvenor Place, SW1 (☎ 020/7235-2171; Tube: Hyde Park Corner), Australia: Australia House, Strand, WC2 (☎ 020/7379-4334; Tube: Charing Cross or Aldwych). New Zealand: New Zealand House, 80 Haymarket at Pall Mall, SW1 (☎ 020/7930-8422; Tube: Charing Cross or Piccadilly Circus).

Emergencies

For police, fire, or an ambulance, call ☎ **999.**

Holidays

Americans may be unfamiliar with some British holidays, particularly the spring and summer Bank Holidays (the last Mondays in May and August), when everyone takes off for a long weekend. Most banks and many shops, museums, historic houses, and other places of interest are closed on Bank Holidays, and public transport services are reduced. The same holds true for other major British holidays: New Year's Day, Good Friday, Easter Monday, May Day (the first Monday in May), Christmas, and Boxing Day (December 26). The London crowds swell during school holidays: mid-July to early September, three weeks at Christmas and at Easter, and a week in mid-October and in mid-February (when are those kids ever in school?).

Hospitals

The following offer 24-hour emergency care, with the first treatment free under the National Health Service: Royal Free Hospital, Pond Street, NW3 (☎ 020/7794-0500; Tube: Belsize Park), and University College Hospital, Grafton Way, WC1 (☎ 020/7387-9300; Tube: Warren St. or Euston Sq.). Many other London hospitals also have accident and emergency departments.

Hotlines

The Rape Crisis Line is ☎ 020/7837-1600, accepting calls after 6 p.m. Samaritans, 46 Marshall St., W1 (☎ 020/7734-2800; Tube: Oxford Circus or Picadilly Circus), maintains a crisis hotline that helps with all kinds of troubles, even threatened suicides. Doors are open from 9 a.m.–9 p.m. daily, but phones are open 24 hours. Alcoholics Anonymous (☎ 020/7833-0022) answers its hotline daily from 10 a.m.–10 p.m. The AIDS 24-hour hotline is ☎ 0800/567-123. If you're in some sort of legal emergency, call Release at ☎ 020/7729-9904, 24 hours a day.

Information

The main Tourist Information Centre, run by the London Tourist Board, is in the forecourt of Victoria Station (Tube: Victoria) and is open daily 8 a.m.–7 p.m.; the center offers booking services and free literature on London attractions and entertainment. Other Tourist Information Centres are in the Liverpool Street Underground Station (open Mon—Fri 8 a.m.–6 p.m., Sat 8 a.m.–5:30 p.m., Sun 9 a.m.–5:30 p.m.); the Arrivals Hall of the Waterloo International Terminal (open daily 8:30 a.m.–10:30 p.m.); the Heathrow Terminal 1, 2, and 3 Underground station (open daily 8 a.m. –6 p.m.), and the Heathrow Terminal 3 Arrivals concourse (open daily 6 a.m. –11 p.m.). See "Where to Get More Informa-tion" later in the appendix for more information.

Internet Access

Office 24, 38 New Oxford St., WC1 (☎ 020/7616-7300; Tube: Tottenham Court Rd. or Holborn) and Net House, 138 Marylebone Rd., NW1 (☎ 020/7224-7008; Tube: Baker St.) have high-speed computers available for Internet/e-mail access. London has many cyber-cafes.

Liquor Laws

No alcohol is served to anyone under 18. Children under 16 aren't allowed in pubs, except in dining rooms, and then only when accompanied by a parent or guardian. Restaurants are allowed to serve liquor during the same hours as pubs (see "Business Hours" earlier in this section for these hours); however, only people who are eating a meal on the premises can be served a drink. In hotels, liquor may be served 11 a.m. – 11 p.m. to both guests and nonguests; after 11 p.m., only guests may be served.

Mail

An airmail letter to North America costs 43p (65¢) for 10 grams, and postcards require a 35p (50¢) stamp; letters generally take seven to ten days to arrive from the U.S., about five to seven days from London to the U.S. Mail within the U.K. can be sent first or second class. See "Post Offices" later in this section.

Maps

The best all-around street directory, *London A to Z* is available at most newsstands and bookstores. You can obtain a bus and Underground map at any Underground station.

Newspapers/Magazines

The *Times, Telegraph, Daily Mail,* and *Evening Standard* are all dailies carrying the latest news. The *International Herald Tribune,* published in Paris, and an international edition of *USA Today,* beamed via satellite, are available daily. Copies of *Time* and *Newsweek* are also sold at most newsstands. Magazines such as *Time Out, City Limits,* and *Where* contain lots of useful information about the latest happenings in London. *Gay Times,* a high-quality news-oriented magazine covering the gay/lesbian community, is available at most news agents. See "Where to Get More Information" later in the Appendix for more info.

Pharmacies

They're called *chemists* in the United Kingdom. The chain Boots has outlets all over London. Bliss the Chemist, 5 Marble Arch, W1 (☎ 020/7723-6116; Tube: Marble Arch), is open daily 9 a.m.–midnight. Zafash Pharmacy, 233–235 Old Brompton Rd., SW5 (☎ 020/7373-2798; Tube: Earl's Court), is London's only 24-hour pharmacy.

Police

In an emergency, dial ☎ 999.

Post Offices

The Main Post Office, 24 William IV St., WC2 (☎ 020/7930-9580; Tube: Charing Cross), is open Monday–Saturday 8:30 a.m.–8 p.m. Other post offices and *sub-post offices* (windows in the back of news agent stores) are open Monday through Friday 9:00 a.m.–5:30 p.m. and Saturday 9:00 a.m.–12:30 p.m. Look for red "Post Office" signs outside.

Radio

You can tune into the following stations while in London: BBC Greater London Radio (94.9) for rock music; BBC4 (95) for classical music; LBC Crown (97.3) for news and reports of what's happening in London; Captial FM (95.8) for U.S.-style pop and rock music, Choice FM (96.9) for jazz, reggae, or salsa; and Jazz FM (102.2) for jazz, blues, and big-band music.

Restrooms

The English often call toilets *loos.* They're marked by "public toilets" signs on streets, parks, and in a few Tube stations. You also find well-maintained lavatories that can be used by anybody in all larger public buildings, such as museums and art galleries, large department stores, and rail stations. Public lavatories are usually free, but you may need a 20p coin to get in or to use a proper wash-room. In some places (like Leicester Square) you find coin-operated "Super Loos" that are sterilized after each use. If all else fails, duck into the nearest pub.

Safety

London is generally a safe city, both on the street and in the Underground. Muggings have increased in recent years, however. As in any large metropolis, use common sense and normal caution when you're in a crowded public area or walking alone at night. The area around Euston Station has more purse-snatchings than anywhere else in London.

Smoking

Most U.S. cigarette brands are available in London. Smoking is forbidden in the Underground (on the cars and the platforms) and on buses. Most restaurants have non-smoking tables, but they're sometimes separated from the smoking section by very little space. Non-smoking rooms are available in more and more hotels, and some B&Bs are now entirely smoke-free.

Taxes

The 17.5% value-added tax (VAT) is added to all hotel and restaurant bills and is included in the price of many items you purchase. This tax can be refunded if you shop at stores that participate in the Retail Export Scheme (signs are posted in the window).

Taxis

You can hail a cab from the street; if the "For Hire" light is lit, the cab is available. You can phone for a radio cab at ☎ 020/7272-0272.

Telephone

For directory assistance in London and the rest of Britain, dial ☎ **192**. The country code for the United Kingdom is 44. The city code for London is 020 within the United Kingdom or 20 outside the United Kingdom. To call England from the United States, dial 011-44-20 and then the 8-digit phone number. If you're dialing a London number within London, drop the 020 city code.

Three types of public pay phones are available: those that take only coins (increasingly rare), those that accept only phonecards (called Cardphones), and those that take both phonecards and credit cards. Phonecards are available in four values — £2 ($3), £4 ($6), £10 ($15), and £20 ($30) — and are reusable until the total value has expired. You can buy the cards from newsstands and post offices. At coin-operated phones, insert your coins before dialing. The minimum charge is 10p (15¢). The credit-call pay phone operates on credit cards — Access (MasterCard), Visa, American Express, and Diners Club — and is most commonly found at airports and large rail stations.

To make an international call from London, dial the inernational access code (00), then the country code followed by the area code and the local number. Or call through one of the following long-distance access codes: AT&T USA Direct (☎0800/890-011), Canada Direct (☎0800/890-016), Australia (☎0800/890-061), and New Zealand

(☎ 0800/890-064). Common country codes are: USA and Canada, 1; Australia, 61; New Zealand, 64.

Time Zone

England follows Greenwich mean time (five hours ahead of eastern standard time). Clocks move forward one hour on March 28 and back one hour on October 24. Most of the year, including summer, Britain is five hours ahead of the time observed on the East Coast of the United States. Because the United States and Britain observe daylight saving time at slightly different times of year, there's a brief period (about a week) in autumn when Britain is only four hours ahead of New York and a brief period in spring when it's six hours ahead of New York.

Tipping

In restaurants, service charges of 15% to 20% are often added to the bill. Sometimes this tip is clearly marked; at other times it isn't. When in doubt, ask. If service isn't included, adding 15% to the bill is customary. Sommeliers get about £1 ($1.50) per bottle of wine served. Tipping in pubs isn't done, but in cocktail bars the server usually gets about £1 ($1.50) per round of drinks. Tipping taxi drivers 10% to 15% of the fare is standard. Barbers and hairdressers expect 10% to 15%. Tour guides expect £2 ($3), although this tip is not mandatory. Theater ushers are not tipped.

Transit Assistance

For 24-hour information on London's Underground, buses, and ferries, call ☎ 020/7222-1234 or go online to www.londontransport.co.uk.

Weather Updates

Call ☎ 020/7922-8844 for current weather information, but chances are the line will be busy. For the daily London weather report before you go, check British Tourist Authority's Web site at www.visitbritain.com.

Toll-Free Numbers and Web Sites

Major airlines serving London

Air Canada
☎ 888/247-2262
www.aircanada.ca

Air New Zealand
☎ 800/262-2468 (U.S.)
☎ 0800/737-767 (New Zealand)
www.airnewzealand.com

American Airlines
☎ 800/433-7300
www.im.aa.com

British Airways
☎ 800/247-9297
☎ 0345/222-111 (U.K.)
www.british-airways.com

British Midland
☎ 0800/788-0555 (U.K.)
www.britishmidland.com

Continental Airlines
☎ 800/625-0280
www.continental.com

Delta Air Lines
☎ 800/221-1212
www.delta.com

Icelandair
☎ 800/223-5500
www.icelandair.is

Northwest Airlines
☎ 800/225-2525
www.nwa.com

Quantas
☎ 800/227-4500 (U.S)
☎ 612/9691-3636 (Australia)
www.qantas.com

Trans World Airlines (TWA)
☎ 800/221-2000
www.twa.com

United Airlines
☎ 800/241-6522
www.united.com

Virgin Atlantic Airways
☎ 800/862-8621 (Continental U.S.)
☎ 0293/747-747 (U.K)
www.virgin-atlantic.com

Major hotel chains in London

Forte & Meridien Hotels & Resorts
☎ 800/225-5843
www.forte-hotels.com
www.lemeridien-hotels.com

Hilton Hotels
☎ 800/HILTONS
www.hilton.com

Hyatt Hotels & Resorts
☎ 800/228-9000
www.hyatt.com

Inter-Continental Hotels & Resorts
☎ 888/567-8725
www.interconti.com

Relais & Chateaux
☎ 800/735-2478
www.relaischateaux.fr

Thistle Hotels Worldwide
☎ 800/847-4358
www.thistlehotels.com

Sheraton Hotels & Resorts
☎ 800/325-3535
www.sheraton.com

Major car rental agencies in London

Alamo
☎ 800/327-9633 (U.S.)
☎ 0800/272-200 (U.K)
www.goalamo.com

Hertz
☎ 800/654-3131 (U.S.)
☎ 0990/6699 (U.K.)
www.hertz.com

Avis
☎ 800/331-1212 (Continental U.S.)
☎ 0990/900-500 (U.K.)
www.avis.com

National
☎ 800/CAR-RENT (U.S.)
☎ 0990/565-656 (U.K.)
www.nationalcar.com

Budget
☎ 800/527-0700 (U.S.)
☎ 0541/565-656 (U.K.)
www.budgetrentacar.com

Where to Get More Information

When it comes to visiting a huge city like London, advanced planning is part of the journey. You've made a wise investment with this guide, which covers all the London basics. For more information, you can contact the agencies in this section. I also include some fun and useful Web sites and books that you can explore for more information on London.

Tourist offices

For general information about London, contact an office of the **British Tourist Authority** (BTA) at one of the following addresses (or on the Web at www.visitbritain.com):

> ✔ **In the United States:** The main BTA office is at 551 Fifth Ave., Suite 701, New York, NY 10176-0799 (☎ **800/462-2748;** Fax: 212/986-1188). The BTA has a branch office at 625 N. Michigan Ave., Suite 1510, Chicago, IL 60611-1977. The Chicago office has no phone; all requests for information go through the toll-free number listed for New York.

✔ **In Canada:** 111 Avenue Rd., Suite 450, Toronto, Ontario M5R 3J8 (☎ 800/847-4885).

✔ **In Australia:** University Centre, 8th floor, 210 Clarence St., Sydney NSW 2000 (☎ 02/267-4555; Fax: 02/267-4442).

✔ **In New Zealand:** Suite 305, Dilworth Building, Queen and Customs streets, Auckland 1 (☎ 09/303-1446; Fax: 09/377-6965).

Surfing the Net

The Web is one of the best places to find information on London. With a click of the mouse you can pull up everything from the latest news emanating from No. 10 Downing Street to current opera and concert schedules. You can even find out what's playing in the West End theaters and book a seat. You find useful and quite specific Web sites scattered throughout this guide. For general information on London, try these sites for starters:

✔ **www.visitbritain.com.** The Web page for the British Tourist Authority is a good resource for visitors to London and the United Kingdom in general.

✔ **www.travelbritain.org.** This British Tourist Authority site offers helpful information for U.S. travelers to Britain.

✔ **www.londontraveller.com.** This site is useful for browsing, with sections on restaurants, nightlife, and hotels.

✔ **www.londontown.com.** The London Tourist Board's site features special offers on hotels, B&Bs, and theater tickets.

✔ **www.timeout.com.** The weekly listings magazine *Time Out* gives you the lowdown on London's cultural events, entertainment, restaurants, and nightlife.

✔ **www.guardian.co.uk.** *The Daily Guardian,* London's left-of-center daily newspaper, provides up-to-the-minute online news coverage.

✔ **www.Sunday-times.co.uk.** The London Times, the oldest and most traditional of London papers, is a good source for gneral news and cultural.

✔ **www.gaylondon.co.uk.** This site provides a useful list of gay and gay-friendly hotels, services, clubs, and restaurants.

✔ **www.heathrow.co.uk.** Information on all of London's airports is available on this site.

✔ **http://metro.ratp.fr:10001/bin/cities/english.** Type in your departure station and arrival station on the London Underground and this nifty site maps out a route and how long the trip will take.

✔ **www.londontransport.co.uk.** This is the Web site for London Transport, which is in charge of all forms of public transportation in the city: Tubes, buses, and ferry service.

✔ **www.royal.gov.uk.** If you want more history, information, and trivia about the Windsors and the British monarchy in general, check out the official Royal Web site.

Hitting the books

Here are a few books that may be useful for your trip.

✔ **Frommer's London** (Hungry Minds, Inc.), updated every year, is an authoritative guide that covers the city and its surroundings.

✔ **Frommer's London from $85 a Day** (Hungry Minds, Inc.) is a time-honored Bible for budget-minded travelers who want to visit London but don't want to spend a fortune doing so.

✔ **Frommer's Memorable Walks in London** (Hungry Minds, Inc.) is an excellent resource for those who want to explore the city in depth and on foot. Each walking tour provides clear, easy-to-follow directions and describes important sights along the way.

✔ **Frommer's Born to Shop London** (Hungry Minds, Inc.) is a must for travelers eager to cruise London with a credit card. The guide covers everything from top department stores to tiny boutiques and helps you find the best, brightest, most unique, and most quintessentially English goods.

✔ **Frommer's Gay & Lesbian Europe** (Hungry Minds, Inc.) contains fun, informative, and up-to-the-minute information on all aspects of gay London, from gay hotels and restaurants to the latest clubs.

✔ **London** (Ballantine Publishing Group) by Edward Rutherford is a sprawling epic novel in which London itself is the main character. The book is a fascinating excursion into the city's 2,000-year-old past.

Making Dollars and Sense of It

Expense	Daily cost	x	Number of days	=	Total
Airfare					
Local transportation					
Car rental					
Lodging (with tax)					
Parking					
Breakfast					
Lunch					
Dinner					
Snacks					
Entertainment					
Babysitting					
Attractions					
Gifts & souvenirs					
Tips					
Other					
Grand Total					

Fare Game: Choosing an Airline

When looking for the best airfare, you should cover all your bases — 1) consult a trusted travel agent; 2) contact the airline directly, via the airline's toll-free number and/or Web site; 3) check out one of the travel-planning Web sites, such as www.frommers.com.

Travel Agency_____ Phone_____
   Agent's Name_____ Quoted fare_____

Airline 1_____ Quoted fare_____
   Toll-free number/Internet_____

Airline 2_____ Quoted fare_____
   Toll-free number/Internet_____

Web site 1_____ Quoted fare_____

Web site 2_____ Quoted fare_____

Departure Schedule & Flight Information

Airline_____ Flight #_____ Confirmation #_____

Departs_____ Date_____ Time_____ a.m./p.m.

Arrives_____ Date_____ Time_____ a.m./p.m.

Connecting Flight (if any)

Amount of time between flights_____ hours/mins

Airline_____ Flight #_____ Confirmation #_____

Departs_____ Date_____ Time_____ a.m./p.m.

Arrives_____ Date_____ Time_____ a.m./p.m.

Return Trip Schedule & Flight Information

Airline_____ Flight #_____ Confirmation #_____

Departs_____ Date_____ Time_____ a.m./p.m.

Arrives_____ Date_____ Time_____ a.m./p.m.

Connecting Flight (if any)

Amount of time between flights_____ hours/mins

Airline_____ Flight #_____ Confirmation #_____

Departs_____ Date_____ Time_____ a.m./p.m.

Arrives_____ Date_____ Time_____ a.m./p.m.

Sweet Dreams: Choosing Your Hotel

Make a list of all the hotels where you'd like to stay and then check online and call the local and toll-free numbers to get the best price. You should also check with a travel agent, who may be able to get you a better rate.

Hotel & page	Location	Internet	Tel. (local)	Tel. (Toll-free)	Quoted rate

Hotel Checklist

Here's a checklist of things to inquire about when booking your room, depending on your needs and preferences.

- ❑ Smoking/smoke-free room
- ❑ Noise (if you prefer a quiet room, ask about proximity to elevator, bar/restaurant, pool, meeting facilities, renovations, and street)
- ❑ View
- ❑ Facilities for children (crib, roll-away cot, babysitting services)
- ❑ Facilities for travelers with disabilities
- ❑ Number and size of bed(s) (king, queen, double/full-size)
- ❑ Is breakfast included? (buffet, continental, or sit-down?)
- ❑ In-room amenities (hair dryer, iron/board, minibar, etc.)
- ❑ Other_____

Places to Go, People to See, Things to Do

Enter the attractions you would most like to see and decide how they'll fit into your schedule. Next, use the "Going My Way" worksheets that follow to sketch out your itinerary.

Attraction/activity	Page	Amount of time you expect to spend there	Best day and time to go

Going "My" Way

Day 1

Hotel_____ Tel. _____

Morning_____

_____

Lunch_____ Tel. _____

Afternoon_____

_____

Dinner_____ Tel. _____

Evening_____

_____

Day 2

Hotel_____ Tel. _____

Morning_____

_____

Lunch_____ Tel. _____

Afternoon_____

_____

Dinner_____ Tel. _____

Evening_____

_____

Day 3

Hotel_____ Tel. _____

Morning_____

_____

Lunch_____ Tel. _____

Afternoon_____

_____

Dinner_____ Tel. _____

Evening_____

_____

Going "My" Way

Day 4

Hotel_____ Tel._____

Morning_____

_____

Lunch_____ Tel._____

Afternoon_____

_____

Dinner_____ Tel._____

Evening_____

_____

Day 5

Hotel_____ Tel._____

Morning_____

_____

Lunch_____ Tel._____

Afternoon_____

_____

Dinner_____ Tel._____

Evening_____

_____

Day 6

Hotel_____ Tel._____

Morning_____

_____

Lunch_____ Tel._____

Afternoon_____

_____

Dinner_____ Tel._____

Evening_____

_____

Index

• *S* •

• Accommodations Index •